Introduction to Networks v6
Companion Guide

Cisco Networking Academy

Cisco Press

800 East 96th Street

Indianapolis, Indiana 46240 USA

Introduction to Networks v6 Companion Guide

Cisco Networking Academy

Published by:
Cisco Press
800 East 96th Street
Indianapolis, IN 46240 USA

Printed in the United States of America

2   17

Library of Congress Control Number: 2016946762

ISBN-13: 978-1-58713-360-2

ISBN-10: 1-58713-360-1

Warning and Disclaimer

This book is designed to provide information about the Cisco Networking Academy Introduction to Networks course. Every effort has been made to make this book as complete and as accurate as possible, but no warranty or fitness is implied.

The information is provided on an "as is" basis. The authors, Cisco Press, and Cisco Systems, Inc. shall have neither liability nor responsibility to any person or entity with respect to any loss or damages arising from the information contained in this book or from the use of the discs or programs that may accompany it.

The opinions expressed in this book belong to the author and are not necessarily those of Cisco Systems, Inc.

Editor-in-Chief
Mark Taub

Product Line Manager
Brett Bartow

Business Operation Manager, Cisco Press
Ronald Fligge

Executive Editor
Mary Beth Ray

Managing Editor
Sandra Schroeder

Development Editor
Ellie C. Bru

Project Editor
Mandie Frank

Copy Editor
Celia McCoy

Technical Editor
Bob Vachon

Editorial Assistant
Vanessa Evans

Designer
Chuti Prasertsith

Composition
codeMantra

Indexer
Cheryl Lenser

Proofreader
Jaikumar

Trademark Acknowledgements

All terms mentioned in this book that are known to be trademarks or service marks have been appropriately capitalized. Cisco Press or Cisco Systems, Inc., cannot attest to the accuracy of this information. Use of a term in this book should not be regarded as affecting the validity of any trademark or service mark.

Special Sales

For government sales inquiries, please contact governmentsales@pearsoned.com.

For questions about sales outside the U.S., please contact intlcs@pearson.com.

Feedback Information

At Cisco Press, our goal is to create in-depth technical books of the highest quality and value. Each book is crafted with care and precision, undergoing rigorous development that involves the unique expertise of members from the professional technical community.

Readers' feedback is a natural continuation of this process. If you have any comments regarding how we could improve the quality of this book, or otherwise alter it to better suit your needs, you can contact us through email at feedback@ciscopress.com. Please make sure to include the book title and ISBN in your message.

We greatly appreciate your assistance.

CISCO™

Americas Headquarters
Cisco Systems, Inc.
170 West Tasman Drive
San Jose, CA 95134-1706
USA
www.cisco.com
Tel: 408 526-4000
800 553-NETS (6387)
Fax: 408 527-0883

Asia Pacific Headquarters
Cisco Systems, Inc.
168 Robinson Road
#28-01 Capital Tower
Singapore 068912
www.cisco.com
Tel: +65 6317 7777
Fax: +65 6317 7799

Europe Headquarters
Cisco Systems International BV
Haarlerbergpark
Haarlerbergweg 13-19
1101 CH Amsterdam
The Netherlands
www-europe.cisco.com
Tel: +31 0 800 020 0791
Fax: +31 0 20 357 1100

Cisco has more than 200 offices worldwide. Addresses, phone numbers, and fax numbers are listed on the Cisco Website at **www.cisco.com/go/offices.**

About the Contributing Authors

Rick Graziani teaches computer science and computer networking courses at Cabrillo College in Aptos, California. Prior to teaching Rick worked in the information technology field for Santa Cruz Operation, Tandem Computers, Lockheed Missiles and Space Corporation, and served in the U.S. Coast Guard. He holds an M.A. in Computer Science and Systems Theory from California State University Monterey Bay. Rick also works as a curriculum developer for the Cisco Networking Academy Curriculum Engineering team. When Rick is not working, he is most likely surfing at one of his favorite Santa Cruz surf breaks.

Allan Johnson entered the academic world in 1999 after 10 years as a business owner/operator to dedicate his efforts to his passion for teaching. He holds both an MBA and an M.Ed. in Occupational Training and Development. He taught CCNA courses at the high school level for seven years and has taught both CCNA and CCNP courses at Del Mar College in Corpus Christi, Texas. In 2003, Allan began to commit much of his time and energy to the CCNA Instructional Support Team, providing services to Networking Academy instructors worldwide and creating training materials. He now works full time for Cisco Networking Academy as a Curriculum Developer.

Contents at a Glance

Contents

Syntax Conventions

The conventions used to present command syntax in this book are the same conventions used in the IOS Command Reference. The Command Reference describes these conventions as follows:

- **Boldface** indicates commands and keywords that are entered literally as shown. In actual configuration examples and output (not general command syntax), boldface indicates commands that are manually input by the user (such as a **show** command).

- *Italics* indicates arguments for which you supply actual values.

- Vertical bars (|) separate alternative, mutually exclusive elements.

- Square brackets ([ ]) indicate an optional element.

- Braces ({ }) indicate a required choice.

- Braces within brackets ([{ }]) indicate a required choice within an optional element.

Introduction

Introduction to Networks: Companion Guide v6 is the official supplemental textbook for the Cisco Network Academy CCNA Introduction to Networks course. Cisco Networking Academy is a comprehensive program that delivers information technology skills to students around the world. The curriculum emphasizes real-world practical application, while providing opportunities for you to gain the skills and hands-on experience needed to design, install, operate, and maintain networks in small- to medium-sized businesses as well as enterprise and service provider environments.

As a textbook, this book provides a ready reference to explain the same networking concepts, technologies, protocols, and devices as the online curriculum. This book emphasizes key topics, terms, and activities and provides some alternate explanations and examples as compared with the course. You can use the online curriculum as directed by your instructor and then use this Companion Guide's study tools to help solidify your understanding of all the topics.

Who Should Read This Book

The book, as well as the course, is designed as an introduction to data network technology for those pursuing careers as network professionals as well as those who need only an introduction to network technology for professional growth. Topics are presented concisely, starting with the most fundamental concepts and progressing to a comprehensive understanding of network communication. The content of this text provides the foundation for additional Cisco Networking Academy courses and preparation for the CCENT and CCNA Routing and Switching certifications.

Book Features

The educational features of this book focus on supporting topic coverage, readability, and practice of the course material to facilitate your full understanding of the course material.

Topic Coverage

The following features give you a thorough overview of the topics covered in each chapter so that you can make constructive use of your study time:

- **Objectives:** Listed at the beginning of each chapter, the objectives reference the core concepts covered in the chapter The question format in the Companion Guide encourages you to think about finding the answers as you read the chapter.

- **"How-to" feature:** When this book covers a set of steps that you need to perform for certain tasks, the text lists the steps as a how-to list. When you are studying, the icon helps you easily refer to this feature as you skim through the book.

- **Notes:** These are short sidebars that point out interesting facts, timesaving methods, and important safety issues.

- **Chapter summaries:** At the end of each chapter is a summary of the chapter's key concepts. It provides a synopsis of the chapter and serves as a study aid.

- **Practice:** At the end of chapter there is a full list of all the labs, class activities, and Packet Tracer activities to refer back to for study time.

Readability

The following features have been updated to assist your understanding of the networking vocabulary:

- **Key terms:** Each chapter begins with a list of key terms along with a page-number reference from inside the chapter. The terms are listed in the order in which they are explained in the chapter. This handy reference allows you to find a term, flip to the page where the term appears, and see the term used in context. The Glossary defines all the key terms.

- **Glossary:** This book contains an all-new Glossary with 253 terms.

Practice

Practice makes perfect. This new Companion Guide offers you ample opportunities to put what you learn into practice. You will find the following features valuable and effective in reinforcing the instruction that you receive:

- **Check Your Understanding questions and answer key:** Updated review questions are presented at the end of each chapter as a self-assessment tool. These questions match the style of questions that you see in the online course. Appendix A, "Answers to the 'Check Your Understanding' Questions," provides an answer key to all the questions and includes an explanation of each answer.

- **Labs and activities:** Throughout each chapter, you will be directed back to the online course to take advantage of the activities created to reinforce concepts. In addition, at the end of each chapter, there is a "Practice" section that collects a list of all the labs and activities to provide practice with the topics introduced in this chapter. The labs and class activities are available in the companion *Introduction to Networking v6 Labs & Study Guide* [ISBN 978-1-58713-361-9]. The Packet Tracer Activities PKA files are found in the online course.

- **Page references to online course:** After headings, you will see, for example, (1.1.2.3). This number refers to the page number in the online course so that you can easily jump to that spot online to view a video, practice an activity, perform a lab, or review a topic.

Labs & Study Guide

The supplementary book *Introduction to Networking v6 Labs & Study Guide*, by Cisco Press (ISBN 978-1-58713-361-9), contains all the labs plus Packet Tracer activities from the course, a command reference, and additional study guide exercises and activities.

About Packet Tracer Software and Activities

Packet Tracer
☐ Activity

Interspersed throughout the chapters you'll find many activities to work with the Cisco Packet Tracer tool. Packet Tracer allows you to create networks, visualize how packets flow in the network, and use basic testing tools to determine whether the network would work. When you see this icon, you can use Packet Tracer with the listed file to perform a task suggested in this book. The activity files are available in the course. Packet Tracer software is available through the Cisco Networking Academy website. Ask your instructor for access to Packet Tracer.

Companion Website

Register this book to get any updates or errata that might become available for this book. Be sure to check the box that you would like to hear from us to receive news of updates and exclusive discounts on related products.

To access this companion website, follow the steps below:

1. Go to www.ciscopress.com/register and log in or create a new account.

2. Enter the ISBN: 9781587133602.

3. Answer the challenge question as proof of purchase.

4. Click the "Access Bonus Content" link in the Registered Products section of your account page, to be taken to the page where your downloadable content is available.

Please note that many of our companion content files can be very large, especially image and video files. If you are unable to locate the files for this title by following the steps, please visit www.ciscopress.com/contact and select the "Site Problems/ Comments" option. Our customer service representatives will assist you.

How This Book Is Organized

This book corresponds closely to the Cisco Academy Introduction to Networking course and is divided into 11 chapters, one appendix, and a glossary of key terms:

- **Chapter 1, "Explore the Network":** Introduces the concept of a network and provides an overview of the different types of networks encountered. It examines how networks impact the way we work, learn, and play. This chapter also examines new trends in networks such as video, cloud computing, and BYOD and how to help ensure that we have a robust, reliable, secure network to support these trends.

- **Chapter 2, "Configure a Network Operating System":** Introduces the operating system used with most Cisco devices: the Cisco IOS. The basic purpose and functions of the IOS are described as well as the methods to access the IOS. The chapter will also present maneuvering through the IOS command-line interface as well as basic IOS device configuration.

- **Chapter 3, "Network Protocols and Communications":** Examines the importance of rules or protocols for network communication. It explores the OSI reference model and the TCP/IP communication suite, examining how these models provide the necessary protocols to allow communication to occur on a modern converged network.

- **Chapter 4, "Network Access":** Introduces the lowest layer of the TCP/IP model: the transport layer. This layer is essentially the equivalent of the OSI data link layer and the physical layer. The chapter discusses how this layer prepares network layer packets for transmission, controls access to the physical media, and transports the data across various media. This chapter includes a description of the encapsulation protocols and processes that occur as data travels across the LAN and the WAN as well as the media used.

- **Chapter 5, "Ethernet":** Examines the functionality of one of the most common LAN protocols in use today. It explores how Ethernet functions and interacts with the TCP/IP protocol suite to provide high-speed data communications.

- **Chapter 6, "Network Layer":** Introduces the function of the network layer—routing—and the basic device that performs this function—the router. The important routing concepts related to addressing, path determination, and data packets for both IPv4 and IPv6 will be presented. The chapter also introduces the construction of a router and the basic router configuration.

- **Chapter 7, "IP Addressing":** Focuses on IPv4 and IPv6 network addressing, including the types of addresses and address assignment. It describes how to use the address mask or prefix length to determine the number of subnetworks and hosts in a network. This chapter also introduces Internet Control Message Protocol (ICMP) tools, such as ping and trace.

- **Chapter 8, "Subnetting IP Networks":** Examines how to improve network performance by optimally dividing the IP address space based on network requirements. It explores the calculation of valid host addresses and the determination of both subnet and subnet broadcast addresses. This chapter examines subnetting for both IPv4 and IPv6.

- **Chapter 9, "Transport Layer":** Introduces Transmission Control Protocol (TCP) and User Datagram Protocol (UDP) and examines how each transports information across the network. It explores how TCP uses segmentation, the three-way handshake, and expectational acknowledgements to ensure reliable delivery of data. It also examines the best-effort delivery mechanism provided by UDP and describes when this would be preferred over TCP.

- **Chapter 10, "Application Layer":** Introduces some protocols of the TCP/IP application layer, which also relates to the top three layers of the OSI model. The chapter focuses on the role of the application layer and how the applications, services, and protocols within the application layer make robust communication across data networks possible. This will be demonstrated by examining some key protocols and services including HTTP, DNS, DHCP, SMTP/POP, Telnet, and FTP.

- **Chapter 11, "Build a Small Network":** Reexamines the various components found in a small network and describes how they work together to allow network growth. Network security and performance issues are examined along with some of the commands that can be used to examine the configuration of devices and the performance of the network. Router and switch file systems are also examined, along with methods for backing up and restoring their configuration files.

- **Appendix A, "Answers to the 'Check Your Understanding' Questions":** This appendix lists the answers to the "Check Your Understanding" review questions that are included at the end of each chapter.

- **Glossary:** The glossary provides you with definitions for all the key terms identified in each chapter.

CHAPTER 1

Explore the Network

Objectives

Upon completion of this chapter, you will be able to answer the following questions:

- How do networks affect the way we interact, learn, work, and play?
- What ways can host devices be used as clients, servers, or both?
- How are network devices used?
- What are the differences between LAN and WAN devices?
- What are the differences between LAN and WAN topologies?
- What is the basic structure of the Internet?
- How do LANs and WANs interconnect to the Internet?

- What is a converged network?
- What are the four basic requirements of a converged network?
- How do trends such as BYOD, online collaboration, video, and cloud computing change the way we interact?
- How are networking technologies changing the home environment?
- What are some basic security threats and solutions for both small and large networks?
- Why is it important to understand the switching and routing infrastructure of a network?

Key Terms

This chapter uses the following key terms. You can find the definitions in the Glossary.

Peer-to-Peer (P2P) file sharing   Page 6

Small Office/Home Office (SOHO) network   Page 8

Medium to large network   Page 8

Server   Page 9

Client   Page 9

End device   Page 14

Medium   Page 8

Network Interface Card (NIC)   Page 18

Physical port   Page 18

Interface   Page 18

Physical topology diagram   Page 19

Logical topology diagram   Page 19

Local area network (LAN)   Page 20

Wide area network (WAN)   Page 20

Internet   Page 23

Intranet   Page 25

Extranet   Page 25

Internet Service Provider (ISP)   Page 26

Converged network   Page 29

Introduction (1.0.1.1)

We now stand at a critical turning point in the use of technology to extend and empower our ability to communicate. The globalization of the Internet has succeeded faster than anyone could have imagined. The manner in which social, commercial, political, and personal interactions occur is rapidly changing to keep up with the evolution of this global network. In the next stage of our development, innovators will use the Internet as a starting point for their efforts, creating new products and services specifically designed to take advantage of the network capabilities. As developers push the limits of what is possible, the capabilities of the interconnected networks that form the Internet will play an increasing role in the success of these projects.

This chapter introduces the platform of data networks upon which our social and business relationships increasingly depend. The material lays the groundwork for exploring the services, technologies, and issues encountered by network professionals as they design, build, and maintain the modern network.

Class Activity 1.0.1.2: Draw Your Concept of the Internet

Refer to Lab Activity for this chapter

Welcome to a new component of our Networking Academy curriculum: Modeling Activities! You will find them at the beginning and end of each chapter.

Some activities can be completed individually (at home or in class), and some will require group or learning-community interaction. Your instructor will be facilitating so that you can obtain the most from these introductory activities.

These activities will help you enhance your understanding by providing an opportunity to visualize some of the abstract concepts that you will be learning in this course. Be creative and enjoy these activities!

Here is your first modeling activity:

Draw Your Concept of the Internet

Draw and label a map of the Internet as you interpret it now. Include your home or school/university location and its respective cabling, equipment, devices, etc. Some items you may wish to include

- Devices/Equipment
- Media (cabling)
- Link Addresses or Names
- Sources and Destinations
- Internet Service Providers

Upon completion, save your work in a hard-copy format, as it will be used for future reference at the end of this chapter. If it is an electronic document, save it to a server location provided by your instructor. Be prepared to share and explain your work in class.

Globally Connected (1.1)

Networks are all around us. They provide us with a way to communicate and share information and resources with individuals in the same location or around the world. This requires an extensive array of technologies and procedures that can readily adapt to varying conditions and requirements.

Networking Today (1.1.1)

For most individuals, the use of networks has become a daily occurrence. The availability of these networks has altered the way in which we interact with each other.

Networks in Our Daily Lives (1.1.1.1)

Among all of the essentials for human existence, the need to interact with others ranks just below our need to sustain life. Communication is almost as important to us as our reliance on air, water, food, and shelter.

In today's world, through the use of networks, we are connected like never before. People with ideas can communicate instantly with others to make those ideas a reality. News events and discoveries are known worldwide in seconds. Individuals can even connect and play games with friends separated by oceans and continents.

Play the video to view how connected we are.

Go to the online course to view this video.

Video

Technology Then and Now (1.1.1.2)

Imagine a world without the Internet. No more Google, YouTube, instant messaging, Facebook, Wikipedia, online gaming, Netflix, iTunes, and easy access to current information. No more price comparison websites, avoiding lines by shopping online, or quickly looking up phone numbers and map directions to various locations at the click of a button. How different would our lives be without all of this? That was the world we lived in just 15 to 20 years ago. But over the years, data networks have slowly expanded and been repurposed to improve the quality of life for people everywhere.

Play the video to watch how the Internet emerged over the last 25 years and see a glimpse into the future! What else do you think we will be able to do using the network as the platform?

Go to the online course to view this video.

Video

No Boundaries (1.1.1.3)

Advancements in networking technologies are perhaps the most significant changes in the world today. They are helping to create a world in which national borders, geographic distances, and physical limitations become less relevant presenting ever-diminishing obstacles.

The Internet has changed the manner in which social, commercial, political, and personal interactions occur. The immediate nature of communications over the Internet encourages the creation of global communities. Global communities allow for social interaction that is independent of location or time zone. The creation of online communities for the exchange of ideas and information has the potential to increase productivity opportunities across the globe.

Cisco refers to this as the human network. The human network centers on the impact of the Internet and networks on people and businesses.

How has the human network affected you?

Networks Support the Way We Learn (1.1.1.4)

Networks have changed the way we learn. Access to high-quality instruction is no longer restricted to students living in proximity to where that instruction is being delivered. Online distance learning has removed geographic barriers and improved student opportunity. Robust and reliable networks support and enrich student learning experiences. They deliver learning material in a wide range of formats including interactive activities, assessments, and feedback.

Play the video to see how the classroom is expanding.

Go to the online course to view this video.

Video

Networks Support the Way We Communicate (1.1.1.5)

The globalization of the Internet has ushered in new forms of communication that empower individuals to create information that can be accessed by a global audience.

Some forms of communication include

- **Texting** – Texting enables instant real-time communication between two or more people.

- **Social Media** – Social media consists of interactive websites where people and communities create and share user-generated content with friends, family, peers, and the world.

- **Collaboration Tools** – Without the constraints of location or time zone, collaboration tools allow individuals to communicate with each other, often across real-time interactive video. The broad distribution of data networks means that people in remote locations can contribute on an equal basis with people in the heart of large population centers.

- **Blogs** – Blogs, which is an abbreviation of the word "weblogs," are web pages that are easy to update and edit. Unlike commercial websites, blogs give anyone a means to communicate their thoughts to a global audience without technical knowledge of web design.

- **Wikis** – Wikis are web pages that groups of people can edit and view together. Whereas a blog is more of an individual, personal journal, a wiki is a group creation. As such, it may be subject to more extensive review and editing. Many businesses use wikis as their internal collaboration tool.

- **Podcasting** – Podcasting allows people to deliver their audio recordings to a wide audience. The audio file is placed on a website (or blog or wiki) where others can download it and play the recording on their computers, laptops, and other mobile devices.

- *Peer-to-Peer (P2P) File Sharing* – Peer-to-Peer file sharing allows people to share files with each other without having to store and download them from a central server. The user joins the P2P network by simply installing the P2P software. P2P file sharing has not been embraced by everyone. Many people are concerned about violating the laws of copyrighted materials.

What other sites or tools do you use to share your thoughts?

Networks Support the Way We Work (1.1.1.6)

In the business world, data networks were initially used by businesses to internally record and manage financial information, customer information, and employee payroll systems. These business networks evolved to enable the transmission of many different types of information services, including email, video, messaging, and telephony.

The use of networks to provide efficient and cost-effective employee training is increasing in acceptance. Online learning opportunities can decrease time-consuming and costly travel yet still ensure that all employees are adequately trained to perform their jobs in a safe and productive manner.

There are many success stories illustrating innovative ways networks are being used to make us more successful in the workplace. Some of these scenarios are available through the Cisco web site at http://www.cisco.com/web/about/success-stories/index.html.

Networks Support the Way We Play (1.1.1.7)

The Internet is used for traditional forms of entertainment. We listen to recording artists, preview or view motion pictures, read entire books, and download material for future offline access. Live sporting events and concerts can be experienced as they are happening or recorded and viewed on demand.

Networks enable the creation of new forms of entertainment, such as online games. Players participate in any kind of online competition that game designers can imagine. We compete with friends and foes around the world as if we were all in the same room.

Even offline activities are enhanced using network collaboration services. Global communities of interest have grown rapidly. We share common experiences and hobbies well beyond our local neighborhood, city, or region. Sports fans share opinions and facts about their favorite teams. Collectors display prized collections and get expert feedback about them.

Whatever form of recreation we enjoy, networks are improving our experience.

How do you play on the Internet?

Lab 1.1.1.8: Researching Network Collaboration Tools

In this lab, you will complete the following objectives:

- Part 1: Use Collaboration Tools
- Part 2: Share Documents with Google Drive
- Part 3: Explore Conferencing and Web Meetings
- Part 4: Create Wiki Pages

Providing Resources in a Network (1.1.2)

To efficiently provide resources to end users, networks occur in many sizes and forms.

Networks of Many Sizes (1.1.2.1)

Networks come in all sizes. They can range from simple networks consisting of two computers to networks connecting millions of devices. Figure 1-1 shows four classifications of networks based on size:

Small Home Networks

Small Office/Home Office Networks

Medium to Large Networks

World Wide Networks

Figure 1-1   Network Sizes

- Small home networks connect a few computers to each other and the Internet.

- The *Small Office/Home Office or SOHO network* enables computers within a home office or a remote office to connect to a corporate network or access centralized, shared resources.

- *Medium to large networks*, such as those used by corporations and schools, can have many locations with hundreds or thousands of interconnected computers.

- The Internet is a network of networks that connects hundreds of millions of computers world-wide.

Simple networks installed in homes enable sharing of resources, such as printers, documents, pictures, and music between a few local computers.

Home office networks and small office networks are often set up by individuals that work from a home or a remote office and need to connect to a corporate network or other centralized resources. Additionally, many self-employed entrepreneurs use home office and small office networks to advertise and sell products, order supplies, and communicate with customers.

In businesses and large organizations, networks can be used on an even broader scale to provide consolidation, storage, and access to information on network servers. Networks also allow for rapid communication such as email, instant messaging, and collaboration among employees. In addition to internal benefits, many organizations use their networks to provide products and services to customers through their connection to the Internet.

The Internet is the largest network in existence. In fact, the term Internet means a 'network of networks.' The Internet is literally a collection of interconnected private and public networks, such as those described above.

Clients and Servers (1.1.2.2)

All computers connected to a network that participate directly in network communication are classified as hosts. Hosts are also called end devices.

Servers are computers with software that enable them to provide information, like email or web pages, to other end devices on the network. Each service requires separate server software. For example, a server requires web server software in order to provide web services to the network. A computer with server software can provide services simultaneously to one or many clients. Additionally, a single computer can run multiple types of server software. In a home or small business, it may be necessary for one computer to act as a file server, a web server, and an email server.

Clients are computers with software installed that enable them to request and display the information obtained from the server. An example of client software is a web browser, like Chrome or Firefox. A single computer can also run multiple types of client software. For example, a user can check email and view a web page while instant messaging and listening to Internet radio.

Figure 1-2 shows different client and server examples.

Figure 1-2   Client/Server Examples

- **Web Client and Server:** The Web Server runs web server software and clients use their browser software, such as Windows Internet Explorer, to access web pages on the server.

- **Email Client and Server:** The Email Server runs email server software and clients use their mail client software, such as Microsoft Outlook, to access email on the server.

- **File Client and Server:** The File Server stores corporate and user files in a central location. The client devices access these files with client software such as Windows Explorer.

Peer-to-Peer (1.1.2.3)

Client and server software usually runs on separate computers, but it is also possible for one computer to carry out both roles at the same time. In small businesses and homes, many computers function as the servers and clients on the network. This type of network is called a *peer-to-peer network*, as shown in Figure 1-3.

Figure 1-3   Peer-to-Peer Example

The advantages of peer-to-peer networking:

- Easy to set up
- Less complexity
- Lower cost since network devices and dedicated servers may not be required
- Can be used for simple tasks such as transferring files and sharing printers

The disadvantages of peer-to-peer networking:

- No centralized administration
- Not as secure
- Not scalable
- All devices may act as both clients and servers, which can slow their performance

LANs, WANs, and the Internet (1.2)

Many different components are required to allow a network to provide services and resources. These various components work together to ensure that resources are delivered in an efficient manner to those requiring the services.

Network Components (1.2.1)

Different network components are used within the network to provide services and resources. These various components work together to ensure that resources are delivered in an efficient manner to those requiring the services.

Overview of Network Components (1.2.1.1)

The path that a message takes from source to destination can be as simple as a single cable connecting one computer to another or as complex as a collection of networks that literally spans the globe. This network infrastructure provides the stable and reliable channel over which these communications occur.

The network infrastructure contains three categories of network components, as shown in Figures 1-4, 1-5, and 1-6.

Figure 1-4 Devices

Figure 1-5 Media

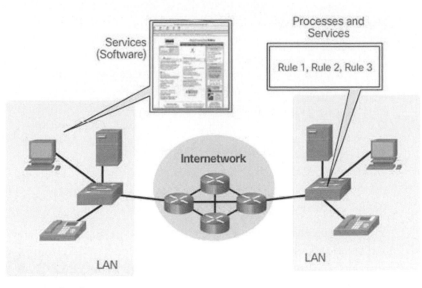

Figure 1-6   Services

Devices and media are the physical elements, or hardware, of the network. Hardware is often the visible components of the network platform such as a laptop, PC, switch, router, wireless access point, or the cabling used to connect the devices.

Services include many of the common network applications people use every day, like email hosting services and web hosting services. Processes provide the functionality that directs and moves the messages through the network. Processes are less obvious to us but are critical to the operation of networks.

End Devices (1.2.1.2)

The network devices that people are most familiar with are called end devices. Some examples of end devices are shown in Figure 1-7.

Figure 1-7   Examples of End Devices

An *end device* is either the source or destination of a message transmitted over the network. To distinguish one end device from another, each end device on a network is identified by an address. When an end device initiates communication, it uses the address of the destination end device to specify where the message should be sent. Devices between the source and destination are responsible for choosing the best path and forwarding messages sent between end devices, as shown in Figure 1-8.

Intermediary Network Devices (1.2.1.3)

Intermediary devices connect the individual end devices to the network and can connect multiple individual networks to form an internetwork. These intermediary devices provide connectivity and ensure that data flows across the network.

Intermediary devices use the destination end device address, in conjunction with information about the network interconnections, to determine the path that messages should take through the network, as shown in Figure 1-8.

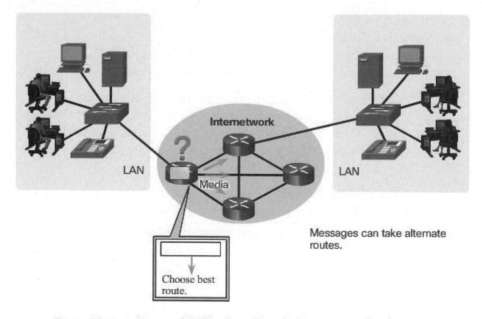

Data originates with an end device, flows through the network, and arrives at an end device.

Figure 1-8 End Devices Communicate Across the Internetwork

Examples of the more common intermediary devices are shown in Figure 1-9.

Figure 1-9   Examples of Intermediary Devices

Intermediary network devices perform some or all of these functions:

- Regenerate and retransmit data signals
- Maintain information about what pathways exist through the network and internetwork
- Notify other devices of errors and communication failures
- Direct data along alternate pathways where there is a link failure
- Classify and direct messages according to priorities
- Permit or deny the flow of data, based on security settings

Network Media (1.2.1.4)

Communication across a network is carried on a medium. The *medium* provides the channel over which the message travels from source to destination.

Modern networks primarily use three types of media to interconnect devices and to provide the pathway over which data can be transmitted. As shown in Figure 1-10, these media are

- **Metallic wires within cables** – data is encoded into electrical impulses
- **Glass or plastic fibers (fiber optic cable)** – data is encoded as pulses of light
- **Wireless transmission** – data is encoded using wavelengths from the electromagnetic spectrum

Figure 1-10 Examples of Network Media

Different types of network media have different features and benefits. Not all network media have the same characteristics, nor are they all appropriate for the same purpose.

Criteria to consider when choosing network media includes the following:

- What is the maximum distance that the media can successfully carry a signal?

- Into what type of environment will the media be installed?

- What is the amount of data and the speed at which it must be transmitted?

- What is the cost of the media and installation?

Network Representations (1.2.1.5)

Diagrams of networks often use symbols, like those shown in Figure 1-11, to represent the different devices and connections that make up a network.

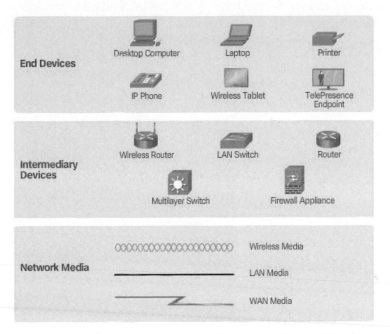

Figure 1-11   Common Icons Use to Represent Network Devices

A diagram provides an easy way to understand how devices in a large network are connected. This type of "picture" of a network is known as a topology diagram. The ability to recognize the logical representations of the physical networking components is critical to being able to visualize the organization and operation of a network.

In addition to these representations, specialized terminology is used when discussing how each of these devices and media connect to each other. Important terms to remember are

- *Network Interface Card* – A NIC, or LAN adapter, provides the physical connection to the network at the PC or other end device. The media that are connecting the PC to the networking device plug directly into the NIC (Figure 1-12).

Figure 1-12   Network Interface Card

- *Physical Port* – A connector or outlet on a networking device where the media is connected to an end device or another networking device.

- *Interface* – Specialized ports on a networking device that connect to individual networks. Because routers are used to interconnect networks, the ports on a router are referred to as network interfaces.

Note

Often, the terms port and interface are often used interchangeably.

Topology Diagrams (1.2.1.6)

Topology diagrams are mandatory for anyone working with a network. They provide a visual map of how the network is connected.

There are two types of topology diagrams:

- *Physical topology diagrams* – Identify the physical location of intermediary devices and cable installation (Figure 1-13).

Figure 1-13   Physical Topology

- *Logical topology diagrams* – Identify devices, ports, and addressing scheme (Figure 1-14).

Figure 1-14   Logical Topology

The topologies shown in the physical and logical diagrams are appropriate for your level of understanding at this point in the course. Search the Internet for "network topology diagrams" to see some more complex examples. If you add the "Cisco" to your search phrase, you will find many topologies using similar icons to what you have seen in this chapter.

Activity 1.2.1.7: Network Component Representations and Functions

Go to the online course to perform this practice activity.

Interactive
Graphic

LANs and WANs (1.2.2)

Network infrastructures can be differentiated is various ways. Two of the most common types of network infrastructures are LANs and WANs.

Types of Networks (1.2.2.1)

Network infrastructures can vary greatly in terms of

- Size of the area covered

- Number of users connected

- Number and types of services available

- Area of responsibility

Figure 1-15 illustrates the two most common types of network infrastructures

- *Local Area Network (LAN)* – A network infrastructure that provides access to users and end devices in a small geographical area, which is typically an enterprise, home, or small business network owned and managed by an individual or IT department.

- *Wide Area Network (WAN)* – A network infrastructure that provides access to other networks over a wide geographical area, which is typically owned and managed by a telecommunications service provider.

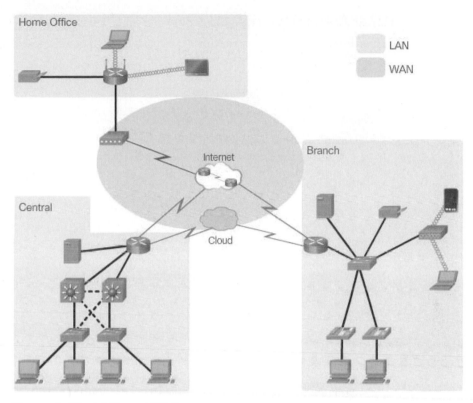

Figure 1-15   LANs and WANs

Play the video to watch Cisco's Jimmy Ray Purser explains the difference between LAN and WAN.

Go to the online course to view this video.

Video

Other types of networks include

- **Metropolitan Area Network (MAN)** – A network infrastructure that spans a physical area larger than a LAN but smaller than a WAN (e.g., a city). MANs are typically operated by a single entity such as a large organization.

- **Wireless LAN (WLAN)** – Similar to a LAN but wirelessly interconnects users and end points in a small geographical area.

- **Storage Area Network (SAN)** – A network infrastructure designed to support file servers and provide data storage, retrieval, and replication.

Local Area Networks (1.2.2.2)

LANs are a network infrastructure that spans a small geographical area, as shown in Figure 1-16.

Figure 1-16   Example of a LAN

Specific features of LANs include

- LANs interconnect end devices in a limited area such as a home, school, office building, or campus.

- A LAN is usually administered by a single organization or individual.

- LANs provide high-speed bandwidth to internal end devices and intermediary devices.

Wide Area Networks (1.2.2.3)

WANs are a network infrastructure that spans a wide geographical area, as shown in Figure 1-17. WANs are typically managed by service providers (SP) or Internet Service Providers (ISP).

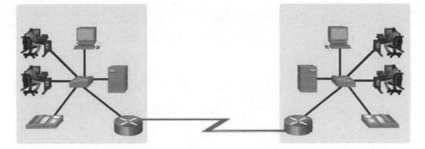

Figure 1-17   Example of a WAN

Specific features of WANs include

■ WANs interconnect LANs over wide geographical areas such as between cities, states, provinces, countries, or continents.

■ WANs are usually administered by multiple service providers.

■ WANs typically provide slower-speed links between LANs.

The Internet, Intranets, and Extranets (1.2.3)

Most individuals need to communicate with a resource on another network, outside of the local network within the home, campus, or organization. This is done using the Internet.

The Internet (1.2.3.1)

The *Internet* is a worldwide collection of interconnected networks (internetworks or internet for short). Figure 1-18 one way to view the Internet as a collection of interconnected LANs and WANs.

LANs use WAN services to interconnect.

Figure 1-18 Collection of Interconnected LANs and WANs

Some of the LAN examples are connected to each other through a WAN connection. WANs are then connected to each other. The red WAN connection lines represent all the varieties of ways we connect networks. WANs can connect through copper wires, fiber optic cables, and wireless transmissions (not shown).

The Internet is not owned by any individual or group. Ensuring effective communication across this diverse infrastructure requires the application of consistent and commonly recognized technologies and standards as well as the cooperation of many network administration agencies. There are organizations that have been developed for the purpose of helping to maintain structure and standardization of Internet protocols and processes. These organizations include the Internet Engineering Task Force (IETF), Internet Corporation for Assigned Names and Numbers (ICANN), and the Internet Architecture Board (IAB), plus many others.

> **Note**
>
> The term internet (with a lower case "i") is used to describe multiple networks interconnected. When referring to the global system of interconnected computer networks or the World Wide Web, the term Internet (with a capital "I") is used.

Intranets and Extranets (1.2.3.2)

There are two other terms that are similar to the term Internet:

- Intranet
- Extranet

Figure 1-19 shows the relationship of the Internet, extranets, and intranets.

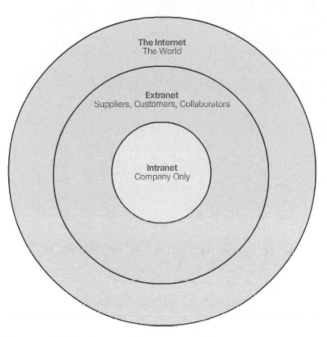

Figure 1-19   Internet, Extranet, and Intranet

Intranet is a term often used to refer to a private connection of LANs and WANs that belongs to an organization and is designed to be accessible only by the organization's members, employees, or others with authorization.

An organization may use an *extranet* to provide secure and safe access to individuals who work for a different organization but require access to the organization's data. Examples of extranets include

- A company that is providing access to outside suppliers and contractors.

- A hospital that is providing a booking system to doctors so they can make appointments for their patients.

- A local office of education that is providing budget and personnel information to the schools in its district.

Internet Connections (1.2.4)

The type of connection to the Internet will depend on the type of network being connected. A business network will usually require a connection with more bandwidth than a home network.

Internet Access Technologies (1.2.4.1)

There are many different ways to connect users and organizations to the Internet.

Home users, teleworkers (remote workers), and small offices typically require a connection to an *Internet Service Provider (ISP)* to access the Internet. Connection options vary greatly between ISP and geographical location. However, popular choices include broadband cable, broadband digital subscriber line (DSL), wireless WANs, and mobile services.

Organizations typically require access to other corporate sites and the Internet. Fast connections are required to support business services including IP phones, video conferencing, and data center storage.

Business-class interconnections are usually provided by service providers (SP). Popular business-class services include business DSL, leased lines, and Metro Ethernet.

Home and Small Office Internet Connections (1.2.4.2)

Figure 1-20 illustrates common connection options for small office and home office users.

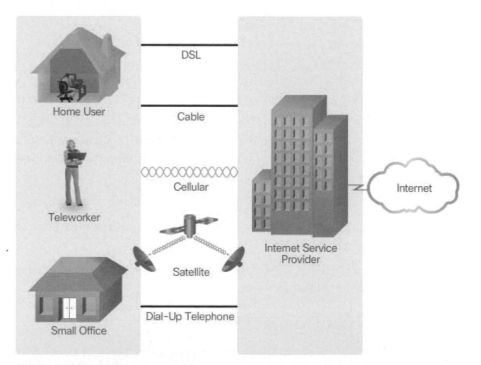

Figure 1-20 Connection Options

- **Cable** – Typically offered by cable television service providers, the Internet data signal is carried on the same cable that delivers cable television. It provides a high bandwidth, always on, connection to the Internet.

- **DSL** – Digital Subscriber Lines provide a high bandwidth, always on, connection to the Internet. DSL runs over a telephone line. In general, small office and home office users connect using Asymmetrical DSL (ADSL), which means that the download speed is faster than the upload speed.

- **Cellular** – Cellular Internet access uses a cell phone network to connect. Wherever you can get a cellular signal, you can get cellular Internet access. Performance will be limited by the capabilities of the phone and the cell tower to which it is connected.

- **Satellite** – The availability of satellite Internet access is a real benefit in those areas that would otherwise have no Internet connectivity at all. Satellite dishes require a clear line of sight to the satellite.

- **Dial-up Telephone** – An inexpensive option that uses any phone line and a modem. The low bandwidth provided by a dial-up modem connection is usually not sufficient for large data transfer, although it is useful for mobile access while traveling.

Many homes and small offices are more commonly being connected directly with fiber optic cables. This enables an ISP to provide higher bandwidth speeds and support more services such as Internet, phone, and TV.

The choice of connection varies depending on geographical location and service provider availability.

Businesses Internet Connections (1.2.4.3)

Corporate connection options differ from home user options. Businesses may require higher bandwidth, dedicated bandwidth, and managed services. Connection options available differ depending on the type of service providers located nearby.

Figure 1-21 illustrates common connection options for businesses.

Figure 1-21   Typical Business Connection Options

- **Dedicated Leased Line** – Leased lines are actually reserved circuits within the service provider's network that connect geographically separated offices for private voice and/or data networking. The circuits are typically rented at a monthly or yearly rate. They can be expensive.

- **Ethernet WAN** – Ethernet WANs extend LAN access technology into the WAN. Ethernet is a LAN technology you will learn about in a later chapter. The benefits of Ethernet are now being extended into the WAN.

- **DSL** – Business DSL is available in various formats. A popular choice is Symmetric Digital Subscriber Lines (SDSL), which is similar to the consumer version of DSL but provides uploads and downloads at the same speeds.

- **Satellite** – Similar to small office and home office users, satellite service can provide a connection when a wired solution is not available.

The choice of connection varies depending on geographical location and service provider availability.

Packet Tracer 1.2.4.4: Help and Navigation Tips

Packet Tracer is a fun, take-home, flexible software program that will help you with your Cisco Certified Network Associate (CCNA) studies. Packet Tracer allows you to experiment with network behavior, build network models, and ask "what if" questions. In this activity, you will explore a relatively complex network that highlights a few of Packet Tracer's features. While doing so, you will learn how to access Help and the tutorials. You will also learn how to switch between various modes and workspaces.

Packet Tracer 1.2.4.5: Network Representation

In this activity, you will explore how Packet Tracer serves as a modeling tool for network representations.

The Network as a Platform (1.3)

The network has become a platform for distributing a wide range of services to end users in a reliable, efficient, and secure manner.

Converged Networks (1.3.1)

Modern networks are constantly evolving to meet user demands. Today's networks are used for data, phone, and video.

Traditional Separate Networks (1.3.1.1)

Consider a school built thirty years ago. Back then, some classrooms were cabled for the data network, telephone network, and video network for televisions. These separate networks could not communicate with each other, as shown in Figure 1-22.

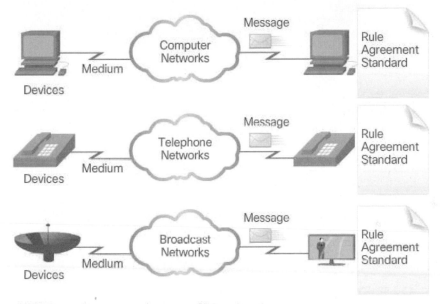

Multiple services are running on multiple networks.

Figure 1-22 Multiple Networks

Each network used different technologies to carry the communication signal. Each network had its own set of rules and standards to ensure successful communication.

The Converging Network (1.3.1.2)

Today, the separate data, telephone, and video networks are converging. Unlike dedicated networks, *converged networks* are capable of delivering data, voice, and video between many different types of devices over the same network infrastructure, as shown in Figure 1-23. This network infrastructure uses the same set of rules, agreements, and implementation standards.

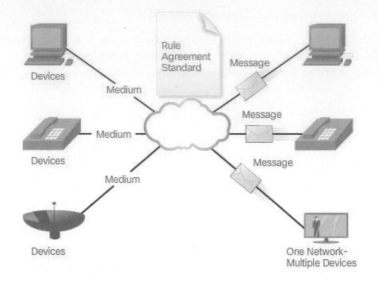

Converged data networks carry multiple services on one network.

Figure 1-23   Converged Networks

Lab 1.3.1.3: Researching Converged Network Services

In this lab, you will complete the following objectives:

- Part 1: Survey Your Understanding of Convergence
- Part 2: Research ISPs Offering Converged Services
- Part 3: Research Local ISPs Offering Converged Services
- Part 4: Select Best Local ISP Converged Service
- Part 5: Research Local Company or Public Institution Using Convergence Technologies

Reliable Network (1.3.2)

With our reliance on networks, certain precautions must be taken to ensure that the network functions as designed, even if things go wrong. Networks must be able to expand to meet the increased needs of an organization. The services provided by the network must be secure and provide the quality of service to meet the expectations of the organization.

Network Architecture (1.3.2.1)

Networks must support a wide range of applications and services as well as operate over many different types of cables and devices, which make up the physical infrastructure. The term *network architecture*, in this context, refers to the technologies that support the infrastructure and the programmed services and rules, or protocols, that move data across the network.

As networks evolve, we are discovering that there are four basic characteristics that the underlying architectures need to address in order to meet user expectations:

- Fault Tolerance
- Scalability
- Quality of Service (QoS)
- Security

Fault Tolerance (1.3.2.2)

The expectation is that the Internet is always available to the millions of users who rely on it. This requires a network architecture that is built to be fault tolerant. A *fault-tolerant network* is one that limits the impact of a failure, so that the fewest number of devices are affected. It is also built in a way that allows quick recovery when such a failure occurs. These networks depend on multiple paths between the source and destination of a message. If one path fails, the messages can be instantly sent over a different link. Having multiple paths to a destination is known as redundancy.

One way reliable networks provide redundancy is by implementing a *packet switched network*. Packet switching splits traffic into packets that are routed over a shared network. A single message, such as an email or a video stream, is broken into multiple message blocks, called packets. Each packet has the necessary addressing information of the source and destination of the message. The routers within the network switch the packets based on the condition of the network at that moment. This means that all the packets in a single message could take very different paths to the destination. In Figure 1-24, the user is not aware and is unaffected by the router dynamically changing the route when a link fails.

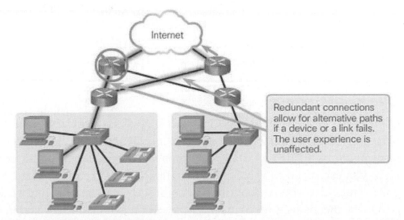

Figure 1-24   Fault Tolerance

This is not the case in circuit-switched networks traditionally used for voice communications. A *circuit-switched network* is one that establishes a dedicated circuit between the source and destination before the users may communicate. If the call is unexpectedly terminated, the users must initiate a new connection.

Scalability (1.3.2.3)

A *scalable network* can expand quickly to support new users and applications without impacting the performance of the service being delivered to existing users. Figure 1-25 shows how a new network can be easily added to an existing network.

Additional users and whole networks can be connected to the Internet without degrading performance for existing users.

Figure 1-25 Scalability

In addition, networks are scalable because the designers follow accepted standards and protocols. This allows software and hardware vendors to focus on improving products and services without worrying about designing a new set of rules for operating within the network.

Quality of Service (1.3.2.4)

Quality of Service (QoS) is also an ever-increasing requirement of networks today. New applications available to users over internetworks, such as voice and live video transmissions, create higher expectations for the quality of the delivered services. Have you ever tried to watch a video with constant breaks and pauses? As data, voice, and video content continue to converge onto the same network, QoS becomes a primary mechanism for managing congestion and ensuring reliable delivery of content to all users.

Congestion occurs when the demand for bandwidth exceeds the amount available. *Network bandwidth* is measured in the number of bits that can be transmitted in a single second, or bits per second (bps). When simultaneous communications are attempted across the network, the demand for network bandwidth can exceed its availability, creating network congestion.

When the volume of traffic is greater than what can be transported across the network, devices queue, or hold, the packets in memory until resources become available to transmit them. In Figure 1-26, one user is requesting a web page and another is on a phone call. With a QoS policy in place, the router can manage the flow of data and voice traffic, giving priority to voice communications if the network experiences congestion.

Figure 1-26   Quality of Service (QoS)

Security (1.3.2.5)

The network infrastructure, services, and the data contained on network-attached devices are crucial personal and business assets. There are two types of network security concerns that must be addressed: network infrastructure security and information security.

Securing a network infrastructure includes the physical securing of devices that provide network connectivity, and preventing unauthorized access to the management software that resides on them, as shown in Figure 1-27.

Figure 1-27   Security

Information security refers to protecting the information contained within the packets being transmitted over the network and the information stored on network attached devices. In order to achieve the goals of network security, there are three primary requirements, as shown in Figure 1-28.

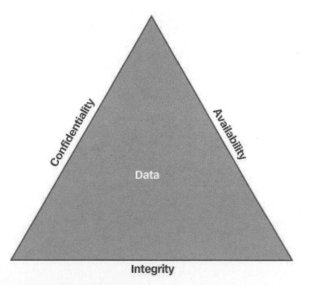

Figure 1-28   CIA Triad

- **Confidentiality** – Data confidentiality means that only the intended and authorized recipients can access and read data.

- **Integrity** – Data integrity means having the assurance that the information has not been altered in transmission, from origin to destination.

- **Availability** – Data availability means having the assurance of timely and reliable access to data services for authorized users.

Interactive Graphic

Activity 1.3.2.6: Reliable Networks

Go to the online course to perform this practice activity.

The Changing Network Environment (1.4)

The network environment continues to evolve, providing new experiences and opportunities for end users. The network is now capable of delivering services and applications in a manner that couldn't be imagined years ago.

Network Trends (1.4.1)

Just as the way we work, play, and learn impacts the network, the availability of a robust reliable network has an impact on our daily lives.

New Trends (1.4.1.1)

As new technologies and end user devices come to market, businesses and consumers must continue to adjust to this ever-changing environment. The role of the network is transforming to enable the connections between people, devices, and information. There are several new networking trends that will affect organizations and consumers. Some of the top trends include

- Bring Your Own Device (BYOD)
- Online collaboration
- Video communication
- Cloud computing

Bring Your Own Device (1.4.1.2)

The concept of any device, to any content, in any manner, is a major global trend that requires significant changes to the way devices are used. This trend is known as *Bring Your Own Device (BYOD)*.

BYOD is about end users having the freedom to use personal tools to access information and communicate across a business or campus network. With the growth of consumer devices, and the related drop in cost, employees and students can be expected to have some of the most advanced computing and networking tools for personal use. These personal tools include laptops, netbooks, tablets, smartphones, and e-readers. These can be devices purchased by the company or school, purchased by the individual, or both.

BYOD means any device, with any ownership, used anywhere. For example, in the past, a student who needed to access the campus network or the Internet had to use one of the school's computers. These devices were typically limited and seen as tools only for work done in the classroom or in the library. Extended connectivity through mobile and remote access to the campus network gives students tremendous flexibility and more learning opportunities for the student.

Online Collaboration (1.4.1.3)

Individuals want to connect to the network, not only for access to data applications, but also to collaborate with one another. *Collaboration* is defined as "the act of working with another or others on a joint project." Collaboration tools, like Cisco WebEx shown in Figure 1-29, give employees, students, teachers, customers, and partners a way to instantly connect, interact, and achieve their objectives.

Figure 1-29 Cisco WebEx

For businesses, collaboration is a critical and strategic priority that organizations are using to remain competitive. Collaboration is also a priority in education. Students need to collaborate to assist each other in learning, to develop team skills used in the work force, and to work together on team-based projects.

Video Communication (1.4.1.4)

Another trend in networking that is critical to the communication and collaboration effort is video. Video is being used for communications, collaboration, and entertainment. Video calls can be made to and from anywhere with an Internet connection. Consider how many people are now using Skype or FaceTime to communicate with friends and family.

Video conferencing is a powerful tool for communicating with others at a distance, both locally and globally. Video is becoming a critical requirement for effective collaboration as organizations extend across geographic and cultural boundaries. Play the video to view how TelePresence can be incorporated into everyday life and business.

Go to the online course to view this video.

Video

Cloud Computing (1.4.1.5)

Cloud computing is another global trend changing the way we access and store data. Cloud computing allows us to store personal files, even backup our entire hard disk drive on servers over the Internet. Applications such as word processing and photo editing can be accessed using the Cloud.

For businesses, Cloud computing extends IT's capabilities without requiring investment in new infrastructure, training new personnel, or licensing new software. These services are available on demand and delivered economically to any device anywhere in the world without compromising security or function.

There are four primary types of Clouds, as shown in Figure 1-30.

Figure 1-30 Types of Clouds

- *Private clouds* – Cloud-based applications and services offered in a private cloud are intended for a specific organization or entity, such as the government. A private cloud can be set up using the organization's private network, although this can be expensive to build and maintain. A private cloud can also be managed by an outside organization with strict access security.

- *Public clouds* – Cloud-based applications and services offered in a public cloud are made available to the general population. Services may be free or are offered on a pay-per-use model, such as paying for online storage. The public cloud uses the Internet to provide services.

- *Hybrid clouds* – A hybrid cloud is made up of two or more clouds (example: part custom, part public), where each part remains a distinctive object, but both are connected using a single architecture. Individuals on a hybrid cloud would be able to have degrees of access to various services based on user access rights.

- *Custom clouds* – These are clouds built to meet the needs of a specific industry, such as healthcare or media. Custom clouds can be private or public.

Cloud computing is possible because of data centers. A *data center* is a facility used to house computer systems and associated components. A data center can occupy one room of a building, one or more floors, or an entire building. Data centers are typically very expensive to build and maintain. For this reason, only large organizations use privately built data centers to house their data and provide services to users. Smaller organizations that cannot afford to maintain their own private data center can reduce the overall cost of ownership by leasing server and storage services from a larger data center organization in the Cloud.

Networking Technologies for the Home (1.4.2)

Today's home networks are used in every aspect of our daily lives, for entertainment, education, communications, and business.

Technology Trends in the Home (1.4.2.1)

Networking trends are not only affecting the way we communicate at work and at school, but they are also changing just about every aspect of the home, as shown in Figure 1-31.

Figure 1-31   Smart Home Technology

The newest home trends include '*smart home technology*.' Smart home technology is technology that is integrated into everyday appliances, allowing them to interconnect with other devices, making them more 'smart' or automated. For example, imagine being able to prepare a dish and place it in the oven for cooking prior to leaving the house for the day. Imagine if the oven was 'aware' of the dish it was cooking and was connected to your 'calendar of events' so that it could determine what time you should be available to eat, and adjust start times and length of cooking accordingly. It could even adjust cooking times and temperatures based on changes in schedule. Additionally, a smartphone or tablet connection allows the user the ability to connect to the oven directly to make any desired adjustments. When the dish is "available," the oven sends an alert message to a specified end user device that the dish is done and warming.

This scenario is not far off in the future. In fact, smart home technology is currently being developed for all rooms within a house. Smart home technology will become more of a reality as home networking and high-speed Internet technology become more widespread. New home networking technologies are being developed daily to meet these types of growing technology needs.

Powerline Networking (1.4.2.2)

Powerline networking is an emerging trend for home networking that uses existing electrical wiring to connect devices, as shown in Figure 1-32.

Figure 1-32 Powerline Networking

The concept of "no new wires" means the ability to connect a device to the network wherever there is an electrical outlet. This saves the cost of installing data cables and without any additional cost to the electrical bill. Using the same wiring that delivers electricity, powerline networking sends information by sending data on certain frequencies.

Using a standard powerline adapter, devices can connect to the LAN wherever there is an electrical outlet. Powerline networking is especially useful when wireless access points cannot be used or cannot reach all the devices in the home. Powerline networking is not designed to be a substitute for dedicated cabling in data networks. However, it is an alternative when data network cables or wireless communications are not a viable option.

Wireless Broadband (1.4.2.3)

Connecting to the Internet is vital in smart home technology. DSL and cable are common technologies used to connect homes and small businesses to the Internet. However, wireless may be another option in many areas.

Wireless Internet Service Provider (WISP) is an ISP that connects subscribers to a designated access point or hot spot using similar wireless technologies found in home wireless local area networks (WLANs). WISPs are more commonly found in rural environments where DSL or cable services are not available.

Although a separate transmission tower may be installed for the antenna, it is common that the antenna is attached to an existing elevated structure, such as a water tower or a radio tower. A small dish or antenna is installed on the subscriber's roof in range of the WISP transmitter. The subscriber's access unit is connected to the wired network inside the home. From the perspective of the home user, the setup is not much different than DSL or cable service. The main difference is that the connection from the home to the ISP is wireless instead of a physical cable.

Another wireless solution for the home and small businesses is wireless broadband, as shown in Figure 1-33.

Figure 1-33 Wireless Broadband Service

This uses the same cellular technology used to access the Internet with a smart phone or tablet. An antenna is installed outside the house providing either wireless or wired connectivity for devices in the home. In many areas, home wireless broadband is competing directly with DSL and cable services.

Network Security (1.4.3)

For a network to be entrusted with the communications of personal and business information, that network must be secure.

Security Threats (1.4.3.1)

Network security is an integral part of computer networking, regardless of whether the network is limited to a home environment with a single connection to the Internet or as large as a corporation with thousands of users. The network security that is implemented must take into account the environment as well as the tools and requirements of the network. It must be able to secure data while still allowing for the quality of service that is expected of the network.

Securing a network involves protocols, technologies, devices, tools, and techniques to secure data and mitigate threats. Threat vectors may be external or internal. Many external network security threats today are spread over the Internet.

The most common external threats to networks include

- **Viruses, worms, and Trojan horses** – malicious software and arbitrary code running on a user device

- **Spyware and adware** – software installed on a user device that secretly collects information about the user

- **Zero-day attacks, also called zero-hour attacks** – an attack that occurs on the first day that a vulnerability becomes known

- **Hacker attacks** – an attack by a knowledgeable person to user devices or network resources

- **Denial of service attacks** – attacks designed to slow or crash applications and processes on a network device

- **Data interception and theft** – an attack to capture private information from an organization's network

- **Identity theft** – an attack to steal the login credentials of a user in order to access private data

It is equally important to consider internal threats. There have been many studies that show that the most common data breaches happen because of internal users of the network. This can be attributed to lost or stolen devices, accidental misuse by employees, and in the business environment, even malicious employees. With the evolving BYOD strategies, corporate data is much more vulnerable. Therefore, when developing a security policy, it is important to address both external and internal security threats.

Security Solutions (1.4.3.2)

No single solution can protect the network from the variety of threats that exist, both internal and external, as shown in Figure 1-34.

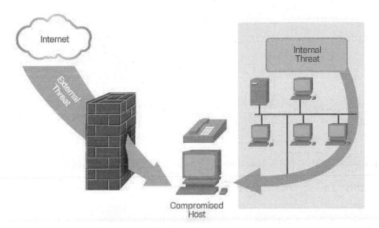

Figure 1-34   Threats to Networks

For this reason, security should be implemented in multiple layers, using more than one security solution. If one security component fails to identify and protect the network, others still stand.

A home network security implementation is usually rather basic. It is generally implemented on the connecting end devices as well as at the point of connection to the Internet and can even rely on contracted services from the ISP.

In contrast, the network security implementation for a corporate network usually consists of many components built into the network to monitor and filter traffic. Ideally, all components work together, which minimizes maintenance and improves security.

Network security components for a home or small office network should include, at a minimum

- **Antivirus and antispyware** – These are used to protect end devices from becoming infected with malicious software.

- **Firewall filtering** – This is used to block unauthorized access to the network. This may include a host-based firewall system that is implemented to prevent unauthorized access to the end device or a basic filtering service on the home router to prevent unauthorized access from the outside world into the network.

In addition to the above, larger networks and corporate networks often have other security requirements:

- **Dedicated firewall systems** – These are used to provide more advanced firewall capabilities that can filter large amounts of traffic with more granularity.

- **Access control lists (ACL)** – These are used to further filter access and traffic forwarding.

- **Intrusion prevention systems (IPS)** – These are used to identify fast-spreading threats, such as zero-day or zero-hour attacks.

- **Virtual private networks (VPN)** – These are used to provide secure access to remote workers.

Network security requirements must take into account the network environment, as well as the various applications, and computing requirements. Both home environments and businesses must be able to secure their data while still allowing for the quality of service that is expected of each technology. Additionally, the security solution implemented must be adaptable to the growing and changing trends of the network.

The study of network security threats and mitigation techniques starts with a clear understanding of the underlying switching and routing infrastructure used to organize network services.

Interactive Graphic

Activity 1.4.3.3: Network Security Terminology

Go to the online course to perform this practice activity.

Network Architecture (1.4.4)

[The role of the network has changed from a data-only network to a system that enables the connections of people, devices, and information in a media-rich, converged network environment. In order for networks to function efficiently and grow in this type of environment, the network must be built upon a standard network architecture.

Cisco Network Architecture (1.4.4.1)

The *network architecture* refers to the devices, connections, and products that are integrated to support the necessary technologies and applications. A well-planned network technology architecture helps ensure the connection of any device across any combination of networks. While ensuring connectivity, it also increases cost efficiency by integrating network security and management and improves business processes. At the foundation of all network architectures, and, in fact, at the foundation of the Internet itself, are routers and switches. Routers and switches transport data, voice, and video communications, as well as allow for wireless access, and provide for security.

Building networks that support our needs of today and the needs and trends of the future starts with a clear understanding of the underlying switching and routing infrastructure. After a basic routing and switching network infrastructure is built, individuals, small businesses, and organizations can grow their network over time, adding features and functionality in an integrated solution.

CCNA (1.4.4.2)

As the use of these integrated, expanding networks increases, so does the need for training for individuals who implement and manage network solutions. This training must begin with the routing and switching foundation. Achieving Cisco Certified Network Associate (CCNA) certification is the first step in helping an individual prepare for a career in networking. Other certifications beyond the Associate are also available, as shown in Figure 1-35.

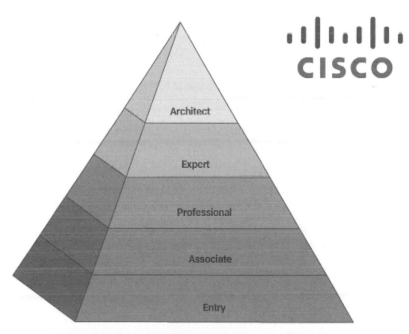

Figure 1-35   Cisco Certification Hierarchy

CCNA certification validates an individual's ability to install, configure, operate, and troubleshoot medium-size routed and switched networks, including implementation and verification of connections to remote sites in a WAN. CCNA curriculum also includes basic mitigation of security threats, introduction to wireless networking concepts and terminology, and performance-based skills. This CCNA curriculum includes the use of various protocols, such as Ethernet, VLANs, IPv4, IPv6, Open Shortest Path First (OSPF), Enhanced Interior Gateway Routing Protocol (EIGRP), access control lists (ACLs) and others.

This course helps set the stage for networking concepts and basic routing and switching configurations and is a start on your path toward CCNA certification.

Lab 1.4.4.3: Researching IT and Networking Job Opportunities

In this lab, you will complete the following objectives:

- Part 1: Research Job Opportunities
- Part 2: Reflect on Research

Summary (1.5)

Class Activity 1.5.1.1: Draw Your Concept of the Internet Now

In this activity, you will use the knowledge you have acquired throughout Chapter 1 and the modeling activity document that you prepared at the beginning of this chapter. You may also refer to the other activities completed in this chapter, including Packet Tracer activities.

Draw a map of the Internet as you see it now. Use the icons presented in the chapter for media, end devices, and intermediary devices.

In your revised drawing, you may wish to include some of the following:

- WANs
- LANs
- Cloud computing
- Internet Service Providers (tiers)

Save your drawing in hard-copy format. If it is an electronic document, save it to a server location provided by your instructor. Be prepared to share and explain your revised work in class.

Warriors of the Net (1.5.1.2)

An entertaining resource to help you visualize networking concepts is the animated movie "Warriors of the Net" by TNG Media Lab. Before viewing the video, there are a few things to consider. In terms of concepts you have learned in this chapter, think about when, in the video, you are on the LAN, on the WAN, on the intranet, on the Internet, and what are end devices versus intermediate devices.

Although all animations often have simplifications in them, there is one outright error in the video. About 5 minutes in, the statement is made "What happens when Mr. IP doesn't receive an acknowledgment, he simply sends a replacement packet." This is not a function of the Layer 3 Internet Protocol, which is an "unreliable," best effort delivery protocol, but rather a function of the transport layer TCP protocol. IP is explained in Chapter 6 and TCP is explained in Chapter 9.

Download the movie from http://www.warriorsofthe.net

Conclusion (1.5.1.3)

Networks and the Internet have changed the way we communicate, learn, work, and even play.

Networks come in all sizes. They can range from simple networks consisting of two computers to networks connecting millions of devices.

The Internet is the largest network in existence. In fact, the term Internet means a 'network of networks.' The Internet provides the services that enable us to connect and communicate with our families, friends, work, and interests.

The network infrastructure is the platform that supports the network. It provides the stable and reliable channel over which communication can occur. It is made up of network components including end devices, intermediate devices, and network media.

Networks must be reliable. This means the network must be fault tolerant, scalable, provide quality of service, and ensure security of the information and resources on the network. Network security is an integral part of computer networking, regardless of whether the network is limited to a home environment with a single connection to the Internet or as large as a corporation with thousands of users. No single solution can protect the network from the variety of threats that exist. For this reason, security should be implemented in multiple layers using more than one security solution.

The network infrastructure can vary greatly in terms of size, number of users, and number and types of services that are supported. The network infrastructure must grow and adjust to support the way the network is used. The routing and switching platform is the foundation of any network infrastructure.

This chapter focused on networking as a primary platform for supporting communication. The next chapter will introduce you to the Cisco Internetwork Operating System (IOS) used to enable routing and switching in a Cisco network environment.

Practice

The following activities provide practice with the topics introduced in this chapter. The Labs and Class Activities are available in the companion Introduction to Networks v5.1 Lab Manual (ISBN 9781587133534). The Packet Tracer Activities PKA files are found in the online course.

Class Activities

Class Activity 1.0.1.2: Draw Your Concept of the Internet

Class Activity 1.5.1.1: Draw Your Concept of the Internet Now

Labs

Lab 1.1.1.8: Researching Network Collaboration Tools

Lab 1.3.1.3: Researching Converged Network Services

Lab 1.4.4.3: Researching IT and Networking Job Opportunities

Packet Tracer Activities

Packet Tracer 1.2.4.4: Help and Navigation Tips

Packet Tracer 1.2.4.5: Network Representation

Check Your Understanding Questions

Complete all the review questions listed here to test your understanding of the topics and concepts in this chapter. The appendix "Answers to 'Check Your Understanding' Questions" lists the answers.

1. What is a group of web pages that groups of individuals can edit and view together called?

   A. Podcasting

   B. Wiki

   C. Weblog (blog)

   D. Instant messaging

   E. Access point

   F. TelePresence endpoint

2. Which of the following are disadvantages of peer-to-peer networking? (Choose two.)

   A. Expensive to set up and maintain

   B. No centralized administration

   C. Complex configuration

   D. Scalability

3. Which devices would be considered end devices on a network? (Choose four.)

   A. Switch

   B. Printer

   C. IP phone

    D. Server

    E. Tablet computer

    F. Wireless access point

4. What type of information would be found on a logical topology diagram?

    A. Location of departmental printer

    B. Length and type of all cable runs

    C. IP addressing scheme

    D. Location of departmental switch

5. What is a network infrastructure that provides access to other networks over a wide geographic area?

    A. LAN

    B. WLAN

    C. MAN

    D. WAN

    E. SAN

6. Which of the following are business-class Internet connection technologies normally supplied by a service provider? (Choose two.)

    A. Leased lines

    B. Broadband cable

    C. Metro Ethernet

    D. Mobile services

    E. Cellular

7. Which technology would be best to provide a home user with a high-speed, always-on Internet connection?

    A. Dial-up

    B. DSL

    C. Satellite

    D. Cellular

8. What is a converged network?

    A. A network that makes use of both fiber-optic and copper connections

    B. A network where voice, video, and data move over the same infrastructure

    C. A network that makes use of both wired and wireless technology

    D. A network that makes use of both satellite and terrestrial connections to move data

9. What is a fault-tolerant network?

    A. A network that can provide priority treatment of voice and video traffic

    B. A network that offers secure transactions

    C. A network that can reroute traffic in case of device failure

    D. A network that is incapable of failing

10. Which type of traffic must receive the highest priority from QoS?

    A. Web traffic

    B. Email

    C. VoIP

    D. Order processing

11. What are the primary requirements of information security? (Choose three.)

    A. Confidentiality

    B. Integrity

    C. Availability

    D. QoS

    E. Scalability

12. In which scenario would the use of a WISP be recommended?

    A. an Internet cafe in a city

    B. a farm in a rural area without wired broadband access

    C. any home with multiple wireless devices

    D. an apartment in a building with cable access to the Internet

13. List four current network trends.

14. Describe some common everyday uses of a modern-day network.

15. In what ways has the network transformed the way we learn?

CHAPTER 2

Configure a Network Operating System

Objectives

Upon completion of this chapter, you will be able to answer the following questions:

- What are the features and functions of the Cisco IOS software?

- What is the purpose of Cisco IOS?

- How is Cisco IOS accessed for configuration purposes?

- How is Cisco IOS navigated?

- What is the command structure of Cisco IOS software?

- How are host names configured on Cisco IOS devices using the CLI?

- How is access to device configuration limited on Cisco IOS devices?

- How is the running configuration saved on Cisco IOS devices?

- How do devices communicate across network media?

- How are Cisco IOS devices configured with an IP address?

- How is connectivity between two end devices verified?

Key Terms

This chapter uses the following key terms. You can find the definitions in the Glossary.

Introduction (2.0.1.1)

Every computer requires an operating system to function, including computer-based network devices such as switches, routers, access points, and firewalls. These network devices use an operating system called a network operating system.

A network operating system enables device hardware to function and provides an interface for users to interact. In the CCNA course of study, students learn to configure both devices that connect to the network (end devices such as PCs) and devices that connect networks together (intermediary devices like routers and switches). Learning to configure the *Cisco Internetwork Operating System (Cisco IOS)* on Cisco routers and switches is a large part of the Cisco CCNA program of study.

The Cisco Internetwork Operating System (IOS) is a generic term for the collection of network operating systems used by Cisco networking devices. Cisco IOS is used for most Cisco devices, regardless of the type or size.

Class Activity 2.0.1.2: It Is Just an Operating System

Refer to Lab Activity for this chapter

In this activity, imagine that you are employed as an engineer for a car manufacturing company. The company is currently working on a new car model. This model will have selected functions that can be controlled by the driver giving specific voice commands.

Design a set of commands used by this voice-activated control system and identify how they are going to be executed. The functions of the car that can be controlled by voice commands are

- Lights
- Wipers
- Radio
- Telephone set
- Air conditioning
- Ignition

IOS Bootcamp (2.1)

This section will provide a concise overview of the Cisco IOS.

Cisco IOS (2.1.1)

This topic will introduce the operating system used in most Cisco devices.

Operating Systems (2.1.1.1)

All end devices and network devices require an operating system (OS). As shown in Figure 2-1, the portion of the OS that interacts directly with computer hardware is known as the *kernel*. The portion that interfaces with applications and the user is known as the *shell*. The user can interact with the shell using a *command-line interface (CLI)* or a *graphical user interface (GUI)*.

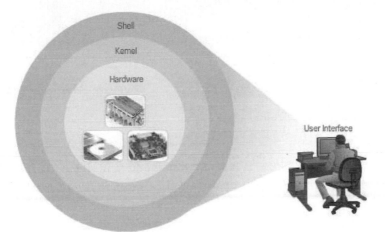

Figure 2-1   Operating System

The definitions of shell, kernel, and hardware are as follows:

- **Shell** – The user interface that allows users to request specific tasks from the computer. These requests can be made either through the CLI or GUI interfaces.

- **Kernel** – Communicates between the hardware and software of a computer and manages how hardware resources are used to meet software requirements.

- **Hardware** – The physical part of a computer including underlying electronics.

When using a CLI as shown for Windows in Figure 2-2, the user interacts directly with the system in a text-based environment by entering commands on the keyboard at a command prompt.

```
Administrator: C:\Windows\system32\cmd.exe

C:\> dir
 Volume in drive C is System
 Volume Serial Number is 808B-CEEA

 Directory of C:\

02/23/2015  08:59 AM                585 CSCOADLS.LOG
07/13/2009  11:08 PM    <JUNCTION>      Documents and Settings [C:\Users]
04/30/2015  07:59 AM             17,453 Install.log
09/12/2014  10:00 AM    <DIR>           Intel
11/23/2015  03:20 PM    <DIR>           IT_Logs
02/23/2015  10:44 AM    <DIR>           LEFTOVERS
02/23/2015  09:38 AM                 81 Newdiskspace.txt
02/23/2015  08:57 AM    <DIR>           OSSource
11/23/2015  03:20 PM    <DIR>           Program Files
12/04/2015  02:32 PM    <DIR>           Program Files (x86)
11/10/2015  06:37 PM    <DIR>           ProgramData
12/27/2015  10:57 AM            524,288 putty.exe
09/04/2015  06:37 AM                  4 ScrubRetValFile.txt
02/23/2015  08:27 PM                142 triggerfullhinv.LOG
02/23/2015  08:54 AM    <DIR>           Users
09/04/2015  06:40 AM    <DIR>           Windows
               6 File(s)        542,553 bytes
              10 Dir(s)  84,617,224,192 bytes free

C:\>
```

Figure 2-2   Windows Command-Line Interface

The system executes the command, often providing textual output. The CLI requires very little overhead to operate. However, it does require that the user have knowledge of the underlying structure that controls the system.

A GUI interface such as Windows, OS X, Apple iOS, or Android allows the user to interact with the system using an environment of graphical icons, menus, and windows. The Windows GUI example in Figure 2-3 is more user-friendly and requires less knowledge of the underlying command structure that controls the system. For this reason, many individuals rely on GUI environments.

However, GUIs may not always be able to provide all of the features available at the CLI. GUIs can also fail, crash, or simply not operate as specified. For these reasons, network devices are typically accessed through a CLI. The CLI is less resource intensive and very stable when compared to a GUI.

The network operating system used on Cisco devices is called the Cisco Internetwork Operating System (IOS). Cisco IOS is used for most Cisco devices regardless of the type or size of the device.

Note

The operating system on home routers is usually called firmware. The most common method for configuring a home router is by using a web browser-based GUI.

Figure 2-3   Windows Graphical User Interface

Purpose of OS (2.1.1.2)

Network operating systems are similar to a PC operating system. Through a GUI, a PC operating system enables a user to

- Use a mouse to make selections and run programs
- Enter text and text-based commands
- View output on a monitor

A CLI-based network operating system like the Cisco IOS on a switch or router enables a network technician to

- Use a keyboard to run CLI-based network programs
- Use a keyboard to enter text and text-based commands
- View output on a monitor

Cisco networking devices run particular versions of the Cisco IOS. The IOS version is dependent on the type of device being used and the required features. Whereas all devices come with a default IOS and feature set, it is possible to upgrade the IOS version or feature set to obtain additional capabilities.

In this course, you will focus primarily on Cisco IOS Release 15.x.

Cisco IOS Access (2.1.2)

This topic investigates the methods of accessing the CLI environment of the Cisco IOS.

Access Methods (2.1.2.1)

A Cisco IOS switch can be implemented with no configuration and still switch data between connected devices. By connecting two PCs to a switch, those PCs will instantly have connectivity with one another.

Even though a Cisco switch will function immediately, configuring initial settings are a recommended best practice. There are several ways to access the CLI environment and configure the device. The most common methods are

- *Console* – This is a physical management port that provides *out-of-band* access to a Cisco device. Out-of-band access refers to access via a dedicated management channel that is used for device maintenance purposes only. The advantage of using a console port is that the device is accessible even if no networking services have been configured, such as when performing an initial configuration of the networking device. When performing an initial configuration, a computer running terminal emulation software is connected to the console port of the device using a special cable. Configuration commands for setting up the switch or router can be entered on the connected computer.

- *Secure Shell (SSH)* – SSH is a method for remotely establishing a secure CLI connection through a virtual interface, over a network. Unlike a console connection, SSH connections require active networking services on the device including an active interface configured with an address. SSH is the recommended method for remote management because it provides a secure connection. SSH provides encrypted password authentication and transport of session data. This keeps the user ID, password, and the details of the management session private. Most versions of Cisco IOS include an SSH server and an SSH client that can be used to establish SSH sessions with other devices.

- *Telnet* – Telnet is an insecure method of remotely establishing a CLI session through a virtual interface, over a network. Unlike SSH, Telnet does not provide a securely encrypted connection. User authentication, passwords, and commands are sent over the network in plaintext. Best practice dictates to use SSH instead of Telnet for remote management CLI connections. Cisco IOS includes a Telnet server and a Telnet client that can be used to establish Telnet sessions with other devices.

Note

Some devices, such as routers, may also support a legacy auxiliary port that was used to establish a CLI session remotely using a modem. Similar to a console connection, the AUX port is out-of-band and does not require networking services to be configured or available.

Terminal Emulation Programs (2.1.2.2)

There are a number of excellent terminal emulation programs available for connecting to a networking device either by a serial connection over a console port or by a SSH/Telnet connection. Some of these include

- PuTTY (Figure 2-4)

- Tera Term (Figure 2-5)

- SecureCRT (Figure 2-6)

- OS X Terminal

Figure 2-4   PuTTY

Figure 2-5 Tera Term

Figure 2-6 SecureCRT

These programs allow you to enhance your productivity by adjusting window sizes, changing font sizes, and changing color schemes.

Activity 2.1.2.3: Accessing Devices

Go to the online course to perform this practice activity.

Navigate the IOS (2.1.3)

To configure, test, and troubleshoot Cisco network devices, technicians need to have a working knowledge of the Cisco IOS. This section introduces the fundamentals of the method and modes of the Cisco IOS.

Cisco IOS Modes of Operation (2.1.3.1)

To initially configure a Cisco device, a console connection must be established. Once consoled in, the network technician will have to navigate through various command modes of the IOS CLI. The Cisco IOS modes use a hierarchical structure and are quite similar for both switches and routers.

Play the video to view a demonstration of how to establish a console connection with a switch.

Go to the online course to view this video.

Primary Command Modes (2.1.3.2)

As a security feature, the Cisco IOS software separates management access into the following two command modes:

- *User EXEC Mode* – This mode has limited capabilities but is useful for basic operations. It allows only a limited number of basic monitoring commands but does not allow the execution of any commands that might change the configuration of the device. The user EXEC mode is identified by the CLI prompt that ends with the > symbol.

- *Privileged EXEC Mode* – To execute configuration commands, a network administrator must access privileged EXEC mode. Higher configuration modes, like global configuration mode, can only be reached from privileged EXEC mode. The privileged EXEC mode can be identified by the prompt ending with the # symbol.

Table 2-1 summarizes the two modes and displays the default CLI prompts of a Cisco switch and router.

Table 2-1   Primary Command Modes

Command Mode	Description	Default Device Prompt
User EXEC Mode	■ Mode allows access to only a limited number of basic monitoring commands.	`Switch>`
	■ It is often referred to as "view-only" mode.	`Router>`
Privileged EXEC Mode	■ Mode allows access to all commands and features.	`Switch#`
	■ The user can use any monitoring commands and execute configuration and management commands.	`Router#`

Configuration Command Modes (2.1.3.3)

To configure the device, the user must enter *Global Configuration Mode*, which is commonly called global config mode.

From global config mode, CLI configuration changes are made that affect the operation of the device as a whole. Global configuration mode is identified by a prompt that ends with (config)# after the device name, such as **Switch(config)#**.

Global configuration mode is accessed before other specific configuration modes. From global config mode, the user can enter different sub-configuration modes. Each of these modes allows the configuration of a particular part or function of the IOS device. Two common sub-configuration modes include

- **Line Configuration Mode** – Used to configure console, SSH, Telnet, or AUX access.

- **Interface Configuration Mode** – Used to configure a switch port or router network interface.

When using the CLI, the mode is identified by the command-line prompt that is unique to that mode. By default, every prompt begins with the device name. Following the name, the remainder of the prompt indicates the mode. For example, the default prompt for line configuration mode is **Switch(config-line)#** and the default prompt for interface configuration mode is **Switch(config-if)#**.

Play the video to view a demonstration of navigating between IOS modes.

Go to the online course to view this video.

Video

Navigate Between IOS Modes (2.1.3.4)

Various commands are used to move in and out of command prompts. To move from user EXEC mode to privileged EXEC mode, use the **enable** command. Use the **disable** privileged EXEC mode command to return to user EXEC mode.

> **Note**
>
> Privileged EXEC mode is sometimes called *enable mode*.

```
Switch> enable
```

```
Switch# disable
```

```
Switch>
```

To move in and out of global configuration mode, use the **configure terminal** privileged EXEC mode command. To return to the privileged EXEC mode, enter the **exit** global config mode command.

There are many different sub-configuration modes. For example, to enter line sub-configuration mode, you use the **line** command followed by the management line type and number you wish to access. To exit a sub-configuration mode and return to global configuration mode, use the **exit** command. Notice the changes in the command prompt.

```
Switch(config)# line console 0
```

```
Switch(config-line)#
```

To move from any sub-configuration mode of the global configuration mode to the mode one step above it in the hierarchy of modes, enter the **exit** command.

```
Switch(config-line)# exit
```

```
Switch(config)#
```

To move from any sub-configuration mode to the privileged EXEC mode, enter the **end** command or enter the key combination **Ctrl+Z**.

```
Switch(config-line)# end
```

```
Switch#
```

You can also move directly from one sub-configuration mode to another. To do so, you must enter a valid global configuration command from the current sub-configuration prompt. The following example displays how to move from line config mode to interface config mode. Notice how after the network device name, the command prompt changes from (config-line)# to (config-if)#.

```
Switch(config-line)# interface FastEthernet 0/1
```

```
Switch(config-if)#
```

Play the video to view a demonstration of how to move between various IOS CLI modes.

Go to the online course to view this video.

Video

The Command Structure (2.1.4)

The Cisco IOS, like programming languages, uses commands that have a specific structure. To configure an IOS device, a network technician needs to understand this structure. This topic will introduce the IOS command structure.

Basic IOS Command Structure (2.1.4.1)

A Cisco IOS device supports many commands. Each IOS command has a specific format or syntax and can only be executed in the appropriate mode. The general syntax for a command is the command followed by any appropriate keywords and arguments, as shown in Figure 2-7.

Figure 2-7   Basic IOS Command Structure

- **Keyword** – a specific parameter defined in the operating system (in the Figure 2-7, **ip protocols**)

- **Argument** – not predefined; a value or variable defined by the user (in the Figure 2-7, **192.168.10.5**)

After entering each complete command, including any keywords and arguments, press the Enter key to submit the command to the command interpreter.

IOS Command Syntax (2.1.4.2)

A command might require one or more arguments. To determine the keywords and arguments required for a command, refer to the command syntax. The syntax provides the pattern or format that must be used when entering a command.

As identified in Table 2-2, boldface text indicates commands and keywords that are entered as shown. Italic text indicates an argument for which the user provides the value.

Table 2-2   IOS Command Conventions

Convention	Description
boldface	Boldface text indicates commands and keywords that you enter literally as shown.
italics	Italic text indicates arguments for which you supply values.
[x]	Square brackets indicate an optional element (keyword or argument).
{x}	Braces indicate a required element (keyword or argument).
[x {y | z}]	Braces and vertical lines within square brackets indicate a required choice within an optional element.

For instance, the syntax for using the **description** command is **description** *string*. The argument is a *string* value provided by the user. The command is typically used to identify the purpose of an interface. For example, entering the command **description Connects to the main headquarter office switch** describes where the other device is at the end of the connection.

The following examples demonstrate conventions used to document and use IOS commands.

- **ping** *ip-address* – The command is *ping* and the user defined argument is the *ip-address* of the destination device. For example, **ping 10.10.10.5**.

- **traceroute** *ip-address* – The command is *traceroute* and the user-defined argument is the *ip-address* of the destination device. For example, **traceroute 192.168.254.254**.

Do an Internet search for the phrase "Cisco IOS Command Reference" to locate the ultimate source of information for a particular IOS command.

IOS Help Features (2.1.4.3)

The IOS has two forms of help available:

- Context Sensitive Help
- Command Syntax Check

Context-sensitive help enables you to quickly find which commands are available in each command mode, which commands start with specific characters or group of characters, and which arguments and keywords are available to particular commands. To access context-sensitive help, simply enter a question mark, **?**, at the CLI.

Command syntax check verifies that a valid command was entered by the user. When a command is entered, the command line interpreter evaluates the command from left to right. If the interpreter understands the command, the requested action is executed, and the CLI returns to the appropriate prompt. However, if the interpreter cannot understand the command being entered, it will provide feedback describing what is wrong with the command.

Play the video to view a demonstration of context-sensitive help and command syntax check.

Go to the online course to view this video.

Video

Hotkeys and Shortcuts (2.1.4.4)

The IOS CLI provides Hotkeys and shortcuts that make configuring, monitoring, and troubleshooting easier. For instance, Table 2-3 lists keyboard shortcuts that can be used at the command prompt to accelerate keyboard input.

Table 2-3   CLI Line Editing

Hotkeys or Shortcut	Description
Tab	Completes a partial command name entry.
Backspace	Erases the character to the left of the cursor.
Ctrl-D	Erases the character at the cursor.
Ctrl-K	Erases all characters from the cursor to the end of the command line.
Esc D	Erases all characters from the cursor to the end of the word.
Ctrl-U or Ctrl-K	Erases all characters from the cursor back to the beginning of the command line.
Ctrl-W	Erases the word to the left of the cursor.
Ctrl-A	Moves the cursor to the beginning of the line.
Left Arrow or Ctrl-B	Moves the cursor one character to the left.
Esc B	Moves the cursor back one word to the left.
Esc F	Moves the cursor forward one word to the right.
Right Arrow or Ctrl-F	Moves the cursor one character to the right.
Ctrl-E	Moves the cursor to the end of the command line.
Up Arrow or Ctrl-P	Recalls the command in the history buffer, beginning with the most recent commands.
Ctrl-R or Ctrl-I or Ctrl-L	Redisplays the system prompt and command line after a console message is received.

Table 2-4 lists the Hotkeys that can be used to change how much text is displayed on the screen.

Table 2-4   At the "——More——" Prompt

Hotkeys	Description
Enter Key	Displays the next line.
Space Bar	Displays the next screen.
Any Key	Ends the display string, returning to privileged EXEC mode.

Table 2-5 list the shortcuts to enter a break command under the described circumstance.

Table 2-5   Break Keys

Shortcut	Description
Ctrl-C	When in any configuration mode, end the configuration mode and returns to privileged EXEC mode. When in setup mode, aborts back to the command prompt.
Ctrl-Z	When in any configuration mode, end the configuration mode and returns to privileged EXEC mode.
Ctrl-Shift-6	All-purpose break sequence. For example, can be used to abort DNS lookups, traceroutes, and pings.

Commands and keywords can be shortened to the minimum number of characters that identify a unique selection. For example, the **configure** command can be shortened to **conf** because **configure** is the only command that begins with **conf**. An even shorter version of **con** will not work because more than one command begins with **con**. Keywords can also be shortened.

Play the video to view a demonstration of the various Hotkeys and shortcuts.

Video Demonstration 2.1.4.5: Hotkeys and Shortcuts

Video

Go to the online course to view this video.

Packet Tracer 2.1.4.6: Navigating the IOS

Packet Tracer
☐ Activity

In this activity, you will practice skills necessary for navigating the Cisco IOS, including different user access modes, various configuration modes, and common commands used on a regular basis. You also practice accessing the context-sensitive help by configuring the clock command.

Lab 2.1.4.7: Establishing a Console Session with Tera Term

Refer to Lab Activity for this chapter

In this lab, you will complete the following objectives:

- Part 1: Access a Cisco Switch through the Serial Console Port
- Part 2: Display and Configure Basic Device Settings
- Part 3: (Optional) Access a Cisco Router Using a Mini-USB Console Cable

Basic Device Configuration (2.2)

Before devices can be used in a network, they will require configuration. This section introduces the basic configuration of Cisco IOS devices.

Hostnames (2.2.1)

An important part of the basic device configuration is assigning the device a name. This topic will discuss the naming of Cisco IOS network devices.

Device Names (2.2.1.1)

When configuring a networking device, one of the first steps is configuring a unique device name or hostname. Hostnames that appear in CLI prompts can be used in various authentication processes between devices and should be used on topology diagrams.

If the device name is not explicitly configured, a factory-assigned default name is used by the Cisco IOS. The default name for a Cisco IOS switch is "Switch." If all network devices were left with their default names, it would be difficult to identify a specific device. For instance, when accessing a remote device using SSH, it is important to have confirmation that you are connected to the proper device.

By choosing names wisely, it is easier to remember, document, and identify network devices. Guidelines for hostname include the following:

- Start with a letter
- End with a letter or digit
- Use only letters, digits, and dashes
- Contain no space
- Be fewer than 64 characters in length

The hostnames used in the device IOS preserve capitalization and lowercase characters. Therefore, it allows you to capitalize a name as you ordinarily would. This contrasts with most Internet naming schemes, where uppercase and lowercase characters are treated identically.

For example, in Figure 2-8, three switches, spanning three different floors, are interconnected together in a network. The naming convention used took into consideration the location and the purpose of each device. Network documentation should explain how these names were chosen so additional devices can be named accordingly.

Figure 2-8 Configuring Device Names

Configure Hostnames (2.2.1.2)

Once the naming convention has been identified, the next step is to apply the names to the devices using the CLI.

As shown in Example 2-1, from the privileged EXEC mode, access the global configuration mode by entering the **configure terminal** command. Notice the change in the command prompt.

From global configuration mode, enter the command **hostname** followed by the name of the switch and press Enter. Notice the change in the command prompt name.

Example 2-1 Configure a Hostname

```
Switch# configure terminal
Switch(config)# hostname Sw-Floor-1
Sw-Floor-1(config)#
```

Note

To remove the configured hostname and return the switch to the default prompt, use the **no hostname** global config command.

Always make sure the documentation is updated each time a device is added or modified. Identify devices in the documentation by their location, purpose, and address.

Limit Access to Device Configurations (2.2.2)

To help ensure the security of a network, access to the network devices should be protected. This topic will examine the basics of limiting device access.

Secure Device Access (2.2.2.1)

The use of weak or easily guessed passwords continues to be a security issue in many facets of the business world. Network devices, including home wireless routers, should always have passwords configured to limit administrative access.

Cisco IOS can be configured to use hierarchical mode passwords to allow different access privileges to a network device.

All networking devices should limit access as follows:

- Securing Administrative Access
  - Secure privileged EXEC access with a password
  - Secure user EXEC access with a password
  - Secure remote Telnet access with a password
- Other tasks
  - Encrypt all passwords
  - Provide legal notification

Use strong passwords that are not easily guessed. When choosing a password, consider the following key points:

- Use passwords that are more than 8 characters in length.
- Use a combination of upper and lowercase letters, numbers, special characters, and/or numeric sequences.
- Avoid using the same password for all devices.
- Don't use common words because these are easily guessed.

Note

Most of the labs in this course use simple passwords such as **cisco** or **class**. These passwords are considered weak and easily guessable and should be avoided in production environments. We only use these passwords for convenience in a classroom setting or to illustrate configuration examples.

Configure Passwords (2.2.2.2)

The most important password to configure secures access to the privileged EXEC mode, as shown in Example 2-2. To secure privileged EXEC access, use the **enable secret** *password* global config command.

Example 2-2 Privileged EXEC Password Configuration

```
Sw-Floor-1> enable
Sw-Floor-1# configure terminal
Sw-Floor-1(config)# enable secret class
Sw-Floor-1(config)# exit
Sw-Floor-1# disable
Sw-Floor-1> enable
Password: <class>
Sw-Floor-1#
```

To secure the user EXEC access, the console port must be configured, as shown in Example 2-3.

Example 2-3 User EXEC Password Configuration

```
Sw-Floor-1(config)# line console 0
Sw-Floor-1(config-line)# password cisco
Sw-Floor-1(config-line)# login
Sw-Floor-1(config-line)# exit
Sw-Floor-1(config)#
```

Enter line console configuration mode using the **line console 0** global configuration command. The zero is used to represent the first (and in most cases the only) console interface. Next, specify the user EXEC mode password using the **password** *password* command. Finally, enable user EXEC access using the **login** command. Console access will now require a password before gaining access to the user EXEC mode.

Virtual terminal (VTY) lines enable remote access to the device. To secure VTY lines used for SSH and Telnet, enter line VTY mode using the **line vty 0 15** global config command, as shown in Example 2-4. Many Cisco switches support up to 16 VTY lines that are numbered 0 to 15. Next, specify the VTY password using the **password** *password* command. Lastly, enable VTY access using the **login** command.

Example 2-4 VTY Line Password Configuration

```
Sw-Floor-1(config)# line vty 0 15
Sw-Floor-1(config-line)# password cisco
Sw-Floor-1(config-line)# login
Sw-Floor-1(config-line)# exit
Sw-Floor-1(config)#
```

Encrypt Passwords (2.2.2.3)

The startup-config and running-config files display most passwords in plaintext. This is a security threat since anyone can see the passwords used if they have access to these files.

To encrypt passwords, use the **service password-encryption** global config command. The command applies weak encryption to all unencrypted passwords. This encryption applies only to passwords in the configuration file, not to passwords as they are sent over the network. The purpose of this command is to keep unauthorized individuals from viewing passwords in the configuration file.

Go to the online course to perform this practice activity.

Interactive Graphic

Banner Messages (2.2.2.4)

Although requiring passwords is one way to keep unauthorized personnel out of a network, it is vital to provide a method for declaring that only authorized personnel should attempt to gain entry into the device. To do this, add a banner to the device output. Banners can be an important part of the legal process in the event that someone is prosecuted for breaking into a device. Some legal systems do not allow prosecution, or even the monitoring of users, unless a notification is visible.

To create a banner message of the day on a network device, use the **banner motd** **#** *the message of the day* **#** global config command. The "#" in the command syntax is called the delimiting character. It is entered before and after the message. The delimiting character can be any character as long as it does not occur in the message. For this reason, symbols such as the "#" are often used. After the command is executed, the banner will be displayed on all subsequent attempts to access the device until the banner is removed.

Because banners can be seen by anyone who attempts to log in, the message must be worded very carefully. The exact content or wording of a banner depends on the local laws and corporate policies. The banner should state that only authorized personnel are allowed to access the device. Any wording that implies a login is "welcome" or "invited" is inappropriate. Further, the banner can include scheduled system shutdowns and other information that affects all network users.

Play the video to view a demonstration of how to secure administrative access to a switch.

Go to the online course to view this video.

Video

Save Configurations (2.2.3)

Configuration changes to Cisco IOS–based devices occur to the running configuration. This working configuration should be backed up to support network recovery. This topic will examine some the methods used to back up and restore the running configuration on Cisco IOS devices.

Save the Running Configuration File (2.2.3.1)

There are two system files that store the device configuration:

- **startup-config** – The file stored in *Non-volatile Random Access Memory (NVRAM)* that contains all of the commands that will be used by the device upon startup or reboot. NVRAM does not lose its contents when the device is powered off.

- **running-config** – The file stored in *Random Access Memory (RAM)* that reflects the current configuration. Modifying a running configuration affects the operation of a Cisco device immediately. RAM is volatile memory. It loses all of its content when the device is powered off or restarted.

As shown Figure 2-9, use the **show running-config** privileged EXEC mode command to view the running configuration file. To view the startup configuration file, use the **show startup-config** privileged EXEC command.

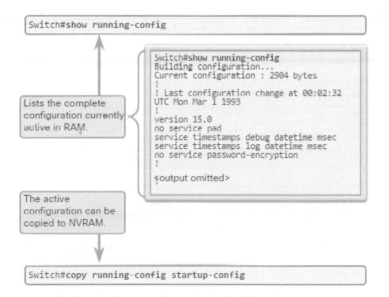

Figure 2-9 Viewing and Saving the Configuration

If power to the device is lost or if the device is restarted, all configuration changes will be lost unless they have been saved. To save changes made to the running configuration to the startup configuration file use the **copy running-config startup-config** privileged EXEC mode command.

```
Sw-Floor-1# copy running-config startup-config
```

Alter the Running Configuration (2.2.3.2)

If changes made to the running configuration do not have the desired effect and the running-config file has not yet been saved, you can

- Restore the device to its previous configuration by removing the changed commands individually.

- Copy the startup configuration file to the running configuration with the **copy startup-config running-config** privileged EXEC mode command.

- Reload the device using the **reload** privileged EXEC mode command.

The downside to using the **reload** command to remove an unsaved running configuration is the brief amount of time the device will be offline, causing network downtime.

When initiating a reload, the IOS will detect that the running config has changes that were not saved to the startup configuration. A prompt will appear to ask whether to save the changes. To discard the changes, enter **n** or **no**.

Alternatively, if undesired changes were saved to the startup configuration, it may be necessary to clear all the configurations. This requires erasing the startup configuration and restarting the device. The startup configuration is removed by using the **erase startup-config** privileged EXEC mode command. After the command is issued, the switch will prompt you for confirmation. Press **Enter** to accept.

After removing the startup configuration from NVRAM, reload the device to remove the current running configuration file from RAM. On reload, a switch will load the default startup configuration that originally shipped with the device.

Play the video to view a demonstration on how to save switch configuration files.

Go to the online course to view this video.

Video

Capture Configuration to a Text File (2.2.3.3)

Configuration files can also be saved and archived to a text document. This sequence of steps ensures that a working copy of the configuration file is available for editing or reuse later.

For example, assume that a switch has been configured and the running configuration has been saved on the device.

■ Open a terminal emulation software such as PuTTY or Tera Term (Figure 2-10) connected to a switch.

Figure 2-10   Using PuTTY to Capture Console Session

■ Enable logging in the terminal software, such as PuTTY or Tera Term, and assign a name and file location to save the log file. Figure 2-11 displays that **All session output** will be captured to the file specified (i.e., MySwitchLogs.log).

Figure 2-11   Enabling Session Logging in PuTTY

■ Execute the **show running-config** or **show startup-config** command at the privileged EXEC prompt. Text displayed in the terminal window will be placed into the chosen file.

■ Disable logging in the terminal software. Figure 2-12 shows how to disable logging by choosing the **None** session logging option.

Figure 2-12   Disabling Session Logging in PuTTY

The text file created can be used as a record of how the device is currently implemented. The file could require editing before being used to restore a saved configuration to a device.

To restore a configuration file to a device

- Enter global configuration mode on the device.

- Copy and paste the text file into the terminal window connected to the switch.

The text in the file will be applied as commands in the CLI and become the running configuration on the device. This is a convenient method of manually configuring a device.

Packet Tracer 2.2.3.4: Configuring Initial Switch Settings

In this activity, you will perform basic switch configurations. You will secure access to the command-line interface (CLI) and console ports using encrypted and plain text passwords. You will learn how to configure messages for users logging in to the switch. These banners are also used to warn unauthorized users that access is prohibited.

Address Schemes (2.3)

In this section, devices are configured with IPv4 addresses.

Ports and Addresses (2.3.1)

For devices to communicate on a network, each device must have addressing information applied. This topic introduces how IPv4 addresses are configured on the devices.

IP Addresses (2.3.1.1)

The use of IP addresses is the primary means of enabling devices to locate one another and establish end-to-end communication on the Internet. Each end device on a network must be configured with an IP address. Examples of end devices that require IP addresses include the following:

- Computers (work stations, laptops, file servers, web servers)
- Network printers
- VoIP phones
- Security cameras
- Smart phones
- Mobile handheld devices (such as wireless barcode scanners)

The structure of an *IPv4 address* is called dotted decimal notation and is represented by four decimal numbers between 0 and 255. IPv4 addresses are assigned to individual devices connected to a network. With the IPv4 address, a *subnet mask* is also necessary. An IPv4 subnet mask is a 32-bit value that separates the network portion of the address from the host portion. Coupled with the IPv4 address, the subnet mask determines the particular subnet of which the device is a member.

Note

IP in this course refers to both the IPv4 and IPv6 protocols. IPv6 is the most recent version of IP and the replacement for the more common IPv4. IPv6 uses the term prefix length instead of subnet mask.

The example in Figure 2-13 displays the IPv4 address (192.168.1.10), subnet mask (255.255.255.0), and default gateway (192.168.1.1) assigned to a host. The default gateway address is the IP address of the router that the host will use to access remote networks, including the Internet.

Figure 2-13   Configuring a Static IP Address on a Host

IP addresses can be assigned to both physical ports and virtual interfaces on devices. A virtual interface means that there is no physical hardware on the device associated with it.

Interfaces and Ports (2.3.1.2)

Network communications depend on end user device interfaces, networking device interfaces, and the cables that connect them. Each physical interface has specifications, or standards, that define it. A cable connecting to the interface must be designed to match the physical standards of the interface. Types of network media include twisted-pair copper cables, fiber-optic cables, coaxial cables, or wireless as shown in Figure 2-14.

Figure 2-14   Interfaces and Ports

Different types of network media have different features and benefits. Not all network media have the same characteristics and are appropriate for the same purpose. Some of the differences among various types of media include

- Distance the media can successfully carry a signal

- Environment in which the media is to be installed

- Amount of data and the speed at which it must be transmitted

- Cost of the media and installation

Not only does each link on the Internet require a specific network media type, but each link also requires a particular network technology. For example, Ethernet is the most common local area network (LAN) technology used today. Ethernet ports are found on end-user devices, switch devices, and other networking devices that can physically connect to the network using a cable.

Cisco IOS Layer 2 switches have physical ports for devices to connect. These ports do not support Layer 3 IP addresses. Therefore, switches have one or more *switch virtual interfaces (SVIs)*. These are virtual interfaces because there is no physical hardware on the device associated with it. An SVI is created in software.

The virtual interface provides a means to remotely manage a switch over a network using IPv4. Each switch comes with one SVI appearing in the default configuration "out-of-the-box." The default SVI is interface VLAN1.

Note

A Layer 2 switch does not need an IP address. The IP address assigned to the SVI is used to remotely access the switch. An IP address is not necessary for the switch to perform its operations.

Configure IP Addressing (2.3.2)

In addition to the IP address, additional addressing information must be configured for devices to communicate on a network. This section introduces how this addressing information is configured on devices.

Manual IP Address Configuration for End Devices (2.3.2.1)

In order for an end device to communicate over the network, it must be configured with a unique IPv4 address and subnet mask. IPv4 address information can be entered into end devices manually, or automatically using *Dynamic Host Configuration Protocol (DHCP)*.

To manually configure an IPv4 address on a Windows host, open the **Control Panel > Network Sharing Center > Change adapter settings** and choose the adapter. Next right-click and select **Properties** to display the **Local Area Connection Properties** shown in Figure 2-15.

Local Area Connection Properties ☒

Networking | Authentication | Sharing

Connect using:

    Intel(R) Ethernet Connection I217-LM

            [_Configure..._]

This connection uses the following items:

- ☑ Client for Microsoft Networks
- ☑ QoS Packet Scheduler
- ☑ File and Printer Sharing for Microsoft Networks
- ☑ Cisco Media Services Interface Protocol Driver
- ☑ Internet Protocol Version 6 (TCP/IPv6)
- ☑ Internet Protocol Version 4 (TCP/IPv4)
- ☑ Link-Layer Topology Discovery Mapper I/O Driver
- ☑ Link-Layer Topology Discovery Responder

[_Install..._]   [_Uninstall_]   [_Properties_]

Description

   Transmission Control Protocol/Internet Protocol. The default wide area network protocol that provides communication across diverse interconnected networks.

[OK]   [Cancel]

Figure 2-15   Ethernet Adapter Properties

Highlight Internet Protocol Version 4 (TCP/IPv4) and click **Properties** to open the **Internet Protocol Version 4 (TCP/IPv4) Properties** window shown in Figure 2-16. Configure the IPv4 address and subnet mask information, and default gateway.

Internet Protocol Version 4 (TCP/IPv4) Properties

General

You can get IP settings assigned automatically if your network supports this capability. Otherwise, you need to ask your network administrator for the appropriate IP settings.

○ Obtain an IP address automatically

● Use the following IP address:

IP address: 192 . 168 . 1 . 10

Subnet mask: 255 . 255 . 255 . 0

Default gateway: 192 . 168 . 1 . 1

○ Obtain DNS server address automatically

● Use the following DNS server addresses

Preferred DNS server: .   .

Alternate DNS server: .   .

☐ Validate settings upon exit   Advanced...

OK   Cancel

Figure 2-16   Manually Assigning IPv4 Address Information

Note

The DNS server addresses are the IP addresses of the *Domain Name System (DNS)* servers, which are used to translate IP addresses to domain names, such as www.cisco.com.

Automatic IP Address Configuration for End Devices (2.3.2.2)

PCs typically default to using DHCP for automatic IPv4 address configuration. DHCP is a technology that is used in almost every network. The best way to understand why DHCP is so popular is by considering all the extra work that would have to take place without it.

In a network, DHCP enables automatic IPv4 address configuration for every end device that has DHCP enabled. Imagine the amount of time it would consume if every time you connected to the network, you had to manually enter the IPv4 address, the subnet mask, the default gateway, and the DNS server. Multiply that by every user and every device in an organization and you see the problem. Manual configuration also increases the chance of misconfiguration by duplicating another device's IPv4 address.

As shown in Figure 2-17, to configure DHCP on a Windows PC, you only need to select "Obtain an IP address automatically" and "Obtain DNS server address automatically." Your PC will search out a DHCP server and be assigned the address settings necessary to communicate on the network.

Figure 2-17 Assigning Dynamic Addresses

It is possible to display the IP configuration settings on a Windows PC by using the **ipconfig** command at the command prompt. The output will show the IPv4 address, subnet mask, and gateway information received from the DHCP server.

Switch Virtual Interface Configuration (2.3.2.3)

To access the switch remotely, an IP address and a subnet mask must be configured on the SVI. To configure an SVI on a switch, use the **interface vlan 1** global configuration command. Vlan 1 is not an actual physical interface but a virtual one. Next assign an IPv4 address using the **ip address** *ip-address subnet-mask* interface configuration command. Finally, enable the virtual interface using the **no shutdown** interface configuration command.

After these commands are configured, the switch has all the IPv4 elements ready for communication over the network.

Play the video to view a demonstration of how to configure a switch virtual interface.

Go to the online course to view this video.

Packet Tracer 2.3.2.5: Implementing Basic Connectivity

In this activity, you will first perform basic switch configurations. Then you will implement basic connectivity by configuring IP addressing on switches and PCs. When the IP addressing configuration is complete, you will use various show commands to verify configurations and use the ping command to verify basic connectivity between devices.

Verifying Connectivity (2.3.3)

A principal troubleshooting technique is to verify the logical connectivity between two or more IPv4 devices. This topic introduces some of the steps used to verify this connectivity.

Interface Addressing Verification (2.3.3.1)

In the same way that you use commands and utilities like **ipconfig** to verify a PC host's network configuration, you also use commands to verify the interfaces and address settings of intermediary devices like switches and routers.

Play the video to view a demonstration of the **show ip interface brief** command. This command is useful for verifying the condition of the switch interfaces.

Go to the online course to view this video.

End-to-End Connectivity Test (2.3.3.2)

The **ping** command can be used to test connectivity to another device on the network or a website on the Internet.

Play the video to view a demonstration using the **ping** command to test connectivity to a switch and to another PC.

Video

Go to the online course to view this video.

Lab 2.3.3.3: Building a Simple Network

In this lab, you will complete the following objectives:

- Part 1: Set Up the Network Topology (Ethernet only)
- Part 2: Configure PC Hosts
- Part 3: Configure and Verify Basic Switch Settings

Lab 2.3.3.4: Configuring a Switch Management Address

In this lab, you will complete the following objectives:

- Part 1: Configure a Basic Network Device
- Part 2: Verify and Test Network Connectivity

Summary (2.4)

Class Activity 2.4.1.1: Tutor Me

Students will work in pairs. Packet Tracer is required for this activity.

Assume that a new colleague has asked you for an orientation to the Cisco IOS CLI. This colleague has never worked with Cisco devices before.

You explain the basic CLI commands and structure because you want your colleague to understand that the CLI is a simple, yet powerful, command language that can be easily understood and navigated.

Use Packet Tracer and one of the activities available in this chapter as a simple network model (for example, Lab – Configuring a Switch Management Address).

Focus on these areas:

While the commands are technical, do they resemble any statements from plain English?

How is the set of commands organized into subgroups or modes? How does an administrator know which mode he or she is currently using?

What are the individual commands to configure the basic settings of a Cisco device? How would you explain this command in simple terms? Use parallels to real life whenever appropriate.

Suggest how to group different commands together according to their modes so that a minimum number of moves between modes will be needed.

Packet Tracer 2.4.1.2: Skills Integration Challenge

Packet Tracer
☐ Activity

As a recently hired LAN technician, your network manager has asked you to demonstrate your ability to configure a small LAN. Your tasks include configuring initial settings on two switches using the Cisco IOS and configuring IP address parameters on host devices to provide end-to-end connectivity. You are to use two switches and two hosts/PCs on a cabled and powered network.

Cisco IOS is a term that encompasses a number of different operating systems, which runs on various networking devices. The technician can enter commands to configure, or program, the device to perform various networking functions. Cisco IOS routers and switches perform functions that network professionals depend upon to make their networks operate as expected.

The services provided by the Cisco IOS are accessed using a command-line interface (CLI), which is accessed by either the console port, the AUX port, or through SSH or Telnet. After connected to the CLI, network technicians can make configuration changes to Cisco IOS devices. The Cisco IOS is designed as a modal operating system, which means a network technician must navigate through various hierarchical modes of the IOS. Each mode supports different IOS commands.

Cisco IOS routers and switches support a similar modal operating system, support similar command structures, and support many of the same commands. In addition, both devices have identical initial configuration steps when implementing them in a network.

This chapter introduced the Cisco IOS. It detailed the various modes of the Cisco IOS and examined the basic command structure that is used to configure it. It also walked through the initial settings of a Cisco IOS switch device, including setting a name, limiting access to the device configuration, configuring banner messages, and saving the configuration.

The next chapter explores how packets are moved across the network infrastructure and introduces you to the rules of packet communication.

Practice

The following activities provide practice with the topics introduced in this chapter. The Labs and Class Activities are available in the companion Introduction to Networks v5.1 Lab Manual (ISBN 9781587133534). The Packet Tracer Activities PKA files are found in the online course.

Class Activities

Class Activity 2.0.1.2: It Is Just an Operating System

Class Activity 2.4.1.1: Tutor Me

Labs

Lab 2.1.4.7: Establishing a Console Session with Tera Term

Lab 2.3.3.3: Building a Simple Network

Lab 2.3.3.4: Configuring a Switch Management Address

Packet Tracer
☐ **Activity**

Packet Tracer Activities

Packet Tracer 2.1.4.6: Navigating the IOS

Packet Tracer 2.2.3.4: Configuring Initial Switch Settings

Packet Tracer 2.3.2.5: Implementing Basic Connectivity

Packet Tracer 2.4.1.2: Skills Integration Challenge

Check Your Understanding Questions

Complete all the review questions listed here to test your understanding of the topics and concepts in this chapter. The appendix "Answers to 'Check Your Understanding' Questions" lists the answers.

1. What is the Cisco IOS?

   A. The memory for the Cisco network device

   B. The configuration for the Cisco network device

   C. The operating system for the Cisco network device

   D. The CPU for the Cisco network device

2. What type of connection to a Cisco IOS switch is used to make the initial configuration?

   A. AUX port

   B. Console port

   C. SSH

   D. Telnet

   E. Web interface

3. What command will display a list of keywords available for viewing the status of an IOS switch?

   A. Switch# **sh?**

   B. Switch# **help**

   C. Switch# **show?**

   D. Switch# **status?**

4. How is the Cisco IOS generally accessed and navigated?

   A. Through the CLI using a terminal emulator

   B. Using a web browser

   C. With a Cisco-proprietary application

   D. By the use of a custom GUI

5. What is initially entered at the CLI of the Cisco IOS when typing a command sequence?

   A. Argument

   B. A space

   C. Command

   D. Keyword

6. When the command "Switch(config)# **hostname EaSt-2+56**" is entered in a Cisco IOS device using the CLI, what will be returned in the CLI?

    A. `Switch(config)#`

    B. `% Invalid input detected`

    C. `EaSt-2+56(config)#`

    D. `EaSt-58(config)#`

    E. `East-2+56(config)#`

    F. `Switch EaSt-2+56(config)#`

7. What is the primary defense against unauthorized remote access to network devices?

    A. Configuring a default gateway

    B. Configuring an IP address

    C. Configuring a VTY password

    D. Configuring a console password

8. Where is the configuration used during startup on Cisco IOS devices located?

    A. Running config

    B. NVRAM

    C. Startup config

    D. Terminal emulator

9. What is the purpose of the following switch configuration?

    `S1(config)# `**`interface vlan 1`**

    `S1(config-if)# `**`ip address 192.168.122.222 255.255.255.0`**

    `S1(config-if)# `**`no shutdown`**

    `S1(config-if)# `**`exit`**

    A. Allows communication to manage the switch

    B. Allows the switch to forward traffic

    C. Allows the switch to provide name resolution

    D. Allows dynamic host configuration

10. From the CLI of a switch with an address of `192.168.1.44`, what command would be used to verify end-to-end connectivity to another host?

    A. **`show ip interface brief`**

    B. **`ping 127.0.0.1`**

    C. **`ping 192.168.1.44`**

    D. **`ping 192.168.1.43`**

CHAPTER 3

Network Protocols and Communications

Objectives

Upon completion of this chapter, you will be able to answer the following questions:

- What are the types of rules that are necessary to successfully communicate?

- Why are protocols necessary in network communication?

- What is the purpose of adhering to a protocol suite?

- What is the role of standards organizations in establishing protocols for network interoperability?

- How are the TCP/IP model and the OSI model used to facilitate standardization in the communication process?

- How does data encapsulation allow data to be transported across the network?

- How do local hosts access local resources on a network?

Key Terms

This chapter uses the following key terms. You can find the definitions in the Glossary.

Introduction (3.0)

More and more, it is networks that connect us. People communicate online from everywhere. Conversations in classrooms spill into instant message chat sessions, and online debates continue at school. New services are being developed daily to take advantage of the network.

Rather than developing unique and separate systems for the delivery of each new service, the network industry as a whole has adopted a developmental framework that allows designers to understand current network platforms and maintain them. At the same time, this framework is used to facilitate the development of new technologies to support future communications needs and technology enhancements.

Central to this developmental framework is the use of generally accepted models that describe network rules and functions.

Within this chapter, you will learn about these models, as well as the standards that make networks work, and how communication occurs over a network.

Class Activity 3.0.1.2: Designing a Communications System

You have just purchased a new automobile for your personal use. After driving the car for a week or so, you find that it is not working correctly.

After discussing the problem with several of your peers, you decide to take it to an automotive repair facility they highly recommend. It is the only repair facility located near you.

When you arrive at the repair facility, you find all of the mechanics speak another language. You are having difficulty explaining the automobile's performance problems, but the repairs really need to be done. You are not sure you can drive it back home to research other options.

You must find a way to work with the repair facility to ensure that your automobile is fixed correctly.

How will you communicate with the mechanics in this form? Design a communications model to ensure the car is properly repaired.

Rules of Communication (3.1)

This section discusses the rules used in network communications.

The Rules (3.1.1)

Computer networks use rules for communications, similar to rules used in human communications. In order for two devices to communicate they must use the same rules.

Communication Fundamentals (3.1.1.1)

A network can be as complex as devices connected across the Internet, or as simple as two computers directly connected to one another with a single cable, and anything in-between. Networks can vary in size, shape, and function. However, simply having a wired or wireless physical connection between end devices is not enough to enable communication. For communication to occur, devices must know "how" to communicate.

People exchange ideas using many different communication methods. However, regardless of the method chosen, all communication methods have three elements in common. The first of these elements is the message *source*, or sender. Message sources are people, or electronic devices, that need to send a message to other individuals or devices. The second element of communication is the *destination*, or receiver, of the message. The destination receives the message and interprets it. A third element, called a *channel*, consists of the media that provides the pathway over which the message travels from source to destination.

Communication begins with a message, or information, that must be sent from a source to a destination. The sending of this message, whether by face-to-face communication or over a network, is governed by rules called *protocols*. These protocols are specific to the type of communication method occurring. In our day-to-day personal communication, the rules we use to communicate over one medium, like a telephone call, are not necessarily the same as the protocols for using another medium, such as sending a letter.

For example, consider two people communicating face-to-face. Prior to communicating, they must agree on how to communicate. If the communication is using voice, they must first agree on the language. Next, when they have a message to share, they must be able to format that message in a way that is understandable. For example, if someone uses the English language, but poor sentence structure, the message can easily be misunderstood. Each of these tasks describe protocols put in place to accomplish communication. This is also true of computer communication.

Many different rules or protocols govern all methods of communication that exist in the world today.

Rule Establishment (3.1.1.2)

Before communicating with one another, individuals must use established rules or agreements to govern the conversation. These rules, or protocols, must be followed in order for the message to be successfully delivered and understood. Protocols must account for the following requirements:

- An identified sender and receiver
- Common language and grammar
- Speed and timing of delivery
- Confirmation or acknowledgment requirements

The protocols that are used in network communications share many of these fundamental traits. In addition to identifying the source and destination, computer and network protocols define the details of how a message is transmitted across a network. Common computer protocols include the requirements shown in Figure 3-1. Each of these will be discussed in more detail.

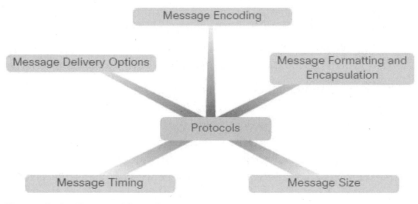

Figure 3-1   Protocol Requirements

Message Encoding (3.1.1.3)

One of the first steps to sending a message is encoding. Encoding is the process of converting information into another acceptable form for transmission. Decoding reverses this process in order to interpret the information.

Imagine a person planning a holiday trip with a friend and calling the friend to discuss the details of where they want to go, as shown in Figure 3-2.

Figure 3-2   Encoding and Decoding Messages Between People

To communicate the message, she converts her thoughts into an agreed-upon language. She then speaks the words using the sounds and inflections of spoken language that convey the message. Her friend listens to the description and decodes the sounds to understand the message he received.

Encoding also occurs in computer communication, as shown in Figure 3-3.

Figure 3-3   Encoding and Decoding Messages Between Computers

Encoding between hosts must be in an appropriate format for the medium. Messages sent across the network are first converted into bits by the sending host. Each bit is encoded into a pattern of sounds, light waves, or electrical impulses depending on the network media over which the bits are transmitted. The destination host receives and decodes the signals in order to interpret the message.

Message Formatting and Encapsulation (3.1.1.4)

When a message is sent from source to destination, it must use a specific format or structure. Message formats depend on the type of message and the channel that is used to deliver the message.

Letter writing is one of the most common forms of written human communication. For centuries, the agreed format for personal letters has not changed. In many cultures, a personal letter contains the following elements:

- An identifier of the recipient

- A salutation or greeting

- The message content

- A closing phrase

- An identifier of the sender

In addition to having the correct format, most personal letters must also be enclosed in an envelope for delivery. The envelope has the address of the sender and receiver, each located at the proper place on the envelope. If the destination address and formatting are not correct, the letter is not delivered. The process of placing one message format (the letter) inside another message format (the envelope) is called *encapsulation*. *De-encapsulation* occurs when the process is reversed by the recipient and the letter is removed from the envelope.

A message that is sent over a computer network follows specific format rules for it to be delivered and processed. Just as a letter is encapsulated in an envelope for delivery, so too are computer messages. Each computer message is encapsulated in a specific format, called a frame, before it is sent over the network. A frame acts like an envelope; it provides the address of the destination and the address of the source host, as shown in Figure 3-4.

Destination (physical / hardware address)	Source (physical / hardware address)	Start Flag (start of message Indicator)	Recipient (destination Identifier)	Sender (source Identifier)	Encapsulated Data (bits)	End of Frame (end of message Indicator)
Frame Addressing		Encapsulated Message				

Figure 3-4 Frame Format

Notice the frame has a source and destination in both the frame addressing portion and in the encapsulated message. The distinction between these two types of addresses will be explained later in this chapter.

The format and contents of a frame are determined by the type of message being sent and the channel over which it is communicated. Messages that are not correctly formatted are not successfully delivered to or processed by the destination host.

Message Size (3.1.1.5)

Another rule of communication is size. When people communicate with each other, the messages that they send are usually broken into smaller parts or sentences. These sentences are limited in size to what the receiving person can process at one time. An individual conversation may be made up of many smaller sentences to ensure that each part of the message is received and understood. Imagine what it would be like to read this course if it all appeared as one long sentence; it would not be easy to read and comprehend.

Likewise, when a long message is sent from one host to another over a network, it is necessary to break the message into smaller pieces, as shown in Figure 3-5.

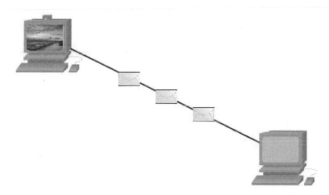

Figure 3-5   Message Is Broken into Smaller Pieces

The rules that govern the size of the pieces, or frames, communicated across the network are very strict. They can also be different, depending on the channel used. Frames that are too long or too short are not delivered.

The size restrictions of frames require the source host to break a long message into individual pieces that meet both the minimum and maximum size requirements. The long message will be sent in separate frames, with each frame containing a piece of the original message. Each frame will also have its own addressing information. At the receiving host, the individual pieces of the message are reconstructed into the original message.

Message Timing (3.1.1.6)

These are the rules of engagement for message timing.

Access Method

Access method determines when someone is able to send a message. If two people talk at the same time, a collision of information occurs and it is necessary for the two to back off and start again. Likewise, it is necessary for computers to define an access method. Hosts on a network need an access method to know when to begin sending messages and how to respond when collisions occur.

Flow Control

Timing also affects how much information can be sent and the speed that it can be delivered. If one person speaks too quickly, it is difficult for the other person to hear and understand the message. In network communication, source and destination hosts use flow control methods to negotiate correct timing for successful communication.

Response Timeout

If a person asks a question and does not hear a response within an acceptable amount of time, the person assumes that no answer is coming and reacts accordingly. The person may repeat the question, or may go on with the conversation. Hosts on the network also have rules that specify how long to wait for responses and what action to take if a response timeout occurs.

Message Delivery Options (3.1.1.7)

A message can be delivered in different ways. Sometimes, a person wants to communicate information to a single individual. At other times, the person may need to send information to a group of people at the same time, or even to all people in the same area.

There are also times when the sender of a message needs to be sure that the message is delivered successfully to the destination. In these cases, it is necessary for the recipient to return an *acknowledgment* to the sender. If no acknowledgment is required, the delivery option is referred to as unacknowledged.

Hosts on a network use similar delivery options to communicate. A one-to-one delivery option is referred to as a *unicast*, meaning there is only a single destination for the message, as shown in Figure 3-6.

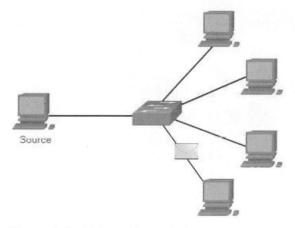

Figure 3-6   Unicast Transmission

When a host needs to send messages using a one-to-many delivery option, it is referred to as a *multicast*. Multicasting is the delivery of the same message to a group of host destinations simultaneously, as shown in Figure 3-7.

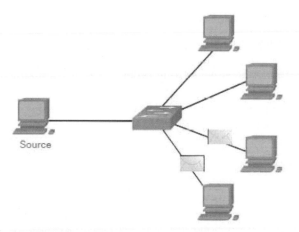

Figure 3-7   Multicast Transmission

If all hosts on the network need to receive the message at the same time, a *broadcast* may be used. Broadcasting represents a one-to-all message delivery option, as shown in Figure 3-8.

Source

Figure 3-8   Broadcast Transmission

Some protocols use a special multicast message that is sent to all devices, making it essentially the same as a broadcast. Additionally, hosts may be required to acknowledge the receipt of some messages while not needing to acknowledge others.

Network Protocols and Standards (3.2)

A strict set of rules must be adhered to in order to allow communication to occur between humans or machines. To ensure that these rules or protocols function together and in a predictable manner, a number of organizations and processes have been developed to provide standards.

Protocols (3.2.1)

Just like in human communication, the various network and computer protocols must be able to interact and work together for network communication to be successful.

Rules that Govern Communications (3.2.1.1)

A group of inter-related protocols necessary to perform a communication function is called a *protocol suite*. Protocol suites are implemented by hosts and networking devices in software, hardware, or both.

One of the best ways to visualize how the protocols within a suite interact is to view the interaction as a stack. A protocol stack shows how the individual protocols within a suite are implemented. The protocols are viewed in terms of layers, with each higher level service depending on the functionality defined by the protocols shown in the lower levels. The lower layers of the stack are concerned with moving data over the network and providing services to the upper layers, which are focused on the content of the message being sent.

As Figure 3-9 shows, we can use layers to describe the activity occurring in our face-to-face communication example.

Figure 3-9   Protocol Suite Example

At the bottom, the physical layer, we have two people, each with a voice that can say words out loud. In the middle, the rules layer, we have an agreement to speak in a common language. At the top, the content layer, there are words that are actually spoken. This is the content of the communication.

Network Protocols (3.2.1.2)

At the human level, some communication rules are formal and others are simply understood based on custom and practice. For devices to successfully communicate, a network protocol suite must describe precise requirements and interactions. Networking protocols define a common format and set of rules for exchanging messages between devices. Some common networking protocols are Hypertext Transfer Protocol (HTTP), Transmission Control Protocol (TCP), and Internet Protocol (IP).

The figures illustrate networking protocols that describe the following processes:

- How the message is formatted or structured, as shown in Figure 3-10.

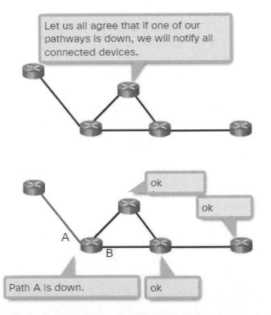

Figure 3-10   Rules for Formatting Messages

- The process by which networking devices share information about pathways with other networks, as shown in Figure 3-11.

Figure 3-11   Rules for Sharing Path Information

■ How and when error and system messages are passed between devices, as shown in Figure 3-12.

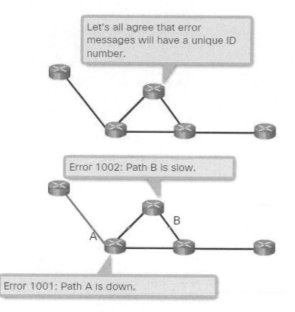

Figure 3-12   Rules for Handling Errors

■ The setup and termination of data transfer sessions, as shown in Figure 3-13.

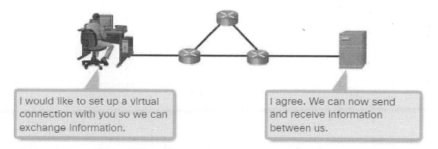

Figure 3-13   Rules for Transferring Data

Protocol Interaction (3.2.1.3)

Communication between a web server and web client is an example of an interaction between several protocols, as shown in Figure 3-14.

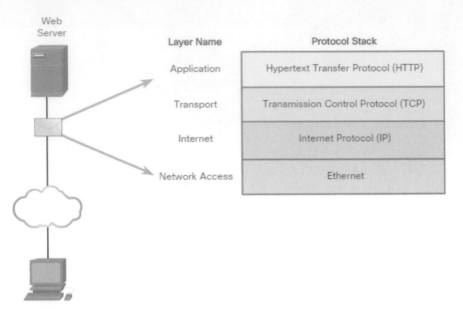

Figure 3-14 Interaction of Protocols Between a Web Server and Web Client

The protocols shown in Figure 3-14 include

- **HTTP –** is an application protocol that governs the way a web server and a web client interact. HTTP defines the content and formatting of the requests and responses that are exchanged between the client and server. Both the client and the web server software implement HTTP as part of the application. HTTP relies on other protocols to govern how the messages are transported between the client and server.

- **TCP –** is the transport protocol that manages the individual conversations. TCP divides the HTTP messages into smaller pieces, called segments. These segments are sent between the web server and client processes running at the destination host. TCP is also responsible for controlling the size and rate at which messages are exchanged between the server and the client.

- **IP –** is responsible for taking the formatted segments from TCP, encapsulating them into packets, assigning them the appropriate addresses, and delivering them to the destination host.

- **Ethernet –** is a network access protocol that describes two primary functions: communication over a data link and the physical transmission of data on the network media. Network access protocols are responsible for taking the packets from IP and formatting them to be transmitted over the media.

Protocol Suites (3.2.2)

As stated previously, a protocol suite is a set of protocols that work together to provide comprehensive network communication services. A protocol suite can be specified by a standards organization or developed by a vendor.

Protocol Suites and Industry Standards (3.2.2.1)

Protocol suites, like the four shown in Figure 3-15, can be a bit overwhelming. However, this course will only cover the protocols of the TCP/IP protocol suite.

Layer Name	TCP/IP	ISO	AppleTalk	Novell Netware
Application	HTTP DNS DHCP FTP	ACSE ROSE TRSE SESE	AFP	NDS
Transport	TCP UDP	TP0 TP1 TP2 TP3 TP4	ATP AEP NBP RTMP	SPX
Internet	IPv4 IPv6 ICMPv4 ICMPv6	CONP/CMNS CLNP/CLNS	AARP	IPX
Network Access	Ethernet PPP Frame Relay ATM WLAN			

Figure 3-15   Protocol Suites and Industry Standards

The TCP/IP protocol suite is an open standard, meaning these protocols are freely available to the public, and any vendor is able to implement these protocols on their hardware or in their software.

A standards-based protocol is a process that has been endorsed by the networking industry and approved by a standards organization. The use of standards in developing and implementing protocols ensures that products from different manufacturers can interoperate successfully. If a protocol is not rigidly observed by a particular manufacturer, their equipment or software may not be able to successfully communicate with products made by other manufacturers.

Some protocols are proprietary, which means one company or vendor controls the definition of the protocol and how it functions. Examples of proprietary protocols are AppleTalk and Novell Netware, which are legacy protocol suites. It is not uncommon for a vendor (or group of vendors) to develop a proprietary protocol to meet the needs of its customers and later assist in making that proprietary protocol an open standard.

For example, search YouTube for "The History of *Ethernet*" to view a presentation by Bob Metcalfe describing the story of how Ethernet was developed.

Development of TCP/IP (3.2.2.2)

The first packet-switching network and predecessor to today's Internet was the Advanced Research Projects Agency Network (ARPANET), which came to life in 1969 by connecting mainframe computers at four locations. ARPANET was funded by the U.S. Department of Defense for use by universities and research laboratories.

Interactive Graphic

Go to the online course to click through a timeline and see details about the development of other network protocols and applications.

TCP/IP Protocol Suite (3.2.2.3)

Today, the TCP/IP protocol suite includes many protocols, as shown in Figure 3-16.

Figure 3-16   TCP/IP Protocols and Standards

Table 3-1 lists the acronym's translation and a brief description of the protocol.

Table 3-1 TCP/IP Protocols and Standards Descriptions

Name	Acronym	Description
Application Layer		
Domain Name System	DNS	■ Translates domain names, such as cisco.com, into IP addresses
Bootstrap Protocol	BOOTP	■ Enables a diskless workstation to discover its own IP address, the IP address of a BOOTP server on the network, and a file to be loaded into memory to boot the machine
		■ BOOTP has been superseded by DHCP
Dynamic Host Configuration Protocol	DHCP	■ Dynamically assigns IP addresses to client stations at start-up
		■ Allows the addresses to be re-used when no longer needed
Simple Mail Transfer Protocol	SMTP	■ Enables clients to send email to a mail server
		■ Enables servers to send email to other servers
Post Office Protocol version 3	POP3	■ Enables clients to retrieve email from a mail server
		■ Downloads email from the mail server to the desktop
Internet Message Access Protocol	IMAP	■ Enables clients to access email stored on a mail server
		■ Maintains email on the server
File Transfer Protocol	FTP	■ A reliable, connection-oriented, and acknowledged file delivery protocol
		■ Sets rules that enable a user on one host to access and transfer files to and from another host over a network
Trivial File Transfer Protocol	TFTP	■ A simple, connectionless file transfer protocol
		■ A best-effort, unacknowledged file delivery protocol
		■ Utilizes less overhead than FTP
Hypertext Transfer Protocol	HTTP	■ Set of rules for exchanging text, graphic images, sound, video, and other multimedia files on the World Wide Web

Continued

Table 3-1   *Continued*

Name	Acronym	Description
Transport Layer		
User Datagram Protocol	UDP	■ Enables a process running on one host to send packets to a process running on another host ■ Does not confirm successful datagram transmission
Transmission Control Protocol	TCP	■ Enables reliable communication between processes running on separate hosts ■ Reliable, acknowledged transmissions that confirm successful delivery
Internet Layer		
Internet Protocol	IP	■ Receives message segments from the transport layer ■ Packages messages into packets ■ Addresses packets for end-to-end delivery over an Internetwork
Network Address Translation	NAT	■ Translates IP addresses from a private network into globally unique public IP addresses
Internet Control Message Protocol	ICMP	■ Provides feedback from a destination host to a source host about errors in packet delivery
Open Shortest Path First	OSPF	■ Link-state routing protocol ■ Hierarchical design based on areas ■ Open standard interior routing protocol
Enhanced Interior Gateway Routing Protocol	EIGRP	■ Cisco proprietary routing protocol ■ Uses composite metric based on bandwidth, delay, load, and reliability
Network Access Layer		
Address Resolution Protocol	ARP	■ Provides dynamic address mapping between an IP address and a hardware address
Point-to-Point Protocol	PPP	■ Provides a means of encapsulating packets for transmission over a serial link
Ethernet	–	■ Defines the rules for wiring and signaling standards of the network access layer
Interface Drivers	–	■ Provides instruction to a machine for the control of a specific interface on a network device

The individual protocols are organized in layers using the TCP/IP protocol model: Application, Transport, Internet, and Network Access Layers. TCP/IP protocols are specific to the Application, Transport, and Internet layers. The network access layer protocols are responsible for delivering the IP packet over the physical medium. These lower layer protocols are developed by various standards organizations.

The TCP/IP protocol suite is implemented as a TCP/IP stack on both the sending and receiving hosts to provide end-to-end delivery of applications over a network. The Ethernet protocols are used to transmit the IP packet over the physical medium used by the LAN.

TCP/IP Communication Process (3.2.2.4)

Figures 3-17 through 3-23 demonstrate the complete communication process using an example of a web server transmitting data to a client. This process and these protocols will be covered in more detail in later chapters.

Interactive Graphic

Go to the online course to view an animation of the TCP/IP communication process.

1. In Figure 3-17, the process begins with the web server preparing the Hypertext Markup Language (HTML) page as data to be sent.

Figure 3-17   Preparing HTML to be Sent

2. The application protocol HTTP header is added to the front of the HTML data. The header contains various information, including the HTTP version the server is using and a status code indicating it has information for the web client.

3. The HTTP application layer protocol delivers the HTML-formatted web page data to the transport layer, as shown in Figure 3-18. TCP adds header information to the HTTP data. The TCP transport layer protocol is used to manage individual conversations, in this example between the web server and web client.

Figure 3-18   Adding the TCP Segment Header

4. Next, the IP information is added to the front of the TCP information, as shown in Figure 3-19. IP assigns the appropriate source and destination IP addresses. This information is known as an IP packet.

Figure 3-19   Adding the IP Packet Header

5. The Ethernet protocol adds information to both ends of the IP packet, known as a data link frame, as shown in Figure 3-20.

Figure 3-20   Adding the Ethernet Frame Header

6. This data is now transported through the internetwork, as shown in Figure 3-21. The internetwork, represented by the cloud in the figure, is a collection of media and intermediary devices.

Figure 3-21   Sending the Frame as Bits to the Destination

7. In Figure 3-22, the client receives the data link frames that contain the data. Each protocol header is processed and then removed in the opposite order it was added. The Ethernet information is processed and removed, followed by the IP protocol information, the TCP information, and finally the HTTP information.

Figure 3-22   Web Client De-Encapsulates the Frame

8. The web page information is then passed on to the client's web browser software, as shown in Figure 3-23.

Figure 3-23   Web Client Sends the Data to the Web Browser

Activity 3.2.2.5: Mapping the Protocols of the TCP/IP Suite

Go to the online course to perform this practice activity.

Standard Organizations (3.2.3)

Standard organizations create the standards that allow devices to communicate independent of any specific vendor. The software or hardware only needs to apply the standard, regardless of vendor.

Open Standards (3.2.3.1)

Open standards encourage interoperability, competition, and innovation. They also guarantee that no single company's product can monopolize the market or have an unfair advantage over its competition.

A good example of this is when purchasing a wireless router for the home. There are many different choices available from a variety of vendors, all of which incorporate standard protocols such as IPv4, DHCP, 802.3 (Ethernet), and 802.11 (Wireless LAN). These open standards also allow a client running Apple's OS X operating system to download a web page from a web server running the Linux operating system. This is because both operating systems implement the open standard protocols, such as those in the TCP/IP protocol suite.

Standards organizations are important in maintaining an open Internet with freely accessible specifications and protocols that can be implemented by any vendor. Standards organizations that are particularly relevant to your networking studies are shown in Figure 3-24.

Figure 3-24   Standards Organizations for the Network Industry

A standards organization may draft a set of rules entirely on its own or in other cases may select a proprietary protocol as the basis for the *standard*. If a *proprietary protocol* is used, it usually involves the vendor who created the protocol.

Standards organizations are usually vendor-neutral, non-profit organizations established to develop and promote the concept of open standards.

Internet Standards (3.2.3.2)

Standards organizations are usually vendor-neutral, non-profit institutions established to develop and promote the concept of open standards. Various organizations have different responsibilities for promoting and creating standards for the TCP/IP protocol.

Internet standards organizations are shown in Figure 3-25.

Figure 3-25   Internet Standards Organizations

- **Internet Society (ISOC)** – Responsible for promoting the open development and evolution of Internet use throughout the world.

- **Internet Architecture Board (IAB)** – Responsible for the overall management and development of Internet standards.

- **Internet Engineering Task Force (IETF)** – Develops, updates, and maintains Internet and TCP/IP technologies. This includes the process and documents for developing new protocols and updating existing protocols know as Request for Comments (RFC) documents.

- **Internet Research Task Force (IRTF)** – Focused on long-term research related to Internet and TCP/IP protocols such as Anti-Spam Research Group (ASRG), Crypto Forum Research Group (CFRG), and Peer-to-Peer Research Group (P2PRG).

Standards organizations responsible for managing IP addresses, domain names, and port numbers are shown in Figure 3-26.

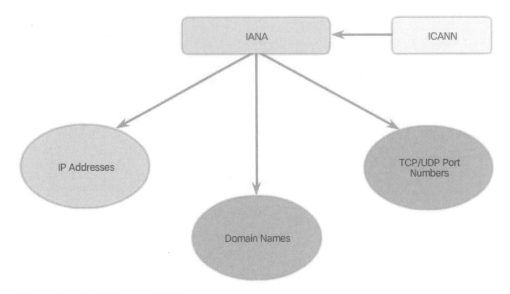

Figure 3-26   IANA and ICANN

- **Internet Corporation for Assigned Names and Numbers (ICANN)** – Based in the United States, coordinates IP address allocation, the management of domain names, and assignment of other information used TCP/IP protocols.

- **Internet Assigned Numbers Authority (IANA)** – Responsible for overseeing and managing IP address allocation, domain name management, and protocol identifiers for ICANN.

Electronics and Communications Standard Organizations (3.2.3.3)

Other standard organizations have responsibilities for promoting and creating the electronic and communication standards used to deliver the IP packets as electronic signals over a wired or wireless medium.

Institute of Electrical and Electronics Engineers (IEEE, pronounced "I-triple-E") – Organization of electrical engineering and electronics dedicated to advancing technological innovation and creating standards in a wide area of industries including power and energy, healthcare, telecommunications, and networking. Standards related to networking belong to the IEEE 802 Working Groups and Study Groups. Common 802 standards include

- 802.1 Higher Layer LAN Protocols Working Group

- 802.3 Ethernet Working Group

- 802.11 Wireless LAN Working Group

- 802.15 Wireless Personal Area Network (WPAN) Working Group

- 802.16 Broadband Wireless Access Working Group

- 802.18 Radio Regulatory TAG

- 802.19 Wireless Coexistence Working Group

- 802.21 Media Independent Handover Services Working Group

- 802.22 Wireless Regional Area Networks

- 802.24 Smart Grid TAG

Electronic Industries Alliance (EIA) – Best known for its standards related to electrical wiring, connectors, and the 19-inch racks used to mount networking equipment.

Telecommunications Industry Association (TIA) – Responsible for developing communication standards in a variety of areas including radio equipment, cellular towers, Voice over IP (VoIP) devices, satellite communications, and more. Figure 3-27 shows an example of an Ethernet cable meeting TIA/EIA standards.

Figure 3-27 EIA/TIA Standards

International Telecommunications Union-Telecommunication Standardization Sector (ITU-T) – One of the largest and oldest communication standard organizations. The ITU-T defines standards for video compression, Internet Protocol Television (IPTV), and broadband communications, such as a digital subscriber line (DSL).

 Lab 3.2.3.4: Researching Networking Standards

In this lab, you will complete the following objectives:

- Part 1: Research Networking Standards Organizations
- Part 2: Reflect on Internet and Computer Networking Experience

Reference Models (3.2.4)

A *reference model* is a conceptual framework to help understand and implement the relationships between various protocols.

The Benefits of Using a Layered Model (3.2.4.1)

The benefits to using a layered model to describe network protocols and operations include

- Assisting in protocol design because protocols that operate at a specific layer have defined information that they act upon and a defined interface to the layers above and below.

- Fostering competition because products from different vendors can work together.

- Preventing technology or capability changes in one layer from affecting other layers above and below.

- Providing a common language to describe networking functions and capabilities.

As shown in Figure 3-28, the TCP/IP model and the Open Systems Interconnection (OSI) model are the primary models used when discussing network functionality.

Figure 3-28   OSI and TCP/IP Models

These two models are differentiated as follows:

- **Protocol model** – This type of model closely matches the structure of a particular protocol suite. The TCP/IP model is a protocol model because it describes the functions that occur at each layer of protocols within the TCP/IP suite. TCP/IP is also used as a reference model.

- **Reference model** – This type of model provides consistency within all types of network protocols and services by describing what has to be done at a particular layer but not prescribing how it should be accomplished. The OSI model is a widely known internetwork reference model, but is also a protocol model for the OSI protocol suite.

The OSI Reference Model (3.2.4.2)

The OSI model provides an extensive list of functions and services that can occur at each layer. It also describes the interaction of each layer with the layers directly above and below. The TCP/IP protocols discussed in this course are structured around both the OSI and TCP/IP models. Table 3-2 lists the description of each layer of the OSI model.

Table 3-2   Layers of the OSI Model

Number	Layer Name	Description
7	Application	The application layer contains protocols used for process-to-process communications.
6	Presentation	The presentation layer provides for common representation of the data transferred between application layer services.
5	Session	The session layer provides services to the presentation layer to organize its dialogue and to manage data exchange.
4	Transport	The transport layer defines services to segment, transfer, and reassemble the data for individual communications between the end devices.
3	Network	The network layer provides services to exchange the individual pieces of data over the network between identified end devices.
2	Data Link	The data link layer protocols describe methods for exchanging data frames between devices over a common media.
1	Physical	The physical layer protocols describe the mechanical, electrical, functional, and procedural means to activate, maintain, and de-activate physical connections for bit transmission to and from a network device.

The functionality of each layer and the relationship between layers will become more evident throughout this course as the protocols are discussed in more detail.

Note

Whereas the TCP/IP model layers are referred to only by name, the seven OSI model layers are more often referred to by number rather than by name. For instance, the physical layer is referred to as Layer 1 of the OSI model.

The TCP/IP Protocol Model (3.2.4.3)

The TCP/IP protocol model for internetwork communications was created in the early 1970s and is sometimes referred to as the Internet model. As shown Figure 3-29, it defines four categories of functions that must occur for communications to be successful.

Figure 3-29   Layers of the TCP/IP Model

The architecture of the TCP/IP protocol suite follows the structure of this model. Because of this, the Internet model is commonly referred to as the TCP/IP model.

Most protocol models describe a vendor-specific protocol stack. Legacy protocol suites, such as Novell Netware and AppleTalk, are examples of vendor-specific protocol stacks. Because the TCP/IP model is an open standard, one company does not control the definition of the model. The definitions of the standard and the TCP/IP protocols are discussed in a public forum and defined in a publicly available set of RFCs.

OSI Model and TCP/IP Model Comparison (3.2.4.4)

The protocols that make up the TCP/IP protocol suite can also be described in terms of the OSI reference model, as shown in Figure 3-30.

Figure 3-30   Comparing the OSI Model and the TCP/IP Model

In the OSI model, the network access layer and the application layer of the TCP/IP model are further divided to describe discrete functions that must occur at these layers.

At the network access layer, the TCP/IP protocol suite does not specify which protocols to use when transmitting over a physical medium; it only describes the handoff from the internet layer to the physical network protocols. OSI Layers 1 and 2 discuss the necessary procedures to access the media and the physical means to send data over a network.

OSI Layer 3, the network layer, maps directly to the TCP/IP Internet layer. This layer is used to describe protocols that address and route messages through an internetwork.

OSI Layer 4, the transport layer, maps directly to the TCP/IP Transport layer. This layer describes general services and functions that provide ordered and reliable delivery of data between source and destination hosts.

The TCP/IP application layer includes a number of protocols that provide specific functionality to a variety of end user applications. The OSI model Layers 5, 6, and 7 are used as references for application software developers and vendors to produce products that operate on networks.

Both the TCP/IP and OSI models are commonly used when referring to protocols at various layers. Because the OSI model separates the data link layer from the physical layer, it is commonly used when referring to these lower layers.

Interactive
Graphic

Activity 3.2.4.5: Identify Layers and Functions

Go to the online course to perform this practice activity.

Packet Tracer
☐ Activity

Packet Tracer 3.2.4.6: Investigating the TCP/IP and OSI Models in Action

This simulation activity is intended to provide a foundation for understanding the TCP/IP protocol suite and the relationship to the OSI model. Simulation mode allows you to view the data contents being sent across the network at each layer.

As data moves through the network, it is broken down into smaller pieces and identified so that the pieces can be put back together when they arrive at the destination. Each piece is assigned a specific name (protocol data unit [PDU]) and associated with a specific layer of the TCP/IP and OSI models. Packet Tracer simulation mode enables you to view each of the layers and the associated PDU. The following steps lead the user through the process of requesting a web page from a web server by using the web browser application available on a client PC.

Even though much of the information displayed will be discussed in more detail later, this is an opportunity to explore the functionality of Packet Tracer and be able to visualize the encapsulation process.

Data Transfer in the Network (3.3)

This section discusses how information is transferred over a network.

Data Encapsulation (3.3.1)

To move through the network, data must be properly encapsulated with sufficient control and addressing information to allow it to move from the sender to the receiver. The actual information required depends on whether the data is destined for a local or remote resource.

Message Segmentation (3.3.1.1)

In theory, a single communication, such as a music video or an email message, could be sent across a network from a source to a destination as one massive, uninterrupted stream of bits. If messages were actually transmitted in this manner, it would mean that no other device would be able to send or receive messages on the same network while this data transfer was in progress. These large streams of data would result in significant delays. Further, if a link in the interconnected network infrastructure failed during the transmission, the complete message would be lost and have to be retransmitted in full.

A better approach is to divide the data into smaller, more manageable pieces to send over the network. This division of the data stream into smaller pieces is called *segmentation*, as shown in Figure 3-31.

Segmentation - breaking communication into pieces.

Figure 3-31   Segmenting a Message

Segmenting messages has two primary benefits:

- By sending smaller individual pieces from source to destination, many different conversations can be interleaved on the network, called multiplexing. Figure 3-32 shows an example of multiplexing.

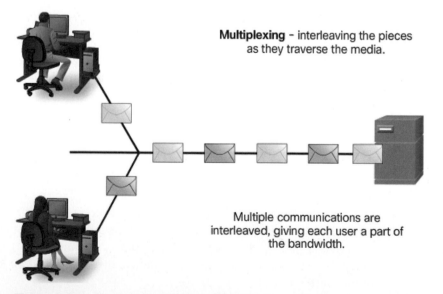

Multiplexing - interleaving the pieces as they traverse the media.

Multiple communications are interleaved, giving each user a part of the bandwidth.

Figure 3-32   Multiplexing Multiple Messages

■ Segmentation can increase the efficiency of network communications. If part of the message fails to make it to the destination, due to failure in the network or network congestion, only the missing parts need to be retransmitted.

The challenge to using segmentation and multiplexing to transmit messages across a network is the level of complexity that is added to the process. Imagine if you had to send a 100-page letter but each envelope would only hold one page. The process of addressing, labeling, sending, receiving, and opening the entire 100 envelopes would be time-consuming for both the sender and the recipient.

In network communications, each segment of the message must go through a similar process to ensure that it gets to the correct destination and can be reassembled into the content of the original message, as shown in Figure 3-33.

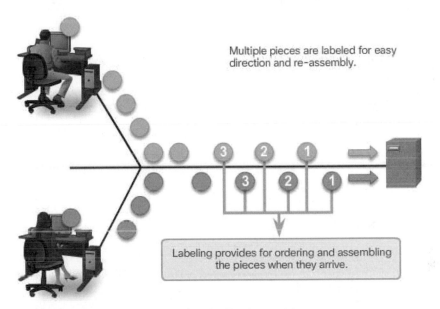

Figure 3-33   Labeling Segments for Re-Assembly

Protocol Data Units (3.3.1.2)

As application data is passed down the protocol stack on its way to be transmitted across the network media, various protocol information is added at each level. This is known as the encapsulation process.

The form that a piece of data takes at any layer is called a *protocol data unit (PDU)*. During encapsulation, each succeeding layer encapsulates the PDU that it receives from the layer above in accordance with the protocol being used. At each stage of the process, a PDU has a different name to reflect its new functions. Although there is no universal naming convention for PDUs, in this course, the PDUs are named according to the protocols of the TCP/IP suite, as shown in Figure 3-34.

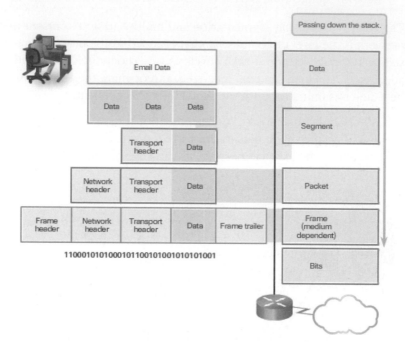

Figure 3-34   Encapsulation

Encapsulation Example (3.3.1.3)

When sending messages on a network, the encapsulation process works from top to bottom. At each layer, the upper layer information is considered data within the encapsulated protocol. For example, the TCP segment is considered data within the IP packet.

De-encapsulation (3.3.1.4)

This process is reversed at the receiving host and is known as de-encapsulation. De-encapsulation is the process used by a receiving device to remove one or more of the protocol headers. The data is de-encapsulated as it moves up the stack toward the end-user application.

Activity 3.3.1.5: Identify the PDU Layer

Go to the online course to perform this practice activity.

Interactive Graphic

Data Access (3.3.2)

To access a network resource, the data must be encapsulated with the correct destination addresses and must also contain proper source addressing information to allow the destination device to reply. Accessing a local network resource requires two types of addresses with different roles.

Network Addresses (3.3.2.1)

The network and data link layers are responsible for delivering the data from the source device to the destination device. As shown in Figure 3-35, protocols at both layers contain a source and destination address, but their addresses have different purposes.

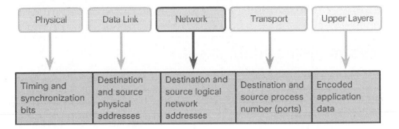

Figure 3-35   Network Addresses and Data Link Addresses

- **Network layer source and destination addresses** – Responsible for delivering the IP packet from the original source to the final destination, either on the same network or to a remote network.

- **Data link layer source and destination addresses** – Responsible for delivering the data link frame from one network interface card (NIC) to another NIC on the same network.

An IP address is the network layer, or Layer 3, logical address used to deliver the IP packet from the original source to the final destination, as shown in Figure 3-36.

Figure 3-36   Layer 3 Network Addresses

The IP packet contains two IP addresses:

■ **Source IP address –** The IP address of the sending device, the original source of the packet.

■ **Destination IP address –** The IP address of the receiving device, the final destination of the packet.

Data Link Addresses (3.3.2.2)

The data link, or Layer 2, physical address has a different role. The purpose of the data link address is to deliver the data link frame from one network interface to another network interface on the same network. This process is illustrated in Figures 3-37 through 3-39.

Figure 3-37   Layer 2 Data Link Addresses – First Hop

Figure 3-38   Layer 2 Data Link Addresses – Second Hop

Figure 3-39   Layer 2 Data Link Addresses – Third Hop

Before an IP packet can be sent over a wired or wireless network, it must be encapsulated in a data link frame so it can be transmitted over the physical medium.

As the IP packet travels from host-to-router, router-to-router, and finally router-to-host, at each point along the way the IP packet is encapsulated in a new data link frame. Each data link frame contains the source data link address of the NIC card sending the frame and the destination data link address of the NIC card receiving the frame.

The Layer 2, data link protocol is only used to deliver the packet from NIC-to-NIC on the same network. The router removes the Layer 2 information as it is received on one NIC and adds new data link information before forwarding out the exit NIC on its way toward the final destination.

The IP packet is encapsulated in a data link frame that contains data link information, including a

- **Source data link address** – The physical address of the device's NIC that is sending the data link frame.

- **Destination data link address** – The physical address of the NIC that is receiving the data link frame. This address is either the next hop router or of the final destination device.

The data link frame also contains a trailer, which will be discussed in later chapters.

Devices on the Same Network (3.3.2.3)

To understand how devices communicate within a network, it is important to understand the roles of both the network layer addresses and the data link addresses.

Role of the Network Layer Addresses

The network layer addresses, or IP addresses, indicate the original source and final destination. An IP address contains two parts:

- **Network portion** – The left-most part of the address that indicates the network of which the IP address is a member. All devices on the same network will have the same network portion of the address.

- **Host portion** – The remaining part of the address that identifies a specific device on the network. The host portion is unique for each device on the network.

Note

The subnet mask is used to identify the network portion of an address from the host portion. The subnet mask is discussed in later chapters.

In this example we have a client computer, PC1, communicating with an FTP server on the same IP network.

- **Source IP address** – The IP address of the sending device, the client computer PC1: 192.168.1.110.

- **Destination IP address** – The IP address of the receiving device, FTP server: 192.168.1.9.

Notice in Figure 3-40 that the network portion of both the source IP address and destination IP address are on the same network.

	Data Link Ethernet Frame Header		Network Layer IP Packet Header		
Destination	Source	Source	Destination		Data
CC-CC-CC-CC- CC-CC	AA-AA-AA-AA- AA-AA	Network 192.168.1. : Host 110	Network 192.168.1. : Host 9		

PC1
192.168.1.110
AA-AA-AA-AA-AA-AA

FTP Server
192.168.1.9
CC-CC-CC-CC-CC-CC

Figure 3-40   Communicating with a Device on the Same Network

Role of the Data Link Layer Addresses

When the sender and receiver of the IP packet are on the same network, the data link frame is sent directly to the receiving device. On an Ethernet network, the data link addresses are known as Ethernet (Media Access Control) addresses. MAC addresses are physically embedded on the Ethernet NIC.

- **Source MAC address** – This is the data link address, or the Ethernet MAC address, of the device that sends the data link frame with the encapsulated IP packet. The MAC address of the Ethernet NIC of PC1 is AA-AA-AA-AA-AA-AA, written in hexadecimal notation.

- **Destination MAC address** – When the receiving device is on the same network as the sending device, this is the data link address of the receiving device. In this example, the destination MAC address is the MAC address of the FTP server: CC-CC-CC-CC-CC-CC, written in hexadecimal notation.

The frame with the encapsulated IP packet can now be transmitted from PC1 directly to the FTP server.

Devices on a Remote Network (3.3.2.4)

But what are the roles of the network layer address and the data link layer address when a device is communicating with a device on a remote network? In this example we have a client computer, PC1, communicating with a server, named Web Server, on a different IP network.

Role of the Network Layer Addresses

When the sender of the packet is on a different network from the receiver, the source and destination IP addresses will represent hosts on different networks. This will be indicated by the network portion of the IP address of the destination host.

- **Source IP address** – The IP address of the sending device, the client computer PC1: 192.168.1.110.

- **Destination IP address** – The IP address of the receiving device, the server, Web Server: 172.16.1.99.

Notice in Figure 3-41 that the network portion of the source IP address and destination IP address are on different networks.

Figure 3-41   Communicating with a Device on a Remote Network

Role of the Data Link Layer Addresses

When the sender and receiver of the IP packet are on different networks, the Ethernet data link frame cannot be sent directly to the destination host because the host is not directly reachable in the network of the sender. The Ethernet frame must be sent to another device known as the router or *default gateway*. In our example, the default gateway is R1. R1 has an Ethernet data link address that is on the same network as PC1. This allows PC1 to reach the router directly.

- **Source MAC address** – The Ethernet MAC address of the sending device, PC1. The MAC address of the Ethernet interface of PC1 is AA-AA-AA-AA-AA-AA.

- **Destination MAC address** – When the receiving device, the destination IP address, is on a different network from the sending device, the sending device uses the Ethernet MAC address of the default gateway or router. In this example, the destination MAC address is the MAC address of R1's Ethernet interface, 11-11-11-11-11-11. This is the interface that is attached to the same network as PC1.

The Ethernet frame with the encapsulated IP packet can now be transmitted to R1. R1 forwards the packet to the destination, Web Server. This may mean that R1 forwards the packet to another router or directly to Web Server if the destination is on a network connected to R1.

It is important that the IP address of the default gateway be configured on each host on the local network. All packets to a destination on remote networks are sent to the default gateway. Ethernet MAC addresses and the default gateway are discussed in later chapters.

Summary (3.4)

Lab 3.4.1.1: Installing Wireshark

Wireshark is a software protocol analyzer, or "packet sniffer" application, used for network troubleshooting, analysis, software and protocol development, and education. Wireshark is used throughout the course to demonstrate network concepts. In this lab, you will download and install Wireshark.

Lab 3.4.1.2: Using Wireshark to View Network Traffic

In this lab, you will use Wireshark to capture and analyze traffic.

Class Activity 3.4.1.3: Guaranteed to Work!

You have just completed the Chapter 3 content regarding network protocols and standards.

Assuming you resolved the beginning of this chapter's modeling activity, how would you compare the following steps taken to design a communications system to the networking models used for communications?

- Establishing a language to communicate
- Dividing the message into small steps, delivered a little at a time, to facilitate understanding of the problem
- Checking to see if the data has been delivered fully and correctly
- Timing needed to ensure quality data communication and delivery

Data networks are systems of end devices, intermediary devices, and the media connecting them. For communication to occur, these devices must know how to communicate.

These devices must comply with communication rules and protocols. TCP/IP is an example of a protocol suite. Most protocols are created by a standards organization such as the IETF or IEEE. The Institute of Electrical and Electronics Engineers is a professional organization for those in the electrical engineering and electronics fields. ISO, the International Organization for Standardization, is the world's largest developer of international standards for a wide variety of products and services.

The most widely used networking models are the OSI and TCP/IP models. Associating the protocols that set the rules of data communications with the different layers of these models is useful in determining which devices and services are applied at specific points as data passes across LANs and WANs.

Data that passes down the stack of the OSI model is segmented into pieces and encapsulated with addresses and other labels. The process is reversed as the pieces are de-encapsulated and passed up the destination protocol stack. The OSI model describes the processes of encoding, formatting, segmenting, and encapsulating data for transmission over the network.

The TCP/IP protocol suite is an open standard protocol that has been endorsed by the networking industry and ratified, or approved, by a standards organization. The Internet Protocol Suite is a suite of protocols required for transmitting and receiving information using the Internet.

Protocol Data Units (PDUs) are named according to the protocols of the TCP/IP suite: data, segment, packet, frame, and bits.

Applying models allows individuals, companies, and trade associations to analyze current networks and plan the networks of the future.

Practice

The following activities provide practice with the topics introduced in this chapter. The Labs and Class Activities are available in the companion Introduction to Networks v5.1 Lab Manual (ISBN 9781587133534). The Packet Tracer Activities PKA files are found in the online course.

Class Activities

Class Activity 3.0.1.2: Designing a Communications System

Class Activity 3.4.1.3: Guaranteed to Work!

Labs

Lab 3.2.3.4: Researching Networking Standards

Lab 3.4.1.1: Installing Wireshark

Lab 3.4.1.2: Using Wireshark to View Network Traffic

Packet Tracer Activities

Packet Tracer 3.2.4.6: Investigating the TCP/IP and OSI Models in Action

Check Your Understanding Questions

Complete all the review questions listed here to test your understanding of the topics and concepts in this chapter. The appendix "Answers to 'Check Your Understanding' Questions" lists the answers.

1. Which of the following elements do both human and computer communication systems have in common? (Choose three.)

    A. Source

    B. Keyboard

    C. Channel

    D. Default gateway

    E. Receiver

2. What happens to frames that are too long or too short for the channel used?

    A. They are broken up into smaller pieces.

    B. They are dropped.

    C. They clog the network and block the delivery of other frames.

    D. They are returned to the sender.

    E. They are delivered but much slower than proper-size frames.

3. Which message timing factor impacts how much information can be sent and the speed at which it can be delivered?

    A. Access method

    B. Delay speed

    C. Flow control

    D. Response timeout

4. What is the name given to a one-to-many message delivery option?

    A. Unicast

    B. Multicast

    C. Broadcast

    D. Manycast

5. What name is given to a group of interrelated protocols necessary to perform a communication function?

    A. Functional collection

    B. Functional protocol

    C. Protocol suite

    D. Protocol stack

6. What type of protocol describes communication over a data link and the physical transmission of data on the network media?

   A. Application protocol

   B. Transport protocol

   C. Internet protocol

   D. Network access protocol

7. Which of the following are examples of proprietary protocols? (Choose two.)

   A. TCP/IP

   B. ISO

   C. AppleTalk

   D. Novell NetWare

8. Which organization is responsible for the standard that defines Media Access Control for wired Ethernet?

   A. ISOC

   B. IAB

   C. IETF

   D. IEEE

   E. ISO

9. What organization is responsible for the overall management and development of Internet standards?

   A. IAB

   B. IETF

   C. IRTF

   D. IEEE

   E. ISO

10. Which organization is responsible for developing communications standards for Voice over IP (VoIP) devices?

   A. The Electronics Industry Alliance (EIA)

   B. The Telecommunications Industry Association (TIA)

   C. The International Telecommunications Union-Telecommunications Standardization Sector (ITU-T)

   D. The Internet Corporation for Assigned Names and Numbers (ICANN)

11. Which of the following TCP/IP protocols exist at the transport layer of the TCP/IP reference model? (Choose two.)

    A. HTTP

    B. FTP

    C. TCP

    D. DNS

    E. UDP

12. Which of the following OSI model layers have the same functionality as the network access layer in the TCP/IP model? (Choose two.)

    A. Application

    B. Transport

    C. Session

    D. Physical

    E. Presentation

    F. Data link

    G. Network

13. Which OSI reference model layer is responsible for common representation of the data transferred between application layer services?

    A. Application

    B. Transport

    C. Session

    D. Physical

    E. Presentation

    F. Data link

    G. Network

14. Which TCP/IP model layer is responsible for providing the best path through the network?

    A. Application

    B. Transport

    C. Internet

    D. Network Access

15. Which application layer protocol allows users on one network to reliably transfer files to and from a host on another network?

    A. HTTP

    B. FTP

    C. IMAP

    D. TFTP

    E. DHCP

16. What is the transport layer PDU?

    A. Data

    B. Segment

    C. Packet

    D. Frame

    E. Bit

17. What is the correct order of data de-encapsulation?

    A. Data > segment > packet > frame > bit

    B. Bit > frame> segment > packet > data

    C. Bit > frame > packet > segment > data

    D. Data > frame > packet > segment > bit

    E. Bit > packet > frame > segment > data

18. What pieces of information are required for a host to access resources on the local network? (Choose three.)

    A. Physical address

    B. Network address

    C. Process number (port)

    D. Default gateway address

    E. Host name

19. What pieces of information are required for a host to access resources on a remote network? (Choose four.)

    A. Physical address

    B. Network address

    C. Process number (port)

    D. Default gateway address

    E. Host name

20. What are some of the four major responsibilities of network protocols?

CHAPTER 4

Network Access

Objectives

Upon completion of this chapter, you will be able to answer the following questions:

- What are options for connecting devices to a data network?

- What are the purpose and functions of the physical layer in data networks?

- What are the basic principles of physical layer standards?

- What are the basic characteristics of copper cabling?

- How are UTP cables built for use in Ethernet networks?

- What are advantages of using fiber-optic cabling over using other media in data networks?

- What are the basic characteristics of using wireless media in data networks?

- What are the purposes and functions of the data link layer in preparing communications for transmission on specific data network media?

- How do the functions of physical topologies compare with the functions of logical topologies?

- What are the basic characteristics of Media Access Control on WAN topologies?

- What are the basic characteristics of Media Access Control on LAN topologies?

- What are the characteristics and functions of the data link layer frame?

Key Terms

This chapter uses the following key terms. You can find the definitions in the Glossary.

Introduction (4.0)

To support our communication, the OSI model divides the functions of a data network into layers. Each layer works with the layers above and below to transmit data. Two layers of the OSI model are so closely tied that according to the TCP/IP model they are in essence one layer. Those two layers are the data link layer and the physical layer.

On the sending device, it is the role of the data link layer to prepare data for transmission and control how that data accesses the *physical media*. However, the physical layer controls how the data is transmitted onto the physical media by encoding the binary digits that represent data into signals.

On the receiving end, the physical layer receives signals across the connecting media. After decoding the signal back into data, the physical layer passes the frame to the data link layer for acceptance and processing.

This chapter begins with the general functions of the physical layer and the standards and protocols that manage the transmission of data across local media. It also introduces the functions of the data link layer and the protocols associated with it.

Class Activity 4.0.1.2: Managing the Medium

You and your colleague are attending a networking conference. There are many lectures and presentations held during this event, and because they overlap, each of you can only choose a limited set of sessions to attend.

Therefore, you decide to split, each of you attending a separate set of presentations. Afterward, you share the slides and the knowledge each of you gained during the event.

Physical Layer Protocols (4.1)

An important element of data networks is the ability to move data across media. Depending on the media, rules are required to govern the use of media to transport data. In this section, these physical layer protocols will be explored.

Physical Layer Connection (4.1.1)

Data in a network will be transported across one of various types of physical media. The rules regarding the physical connections and the representation of data on the media are defined by protocols. This topic will introduce the basic elements of making network connectivity.

Types of Connections (4.1.1.1)

Whether connecting to a local printer in the home or a web site in another country, before any network communications can occur, a physical connection to a local network must be established. A physical connection can be a wired connection using a cable or a wireless connection using radio waves.

The type of physical connection used is dependent upon the setup of the network. For example, in many corporate offices employees have desktop or laptop computers that are physically connected, via cable, to a shared switch. This type of setup is a wired network. Data is transmitted through a physical cable.

In addition to wired connections, many businesses also offer wireless connections for laptops, tablets, and smartphones. With wireless devices, data is transmitted using radio waves. The use of wireless connectivity is common as individuals, and businesses alike, discover the advantages of offering this type of service. To offer wireless capability, devices on a wireless network must be connected to a *wireless access point (AP)*.

Switch devices and wireless access points are often two separate dedicated devices within a network implementation. However, there are also devices that offer both wired and wireless connectivity. In many homes, for example, individuals are implementing home integrated service routers (ISRs), as shown in Figure 4-1.

Figure 4-1   Connections on a Home Router

ISRs offer a switching component with multiple ports, allowing multiple devices to be connected to the local area network (LAN) using cables, as shown in Figure 4-2. Additionally, many ISRs also include an AP, which allows wireless devices to connect as well.

Figure 4-2   Connecting to the Wired LAN

Network Interface Cards (4.1.1.2)

Network Interface Cards (NICs) connect a device to the network. Ethernet NICs are used for a wired connection, as shown in Figure 4-3, whereas WLAN (Wireless Local Area Network) NICs are used for wireless.

Figure 4-3   Wired Connection Using an Ethernet NIC

An end-user device may include one or both types of NICs. A network printer, for example, may only have an Ethernet NIC, and therefore, must connect to the network using an Ethernet cable. Other devices, such as tablets and smartphones, might only contain a WLAN NIC and must use a wireless connection.

Not all physical connections are equal, in terms of the performance level, when connecting to a network.

For example, a wireless device will experience degradation in performance based on its distance from a wireless access point. The further the device is from the access point, the weaker the wireless signal it receives. This can mean less bandwidth or no wireless connection at all. Figure 4-4 shows that a wireless range extender can be used to regenerate the wireless signal to other parts of the house that are too far from the wireless access point. Alternatively, a wired connection will not degrade in performance.

Figure 4-4   Connecting to the Wireless LAN with a Range Extender

All wireless devices must share access to the airwaves connecting to the wireless access point. This means slower network performance may occur as more wireless devices access the network simultaneously. A wired device does not need to share its access to the network with other devices. Each wired device has a separate communications channel over its Ethernet cable. This is important when considering some applications, such as online gaming, streaming video, and video conferencing, which require more dedicated bandwidth than other applications.

Over the next couple of topics, you will learn more about the physical layer connections that occur and how those connections affect the transportation of data.

Purpose of the Physical Layer (4.1.2)

All data being transferred over a network must be represented on a medium by the sending node and interpreted on a medium by the receiving node. The physical layer is responsible for these functions. In this topic, the physical layer will be explored.

The Physical Layer (4.1.2.1)

The OSI physical layer provides the means to transport the bits that make up a data link layer frame across the network media. This layer accepts a complete frame from the data link layer and encodes it as a series of signals that are transmitted onto the local media, as shown in Figure 4-5.

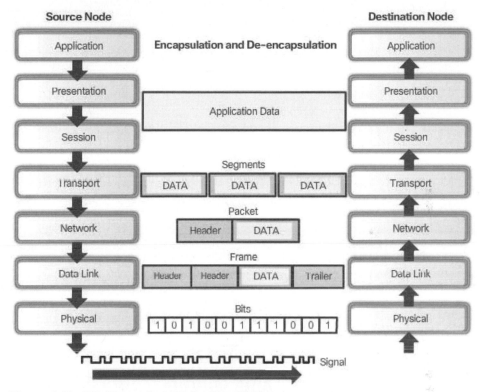

Figure 4-5   Bits Transmitted at the Physical Layer

The encoded bits that comprise a frame are received by either an end device or an intermediate device.

The process that data undergoes from a source node to a destination node is

- The user data is segmented by the transport layer, placed into packets by the network layer, and further encapsulated into frames by the data link layer.

- The physical layer encodes the frames and creates the electrical, optical, or radio wave signals that represent the bits in each frame.

- These signals are then sent on the media, one at a time.

- The destination node physical layer retrieves these individual signals from the media, restores them to their bit representations, and passes the bits up to the data link layer as a complete frame.

Physical Layer Media (4.1.2.2)

There are three basic forms of network media. The physical layer produces the representation and groupings of bits for each type of media as

- **Copper cable** – The signals are patterns of electrical pulses.
- **Fiber-optic cable** – The signals are patterns of light.
- **Wireless** – The signals are patterns of microwave transmissions.

Figure 4-6 displays signaling examples for copper, fiber-optic, and wireless.

Figure 4-6   Examples of Physical Layer Signals

To enable physical layer interoperability, all aspects of these functions are governed by standards organizations.

Physical Layer Standards (4.1.2.3)

The protocols and operations of the upper OSI layers are performed in software designed by software engineers and computer scientists. The services and protocols in the TCP/IP suite are defined by the Internet Engineering Task Force (IETF), as shown in Figure 4-7.

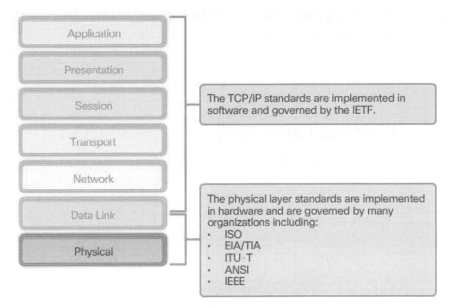

Figure 4-7   Standards at the Physical Layer

The physical layer consists of electronic circuitry, media, and connectors developed by engineers. Therefore, it is appropriate that the standards governing this hardware are defined by the relevant electrical and communications engineering organizations.

There are many different international and national organizations, regulatory government organizations, and private companies involved in establishing and maintaining physical layer standards. For instance, the physical layer hardware, media, encoding, and signaling standards are defined and governed by the

- *International Organization for Standardization (ISO)*
- *Telecommunications Industry Association/Electronic Industries Association (TIA/EIA)*
- *International Telecommunication Union (ITU)*
- *American National Standards Institute (ANSI)*
- *Institute of Electrical and Electronics Engineers (IEEE)*
- National telecommunications regulatory authorities including the Federal Communication Commission (FCC) in the USA and the European Telecommunications Standards Institute (ETSI)

In addition to these, there are often regional cabling standards groups such as CSA (Canadian Standards Association), CENELEC (European Committee for Electrotechnical Standardization), and JSA/JIS (Japanese Standards Association), developing local specifications.

Lab 4.1.2.4: Identifying Network Devices and Cabling

In this lab, you will complete the following objectives:

- Part 1: Identify Network Devices
- Part 2: Identify Network Media

Physical Layer Characteristics (4.1.3)

At the foundation of network communications is the physical layer, Layer 1. This topic examines components that make up the physical layer.

Functions (4.1.3.1)

The physical layer standards address three functional areas.

Physical Components

The physical components are the electronic hardware devices, media, and other connectors that transmit and carry the signals to represent the bits. Hardware components such as NICs, interfaces and connectors, cable materials, and cable designs are all specified in standards associated with the physical layer. The various ports and interfaces on a Cisco 1941 router are also examples of physical components with specific connectors and pinouts resulting from standards.

Encoding

Encoding or line encoding is a method of converting a stream of data bits into a predefined "code." Codes are groupings of bits used to provide a predictable pattern that can be recognized by both the sender and the receiver. In the case of networking, encoding is a pattern of voltage or current used to represent bits, the 0s and 1s.

For example, *Manchester encoding* represents a 0 bit by a high-to-low voltage transition, and a 1 bit is represented as a low-to-high voltage transition. An example of Manchester encoding is illustrated in Figure 4-8. The transition occurs at the middle of each bit period. This type of encoding is used in 10 b/s Ethernet. Faster data rates require more complex encoding.

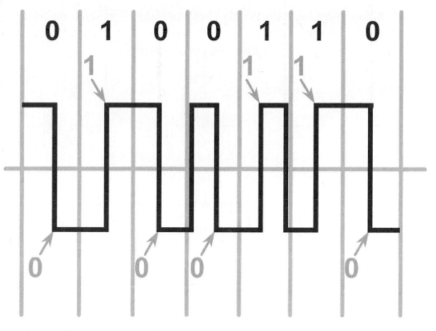

The transition occurs at the middle of each bit period.

Figure 4-8   Manchester Encoding

Signaling

The physical layer must generate the electrical, optical, or wireless signals that represent the "1" and "0" on the media. The method of representing the bits is called the signaling method. The physical layer standards must define what type of signal represents a "1" and what type of signal represents a "0." This can be as simple as a change in the level of an electrical signal or optical pulse. For example, a long pulse might represent a 1, whereas a short pulse represents a 0.

This is similar to how Morse code is used for communication. Morse code is another signaling method that uses a series of on-off tones, lights, or clicks to send text over telephone wires or between ships at sea.

There are many ways to transmit signals. A common method to send data is using modulation techniques. Modulation is the process by which the characteristic of one wave (the signal) modifies another wave (the carrier).

The nature of the actual signals representing the bits on the media will depend on the signaling method in use.

Figure 4-9 illustrates the how AM and FM techniques are used to send a signal.

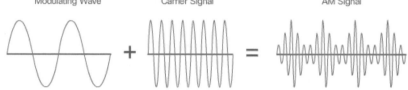

Figure 4-9   Modulation Techniques

Bandwidth (4.1.3.2)

Different physical media support the transfer of bits at different rates. Data transfer is usually discussed in terms of bandwidth and throughput.

Bandwidth is the capacity of a medium to carry data. Digital bandwidth measures the amount of data that can flow from one place to another in a given amount of time. Bandwidth is typically measured in kilobits per second (kb/s), megabits per second (Mb/s), or gigabits per second (Gb/s). Bandwidth is sometimes thought of as the speed that bits travel; however, this is not accurate. For example, in both 10 Mb/s and 100 Mb/s Ethernet, the bits are sent at the speed of electricity. The difference is the number of bits that are transmitted per second.

A combination of factors determines the practical bandwidth of a network:

- The properties of the physical media
- The technologies chosen for signaling and detecting network signals

Physical media properties, current technologies, and the laws of physics all play a role in determining the available bandwidth.

Table 4-1 shows the commonly used units of measure for bandwidth.

Table 4-1   Bandwidth Measurements

Unit of Bandwidth	Abbreviation	Equivalence
Bits per second	b/s	1 b/s = fundamental unit of bandwidth
Kilobits per second	kb/s	1 kb/s = 1,000 b/s = 10^3 b/s
Megabits per second	Mb/s	1 Mb/s = 1,000,000 b/s = 10^6 b/s
Gigabits per second	Gb/s	1 Gb/s = 1,000,000,000 b/s = 10^9 b/s
Terabits per second	Tb/s	1 Tb/s = 1,000,000,000,000 = 10^{12} b/s

Throughput (4.1.3.3)

Throughput is the measure of the transfer of bits across the media over a given period of time.

Due to a number of factors, throughput usually does not match the specified bandwidth in physical layer implementations. Many factors influence throughput, including

- The amount of traffic

- The type of traffic

- The latency created by the number of network devices encountered between source and destination

Latency refers to the amount of time, to include delays, for data to travel from one given point to another.

In an internetwork or network with multiple segments, throughput cannot be faster than the slowest link in the path from source to destination. Even if all or most of the segments have high bandwidth, it will only take one segment in the path with low throughput to create a bottleneck to the throughput of the entire network.

There are many online speed tests that can reveal the throughput of an Internet connection. Figure 4-10 provides sample results from a speed test.

Figure 4-10   Speed Test

There is a third measurement to assess the transfer of usable data that is known as goodput. Goodput is the measure of usable data transferred over a given period of time. Goodput is throughput minus traffic overhead for establishing sessions, acknowledgments, and encapsulation.

Types of Physical Media (4.1.3.4)

The physical layer produces the representation and groupings of bits as voltages, radio frequencies, or light pulses. Various standards organizations have contributed to the definition of the physical, electrical, and mechanical properties of the media available for different data communications. These specifications guarantee that cables and connectors will function as anticipated with different data link layer implementations.

As an example, standards for copper media are defined for the

- Type of copper cabling used

- Bandwidth of the communication

- Type of connectors used

- Pinout and color codes of connections to the media

- Maximum distance of the media

Figure 4-11 shows different types of interfaces and ports available on a 1941 router.

Figure 4-11   Cisco 1941 Router Connections

Activity 4.1.3.5: Physical Layer Terminology

Go to the online course to perform this practice activity.

Network Media (4.2)

Much of the aspects of the physical layer are dependent on the type of media used. The characteristics of media types will be explored in this section.

Copper Cabling (4.2.1)

One of the oldest and most used media for communications is copper cabling. The characteristics and use of copper media in data networks will be examined in this topic.

Characteristics of Copper Cabling (4.2.1.1)

Networks use copper media because it is inexpensive and easy to install and has low resistance to electrical current. However, copper media is limited by distance and signal interference.

Data is transmitted on copper cables as electrical pulses. A detector in the network interface of a destination device must receive a signal that can be successfully decoded to match the signal sent. However, the longer the signal travels, the more it deteriorates. This is referred to as signal attenuation. For this reason, all copper media must follow strict distance limitations as specified by the guiding standards.

The timing and voltage values of the electrical pulses are also susceptible to interference from two sources:

■ *Electromagnetic interference (EMI)* or *radio frequency interference (RFI)* – EMI and RFI signals can distort and corrupt the data signals being carried by copper media. Potential sources of EMI and RFI include radio waves and electromagnetic devices, such as fluorescent lights or electric motors, as shown in the figure.

■ *Crosstalk* – Crosstalk is a disturbance caused by the electric or magnetic fields of a signal on one wire to the signal in an adjacent wire. In telephone circuits, crosstalk can result in hearing part of another voice conversation from an adjacent circuit. Specifically, when an electrical current flows through a wire, it creates a small, circular magnetic field around the wire, which can be picked up by an adjacent wire.

■ Figure 4-12 illustrates how data transmission can be affected by interference.

Figure 4-12   An Interference Signal can Change a Digital Signal

1. The NIC generates a pure digital signal and sends it out on the media.

2. The pure digital signal encounters an interference signal in transit to the destination.

3. The pure digital signal mixes with the interference signal.

4. The destination computer receives a corrupted signal. In this case, a "0" bit has turned into a "1" bit.

To counter the negative effects of EMI and RFI, some types of copper cables are wrapped in metallic shielding and require proper grounding connections.

To counter the negative effects of crosstalk, some types of copper cables have opposing circuit wire pairs twisted together, which effectively cancels the crosstalk.

The susceptibility of copper cables to electronic noise can also be limited by

- Selecting the cable type or category most suited to a given networking environment.

- Designing a cable infrastructure to avoid known and potential sources of interference in the building structure.

- Using cabling techniques that include the proper handling and termination of the cables.

Copper Media (4.2.1.2)

There are three main types of copper media used in networking:

- **Unshielded Twisted-Pair (UTP)**

- **Shielded Twisted-Pair (STP)**

- **Coaxial**

Examples of these copper media are shown in Figure 4-13.

Unshielded Twisted-Pair (UTP) cable   Shielded Twisted-Pair
                                                  (STP) cable

Coaxial cable

Figure 4-13   Examples of Copper Media

These cables are used to interconnect nodes on a LAN and infrastructure devices such as switches, routers, and wireless access points. Each type of connection and the accompanying devices has cabling requirements stipulated by physical layer standards.

Different physical layer standards specify the use of different connectors. These standards specify the mechanical dimensions of the connectors and the acceptable electrical properties of each type. Networking media use modular jacks and plugs to provide easy connection and disconnection. Also, a single type of physical connector may be used for multiple types of connections. For example, the RJ-45 connector is widely used in LANs with one type of media and in some WANs with another media type.

Unshielded Twisted-Pair Cable (4.2.1.3)

Unshielded twisted-pair (UTP) cabling is the most common networking media. UTP cabling, terminated with RJ-45 connectors, is used for interconnecting network hosts with intermediate networking devices, such as switches and routers.

In LANs, UTP cable consists of four pairs of color-coded wires that have been twisted together and then encased in a flexible plastic sheath that protects from minor physical damage. The twisting of wires helps protect against signal interference from other wires.

Figure 4-14 shows some of the properties of UTP cable.

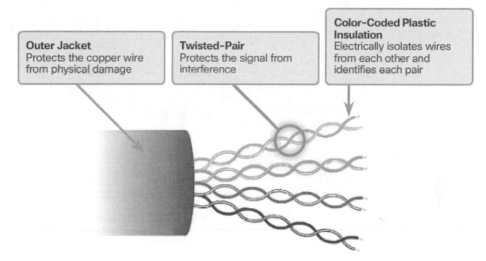

Outer Jacket
Protects the copper wire from physical damage

Twisted-Pair
Protects the signal from interference

Color-Coded Plastic Insulation
Electrically isolates wires from each other and identifies each pair

Figure 4-14   UTP Cable

Shielded Twisted-Pair Cable (4.2.1.4)

Shielded twisted-pair (STP) provides better noise protection than UTP cabling. However, compared to UTP cable, STP cable is significantly more expensive and difficult to install. Like UTP cable, STP uses an RJ-45 connector.

STP cables combine the techniques of shielding to counter EMI and RFI, and wire twisting to counter crosstalk. To gain the full benefit of the shielding, STP cables are terminated with special shielded STP data connectors. If the cable is improperly grounded, the shield may act as an antenna and pick up unwanted signals.

The STP cable shown in Figure 4-15 uses four pairs of wires, each wrapped in a foil shield, which are then wrapped in an overall metallic braid or foil.

Figure 4-15   STP Cable

Coaxial Cable (4.2.1.5)

Coaxial cable, or *coax* for short, gets its name from the fact that there are two conductors that share the same axis. As shown in Figure 4-16, coaxial cable consists of

- A copper conductor used to transmit the electronic signals.

- A layer of flexible plastic insulation surrounding a copper conductor.

- The insulating material is surrounded in a woven copper braid, or metallic foil, that acts as the second wire in the circuit and as a shield for the inner conductor. This second layer, or shield, also reduces the amount of outside electromagnetic interference.

- The entire cable is covered with a cable jacket to prevent minor physical damage.

Figure 4-16   Coaxial Cable and Connectors

There are different types of connectors used with coax cable.

Although UTP cable has essentially replaced coaxial cable in modern Ethernet installations, the coaxial cable design is used in

- **Wireless installations –** Coaxial cables attach antennas to wireless devices. The coaxial cable carries radio frequency (RF) energy between the antennas and the radio equipment.

- **Cable Internet installations –** Cable service providers provide Internet connectivity to their customers by replacing portions of the coaxial cable and supporting amplification elements with *fiber-optic cable*. However, the wiring inside the customer's premises is still coax cable.

Copper Media Safety (4.2.1.6)

All three types of copper media are susceptible to fire and electrical hazards.

Fire hazards exist because cable insulation and sheaths may be flammable, or produce toxic fumes when heated or burned. Building authorities or organizations may stipulate related safety standards for cabling and hardware installations.

Electrical hazards are a potential problem because copper wires can conduct electricity in undesirable ways. This could subject personnel and equipment to a range of electrical hazards. For example, a defective network device could conduct currents to the chassis of other network devices. Additionally, network cabling could present undesirable voltage levels when used to connect devices that have power sources with different ground potentials. Such situations are possible when copper cabling is used to connect networks in different buildings or on separate floors that use disparate power facilities. Finally, copper cabling may conduct voltages caused by lightning strikes to network devices.

The result of undesirable voltages and currents can include damage to network devices and connected computers or injury to personnel. It is important that copper cabling be installed appropriately, and according to the relevant specifications and building codes, in order to avoid potentially dangerous and damaging situations.

Figure 4-17 displays proper cabling practices that help to prevent potential fire and electrical hazards.

The separation of data and electrical power cabling must comply with safety codes.

Cables must be connected correctly.

Installations must be inspected for damage.

Equipment must be grounded correctly.

Figure 4-17   Examples of Safety Procedures for Copper Cable

Interactive Graphic

Activity 4.2.1.7: Copper Media Characteristics

Go to the online course to perform this practice activity.

UTP Cabling (4.2.2)

Copper media has some inherent issues. Twisting the internal pairs of the copper media, as used in UTP, is a low-cost solution to improve some of the cabling performance. This section will further explore UTP cabling.

Properties of UTP Cabling (4.2.2.1)

When used as a networking medium, unshielded twisted-pair (UTP) cabling consists of four pairs of color-coded copper wires that have been twisted together and then encased in a flexible plastic sheath. Its small size can be advantageous during installation.

UTP cable does not use shielding to counter the effects of EMI and RFI. Instead, cable designers have discovered that they can limit the negative effect of crosstalk by

- **Cancellation** – Designers now pair wires in a circuit. When two wires in an electrical circuit are placed close together, their magnetic fields are the exact opposite of each other. Therefore, the two magnetic fields cancel each other and also cancel out any outside EMI and RFI signals.

- **Varying the number of twists per wire pair** – To further enhance the cancellation effect of paired circuit wires, designers vary the number of twists of each wire pair in a cable. UTP cable must follow precise specifications governing how many twists or braids are permitted per meter (3.28 feet) of cable. Notice in Figure 4-18 that each pair has a different number of twists per meter.

Figure 4-18   UTP Pairs Have Different Number of Twists per Inch

UTP cable relies solely on the cancellation effect produced by the twisted wire pairs to limit signal degradation and effectively provide self-shielding for wire pairs within the network media.

UTP Cabling Standards (4.2.2.2)

UTP cabling conforms to the standards established jointly by the TIA/EIA. Specifically, TIA/EIA-568 stipulates the commercial cabling standards for LAN installations and is the standard most commonly used in LAN cabling environments. Some of the elements defined are

- Cable types

- Cable lengths

- Connectors

- Cable termination

- Methods of testing cable

The electrical characteristics of copper cabling are defined by the Institute of Electrical and Electronics Engineers (IEEE). IEEE rates UTP cabling according to its performance. Cables are placed into categories based on their ability to carry higher bandwidth rates. For example, Category 5 (Cat5) cable is used commonly in 100BASE-TX Fast Ethernet installations. Other categories include Enhanced Category 5 (Cat5e) cable, Category 6 (Cat6), and Category 6a.

Cables in higher categories are designed and constructed to support higher data rates. As new gigabit-speed Ethernet technologies are being developed and adopted, Cat5e is now the minimally acceptable cable type, with Cat6 being the recommended type for new building installations.

Table 4-2 lists the properties for the three major UTP categories.

Table 4-2   UTP Categories

UTP Cable	Properties
Category 3 Cable (UTP)	■ Used for voice communication ■ Most often used for phone lines
Category 5 and 5e (UTP)	■ Used for data transmission ■ Cat5 supports 100 Mb/s and can support 1000 Mb/s, but it is not recommended ■ Cat5e supports 1000 Mb/s
Category 6 Cable (UTP)	■ Used for data transmission ■ An added separator is between each pair of wires allowing it to function at higher speeds ■ Supports 1000 Mb/s–10 Gb/s, although 10 Gb/s is not recommended

Some manufacturers are making cables exceeding the TIA/EIA Category 6a specifications and refer to these as Category 7.

UTP Connectors (4.2.2.3)

UTP cable is usually terminated with an RJ-45 connector. This connector is used for a range of physical layer specifications, one of which is Ethernet. The TIA/EIA-568 standard describes the wire color codes to pin assignments (pinouts) for Ethernet cables.

As shown in Figure 4-19, the RJ-45 connector is the male component, crimped at the end of the cable. The socket is the female component of a network device, wall, cubicle partition outlet, or patch panel.

RJ-45 UTP Plugs

RJ-45 UTP Socket

Figure 4-19   Examples of UTP Connectors

Each time copper cabling is terminated, there is the possibility of signal loss and the introduction of noise into the communication circuit. When terminated improperly, each cable is a potential source of physical layer performance degradation. It is essential that all copper media terminations be of high quality to ensure optimum performance with current and future network technologies.

Figure 4-20 displays an example of a badly terminated UTP cable and a well-terminated UTP cable.

Bad connector – Wires are exposed, untwisted, and not entirely covered by the sheath.

Good connector – Wires are untwisted to the extent necessary to attach the connector.

Figure 4-20   Examples of Poor and Proper Cable Termination

Types of UTP Cable (4.2.2.4)

Different situations may require UTP cables to be wired according to different wiring conventions. This means that the individual wires in the cable have to be connected in different orders to different sets of pins in the RJ-45 connectors.

The following are the main cable types that are obtained by using specific wiring conventions:

- **Ethernet Straight-through** – The most common type of networking cable. It is commonly used to interconnect a host to a switch and a switch to a router.

- **Ethernet Crossover** – A cable used to interconnect similar devices, for example, to connect a switch to a switch, a host to a host, or a router to a router.

- **Rollover** – A Cisco proprietary cable used to connect a workstation to a router or switch console port.

Table 4-3 shows the UTP cable type, related standards, and typical application of these cables.

Table 4-3 Copper Cable Types

Cable Type	Standard	Application
Ethernet Straight-through	Both ends T568A or both ends T568B	■ Connects a network host to a network device such as a switch or a hub.
Ethernet Crossover	One end T568A, other end T568B	■ Connects two network hosts ■ Connects two network intermediary devices (switch to switch or router to router)
Rollover	Cisco proprietary	■ Connects a workstation serial port to a router console port using an adapter

Figure 4-21 identifies the individual wire pairs for the TIA-568A and TIA-568B standards.

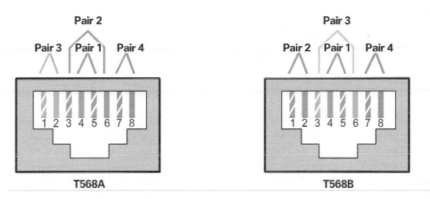

Figure 4-21   T568A and T568B Pinouts

Using a crossover or straight-through cable incorrectly between devices may not damage the devices, but connectivity and communication between the devices will not take place. This is a common error in the lab, and checking that the device connections are correct should be the first troubleshooting action if connectivity is not achieved.

Testing UTP Cables (4.2.2.5)

After installation, a UTP cable tester, like the one shown in Figure 4-22, should be used to test for the following parameters:

- Wire map
- Cable length
- Signal loss due to attenuation
- Crosstalk

Figure 4-22   Using a Cable Tester

It is recommended to check thoroughly that all UTP installation requirements have been met.

Activity 4.2.2.6: Cable Pinouts

Go to the online course to perform this practice activity.

Lab 4.2.2.7: Building an Ethernet Crossover Cable

In this lab, you will complete the following objectives:

- Part 1: Analyze Ethernet Cabling Standards and Pinouts
- Part 2: Build an Ethernet Crossover Cable
- Part 3: Test an Ethernet Crossover Cable

Fiber-Optic Cabling (4.2.3)

Networking media selection is being driven by the growing needs for network bandwidth. The distance and performance of fiber-optic cable make it a good media choice to support these network needs. This topic will examine the characteristics of fiber-optic cabling use in data networks.

Properties of Fiber-Optic Cabling (4.2.3.1)

Optical fiber cable transmits data over longer distances and at higher bandwidths than any other networking media. Unlike copper wires, fiber-optic cable can transmit signals with less attenuation and is completely immune to EMI and RFI. Optical fiber is commonly used to interconnect network devices, as shown in Figure 4-23.

Interactive
Graphic

Figure 4-23   Fiber Connection to a Networking Device

Optical fiber is a flexible, but extremely thin, transparent strand of very pure glass, not much bigger than a human hair. Bits are encoded on the fiber as light impulses. The fiber-optic cable acts as a waveguide, or "light pipe," to transmit light between the two ends with minimal loss of signal.

As an analogy, consider an empty paper towel roll with the inside coated like a mirror. It is a thousand meters in length, and a small laser pointer is used to send Morse code signals at the speed of light. Essentially that is how a fiber-optic cable operates, except that it is smaller in diameter and uses sophisticated light technologies.

Fiber-optic cabling is now being used in four types of industry:

- **Enterprise Networks** – Used for backbone cabling applications and interconnecting infrastructure devices.

- **Fiber-to-the-Home (FTTH)** – Used to provide always-on broadband services to homes and small businesses.

- **Long-Haul Networks** – Used by service providers to connect countries and cities.

- **Submarine Cable Networks** – Used to provide reliable high-speed, high-capacity solutions capable of surviving in harsh undersea environments up to transoceanic distances.

Our focus in this course is the use of fiber within the enterprise.

Fiber Media Cable Design (4.2.3.2)

Optical fiber is composed of two kinds of glass (core and cladding) and a protective outer shield (jacket), as shown in Figure 4-24.

Figure 4-24 Cross-section and Isometric View of Fiber Cable

Table 4-4 lists and describes each component shown in Figure 4-24.

Table 4-4 Fiber Cable Components

Component	Description
Core	The core is actually the light transmission element at the center of the optical fiber. This core is typically silica or glass. Light pulses travel through the fiber core.
Cladding	Made from slightly different chemicals than those used to create the core. It tends to act like a mirror by reflecting light back into the core of the fiber. This keeps light in the core as it travels down the fiber.
Buffer	Used to help shield the core and cladding from damage.
Strengthening material	Surrounds the buffer, prevents the fiber cable from being stretched when it is being pulled. The material used is often the same material used to produce bulletproof vests.
Jacket	Typically a PVC jacket that protects the fiber against abrasion, moisture, and other contaminants. This outer jacket composition can vary depending on the cable usage.

Although the optical fiber is very thin and susceptible to sharp bends, the properties of the core and cladding make it very strong. Optical fiber is durable and is deployed in harsh environmental conditions in networks all around the world.

Types of Fiber Media (4.2.3.3)

Light pulses representing the transmitted data as bits on the media are generated by either

- Lasers

- Light emitting diodes (LEDs)

Electronic semiconductor devices called photodiodes detect the light pulses and convert them to voltages. The laser light transmitted over fiber-optic cabling can damage the human eye. Care must be taken to avoid looking into the end of an active optical fiber.

Fiber-optic cables are broadly classified into two types:

- **Single-mode fiber (SMF)** – Consists of a very small core and uses expensive laser technology to send a single ray of light, as shown in Figure 4-25. Popular in long-distance situations spanning hundreds of kilometers, such as those required in long-haul telephony and cable TV applications. Characteristics of single-mode fiber include

  o Small core

  o Less dispersion

  o Suited for long-distance applications

  o Uses lasers as the light source

  o Commonly used with campus backbones for distances of several thousand meters

Produces single straight path for light

Glass Core=9 microns

Glass Cladding 125 microns diameter

Polymeric coating

Figure 4-25   Single Mode Fiber

- **Multimode fiber (MMF)** – Consists of a larger core and uses LED emitters to send light pulses. Specifically, light from an LED enters the multimode fiber at different angles, as shown in Figure 4-26. Popular in LANs because they can be powered by low-cost LEDs. It provides bandwidth up to 10 Gb/s over link lengths of up to 550 meters. Characteristics of multimode fiber include

  ○ Larger core than single-mode cable

  ○ Allows greater dispersion and therefore, loss of signal

  ○ Suited for long-distance applications, but shorter than single mode

  ○ Uses LEDs as the light source

  ○ Commonly used with LANs or distances of a couple hundred meters within a campus network

Figure 4-26   Multimode Fiber

One of the highlighted differences between multimode and single-mode fiber is the amount of dispersion. Dispersion refers to the spreading out of a light pulse over time. The more dispersion there is, the greater the loss of signal strength.

Fiber-Optic Connectors (4.2.3.4)

An optical fiber connector terminates the end of an optical fiber. A variety of optical fiber connectors are available. The main differences among the types of connectors are dimensions and methods of coupling. Businesses decide on the types of connectors that will be used, based on their equipment.

Figure 4-27 shows the most popular fiber-optics connectors.

ST Connectors   SC Connectors

LC Connectors   Duplex Multimode LC
                                       Connectors

Figure 4-27   Fiber-Optic Connectors

A description of the connectors in Figure 4-27 is as follows:

- **Straight-Tip (ST) Connectors** – One of the first connector types used. The connector locks securely with a "twist-on/twist-off" bayonet-style mechanism.

- **Subscriber Connector (SC)** – Sometimes referred to as square connector or standard connector. It is a widely adopted LAN and WAN connector that uses a push-pull mechanism to ensure positive insertion. This connector type is used with multimode and single-mode fiber.

- **Lucent Connector (LC) Simplex Connector** – A smaller version of the fiber-optic SC connector. It is sometimes called a little or local connector and is quickly growing in popularity due to its smaller size.

- **Duplex Multimode LC Connectors** – Similar to a LC simplex connector, but using a duplex connector.

Because light can only travel in one direction over optical fiber, two fibers are required to support the full duplex operation. Therefore, fiber-optic patch cables bundle together two optical fiber cables and terminate them with a pair of standard single fiber connectors. Some fiber connectors accept both the transmitting and receiving fibers in a single connector known as a duplex connector, as shown in the Duplex Multimode LC Connector.

Fiber patch cords are required for interconnecting infrastructure devices. Figure 4-28 displays various common patch cords.

Figure 4-28 Command Fiber Patch Cords

The use of color distinguishes between single-mode and multimode patch cords. A yellow jacket is for single-mode fiber cables and orange (or aqua) for multimode fiber cables.

Fiber cables should be protected with a small plastic cap when not in use.

Testing Fiber Cables (4.2.3.5)

Terminating and splicing fiber-optic cabling requires special training and equipment. Incorrect termination of fiber-optic media will result in diminished signaling distances or complete transmission failure.

Three common types of fiber-optic termination and splicing errors are

- **Misalignment** – The fiber-optic media are not precisely aligned to one another when joined.

- **End gap** – The media does not completely touch at the splice or connection.

- **End finish** – The media ends are not well polished, or dirt is present at the termination.

A quick and easy field test can be performed by shining a bright flashlight into one end of the fiber while observing the other end. If light is visible, the fiber is capable of passing light. Although this does not ensure performance, it is a quick and inexpensive way to find a broken fiber.

An Optical Time Domain Reflectometer (OTDR), such as the one shown in Figure 4-29, can be used to test each fiber-optic cable segment.

Figure 4-29   Optical Time Domain Reflectometer (OTDR)

This device injects a test pulse of light into the cable and measures backscatter and reflection of light detected as a function of time. The OTDR will calculate the approximate distance at which these faults are detected along the length of the cable.

Fiber versus Copper (4.2.3.6)

There are many advantages to using fiber-optic cable compared to copper cables. Table 4-5 highlights some of these differences.

Table 4-5   UTP and Fiber-Optic Cable Comparison

Implementation Issues	UTP Cabling	Fiber-Optic Cabling
Bandwidth supported	10 Mb/s–10 Gb/s	10 Mb/s–100 Gb/s
Distance	Relatively short (1–100 meters)	Relatively long (1–100,000 meters)
Immunity to EMI and RFI	Low	High (completely immune)
Immunity to electrical hazards	Low	High (completely immune)
Media and connector costs	Lowest	Highest
Installation skills required	Lowest	Highest
Safety precautions	Lowest	Highest

Given that the fibers used in fiber-optic media are not electrical conductors, the media is immune to electromagnetic interference and will not conduct unwanted electrical currents due to grounding issues. Optical fibers are thin and have a relatively low signal loss and can be operated at much greater lengths than copper media. Some optical fiber physical layer specifications allow lengths that can reach multiple kilometers.

At present, in most enterprise environments, optical fiber is primarily used as backbone cabling for high-traffic, point-to-point connections between data distribution facilities and for the interconnection of buildings in multi-building campuses. Because optical fiber does not conduct electricity and has a low signal loss, it is well suited for these uses.

Interactive Graphic

Activity 4.2.3.7: Fiber Optics Terminology

Go to the online course to perform this practice activity.

Wireless Media (4.2.4)

With more mobile devices being used, wireless networking is also growing in demand. This topic explores wireless media characteristic and uses.

Properties of Wireless Media (4.2.4.1)

Wireless media carry electromagnetic signals that represent the binary digits of data communications using radio or microwave frequencies.

Wireless media provides the greatest mobility options of all media, and the number of wireless-enabled devices continues to increase. As network bandwidth options increase, wireless is quickly gaining in popularity in enterprise networks.

Wireless does have some areas of concern, including

- **Coverage area** – Wireless data communication technologies work well in open environments. However, certain construction materials used in buildings and structures, and the local terrain, will limit the effective coverage.

- **Interference** – Wireless is susceptible to interference and can be disrupted by such common devices as household cordless phones, some types of fluorescent lights, microwave ovens, and other wireless communications.

- **Security** – Wireless communication coverage requires no access to a physical strand of media. Therefore, devices and users, not authorized for access to the network, can gain access to the transmission. Network security is a major component of wireless network administration.

- **Shared medium** – WLANs operate in half-duplex, which means only one device can send or receive at a time. The wireless medium is shared among all wireless users. The more users needing to access the WLAN simultaneously results in less bandwidth for each user. Half-duplex is discussed later in this chapter.

Although wireless is increasing in popularity for desktop connectivity, copper and fiber are the most popular physical layer media for network deployments.

Types of Wireless Media (4.2.4.2)

The IEEE and telecommunications industry standards for wireless data communications cover both the data link and physical layers. IEEE wireless standards include the following:

- **WiFi (IEEE 802.11 standard)** – Wireless LAN (WLAN) technology, commonly referred to as Wi-Fi. WLAN uses a contention-based protocol known as Carrier Sense Multiple Access/Collision Avoidance (CSMA/CA). The wireless NIC must first listen before transmitting to determine if the radio channel is clear. If another wireless device is transmitting, then the NIC must wait until the channel is clear. CSMA/CA is discussed later in this chapter.

- **Bluetooth (IEEE 802.15 standard)** – Wireless Personal Area Network (WPAN) standard, commonly known as "Bluetooth," uses a device-pairing process to communicate over distances from 1 to 100 meters.

- **Wi Max (IEEE 802.16 Standard)** – Commonly known as Worldwide Interoperability for Microwave Access (WiMAX), uses a point-to-multipoint topology to provide wireless broadband access.

Note

Other wireless technologies such as cellular and satellite communications can also provide data network connectivity. However, these wireless technologies are out of scope for this chapter.

In each of these standards, physical layer specifications are applied to areas that include

- Data-to-radio signal encoding

- Frequency and power of transmission

- Signal reception and decoding requirements

- Antenna design and construction

Wi-Fi is a trademark of the Wi-Fi Alliance. Wi-Fi is used with certified products that belong to WLAN devices that are based on the IEEE 802.11 standards.

Wireless LAN (4.2.4.3)

A common wireless data implementation is enabling devices to connect wirelessly via a LAN. In general, a wireless LAN requires the following network devices:

- **Wireless Access Point (AP)** – Concentrates the wireless signals from users and connects to the existing copper-based network infrastructure, such as Ethernet. Home and small business wireless routers integrate the functions of a router, switch, and access point into one device, such as the Cisco router in Figure 4-30.

Figure 4-30   Cisco WRP500 Wireless Broadband Router

- **Wireless NIC adapters** – Provide wireless communication capability to each network host.

As the technology has developed, a number of WLAN Ethernet-based standards have emerged. Care needs to be taken in purchasing wireless devices to ensure compatibility and interoperability.

The benefits of wireless data communications technologies are evident, especially the savings on costly premises wiring and the convenience of host mobility. Network administrators need to develop and apply stringent security policies and processes to protect wireless LANs from unauthorized access and damage.

Packet Tracer
☐ **Activity**

Packet Tracer 4.2.4.4: Connecting a Wired and Wireless LAN

When working in Packet Tracer, a lab environment, or a corporate setting, you should know how to select the appropriate cable and how to properly connect devices. This activity will examine device configurations in Packet Tracer, selecting the proper cable based on the configuration, and connecting the devices. This activity will also explore the physical view of the network in Packet Tracer.

Lab 4.2.4.5: Viewing Wired and Wireless NIC Information

In this lab, you will complete the following objectives:

- Part 1: Identify and Work with PC NICs
- Part 2: Identify and Use the System Tray Network Icons

Data Link Layer Protocols (4.3)

This section introduces the role of the data link layer in sending and receiving data over the physical layer.

Purpose of the Data Link Layer (4.3.1)

Just above the physical layer is the data link layer. This layer provides structure to the 1s and 0s that are sent over the media. By adding grouping to the seemingly arbitrary bits being placed on and extracted from the network media, the data link layer provides meaningful data between the upper layers of the sending and receiving nodes. This topic will inspect the important functions of the data link layer.

The Data Link Layer (4.3.1.1)

The data link layer of the OSI model (Layer 2), as shown Figure 4-31, is responsible for

- Allowing the upper layers to access the media
- Accepting Layer 3 packets and packaging them into frames
- Preparing network data for the physical network
- Controlling how data is placed and received on the media
- Exchanging frames between nodes over a physical network media, such as UTP or fiber-optic
- Receiving and directing packets to an upper layer protocol
- Performing error detection

Figure 4-31   Purpose of the Data Link Layer

The Layer 2 notation for network devices connected to a common media is called a node. Nodes build and forward frames. As shown in Figure 4-32, the OSI data link layer is responsible for the exchange of Ethernet frames between source and destination nodes over a physical network media.

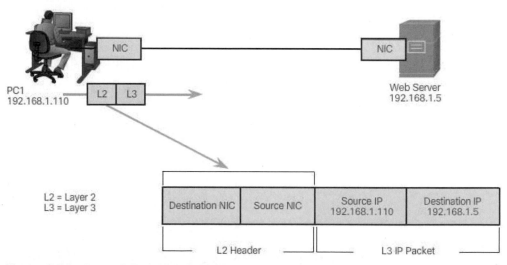

Figure 4-32   Layer 2 Data Link Addresses

The data link layer effectively separates the media transitions that occur as the packet is forwarded from the communication processes of the higher layers. The data link layer receives packets from and directs packets to an upper layer protocol, in this case IPv4 or IPv6. This upper layer protocol does not need to be aware of which media the communication will use.

Data Link Sublayers (4.3.1.2)

The data link layer is divided into two sublayers:

- *Logical Link Control (LLC)* – This upper sublayer communicates with the network layer. It places information in the frame that identifies which network layer protocol is being used for the frame. This information allows multiple Layer 3 protocols, such as IPv4 and IPv6, to utilize the same network interface and media.

- *Media Access Control (MAC)* – This lower sublayer defines the media access processes performed by the hardware. It provides data link layer addressing and access to various network technologies.

Figure 4-33 illustrates how the data link layer is separated into the LLC and MAC sublayers.

Figure 4-33   The LLC and MAC Sublayers

The LLC communicates with the network layer while the MAC sublayer allows various network access technologies. For instance, the MAC sublayer communicates with Ethernet LAN technology to send and receive frames over copper or fiber-optic cable. The MAC sublayer also communicates with wireless technologies such as Wi-Fi and Bluetooth to send and receive frames wirelessly.

Media Access Control (4.3.1.3)

Layer 2 protocols specify the encapsulation of a packet into a frame and the techniques for getting the encapsulated packet on and off each medium. The technique used for getting the frame on and off the media is called the media access control method.

As packets travel from the source host to the destination host, they typically traverse over different physical networks. These physical networks can consist of different types of physical media such as copper wires, optical fibers, and wireless consisting of electromagnetic signals, radio and microwave frequencies, and satellite links.

Without the data link layer, network layer protocols such as IP would have to make provisions for connecting to every type of media that could exist along a delivery path. Moreover, IP would have to adapt every time a new network technology or medium was developed. This process would hamper protocol and network media innovation and development. This is a key reason for using a layered approach to networking.

Figure 4-34 shows an example of a PC in Paris connecting to a laptop in Japan.

Figure 4-34   Frame Format Changes Based on the Data Link Layer

Although the two hosts are communicating using IP exclusively, it is likely that numerous data link layer protocols are being used to transport the IP packets over various types of LANs and WANs. Each transition at a router may require a different data link layer protocol for transport on a new medium.

Providing Access to Media (4.3.1.4)

Different media access control methods may be required during a single communication. Each network environment that packets encounter as they travel from a local host to a remote host can have different characteristics. For example, an Ethernet LAN consists of many hosts contending to access the network medium. Serial links consist of a direct connection between only two devices.

Router interfaces encapsulate the packet into the appropriate frame, and a suitable media access control method is used to access each link. In any given exchange of network layer packets, there may be numerous data link layers and media transitions.

At each hop along the path, a router

- Accepts a frame from a medium

- De-encapsulates the frame

- Re-encapsulates the packet into a new frame

- Forwards the new frame appropriate to the medium of that segment of the physical network

The router in Figure 4-35 has an Ethernet interface to connect to the LAN and a serial interface to connect to the WAN.

Figure 4-35   Router Changes the Frame Format Before Sending to Next Router

As the router processes frames, it will use data link layer services to receive the frame from one medium, de-encapsulate it to the Layer 3 PDU, re-encapsulate the PDU into a new frame, and place the frame on the medium of the next link of the network.

Data Link Layer Standards (4.3.1.5)

Unlike the protocols of the upper layers of the TCP/IP suite, data link layer protocols are generally not defined by *Request for Comments (RFCs)*. Although the Internet Engineering Task Force (IETF) maintains the functional protocols and services for the TCP/IP protocol suite in the upper layers, the IETF does not define the functions and operation of that model's network access layer.

Engineering organizations that define open standards and protocols that apply to the network access layer include the ones shown in Figure 4-36.

Figure 4-36   Standards Organization for the Data Link Layer

- Institute of Electrical and Electronics Engineers (IEEE)
- International Telecommunication Union (ITU)
- International Organization for Standardization (ISO)
- American National Standards Institute (ANSI)

Media Access Control (4.4)

The data entering and exiting nodes is connected; the network media requires coordination. This section will provide an overview of the data link sublayer, which provides this function: Media Access Control.

Topologies (4.4.1)

Nodes on a network can be interconnected in numerous ways. How these nodes are connected or how they communicate is described by the topology of the network. This topic will provide an overview of network topologies and how data access to the media is regulated.

Controlling Access to the Media (4.4.1.1)

Regulating the placement of data frames onto the media is controlled by the media access control sublayer. Media access control requires rules to share the media, as shown in Figure 4-37.

Figure 4-37   Sharing the Media

Media access control is the equivalent of traffic rules that regulate the entrance of motor vehicles onto a roadway. The absence of any media access control would be the equivalent of vehicles ignoring all other traffic and entering the road without regard to the other vehicles. However, not all roads and entrances are the same. Traffic can enter the road by merging, by waiting for its turn at a stop sign, or by obeying signal lights. A driver follows a different set of rules for each type of entrance.

In the same way, there are different methods to regulate placing frames onto the media. The protocols at the data link layer define the rules for access to different media. These media access control techniques define if and how the nodes share the media.

The actual media access control method used depends on

- **Topology** – How the connection between the nodes appears to the data link layer.

- **Media sharing** – How the nodes share the media. The media sharing can be point-to-point, such as in WAN connections, or shared such as in LAN networks.

Physical and Logical Topologies (4.4.1.2)

The topology of a network is the arrangement or relationship of the network devices and the interconnections between them. LAN and WAN topologies can be viewed in two ways:

- *Physical topology* – Refers to the physical connections and identifies how end devices and infrastructure devices such as routers, switches, and wireless access points are interconnected. Physical topologies are usually point-to-point or star. See Figure 4-38.

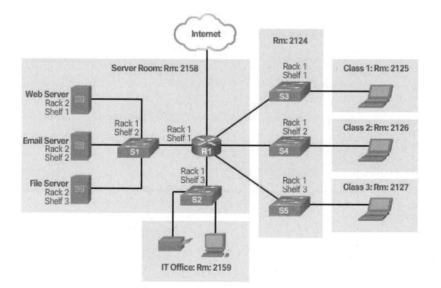

Figure 4-38   Physical Topology

- *Logical topology* – Refers to the way a network transfers frames from one node to the next. This arrangement consists of virtual connections between the nodes of a network. These logical signal paths are defined by data link layer protocols. The logical topology of point-to-point links is relatively simple while shared media offers different access control methods. See Figure 4-39.

Figure 4-39 Logical Topology

The data link layer "sees" the logical topology of a network when controlling data access to the media. It is the logical topology that influences the type of network framing and media access control used.

WAN Topologies (4.4.2)

Traditional WANs technologies have some common methods of interconnection and associated Media Access Control. This topic will introduce some of these physical and logical topologies.

Common Physical WAN Topologies (4.4.2.1)

WANs are commonly interconnected using the following physical topologies:

- **Point-to-Point** – This is the simplest topology that consists of a permanent link between two endpoints. For this reason, this is a very popular WAN topology.

- **Hub and Spoke** – A WAN version of the star topology in which a central site interconnects branch sites using point-to-point links.

- **Mesh** – This topology provides high availability but requires that every end system be interconnected to every other system. Therefore, the administrative and physical costs can be significant. Each link is essentially a point-to-point link to the other node.

A hybrid is a variation or combination of any of the above topologies. For example, a partial mesh is a hybrid topology in which some, but not all, end devices are interconnected.

The three common physical WAN topologies are illustrated in Figure 4-40.

Point-to-point topology

Hub and spoke topology

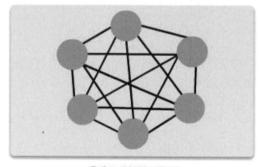

Full mesh topology

Figure 4-40   Physical WAN Topologies

Physical Point-to-Point Topology (4.4.2.2)

Physical point-to-point topologies directly connect two nodes as shown in Figure 4-41.

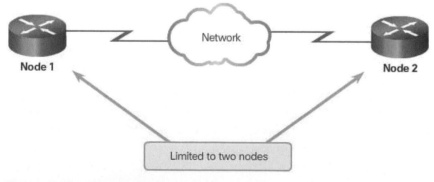

Figure 4-41   Point-to-Point

In this arrangement, two nodes do not have to share the media with other hosts. Additionally, a node does not have to make any determination about whether an incoming frame is destined for it or another node. Therefore, the logical data link protocols can be very simple, as all frames on the media can only travel to or from the two nodes. The frames are placed on the media by the node at one end and taken from the media by the node at the other end of the point-to-point circuit.

Logical Point-to-Point Topology (4.4.2.3)

The end nodes communicating in a point-to-point network can be physically connected via a number of intermediate devices. However, the use of physical devices in the network does not affect the logical topology.

As shown in Figure 4-42, the source and destination node may be indirectly connected to each other over some geographical distance.

Figure 4-42   Logical Connection

In some cases, the logical connection between nodes forms what is called a *virtual circuit*. A virtual circuit is a logical connection created within a network between two network devices. The two nodes on either end of the virtual circuit exchange the frames with each other. This occurs even if the frames are directed through intermediary devices, as shown in Figure 4-43. Virtual circuits are important logical communication constructs used by some Layer 2 technologies.

Figure 4-43 Physical Layer Details of a Logical Connection

The media access method used by the data link protocol is determined by the logical point-to-point topology, not the physical topology. This means that the logical point-to-point connection between two nodes may not necessarily be between two physical nodes at each end of a single physical link.

LAN Topologies (4.4.3)

Like WANs, some physical and logical topologies are more predominately used in LANs. These topologics will be examined in this topic.

Physical LAN Topologies (4.4.3.1)

Physical topology defines how the end systems are physically interconnected. In shared media LANs, end devices can be interconnected using the following physical topologies:

- **Star** – End devices are connected to a central intermediate device. Early star topologies interconnected end devices using Ethernet hubs. However, star topologies now use Ethernet switches. The star topology is easy to install, very scalable (easy to add and remove end devices), and easy to troubleshoot.

- **Extended Star** – In an extended star topology, additional Ethernet switches interconnect other star topologies.

- **Bus** – All end systems are chained to each other and terminated in some form on each end. Infrastructure devices such as switches are not required to interconnect the end devices. Bus topologies using coax cables were used in legacy Ethernet networks because it was inexpensive and easy to set up.

- **Ring** – End systems are connected to their respective neighbor forming a ring. Unlike the bus topology, the ring does not need to be terminated. Ring topologies were used in legacy Fiber Distributed Data Interface (FDDI) and Token Ring networks.

Figure 4-44 illustrates how end devices are interconnected on LANs. It is common for a straight line in networking graphics to represent an Ethernet LAN including a simple star and an extended star.

Star topology   Extended star topology

Bus topology   Ring topology

Figure 4-44   Physical LAN Topologies

Half and Full Duplex (4.4.3.2)

Duplex communications refer to the direction of data transmission between two devices. Half-duplex communications restrict the exchange of data to one direction at a time while full-duplex allows the sending and receiving of data to happen simultaneously.

■ *Half-duplex communication* – Both devices can transmit and receive on the media but cannot do so simultaneously. The half-duplex mode is used in legacy bus topologies and with Ethernet hubs. WLANs also operate in half-duplex. Half-duplex allows only one device to send or receive at a time on the shared medium and is used with contention-based access methods. Figure 4-45 shows half-duplex communication.

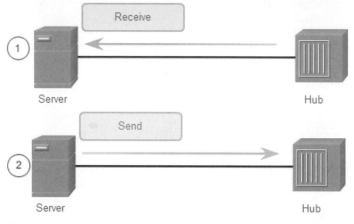

Figure 4-45   Half-Duplex Communication

■ *Full-duplex communication* – Both devices can transmit and receive on the media at the same time. The data link layer assumes that the media is available for transmission for both nodes at any time. Ethernet switches operate in full-duplex mode by default but can operate in half-duplex if connecting to a device such as an Ethernet hub. Figure 4-46 shows full-duplex communication.

Figure 4-46   Full-Duplex Communication

It is important that two interconnected interfaces, such as a host's NIC and an interface on an Ethernet switch, operate using the same duplex mode. Otherwise, there will be a duplex mismatch creating inefficiency and latency on the link.

Media Access Control Methods (4.4.3.3)

Some network topologies share a common medium with multiple nodes. These are called multi-access networks. Ethernet LANs and WLANs are examples of a multi-access network. At any one time, there may be a number of devices attempting to send and receive data using the same network media.

Some multi-access networks require rules to govern how devices share the physical media. There are two basic access control methods for shared media:

- **Contention-based access** – All nodes operating in half-duplex compete for the use of the medium, but only one device can send at a time. However, there is a process if more than one device transmits at the same time. Ethernet LANs using hubs and WLANs are examples of this type of access control. Figure 4-47 shows contention-based access.

Figure 4-47 Contention-Based Access

- **Controlled access** – Each node has its own time to use the medium. These deterministic types of networks are inefficient because a device must wait its turn to access the medium. Legacy Token Ring LANs are an example of this type of access control. Figure 4-48 shows controlled access.

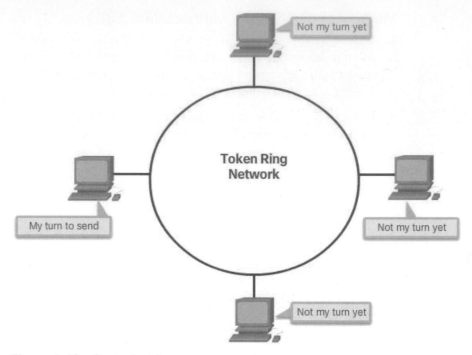

Figure 4-48   Controlled Access

By default, Ethernet switches operate in full-duplex mode. This allows the switch and the full-duplex connected device to send and receive simultaneously.

Contention-Based Access – CSMA/CD (4.4.3.4)

WLANs, Ethernet LANs with hubs, and legacy Ethernet bus networks are all examples of contention-based access networks. All of these networks operate in half-duplex mode. This requires a process to govern when a device can send and what happens when multiple devices send at the same time.

The *Carrier Sense Multiple Access/Collision Detection (CSMA/CD)* process is used in half-duplex Ethernet LANs. Figure 4-49 shows an example of CSMA/CD.

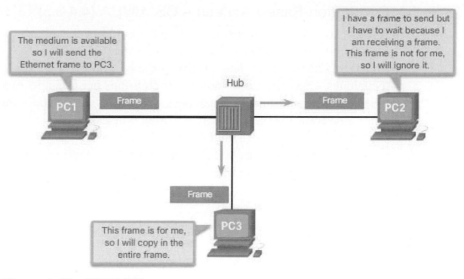

Figure 4-49   CSMA/CD

The CSMA process is as follows:

1. PC1 has an Ethernet frame to send to PC3.

2. PC1's NIC needs to determine if anyone is transmitting on the medium. If it does not detect a carrier signal, in other words, it is not receiving transmissions from another device, it will assume the network is available to send.

3. PC1's NIC sends the Ethernet Frame.

4. The Ethernet hub receives the frame. An Ethernet hub is also known as a multiport repeater. Any bits received on an incoming port are regenerated and sent out all other ports.

5. If another device, such as PC2, wants to transmit, but is currently receiving a frame, it must wait until the channel is clear.

6. All devices attached to the hub will receive the frame. Because the frame has a destination data link address for PC3, only that device will accept and copy in the entire frame. All other devices' NICs will ignore the frame.

If two devices transmit at the same time, a collision will occur. Both devices will detect the collision on the network; this is the collision detection (CD). This is done by the NIC comparing data transmitted with data received or by recognizing the signal amplitude is higher than normal on the media. The data sent by both devices will be corrupted and will need to be resent.

Contention-Based Access – CSMA/CA (4.4.3.5)

Another form of CSMA that is used by IEEE 802.11 WLANs is *Carrier Sense Multiple Access/Collision Avoidance (CSMA/CA)*. CSMA/CA uses a method similar to CSMA/CD to detect if the media is clear. CSMA/CA also uses additional techniques. CSMA/CA does not detect collisions but attempts to avoid them by waiting before transmitting. Each device that transmits includes the time duration that it needs for the transmission. All other wireless devices receive this information and know how long the medium will be unavailable, as shown in Figure 4-50. After a wireless device sends an 802.11 frame, the receiver returns an acknowledgment so that the sender knows the frame arrived.

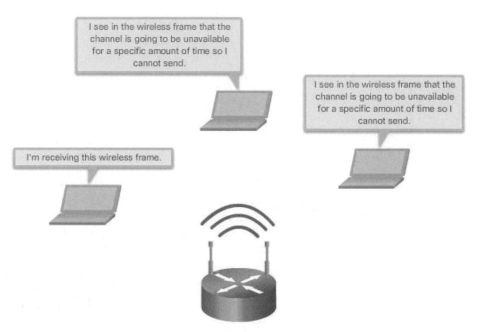

Figure 4-50   CSMA/CA

Whether it is an Ethernet LAN using hubs or a WLAN, contention-based systems do not scale well under heavy media use. It is important to note that Ethernet LANs using switches do not use a contention-based system because the switch and the host NIC operate in full-duplex mode.

Data Link Frame (4.4.4)

The data link layer needs to provide intelligible data between the Layer 3 of the sending host and the Layer 3 of the receiving host. To do this, the Layer 3 PDU is wrapped with a header and trailer to form the Layer 2 frame. This topic will examine the common elements of within the frame structure as well as explore some of the commonly used data link layer protocols.

The Frame (4.4.4.1)

The data link layer prepares a packet for transport across the local media by encapsulating it with a header and a trailer to create a frame. The description of a frame is a key element of each data link layer protocol. Although there are many different data link layer protocols that describe data link layer frames, each frame type has three basic parts:

- Header
- Data
- Trailer

All data link layer protocols encapsulate the Layer 3 PDU within the data field of the frame. However, the structure of the frame and the fields contained in the header and trailer vary according to the protocol.

There is no one frame structure that meets the needs of all data transportation across all types of media. Depending on the environment, the amount of control information needed in the frame varies to match the access control requirements of the media and logical topology.

As shown in Figure 4-51, a fragile environment requires more control.

Figure 4-51   Fragile Environment

Frame Fields (4.4.4.2)

Framing breaks the stream into decipherable groupings, with control information inserted in the header and trailer as values in different fields. This format gives the physical signals a structure that can be received by nodes and decoded into packets at the destination.

Figure 4-52 shows the fields of a generic frame.

Figure 4-52   Frame Fields

The generic frame field types include

- **Frame start and stop indicator flags** – Used to identify the beginning and end limits of the frame.

- **Addressing** – Indicates the source and destination nodes on the media.

- **Type** – Identifies the Layer 3 protocol in the data field.

- **Control** – Identifies special flow control services such as quality of service (QoS). QoS is used to give forwarding priority to certain types of messages. Data link frames carrying voice over IP (VoIP) packets normally receive priority because they are sensitive to delay.

- **Data** – Contains the frame payload (i.e., packet header, segment header, and the data).

- **Error Detection** – These frame fields are used for error detection and are included after the data to form the trailer.

Not all protocols include all of these fields. The standards for a specific data link protocol define the actual frame format.

Data link layer protocols add a trailer to the end of each frame. The trailer is used to determine if the frame arrived without error. This process is called error detection and is accomplished by placing a logical or mathematical summary of the bits that comprise the frame in the trailer. Error detection is added at the data link layer because the signals on the media could be subject to interference, distortion, or loss that would substantially change the bit values that those signals represent.

A transmitting node creates a logical summary of the contents of the frame, known as the cyclic redundancy check (CRC) value. This value is placed in the Frame Check Sequence (FCS) field to represent the contents of the frame. In the Ethernet trailer, the FCS provides a method for the receiving node to determine whether the frame experienced transmission errors.

Activity 4.4.4.3: Generic Frame Fields

Go to the online course to perform this practice activity.

Layer 2 Address (4.4.4.4)

The data link layer provides addressing that is used in transporting a frame across a shared local media. Device addresses at this layer are referred to as physical addresses. Data link layer addressing is contained within the frame header and specifics the frame destination node on the local network. The frame header may also contain the source address of the frame.

Unlike Layer 3 logical addresses, which are hierarchical, physical addresses do not indicate on what network the device is located. Rather, the physical address is unique to the specific device. If the device is moved to another network or subnet, it will still function with the same Layer 2 physical address.

Figures 4-53 through 4-55 illustrate the function of the Layer 2 and Layer 3 addresses.

Figure 4-53   Data Link Addresses – First Hop

Figure 4-54   Data Link Addresses – Second Hop

Figure 4-55   Data Link Addresses – Third Hop

As the IP packet travels from host-to-router, router-to-router, and finally router-to-host, at each point along the way the IP packet is encapsulated in a new data link frame. Each data link frame contains the source data link address of the NIC card sending the frame and the destination data link address of the NIC card receiving the frame.

An address that is device-specific and non-hierarchical cannot be used to locate a device on large networks or the Internet. This would be like trying to find a single house within the entire world, with nothing more than a house number and street name. The physical address, however, can be used to locate a device within a limited area. For this reason, the data link layer address is only used for local delivery. Addresses at this layer have no meaning beyond the local network. Compare this to Layer 3, where addresses in the packet header are carried from the source host to the destination host, regardless of the number of network hops along the route.

If the data must pass onto another network segment, an intermediate device, such as a router, is necessary. The router must accept the frame based on the physical address and de-encapsulate the frame in order to examine the hierarchical address, or IP address. Using the IP address, the router is able to determine the network location of the destination device and the best path to reach it. When it knows where to forward the packet, the router then creates a new frame for the packet, and the new frame is sent on to the next network segment toward its final destination.

LAN and WAN Frames (4.4.4.5)

In a TCP/IP network, all OSI Layer 2 protocols work with IP at OSI Layer 3. However, the Layer 2 protocol used depends on the logical topology and the physical media.

Each protocol performs media access control for specified Layer 2 logical topologies. This means that a number of different network devices can act as nodes that operate at the data link layer when implementing these protocols. These devices include the NICs on computers as well as the interfaces on routers and Layer 2 switches.

The Layer 2 protocol used for a particular network topology is determined by the technology used to implement that topology. The technology is, in turn, determined by the size of the network – in terms of the number of hosts and the geographic scope – and the services to be provided over the network.

A LAN typically uses a high bandwidth technology that is capable of supporting large numbers of hosts. A LAN's relatively small geographic area (a single building or a multi-building campus) and its high density of users make this technology cost-effective.

However, using a high-bandwidth technology is usually not cost-effective for WANs that cover large geographic areas (cities or multiple cities, for example). The cost of the long-distance physical links and the technology used to carry the signals over those distances typically results in lower bandwidth capacity.

The difference in bandwidth normally results in the use of different protocols for LANs and WANs.

Data link layer protocols include

- Ethernet
- 802.11 Wireless
- Point-to-Point Protocol (PPP)
- HDLC
- Frame Relay

Figure 4-56 shows an example of data link layer protocols changing from hop to hop on the way to the destination.

Figure 4-56   Examples of Layer 2 Protocols

Summary (4.5)

Class Activity 4.5.1.1: Linked In!

Your small business is moving to a new location! Your building is brand new, and you must come up with a physical topology so that network port installation can begin.

Your instructor will provide you with a blueprint created for this activity. The area on the blueprint, indicated by Number 1, is the reception area and the area numbered RR is the restroom area.

All rooms are within Category 6 UTP specifications (100 meters), so you have no concerns about hard-wiring the building to code. Each room in the diagram must have at least one network connection available for users/intermediary devices.

Do not go into excessive detail on your design. Just use the content from the chapter to be able to justify your decisions to the class.

The TCP/IP network access layer is the equivalent of the OSI data link layer (Layer 2) and the physical layer (Layer 1).

The OSI physical layer provides the means to transport the bits that make up a data link layer frame across the network media. The physical components are the electronic hardware devices, media, and other connectors that transmit and carry the signals to represent the bits. Hardware components such as network adapters (NICs), interfaces and connectors, cable materials, and cable designs are all specified in standards associated with the physical layer. The physical layer standards address three functional areas: physical components, frame encoding technique, and signaling method.

Using the proper media is an important part of network communications. Without the proper physical connection, either wired or wireless, communications between any two devices will not occur.

Wired communication consists of copper media and fiber cable:

- There are three main types of copper media used in networking: unshielded-twisted pair (UTP), shielded-twisted pair (STP), and coaxial cable. UTP cabling is the most common copper networking media.

- Optical fiber cable has become very popular for interconnecting infrastructure network devices. It permits the transmission of data over longer distances and at higher bandwidths (data rates) than any other networking media. Unlike copper wires, fiber-optic cable can transmit signals with less attenuation and is completely immune to EMI and RFI.

Wireless media carry electromagnetic signals that represent the binary digits of data communications using radio or microwave frequencies.

The number of wireless-enabled devices continues to increase. For this reason, wireless has become the medium of choice for home networks and is quickly gaining in popularity in enterprise networks.

The data link layer handles the exchange of frames between nodes over a physical network media. It allows the upper layers to access the media and controls how data is placed and received on the media.

Among the different implementations of the data link layer protocols, there are different methods of controlling access to the media. These media access control techniques define if and how the nodes share the media. The actual media access control method used depends on the topology and media sharing. LAN and WAN topologies can be physical or logical. It is the logical topology that influences the type of network framing and media access control used. WANs are commonly interconnected using the point-to-point, hub and spoke, or mesh physical topologies. In shared-media LANs, end devices can be interconnected using the star, bus, ring, or extended star physical topologies.

All data link layer protocols encapsulate the Layer 3 PDU within the data field of the frame. However, the structure of the frame and the fields contained in the header and trailer vary according to the protocol.

Practice

The following activities provide practice with the topics introduced in this chapter. The Labs and Class Activities are available in the companion Introduction to Networks v5.1 Lab Manual (ISBN 9781587133534). The Packet Tracer Activities PKA files are found in the online course.

Class Activities

Class Activity 4.0.1.2: Managing the Medium

Class Activity 4.5.1.1: Linked In!

Labs

Lab 4.1.2.4: Identifying Network Devices and Cabling

Lab 4.2.2.7: Building an Ethernet Crossover Cable

Lab 4.2.4.5: Viewing Wired and Wireless NIC Information

Packet Tracer
☐ Activity

Packet Tracer Activities

Packet Tracer 4.2.4.4: Connecting a Wired and Wireless LAN

Check Your Understanding Questions

Complete all the review questions listed here to test your understanding of the topics and concepts in this chapter. The appendix "Answers to 'Check Your Understanding' Questions" lists the answers.

1. What are the purpose and functions of the physical layer in data networks? (Choose two.)

   A. Controls how the data is transmitted onto the physical media

   B. Encodes the data into signals

   C. Provides logical addressing

   D. Packages bits into data units

   E. Controls media access

2. Which of these statements regarding UTP network cabling are true? (Choose two.)

   A. Uses light to transmit data

   B. Susceptible to EMI and RFI

   C. Commonly used between buildings

   D. Most difficult type of networking cable to install

   E. Most commonly used type of networking cable

3. What is the purpose of cladding in fiber-optic cables?

   A. Cable grounding

   B. Noise cancellation

   C. Prevention of light loss by keeping light in the core

   D. EMI protection

4. Which statement describes a characteristic of the frame header fields of the data link layer?

   A. They all include the flow control and logical connection fields.

   B. Ethernet frame header fields contain Layer 3 source and destination addresses.

   C. They vary depending on protocols.

   D. They include information on user applications.

5. What are the advantages of using fiber-optic cable over copper cable? (Choose three.)

   A. Copper is more expensive.

   B. Immunity to electromagnetic interference.

   C. Careful cable handling.

   D. Longer maximum cable length.

   E. Efficient electrical current transfer.

   F. Greater bandwidth potential.

6. What occurs when another wireless device connects to a wireless access point (WAP)?

   A. The WAP adds an additional channel to support the new client.

   B. The WAP throughput for all the connected clients decreases.

   C. The WAP decreases the radio coverage area.

   D. The WAP will change frequencies to reduce interference caused by the new client.

7. Which is a function of the Logical Link Control (LLC) sublayer?

   A. To define the media access processes that are performed by the hardware

   B. To provide data link layer addressing

   C. To identify which network layer protocol is being used

   D. To accept segments and package them into data units that are called packets

8. What are the contents of the data field in a frame?

   A. A CRC

   B. The network layer PDU

   C. The Layer 2 source address

   D. The length of the frame

9. Which of the following is true about the logical topology of a network?

    A. Is always multi-access

    B. Provides the physical addressing

    C. Is determined by how the nodes in the network are connected

    D. Defines how frames are transferred from one node to the next

10. Which of the following is a characteristic of contention-based MAC?

    A. Used in point-to-point topologies.

    B. Nodes compete for the use of the medium.

    C. Leaves MAC to the upper layer.

    D. Each node has a specific time to use the medium.

CHAPTER 5

Ethernet

Objectives

Upon completion of this chapter, you will be able to answer the following questions:

- What is the function of each of the Ethernet sublayers?

- What are the characteristics and purpose of the Ethernet MAC address?

- How does an Ethernet switch build its MAC address table and how is it used to forward frames?

- What are the available forwarding methods and port settings on an Ethernet switch?

- What are the functions and differences between MAC and IP addresses?

- What is the role of ARP in an Ethernet network?

- How do ARP requests impact network and host performance?

Key Terms

This chapter uses the following key terms. You can find the definitions in the Glossary.

Introduction (5.0)

The OSI physical layer provides the means to transport the bits that make up a data link layer frame across the network media.

Ethernet is now the predominant LAN technology in the world. Ethernet operates in the data link layer and the physical layer. The Ethernet protocol standards define many aspects of network communication including frame format, frame size, timing, and encoding. When messages are sent between hosts on an Ethernet network, the hosts format the messages into the frame layout that is specified by the standards.

Because Ethernet is comprised of standards at these lower layers, it may best be understood in reference to the OSI model. The OSI model separates the data link layer functionalities of addressing, framing, and accessing the media from the physical layer standards of the media. Ethernet standards define both the Layer 2 protocols and the Layer 1 technologies. Although Ethernet specifications support different media, bandwidths, and other Layer 1 and 2 variations, the basic frame format and address scheme is the same for all varieties of Ethernet.

This chapter examines the characteristics and operation of Ethernet as it has evolved from a shared media, contention-based data communications technology to today's high bandwidth, full-duplex technology.

Class Activity 5.0.1.2: Join My Social Circle!

Refer to Lab Activity for this chapter

Much of our network communication takes the form of messaging (text or instant), video contact, social media postings, etc.

For this activity, choose one of the communication networks you use most:

- Text (or instant) messaging

- Audio/video conferencing

- Emailing

- Gaming

Now that you have selected a network communication type, record your answers to the following questions:

- Is there a procedure you must follow to register others and yourself so that you form a communications group?

- How do you initiate contact with the person/people with whom you wish to communicate?

- How do you limit your conversations so they are received by only those with whom you wish to communicate?

Be prepared to discuss your recorded answers in class.

Ethernet Protocol (5.1)

As previously stated, Ethernet is the most widely used LAN technology today. It provides high-speed communications between end devices in most local area networks. For this reason, a good understanding of Ethernet technology is a requirement for anyone working with LAN technology.

Ethernet Frame (5.1.1)

Ethernet operates in the data link layer and the physical layer. It is a family of networking technologies that are defined in the IEEE 802.2 and 802.3 standards.

Ethernet Encapsulation (5.1.1.1)

Ethernet is the most widely used LAN technology today.

Ethernet operates in the data link layer and the physical layer. It is a family of networking technologies that are defined in the IEEE 802.2 and 802.3 standards. Ethernet supports data bandwidths of

- 10 Mb/s
- 100 Mb/s
- 1000 Mb/s (1 Gb/s)
- 10,000 Mb/s (10 Gb/s)
- 40,000 Mb/s (40 Gb/s)
- 100,000 Mb/s (100 Gb/s)

As shown in Figure 5-1, Ethernet standards define both the Layer 2 protocols and the Layer 1 technologies. For the Layer 2 protocols, as with all 802 IEEE standards, Ethernet relies on the two separate sublayers of the data link layer to operate, the Logical Link Control (LLC) and the MAC sublayers.

Figure 5-1   Ethernet in the OSI Model

LLC sublayer

The Ethernet LLC sublayer handles the communication between the upper layers and the lower layers. This is typically between the networking software and the device hardware. The LLC sublayer takes the network protocol data, which is typically an IPv4 packet, and adds control information to help deliver the packet to the destination node. The LLC is used to communicate with the upper layers of the application and transition the packet to the lower layers for delivery.

LLC is implemented in software, and its implementation is independent of the hardware. In a computer, the LLC can be considered the driver software for the NIC. The NIC driver is a program that interacts directly with the hardware on the NIC to pass the data between the MAC sublayer and the physical media.

MAC sublayer

MAC constitutes the lower sublayer of the data link layer. MAC is implemented by hardware, typically in the computer NIC. The specifics are listed in the IEEE 802.3 standards. Figure 5-2 lists common IEEE Ethernet standards.

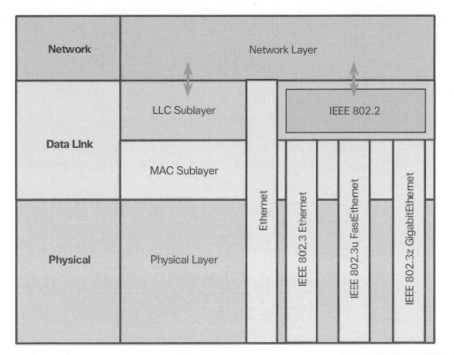

Figure 5-2   IEEE Ethernet Standards in the OSI Model

MAC Sublayer (5.1.1.2)

The Ethernet MAC sublayer highlighted in Figure 5-3 has two primary responsibilities:

- Data encapsulation
- Media access control

Figure 5-3   Details of the MAC Sublayer

Data encapsulation

The data encapsulation process includes frame assembly before transmission and frame disassembly upon reception of a frame. In forming the frame, the MAC layer adds a header and trailer to the network layer PDU.

Data encapsulation provides three primary functions:

- **Frame delimiting** – The framing process provides important delimiters that are used to identify a group of bits that make up a frame. These delimiting bits provide synchronization between the transmitting and receiving nodes.

- **Addressing** – The encapsulation process contains the Layer 3 PDU and also provides for data link layer addressing.

- **Error detection** – Each frame contains a trailer used to detect any errors in transmissions.

The use of frames aids in the transmission of bits as they are placed on the media and in the grouping of bits at the receiving node.

Media Access Control

The second responsibility of the MAC sublayer is media access control. Media access control is responsible for the placement of frames on the media and the removal of frames from the media. As its name implies, it controls access to the media. This sublayer communicates directly with the physical layer.

The underlying logical topology of Ethernet is a multi-access bus; therefore, all nodes (devices) on a single network segment share the medium. Ethernet is a *contention-based* method of networking. A contention-based method means that any device can try to transmit data across the shared medium whenever it has data to send. The Carrier Sense Multiple Access/Collision Detection (CSMA/CD) process is used in half-duplex Ethernet LANs to detect and resolve collisions. Today's Ethernet LANs use full-duplex switches, which allow multiple devices to send and receive simultaneously with no collisions.

Ethernet Evolution (5.1.1.3)

Since the creation of Ethernet in 1973, standards have evolved for specifying faster and more flexible versions of the technology. This ability for Ethernet to improve over time is one of the main reasons it has become so popular. Early versions of Ethernet were relatively slow at 10 Mbps. The latest versions of Ethernet operate at 10 Gigabits per second and faster.

Interactive Graphic

Go to the online course to view an interactive timeline of the various versions of Ethernet.

At the data link layer, the frame structure is nearly identical for all speeds of Ethernet. The Ethernet frame structure adds headers and trailers around the Layer 3 PDU to encapsulate the message being sent, as shown in Figure 5-4.

Ethernet II					
8 Bytes	6 Bytes	6 Bytes	2 Bytes	46 to 1500 Bytes	4 Bytes
Preamble	Destination Address	Source Address	Type	Data	Frame Check Sequence

Figure 5-4 Ethernet II Frame Structure and Field Size

Ethernet II is the Ethernet frame format used in TCP/IP networks.

Ethernet Frame Fields (5.1.1.4)

The minimum Ethernet frame size is 64 bytes and the maximum is 1518 bytes. This includes all bytes from the Destination MAC Address field through the Frame Check Sequence (FCS) field. The Preamble field is not included when describing the size of a frame.

Any frame less than 64 bytes in length is called a "*collision fragment*" or "*runt frame*" and is automatically discarded by receiving stations. Frames with more than 1500 bytes of data are called "*jumbo frames*" or "*baby giant frames*."

If the size of a transmitted frame is less than the minimum or greater than the maximum, the receiving device drops the frame. Dropped frames are likely to be the result of collisions or other unwanted signals and are therefore considered invalid.

The function of each field in the Ethernet frame is as follows:

- **Preamble –** The Preamble (7 bytes) and Start Frame Delimiter (SFD), also called the Start of Frame (1 byte), fields are used for synchronization between the sending and receiving devices. These first eight bytes of the frame are used to get the attention of the receiving nodes. Essentially, the first few bytes tell the receivers to get ready to receive a new frame.

- **Destination MAC Address –** This 6-byte field is the identifier for the intended recipient. As you will recall, this address is used by Layer 2 to assist devices in determining if a frame is addressed to them. The address in the frame is compared to the MAC address in the device. If there is a match, the device accepts the frame. It can be a unicast, multicast, or broadcast address.

- **Source MAC Address –** This 6-byte field identifies the frame's originating NIC or interface. It must be a unicast address.

- **EtherType Field** – This 2-byte field identifies the upper layer protocol encapsulated in the Ethernet frame. Common values are, in hexadecimal, 0 × 800 for IPv4, 0 × 86DD for IPv6 and 0 × 806 for ARP.

- **Data** – This field (46–1500 bytes) contains the encapsulated data from a higher layer, which is a generic Layer 3 PDU, or more commonly, an IPv4 packet. All frames must be at least 64 bytes long. If a small packet is encapsulated, additional bits called a pad are used to increase the size of the frame to this minimum size.

- **FCS** – The Frame Check Sequence (FCS) field (4 bytes) is used to detect errors in a frame. It uses a *cyclic redundancy check (CRC)*. The sending device includes the results of a CRC in the FCS field of the frame. The receiving device receives the frame and generates a CRC to look for errors. If the calculations match, no error occurred. Calculations that do not match are an indication that the data has changed; therefore, the frame is dropped. A change in the data could be the result of a disruption of the electrical signals that represent the bits.

Interactive Graphic

Activity 5.1.1.5: MAC and LLC Sublayers

Go to the online course to perform this practice activity.

Interactive Graphic

Activity 5.1.1.6: Ethernet Frame Fields

Go to the online course to perform this practice activity.

Lab 5.1.1.7: Using Wireshark to Examine Ethernet Frames

In this lab, you will complete the following objectives:

- Part 1: Examine the Header Fields in an Ethernet II Frame
- Part 2: Use Wireshark to Capture and Analyze Ethernet Frames

Ethernet MAC Addresses (5.1.2)

Ethernet technology relies on MAC addresses to function. MAC addresses are used to identify the frame source and destination.

MAC Address and Hexadecimal (5.1.2.1)

An Ethernet MAC address is a 48-bit binary value expressed as 12 hexadecimal digits (4 bits per hexadecimal digit).

Just as decimal is a base ten number system, hexadecimal is a base sixteen system. The base sixteen number system uses the numbers 0 to 9 and the letters A to F. Table 5-1 shows the equivalent decimal and hexadecimal values for binary 0000 to 1111. It is easier to express a value as a single hexadecimal digit than as four binary bits.

Table 5-1   Decimal to Binary to Hexadecimal Conversion

Decimal	Binary	Hexadecimal
0	0000	0
1	0001	1
2	0010	2
3	0011	3
4	0100	4
5	0101	5
6	0110	6
7	0111	7
8	1000	8
9	1001	9
10	1010	A
11	1011	B
12	1100	C
13	1101	D
14	1110	E
15	1111	F

Given that 8 bits (one byte) is a common binary grouping, binary 00000000 to 11111111 can be represented in hexadecimal as the range 00 to FF, as shown in Table 5-2. Leading zeroes are always displayed to complete the 8-bit representation. For example, the binary value 0000 1010 is shown in hexadecimal as 0A.

Table 5-2   Selected Examples of Decimal to Binary to Hexadecimal Conversions

Decimal	Binary	Hexadecimal
0	0000 0000	00
1	0000 0001	01
2	0000 0010	02
3	0000 0011	03
4	0000 0100	04
5	0000 0101	05

Continued

Table 5-2 *Continued*

Decimal	Binary	Hexadecimal
6	0000 0110	06
7	0000 0111	07
8	0000 1000	08
10	0000 1010	0A
15	0000 1111	0F
16	0001 0000	10
32	0010 0000	20
64	0100 0000	40
128	1000 0000	80
192	1100 0000	C0
202	1100 1010	CA
240	1111 0000	F0
255	1111 1111	FF

Note

It is important to distinguish hexadecimal values from decimal values regarding the characters 0 to 9, as shown in the figure.

Representing Hexadecimal Values

Hexadecimal is usually represented in text by the value preceded by 0× (for example 0×73) or a subscript 16. Less commonly, it may be followed by an H (for example 73H). However, because subscript text is not recognized in command line or programming environments, the technical representation of hexadecimal is preceded with "0×" (zero ×). Therefore, the examples above would be shown as 0×0A and 0×73, respectively.

Hexadecimal is used to represent Ethernet MAC addresses and IP Version 6 addresses.

Hexadecimal Conversions

Number conversions between decimal and hexadecimal values are straightforward, but quickly dividing or multiplying by 16 is not always convenient. If such conversions are required, it is usually easier to convert the decimal or hexadecimal value to binary and then to convert the binary value to either decimal or hexadecimal as appropriate.

MAC Address: Ethernet Identity (5.1.2.2)

In Ethernet, every network device is connected to the same, shared media. Ethernet was once predominantly a half-duplex topology using a multi-access bus or later Ethernet hubs. This meant that all nodes would receive every frame transmitted. To prevent the excessive overhead involved in the processing of every frame, MAC addresses were created to identify the actual source and destination. MAC addressing provides a method for device identification at the lower level of the OSI model. Although Ethernet has now transitioned to full-duplex NICs and switches, it is still possible that a device that is not the intended destination will receive an Ethernet frame.

MAC Address Structure

The MAC address value is a direct result of IEEE-enforced rules for vendors to ensure globally unique addresses for each Ethernet device. The rules established by IEEE require any vendor that sells Ethernet devices to register with IEEE. The IEEE assigns the vendor a 3-byte (24-bit) code, called the *Organizationally Unique Identifier (OUI)*.

IEEE requires a vendor to follow two simple rules, as shown in Figure 5-5:

- All MAC addresses assigned to a NIC or other Ethernet device must use that vendor's assigned OUI as the first 3 bytes.

- All MAC addresses with the same OUI must be assigned a unique value in the last 3 bytes.

Figure 5-5   The Ethernet MAC Address Structure

> **Note**
>
> It is possible for duplicate MAC addresses to exist due to mistakes during manufacturing or in some virtual machine implementation methods. In either case, it will be necessary to modify the MAC address with a new NIC or in software.

Frame Processing (5.1.2.3)

The MAC address is often referred to as a *burned-in address (BIA)* because, historically, this address is burned into ROM (Read-Only Memory) on the NIC. This means that the address is encoded into the ROM chip permanently.

> **Note**
>
> On modern PC operating systems and NICs, it is possible to change the MAC address in software. This is useful when attempting to gain access to a network that filters based on BIA. Consequently, filtering or controlling traffic based on the MAC address is no longer as secure.

When the computer starts up, the first thing the NIC does is copy the MAC address from ROM into RAM. When a device is forwarding a message to an Ethernet network, it attaches header information to the frame. The header information contains the source and destination MAC address, as shown in Figure 5-6.

Figure 5-6   Source Prepares a Frame to Send to the Destination

When a NIC receives an Ethernet frame, it examines the destination MAC address to see if it matches the device's physical MAC address stored in RAM. If there is no match, the device discards the frame. In Figure 5-7, H2 and H4 discard the frame. The MAC matches H4, so it passes the frame up the OSI layers, where the de-encapsulation process takes place.

Figure 5-7   All Devices Receive the Frame but Only the Destination Processes It

Note

Ethernet NICs will also accept frames if the destination MAC address is a broadcast or a multicast group of which the host is a member.

Any device that can be the source or destination of an Ethernet frame must be assigned a MAC address. This includes workstations, servers, printers, mobile devices, and routers.

MAC Address Representations (5.1.2.4)

On a Windows host, the **ipconfig /all** command can be used to identify the MAC address of an Ethernet adapter. In Example 5-1, notice the Physical Address (MAC) of the computer is 00-18-DE-DD-A7-B2. If you have access, you may wish to try this on your own computer. On a MAC or Linux host, the **ifconfig** command is used.

Example 5-1 Physical Address of a Host

```
C:\> ipconfig/all

Ethernet adapter Local Area Connection:

 Connection-specific DNS Suffix  . :
 Description . . . . . . . . . . . : Intel(R) Ethernet Connection I217-LM
 Physical Address. . . . . . . . . : 00-18-DE-DD-A7-B2
 DHCP Enabled. . . . . . . . . . . : Yes
 Autoconfiguration Enabled . . . . : Yes
 Link-local IPv6 Address . . . . . : fe80::487a:32ba:8937:f07b%11(Preferred)
 IPv4 Address. . . . . . . . . . . : 10.10.10.12(Preferred)
 Subnet Mask . . . . . . . . . . . : 255.255.255.0
 Lease Obtained. . . . . . . . . . : Monday, December 28, 2015 8:42:28 PM
 Lease Expires . . . . . . . . . . : Thursday, December 31, 2015 8:42:30 AM
 Default Gateway . . . . . . . . . : 10.10.10.1
 DHCP Server . . . . . . . . . . . : 10.10.10.1
 DNS Servers . . . . . . . . . . . : 10.10.10.1
```

Depending on the device and the operating system, you will see various representations of MAC addresses, as displayed in Figure 5-8. Cisco routers and switches use the form XXXX.XXXX.XXXX where X is a hexadecimal character.

| With Dashes 00-60-2F-3A-07-BC |
| With Colons 00:60:2F:3A:07:BC |
| With Periods 0060.2F3A.07BC |

Figure 5-8   Different Representations of MAC Addresses

Unicast MAC Address (5.1.2.5)

In Ethernet, different MAC addresses are used for Layer 2 unicast, broadcast, and multicast communications.

A unicast MAC address is the unique address used when a frame is sent from a single transmitting device to a single destination device, as shown in Figure 5-9.

Figure 5-9   Unicast Frame Transmission

The source host with IPv4 address 192.168.1.5 requests a web page from the server at IPv4 unicast address 192.168.1.200. For a unicast packet to be sent and received, a destination IP address must be in the IP packet header. A corresponding destination MAC address must also be present in the Ethernet frame header. The IP address and MAC address combine to deliver data to one specific destination host.

The process that a source host uses to determine the destination MAC address is known as *Address Resolution Protocol (ARP)*. ARP is discussed later in this chapter.

Although the destination MAC address can be a unicast, broadcast, or multicast address, the source MAC address must always be a unicast.

Broadcast MAC Address (5.1.2.6)

A broadcast packet contains a destination IPv4 address that has all ones (1s) in the host portion. This numbering in the address means that all hosts on that local network (broadcast domain) will receive and process the packet, as shown in Figure 5-10. Many network protocols, such as DHCP and ARP, use broadcasts.

Figure 5-10   Broadcast Frame Transmission

The source host sends an IPv4 broadcast packet to all devices on its network. The IPv4 destination address is a broadcast address, 192.168.1.255. When the IPv4 broadcast packet is encapsulated in the Ethernet frame, the destination MAC address is the broadcast MAC address of FF-FF-FF-FF-FF-FF in hexadecimal (48 binary ones).

Multicast MAC Address (5.1.2.7)

Multicast addresses allow a source device to send a packet to a group of devices, as shown in Figure 5-11.

Figure 5-11   Multicast Frame Transmission

Devices that belong to a multicast group are assigned a multicast group IP address. The range of IPv4 multicast addresses is 224.0.0.0 to 239.255.255.255. The range of IPv6 multicast addresses begins with FF00::/8. Because multicast addresses represent a group of addresses (sometimes called a host group), they can only be used as the destination of a packet. The source will always be a unicast address.

Multicast addresses would be used in remote gaming, where many players are connected remotely but playing the same game. Another use of multicast addresses is in distance learning through video conferencing, where many students are connected to the same class.

As with the unicast and broadcast addresses, the multicast IP address requires a corresponding multicast MAC address to actually deliver frames on a local network. The multicast MAC address associated with an IPv4 multicast address is a special value that begins with 01-00-5E in hexadecimal. The remaining portion of the multicast MAC address is created by converting the lower 23 bits of the IP multicast group address into 6 hexadecimal characters.

Note

For an IPv6 address, the multicast MAC address begins with 33-33.

For example, refer to the multicast hexadecimal address 01-00-5E-00-00-C8 shown in Figure 5-11. The last byte, or eight bits, of the IPv4 address 224.0.0.200 is the decimal value 200. The easiest way to see the hexadecimal equivalent is to first convert it to binary with a space between each four bits, 200 (decimal) = 1100 1000 (binary). Using the binary to hexadecimal conversion chart shown earlier, 1100 1000 (binary) = 0×C8.

Lab 5.1.2.8: Viewing Network Device MAC Addresses

In this lab, you will complete the following objectives:

- Part 1: Set Up the Topology and Initialize Devices

- Part 2: Configure Devices and Verify Connectivity

- Part 3: Display, Describe, and Analyze Ethernet MAC Addresses

LAN Switches (5.2)

Switches are used in Ethernet networks to improve both security and efficiency. Although traditionally most LAN switches operate at Layer 2 of the OSI model, an increasing number of Layer 3 switches are now being implemented. This section focuses on Layer 2 switches. Layer 3 switches are beyond the scope of this book.

The MAC Address Table (5.2.1)

Switches use MAC addresses to direct network communications through their switch fabric toward the destination node. The *switch fabric* is the integrated circuits and the accompanying machine programming that allows the data paths through the switch to be controlled. For a switch to know which port to use to transmit a unicast frame, it must first learn which nodes exist on each of its ports.

Switch Fundamentals (5.2.1.1)

A Layer 2 Ethernet switch uses MAC addresses to make forwarding decisions. It is completely unaware of the protocol being carried in the data portion of the frame, such as an IPv4 packet. The switch makes its forwarding decisions based only on the Layer 2 Ethernet MAC addresses.

Unlike legacy Ethernet hubs that repeat bits out all ports except the incoming port, an Ethernet switch consults a *MAC address table* to make a forwarding decision for each frame. In Figure 5-12, the four-port switch was just powered on. It has not yet learned the MAC addresses for the four attached PCs.

Figure 5-12   Switch Powers Up with an Empty MAC Address Table

---

Note

The MAC address table is sometimes referred to as a content addressable memory (CAM) table. Whereas the term CAM table is fairly common, for the purposes of this course, we will refer to it as a MAC address table.

Learning MAC Addresses (5.2.1.2)

The switch dynamically builds the MAC address table by examining the source MAC address of the frames received on a port. The switch forwards frames by searching for a match between the destination MAC address in the frame and an entry in the MAC address table.

The following process is performed on every Ethernet frame that enters a switch.

Learn – Examining the Source MAC Address

Every frame that enters a switch is checked for new information to learn. It does this by examining the frame's source MAC address and port number where the frame entered the switch.

- If the source MAC address does not exist, it is added to the table along with the incoming port number. In Figure 5-13, PC-A is sending an Ethernet frame to PC-D. The switch adds the MAC address for PC-A to the table.

- If the source MAC address does exist, the switch updates the refresh timer for that entry. By default, most Ethernet switches keep an entry in the table for 5 minutes.

Figure 5-13   Switch Learns the MAC Address for PC-A

Note

If the source MAC address does exist in the table but on a different port, the switch treats this as a new entry. The entry is replaced using the same MAC address but with the more current port number.

Forward – Examining the Destination MAC Address

Next, if the destination MAC address is a unicast address, the switch will look for a match between the destination MAC address of the frame and an entry in its MAC address table.

- If the destination MAC address is in the table, it will forward the frame out the specified port.

- If the destination MAC address is not in the table, the switch will forward the frame out all ports except the incoming port. This is known as an *unknown unicast*. As shown in Figure 5-14, the switch does not have the destination MAC address in its table for PC-D, so it sends the frame out all ports except port 1.

Figure 5-14 Switch Forwards the Frame Out All Other Ports

Filtering Frames (5.2.1.3)

As a switch receives frames from different devices, it is able to populate its MAC address table by examining the source MAC address of every frame. When the switch's MAC address table contains the destination MAC address, it is able to filter the frame and forward out a single port.

Figure 5-15 shows PC-D sending a frame back to PC-A. The switch will first learn PC-D's MAC address.

Figure 5-15   Switch Learns the MAC Address for PC-D

Next, because the switch has PC-A's MAC address in its table, it will send the frame only out port 1, as shown in Figure 5-16.

Figure 5-16   Switch Forwards the Frame Out the Port Belonging to PC-A

Figure 5-17 shows PC-A sending another frame to PC-D. The MAC address table already contains PC-A's MAC address, so the five-minute refresh timer for that entry is reset. Next, because the switch's table contains PC-D's MAC address, it sends the frame only out port 4.

MAC Address Table	
Port	MAC Address
1	00-0A
4	00-0D

Destination MAC 00-0D	Source MAC 00-0A	Type	Data	FCS

Figure 5-17   Switch Forwards the Frame out the Port Belonging to PC-D

MAC Address Tables on Connected Switches (5.2.1.4)

A switch can have multiple MAC addresses associated with a single port. This is common when the switch is connected to another switch. The switch will have a separate MAC address table entry for each frame received with a different source MAC address.

Using Figures 5-18 through 5-24, we will examine the process of PC-A sending an Ethernet frame to PC-B, and then PC-B is sending an Ethernet frame to PC-A. We will examine how switches S1 and S2 build their MAC address tables and also how they forward frames based on the information in their MAC address tables.

Note

The MAC addresses in Figures 5-18 through 5-24 have been shortened for brevity.

In Figure 5-18, PC-A has an Ethernet frame to send to PC-B. The source MAC address of the frame is 00-0A, and the destination MAC address is 00-0B. The Ethernet frame is sent to switch S1. S1 receives the Ethernet frame, examines the source MAC address, and notices that this MAC address is not in its MAC address table, so it adds the source MAC address and the incoming port number to the table.

Figure 5-18   S1 Adds PC-A's MAC Address

Next in Figure 5-19, switch S1 examines the destination MAC address and notices that this MAC address is not in its table, so it floods it out all ports, except the port it was received on. PC-B receives the Ethernet frame, compares the destination MAC address with its own MAC address, notices that it is a match, and receives the rest of the frame.

Switch S1 is also connected to switch S2. Because the frame is flooded out all ports, the Ethernet frame is forwarded to switch S2.

Figure 5-19   S1 Floods the Frame

In Figure 5-20, switch S2 examines the source MAC address to the frame and notices it is not in its MAC address table, so it adds the source MAC address and the incoming port to its MAC address table.

Figure 5-20   S2 Adds PC-A's MAC Address

Next in Figure 5-21, switch S2 examines the destination MAC address and notices that is not in its MAC address table, so it floods it out all ports except the incoming port.

Figure 5-21   S2 Floods the Frame

In Figure 5-22, PC-C receives the Ethernet frame, and its MAC address does not match the destination MAC address of the Ethernet frame, so it discards the rest of the frame. The router receives the Ethernet frame, compares the destination MAC address with its own MAC address, and notices it is not a match, so it discards the rest of the frame.

Figure 5-22   PC-C and Router Receive the Frame

Now let's examine the process of PC-B sending a frame back to PC-A. As shown in Figure 5-23, the source MAC address of the frame is 00-0B, and the destination MAC address is 00-0A. PC-B sends it to switch S1. S1 notices that the source MAC address is not in its MAC address table, so it adds the source MAC address and the incoming port number to the table.

Figure 5-23   S2 Adds PC-B's MAC Address

Next in Figure 5-24, switch S1 examines the destination MAC address and notices that MAC address is in its MAC address table. So it only sends it out port 1. PC-A receives the Ethernet frame, compares the destination MAC address against its own MAC address, and notices it is a match, so it receives the rest of the frame.

Figure 5-24   S1 Filters Frame

Video

Video Demonstration 5.2.1.4: MAC Address Tables on Connected Switches

Go to the online course to view this video.

Sending a Frame to the Default Gateway (5.2.1.5)

When a device has an IP address that is on a remote network, the Ethernet frame cannot be sent directly to the destination device. Instead, the Ethernet frame is sent to the MAC address of the default gateway, the router.

Refer to Figures 5-25 through 5-30 to see how PC-A sends a packet to a device on another network.

> **Note**
>
> The MAC addresses in Figures 5-25 through 5-30 have been shortened for brevity. Switch S1 and S2 MAC address tables are still populated with the MAC addresses previously learned in the communications between PC-A and PC-B.

In Figure 5-25, the source MAC address is that of PC-A and the destination MAC address is that of the router, 00-0D. The Ethernet frame is sent to switch S1. Switch S1 receives the frame and examines the source MAC address, which is in its MAC address table. So it just simply refreshes its 5-minute timer for this entry.

Figure 5-25   S1 Receives Frame from PC-A

In Figure 5-26, S1 examines the destination MAC address, and because that destination MAC address is not in its MAC address table, it floods it out all ports except the receiving port. PC-B receives the Ethernet frame, and because the destination MAC address does not match its own MAC address, it discards the rest of the frame. Switch S2 receives the Ethernet frame and examines the source MAC address, which is in its MAC address table, so it also simply refreshes this entry's 5-minute timer.

Figure 5-26   S1 Floods Frame

In Figure 5-27, switch S2 examines the destination MAC address of the frame. The destination MAC address is not in its MAC address table, so it floods it out all ports except the receiving port. PC-C receives the Ethernet frame, and because the destination MAC address does not match its own MAC address, it discards the rest of the Ethernet frame. The router receives the Ethernet frame. The destination MAC address does match the router's MAC address, so it accepts the rest of the frame.

The router will next de-encapsulate the packet from the Ethernet frame, use its routing table to look up the destination IP address, and forward the frame toward the final destination.

Figure 5-27   S2 Floods Frame

Next, we'll examine the process of an Ethernet frame originating from a remote network being sent to PC-A. The frame is at the router in Figure 5-28. The source IP address is the IP address of a device on the remote network. The destination IP address is PC-A's address.

The router will now forward the frame toward PC-A. The source MAC address is that of the Ethernet interface of the router, 00-0D, and the destination MAC address is that of PC-A, 00-0A. The frame is sent to switch S2.

Switch S2 receives the frame and examines the source MAC address. The source MAC address is not in its MAC address table, so it adds it and the incoming port number to the table.

Figure 5-28   S2 Receives Frame from Router

Next in Figure 5-29, switch S2 examines the destination MAC address. The destination MAC address is in its MAC address table, so it only forwards it out port 1. Switch S1 receives the Ethernet frame and examines the source MAC address, which is not in its MAC address table, so it adds it and the incoming port number to its MAC address table.

Figure 5-29   S2 Filters Frame

In Figure 5-30, switch S1 examines the destination MAC address. The destination MAC address is in its MAC address table, so it only forwards it out port 1 towards PC-A. PC-A examines the destination MAC address, and because it is a match, it accepts the rest of the frame.

Figure 5-30 S1 Filters Frame

Video

Video Demonstration 5.2.1.5: Sending a Frame to the Default Gateway

Go to the online course to view this video.

Interactive Graphic

Activity 5.2.1.6: Switch It!

Go to the online course to perform this practice activity.

Lab 5.2.1.7: Viewing the Switch MAC Address Table

In this lab, you will complete the following objectives:

- Part 1: Build and Configure the Network
- Part 2: Examine the Switch MAC Address Table

Switch Forwarding Methods (5.2.2)

Switches may have the capability to implement various forwarding methods to increase performance.

Frame Forwarding Methods on Cisco Switches (5.2.2.1)

Switches use one of the following forwarding methods for switching data between network ports:

- Store-and-forward switching

- Cut-through switching

Figure 5-31 highlights differences between these two methods.

Store-and-forward

Cut-through

A store-and-forward switch receives the entire frame, and computes the CRC. If the CRC is valid, the switch looks up the destination address, which determines the outgoing interface. The frame is then forwarded out the correct port.

A cut-through switch forwards the frame before it is entirely received. At a minimum, the destination address of the frame must be read before the frame can be forwarded.

Figure 5-31   Switch Forwarding Methods

In store-and-forward switching, when the switch receives the frame, it stores the data in buffers until the complete frame has been received. During the storage process, the switch analyzes the frame for information about its destination. In this process, the switch also performs an error check using the CRC trailer portion of the Ethernet frame.

CRC uses a mathematical formula, based on the number of bits (1s) in the frame, to determine whether the received frame has an error. After confirming the integrity of the frame, the frame is forwarded out the appropriate port, toward its destination. When an error is detected in a frame, the switch discards the frame. Discarding frames with errors reduces the amount of bandwidth consumed by corrupt data. Store-and-forward switching is required for Quality of Service (QoS) analysis on converged networks where frame classification for traffic prioritization is necessary. For example, voice over IP data streams need to have priority over web-browsing traffic.

In Figure 5-32 shows the store-and-forward process.

A store-and-forward switch receives the entire frame, and computes the CRC. If the CRC is valid, the switch looks up the destination address, which determines the outgoing interface. The frame is then forwarded out the correct port.

Figure 5-32   Store-and-Forward Switching

Cut-Through Switching (5.2.2.2)

In cut-through switching, the switch acts upon the data as soon as it is received, even if the transmission is not complete. The switch buffers just enough of the frame to read the destination MAC address so that it can determine to which port to forward the data. The destination MAC address is located in the first 6 bytes of the frame following the preamble. The switch looks up the destination MAC address in its switching table, determines the outgoing interface port, and forwards the frame onto its destination through the designated switch port. The switch does not perform any error checking on the frame.

Figure 5-33 shows the cut-through switching process.

A cut-through switch forwards the frame before it is entirely received. At a minimum, the destination address of the frame must be read before the frame can be forwarded.

Figure 5-33   Cut-Through Switching

There are two variants of cut-through switching:

- **Fast-forward switching** – Fast-forward switching offers the lowest level of latency. Fast-forward switching immediately forwards a packet after reading the destination address. Because fast-forward switching starts forwarding before the entire packet has been received, there may be times when packets are relayed with errors. This occurs infrequently, and the destination network adapter discards the faulty packet upon receipt. In fast-forward mode, latency is measured from the first bit received to the first bit transmitted. Fast-forward switching is the typical cut-through method of switching.

- **Fragment-free switching** – In fragment-free switching, the switch stores the first 64 bytes of the frame before forwarding. Fragment-free switching can be viewed as a compromise between store-and-forward switching and fast-forward switching. The reason fragment-free switching stores only the first 64 bytes of the frame is that most network errors and collisions occur during the first 64 bytes. Fragment-free switching tries to enhance fast-forward switching by performing a small error check on the first 64 bytes of the frame to ensure that a collision has not occurred before forwarding the frame. Fragment-free switching is a compromise between the high latency and high integrity of store-and-forward switching, and the low latency and reduced integrity of fast-forward switching.

Some switches are configured to perform cut-through switching on a per-port basis until a user-defined error threshold is reached, and then they automatically change to store-and-forward. When the error rate falls below the threshold, the port automatically changes back to cut-through switching.

Memory Buffering on Switches (5.2.2.3)

An Ethernet switch may use a buffering technique to store frames before forwarding them. Buffering may also be used when the destination port is busy due to congestion and the switch stores the frame until it can be transmitted.

There are two methods of memory buffering:

Port based Memory Buffering

In port-based memory buffering, frames are stored in queues that are linked to specific incoming and outgoing ports. A frame is transmitted to the outgoing port only when all the frames ahead of it in the queue have been successfully transmitted. It is possible for a single frame to delay the transmission of all the frames in memory because of a busy destination port. This delay occurs even if the other frames could be transmitted to open destination ports.

Shared Memory Buffering

Shared memory buffering deposits all frames into a common memory buffer that all the ports on the switch share. The amount of buffer memory required by a port is dynamically allocated. The frames in the buffer are linked dynamically to the destination port. This allows the packet to be received on one port and then transmitted on another port without moving it to a different queue.

The switch keeps a map of frame-to-port links showing where a packet needs to be transmitted. The map link is cleared after the frame has been successfully transmitted. The number of frames stored in the buffer is restricted by the size of the entire memory buffer and not limited to a single port buffer. This permits larger frames to be transmitted with fewer dropped frames. This is especially important to *Asymmetric switching*. Asymmetric switching allows for different data rates on different ports. This allows more bandwidth to be dedicated to certain ports, such as a port connected to a server.

Activity 5.2.2.4: Frame Forwarding Methods

Go to the online course to perform this practice activity.

> **Interactive Graphic**

Switch Port Settings (5.2.3)

Although transparent to network protocols and user applications, switches can operate in different modes that can have both positive and negative effects when forwarding Ethernet frames on a network. Two of the most basic settings of a switch are the duplex and bandwidth (speed) settings on individual ports connected to each host device.

Duplex and Speed Settings (5.2.3.1)

It is critical that the duplex and bandwidth settings match between the switch port and the connected devices, such as a computer or another switch.

There are two types of duplex settings used for communications on an Ethernet network: half-duplex and full-duplex.

- **Full-duplex** – Both ends of the connection can send and receive simultaneously.
- **Half-duplex** – Only one end of the connection can send at a time.

Autonegotiation is an optional function found on most Ethernet switches and NICs. Autonegotiation enables two devices to automatically exchange information about speed and duplex capabilities. The switch and the connected device will choose the highest performance mode. Full-duplex is chosen if both devices have the capability along with their highest common bandwidth.

For example, in Figure 5-34 PC-A's Ethernet NIC can operate in full-duplex or half-duplex and in 10 Mb/s or 100 Mb/s. PC-A is connected to switch S1 on port 1, which can operate in full-duplex or half-duplex and in 10 Mb/s, 100 Mb/s, or 1000 Mb/s (1 Gb/s). If both devices are using autonegotiation, the operating mode will be full-duplex and 100 Mb/s.

Figure 5-34   Duplex and Speed Settings

Note

Most Cisco switches and Ethernet NICs default to autonegotiation for speed and duplex. Gigabit Ethernet ports only operate in full-duplex.

Duplex Mismatch

One of the most common causes of performance issues on 10/100 Mb/s Ethernet links occurs when one port on the link operates at half-duplex while the other port operates at full-duplex, as shown in Figure 5-35.

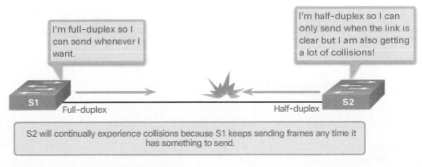

Figure 5-35   Duplex Mismatch

This occurs when one or both ports on a link are reset and the autonegotiation process does not result in both link partners having the same configuration. It also can occur when users reconfigure one side of a link and forget to reconfigure the other. Both sides of a link should have autonegotiation on or both sides should have it off.

Auto-MDIX (5.2.3.2)

In addition to having the correct duplex setting, it is also necessary to have the correct cable type defined for each port. Connections between specific devices, such as switch-to-switch, switch-to-router, switch-to-host, and router-to-host devices, once required the use of specific cable types (crossover or straight-through). Most switch devices now support the mdix auto interface configuration command in the CLI to enable the *automatic medium-dependent interface crossover (auto-MDIX)* feature.

When the auto-MDIX feature is enabled, the switch detects the type of cable attached to the port and configures the interfaces accordingly, as shown in Figure 5-36. Therefore, you can use either a crossover or a straight-through cable for connections to a copper 10/100/1000 port on the switch, regardless of the type of device on the other end of the connection.

MDIX auto detects the type of connection required and configures the interface accordingly.

Figure 5-36   Auto-MDIX

Note

The auto-MDIX feature is enabled by default on switches running Cisco IOS Release 12.2(18) SE or later.

Address Resolution Protocol (5.3)

This section discusses the relationship between MAC and IP addresses, and the how the Address Resolution Protocol (ARP) is used to map the two addresses.

MAC and IP (5.3.1)

Two different types of address have been discussed, MAC addresses and IP addresses. This topic helps distinguish the functions and differences of each.

Destination on Same Network (5.3.1.1)

There are two primary addresses assigned to a device on an Ethernet LAN:

- **Physical address (the MAC address)** – Used for Ethernet NIC to Ethernet NIC communications on the same network.

- **Logical address (the IP address)** – Used to send the packet from the original source to the final destination.

IP addresses are used to identify the address of the original source and the final destination. The destination IP address may be on the same IP network as the source or may be on a remote network.

Note

Most applications use DNS (Domain Name System) to determine the IP address when given a domain name such as www.cisco.com. DNS is discussed in a later chapter.

Layer 2 or physical addresses, like Ethernet MAC addresses, have a different purpose. These addresses are used to deliver the data link frame with the encapsulated IP packet from one NIC to another NIC on the same network. If the destination IP address is on the same network, the destination MAC address will be that of the destination device.

Figure 5-37 shows the Ethernet MAC addresses and IP address for PC-A sending an IP packet to the file server on the same network.

Figure 5-37   Communicating on a Local Network

The Layer 2 Ethernet frame contains

- **Destination MAC address –** This is the MAC address of the file server's Ethernet NIC.

- **Source MAC address –** This is the MAC address of PC-A's Ethernet NIC.

The Layer 3 IP packet contains

- **Source IP address –** This is the IP address of the original source, PC-A.

- **Destination IP address –** This is the IP address of the final destination, the file server.

Destination Remote Network (5.3.1.2)

When the destination IP address is on a remote network, the destination MAC address will be the address of the host's default gateway, the router's NIC, as shown in Figure 5-38.

Figure 5-38   Communicating to a Remote Network

Using a postal analogy, this would be similar to a person taking a letter to their local post office. All they need to do is take the letter to the post office and then it becomes the responsibility of the post office to forward the letter on toward its final destination.

The figure shows the Ethernet MAC addresses and IPv4 addresses for PC-A sending an IPv4 packet to a web server on a remote network. Routers examine the destination IP address to determine the best path to forward the IP packet. This is similar to how the postal service forwards mail based on the address of the recipient.

When the router receives the Ethernet frame, it de-encapsulates the Layer 2 information. Using the destination IP address, it determines the next-hop device and then encapsulates the IP packet in a new data link frame for the outgoing interface. Along each link in a path, an IP packet is encapsulated in a frame specific to the particular data link technology associated with that link, such as Ethernet. If the next-hop device is the final destination, the destination MAC address will be that of the device's Ethernet NIC.

How are the IPv4 addresses of the IPv4 packets in a data flow associated with the MAC addresses on each link along the path to the destination? This is done through a process called Address Resolution Protocol (ARP).

Packet Tracer 5.3.1.3: Identify MAC and IP Addresses

This activity is optimized for viewing PDUs. The devices are already configured. You will gather PDU information in simulation mode and answer a series of questions about the data you collect.

Packet Tracer
☐ Activity

ARP (5.3.2)

Recall that each node on an IPv4 network has both a MAC address and an IPv4 address. To send data, the node must use both of these addresses. The node will use its own MAC and IPv4 addresses in the source fields and must also provide both a destination MAC address and a destination IPv4 address. Whereas the IPv4 address of the destination will be provided by a higher OSI layer, the sending node needs to use a destination MAC address to forward the frame. This is the purpose of ARP.

Introduction to ARP (5.3.2.1)

Recall that every device with an IP address on an Ethernet network also has an Ethernet MAC address. When a device sends an Ethernet frame, it contains these two addresses:

- **Destination MAC address** – The MAC address of the Ethernet NIC, which will be either the MAC address of the final destination device or the router.

- **Source MAC address** – The MAC address of the sender's Ethernet NIC.

Sometimes, a device will not know the destination MAC address, as shown in Figure 5-39.

Figure 5-39   End Devices Need Both Layer 2 and Layer 3 Addresses

To determine the destination MAC address, the device uses ARP. ARP provides two basic functions:

- Resolving IPv4 addresses to MAC addresses
- Maintaining a table of mappings

ARP Functions (5.3.2.2)

Resolving IPv4 Addresses to MAC Addresses

When a packet is sent to the data link layer to be encapsulated into an Ethernet frame, the device refers to a table in its memory to find the MAC address that is mapped to the IPv4 address. This table is called the *ARP table* or the *ARP cache*. The ARP table is stored in the RAM of the device.

The sending device will search its ARP table for a destination IPv4 address and a corresponding MAC address.

- If the packet's destination IPv4 address is on the same network as the source IPv4 address, the device will search the ARP table for the destination IPv4 address.

- If the destination IPv4 address is on a different network than the source IPv4 address, the device will search the ARP table for the IPv4 address of the *default gateway*.

In both cases, the search is for an IPv4 address and a corresponding MAC address for the device.

Each entry, or row, of the ARP table binds an IPv4 address with a MAC address. We call the relationship between the two values a map—it simply means that you can locate an IPv4 address in the table and discover the corresponding MAC address. The ARP table temporarily saves (caches) the mapping for the devices on the LAN.

If the device locates the IPv4 address, its corresponding MAC address is used as the destination MAC address in the frame. If there is no entry is found, then the device sends an ARP request, as shown in Figure 5-40.

Figure 5-40   H1 Sends a Broadcast ARP Request

The destination responds with an ARP reply, as shown in Figure 5-41.

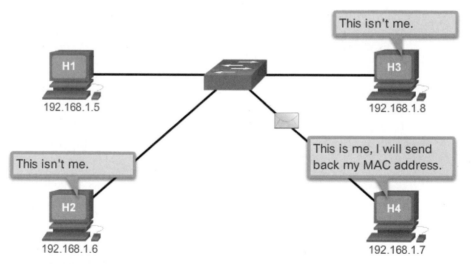

Figure 5-41   H4 Sends a Unicast ARP Reply

ARP Request (5.3.2.3)

An ARP request is sent when a device needs a MAC address associated with an IPv4 address, and it does not have an entry for the IPv4 address in its ARP table.

ARP messages are encapsulated directly within an Ethernet frame. There is no IPv4 header. The ARP request message includes

- **Target IPv4 address** – This is the IPv4 address that requires a corresponding MAC address.

- **Target MAC address** – This is the unknown MAC address and will be empty in the ARP request message.

The ARP request is encapsulated in an Ethernet frame using the following header information:

- **Destination MAC address** – This is a broadcast address requiring all Ethernet NICs on the LAN to accept and process the ARP request.

- **Source MAC address** – This is the sender of the ARP request's MAC address.

- **Type** – ARP messages have a type field of 0×806. This informs the receiving NIC that the data portion of the frame needs to be passed to the ARP process.

Because ARP requests are broadcasts, they are flooded out all ports by the switch except the receiving port. All Ethernet NICs on the LAN process broadcasts. Every device must process the ARP request to see if the target IPv4 address matches its own. A router will not forward broadcasts out other interfaces.

Only one device on the LAN will have an IPv4 address that matches the target IPv4 address in the ARP request. All other devices will not reply.

Using Figures 5-42 through 5-46, we will examine the ARP process when PC-A has an IPv4 packet for another device on its network, PC-C.

Note

The MAC addresses in Figures 5-18 through 5-24 have been shortened for brevity.

In Figure 5-42, PC-A has an IPv4 packet with its source IPv4 address 192.168.1.110 and the destination IP address of PC-C at 192.168.1.50. This packet needs to be encapsulated in an Ethernet frame with a destination MAC address. Because the source and destination IPv4 addresses are on the same network, the destination MAC address will be that of the destination IPv4 address of PC-C at 192.168.1.50. The source MAC address will be that of PC-A, 00-0A. PC-A checks its ARP cache for the IPv4 address 192.168.1.50.

Figure 5-42   PC-A's IPv4 Packet Destined for Local Network

The IPv4 address 192.168.1.50 is not in its ARP cache so PC-A puts the packet on hold and creates an ARP request, shown in Figure 5-43. The ARP request contains the target IPv4 address, the known IPv4 address of PC-A, and the target MAC address, which is unknown. The target MAC address is the address PC-A needs to discover. The ARP request is sent as a broadcast, so every IPv4 device on the network will need to examine this Ethernet frame and process the ARP request. PC-A sends the Ethernet broadcast to the switch. The switch will flood the Ethernet broadcast out all ports except for the receiving port.

Figure 5-43   PC-A's ARP Request for PC-C

In Figure 5-44 PC-B receives the Ethernet broadcast, which must be received by its Ethernet NIC. The ARP message is sent to PC-B's ARP process. It compares its own IPv4 address with the target IPv4 address and determines it is not a match, so it doesn't need to send an ARP reply.

Figure 5-44   PC-B Receives ARP Request

In Figure 5-45 router R1 also receives and accepts the same ARP request. Its ARP process examines its own IPv4 address and compares it to the target IPv4 address. The router also determines there is not a match, so it does not need to send an ARP reply. Routers do not forward broadcasts out other ports.

Figure 5-45   R1 Receives ARP Request

In Figure 5-46, PC-C receives the ARP request, compares its IPv4 address against the target IPv4 address, and notices that it is the intended target of the ARP request. In other words, the target IPv4 address does match its own IPv4 address. Therefore, PC-C will need to send an ARP reply.

Figure 5-46   PC-C Receives ARP Request

Video Demonstration 5.3.2.3: ARP Request

Go to the online course to view this video.

ARP Reply (5.3.2.4)

Only the device with an IPv4 address associated with the target IPv4 address in the ARP request will respond with an ARP reply. The ARP reply message includes

- **Sender's IPv4 address** – This is the IPv4 address of the sender, the device whose MAC address was requested.

- **Sender's MAC address** – This is the MAC address of the sender, the MAC address needed by the sender of the ARP request.

The ARP reply is encapsulated in an Ethernet frame using the following header information:

- **Destination MAC address** – This is the MAC address of the sender of the ARP request.

- **Source MAC address** – This is the sender of the ARP reply's MAC address.

- **Type** – ARP messages have a type field of 0×806. This informs the receiving NIC that the data portion of the frame needs to be passed to the ARP process.

Only the device that originally sent the ARP request will receive the unicast ARP reply. Once the ARP reply is received, the device will add the IPv4 address and the corresponding MAC address to its ARP table. Packets destined for that IPv4 address can now be encapsulated in frames using its corresponding MAC address.

If no device responds to the ARP request, the packet is dropped because a frame cannot be created.

Entries in the ARP table are time stamped. If a device does not receive a frame from a particular device by the time the timestamp expires, the entry for this device is removed from the ARP table.

Additionally, static map entries can be entered in an ARP table, but this is rarely done. Static ARP table entries do not expire over time and must be manually removed.

Note

Pv6 uses a similar process to ARP for IPv4, known as ICMPv6 neighbor discovery. IPv6 uses neighbor solicitation and neighbor advertisement messages, similar to IPv4 ARP requests and ARP replies.

Continuing the process from the previous ARP request, Figures 5-47 through 5-49 illustrate the corresponding ARP reply.

Previously, PC-C received an ARP request, examined the target IPv4 address, and compared it to its own IPv4 address and noticed that it was the intended target. PC-C will generate an ARP reply in response to that ARP request.

As shown in Figure 5-47, the ARP reply includes PC-C's own IPv4 address and its own MAC address. The ARP reply is sent as a unicast directly to PC-A, with a destination MAC address of PC-A.

Figure 5-47   PC-C's ARP Reply

In Figure 5-48, PC-A receives the ARP reply in response to its previous ARP request. PC-A uses the information in the ARP reply, the sender IPv4 address and the sender MAC address, and adds this information to its ARP cache. PC-A can now take the packet, the original packet destined for PC-C, off hold. PC-A now has the information it needs to send that packet to PC-C. PC-A uses this new information in its ARP cache and adds the destination MAC address to the Ethernet frame.

Figure 5-48   PC-A Receives ARP Reply

Figure 5-49 shows PC-A can now forward this packet in the proper Ethernet frame on to PC-C.

Figure 5-49   PC-A Sends IPv4 Packet to PC-C

Video Demonstration 5.3.2.4: ARP Reply

Go to the online course to view this video.

ARP Role in Remote Communication (5.3.2.5)

When the destination IPv4 address is not on the same network as the source IPv4 address, the source device needs to send the frame to its default gateway. This is the interface of the local router. Whenever a source device has a packet with an IPv4 address on another network, it will encapsulate that packet in a frame using the destination MAC address of the router.

The IPv4 address of the default gateway address is stored in the IPv4 configuration of the hosts. When a host creates a packet for a destination, it compares the destination IPv4 address and its own IPv4 address to determine if the two IPv4 addresses are located on the same Layer 3 network. If the destination host is not on its same network, the source checks its ARP table for an entry with the IPv4 address of the default gateway. If there is not an entry, it uses the ARP process to determine a MAC address of the default gateway.

Using Figures 5-50 through 5-54, we will examine the ARP process when PC-A has a packet for a device on another network.

Note

The MAC addresses in Figures 5-18 through 5-24 have been shortened for brevity.

In Figure 5-50, PC-A has a packet, source IPv4 address 192.168.1.110, and destination IPv4 address 10.1.1.10. The destination IPv4 address is on a remote network. Therefore, the destination MAC address will be that of its default gateway, router R1, 192.168.1.1. PC-A examines its ARP cache for the IPv4 address of the default gateway 192.168.1.1 and determines it does not have this entry.

Figure 5-50   PC-A's IPv4 Packet Destined for a Remote Network

In Figure 5-51 PC-A puts the packet on hold and creates an ARP request. The ARP request includes the target IPv4 address of the default gateway, 192.168.1.1, and the target MAC address, which is unknown. The destination MAC address of an ARP request is a broadcast.

The switch will flood the Ethernet broadcast out all ports except for the incoming port.

PC-B receives the ARP request and compares its own IPv4 address against the target IPv4 address in the ARP request. PC-B determines it does not a match, so it is not the intended target.

PC-C receives the ARP request, compares its IPv4 address against the target IPv4 address, and determines that it not the intended target either.

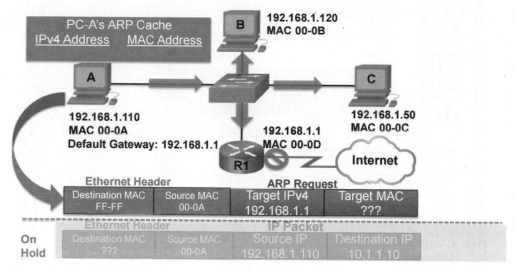

Figure 5-51 PC-A's ARP Request for Default Gateway

In Figure 5-52, router R1 receives the ARP request, compares its IPv4 address to the target IPv4 address, and determines there is a match. In other words, it is the intended target of the ARP request.

Figure 5-52 R1 Receives ARP Request

Router R1 will issue an ARP reply in response, shown in Figure 5-53. R1 includes its own MAC address, 00-0D, along with its IPv4 address. The ARP reply is sent as a unicast directly to PC-A, with a destination MAC address of PC-A.

PC-A receives the ARP reply in response to its ARP request. R1 adds the target IPv4 address and the target MAC address to its ARP cache.

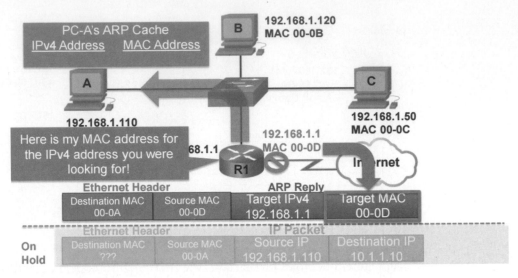

Figure 5-53 PC-A Receives ARP Reply

As shown in Figure 5-54, R1 now has the information it needs to forward the packet that was on hold. The destination MAC address is 00-0D, router R1's MAC address.

Figure 5-54 PC-A Sends IPv4 Packet to Default Gateway

Video Demonstration 5.3.2.5: ARP Role in Remote Communication

Go to the online course to view this video.

Removing Entries from an ARP Table (5.3.2.6)

For each device, an ARP cache timer removes ARP entries that have not been used for a specified period of time. The times differ depending on the device's operating system. For example, some Windows operating systems store ARP cache entries for 2 minutes, as shown in Figure 5-55.

Figure 5-55 Removing MAC-to-IP Address Mappings

Commands may also be used to manually remove all or some of the entries in the ARP table. After an entry has been removed, the process for sending an ARP request and receiving an ARP reply must occur again to enter the map in the ARP table.

ARP Tables (5.3.2.7)

On a Cisco router, the **show ip arp** command is used to display the ARP table, as shown in Example 5-2.

Example 5-2 Viewing a Router ARP Cache

```
Router# show ip arp

Protocol Address Age (min) Hardware Addr Type Interface
Internet 172.16.1.1 - 0060.7027.0301 ARPA Ethernet0/0
Internet 172.16.1.10 0 0090.21B5.B1CB ARPA Ethernet0/0
Internet 172.16.1.100 0 0002.169C.7A07 ARPA Ethernet0/0
```

On a Windows 7 PC, the **arp –a** command is used to display the ARP table, as shown in Example 5-3.

Example 5-3 Viewing a Windows PC ARP

```
C:\> arp -a

Interface: 10.10.10.12 —- 0×b
 Internet Address Physical Address Type
 10.10.10.1 e4-f4-c6-12-2b-c9 dynamic
 10.10.10.9 f0-4d-a2-dd-a7-b2 dynamic
 10.10.10.255 ff-ff-ff-ff-ff-ff static
 224.0.0.2 01-00-5e-00-00-02 static
 224.0.0.22 01-00-5e-00-00-16 static
 224.0.0.251 01-00-5e-00-00-fb static
 224.0.0.252 01-00-5e-00-00-fc static
 224.0.1.60 01-00-5e-00-01-3c static
 239.255.255.250 01-00-5e-7f-ff-fa static
 255.255.255.255 ff-ff-ff-ff-ff-ff static
```

Packet Tracer
☐ Activity

Packet Tracer 5.3.2.8: Examine the ARP Table

This activity is optimized for viewing PDUs. The devices are already configured. You will gather PDU information in simulation mode and answer a series of questions about the data you collect.

ARP Issues (5.3.3)

This topic discusses some of the ARP performance and security issues.

ARP Broadcasts (5.3.3.1)

As a broadcast frame, an ARP request is received and processed by every device on the local network. On a typical business network, these broadcasts would probably have minimal impact on network performance. However, if a large number of devices were to be powered up and all start accessing network services at the same time, there could be some reduction in performance for a short period of time, as shown in Figure 5-56. After the devices send out the initial ARP broadcasts and have learned the necessary MAC addresses, any impact on the network will be minimized.

All devices powered on at the same time

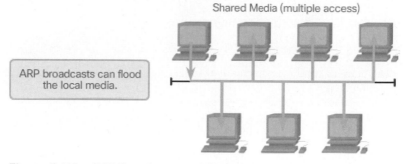

Figure 5-56   ARP Broadcasts and Security

ARP Spoofing (5.3.3.2)

In some cases, the use of ARP can lead to a potential security risk known as ARP spoofing or ARP poisoning. This is a technique used by an attacker to reply to an ARP request for an IPv4 address belonging to another device, such as the default gateway, as shown in Figure 5-57. The attacker sends an ARP reply with its own MAC address. The receiver of the ARP reply will add the wrong MAC address to its ARP table and send these packets to the attacker.

MAC addresses are shortened for demonstration purposes.

Figure 5-57   Example of ARP Spoofing

Enterprise level switches include mitigation techniques known as dynamic ARP inspection (DAI) and IP Source Guard (IPSG). DAI and IPSG are beyond the scope of this course.

Summary (5.4)

Class Activity 5.4.1.1: MAC and Choose...

Note

This activity can be completed individually, in small groups, or in a full-classroom learning environment.

Please search YouTube and view the video "The History of Ethernet."

Topics discussed include not only where we have come from in Ethernet development but where we are going with Ethernet technology (a futuristic approach).

After viewing the video and comparing its contents to Chapter 5, go to the web and search for information about Ethernet. Use a constructivist approach:

- What did Ethernet look like when it was first developed?

- How has Ethernet stayed the same over the past 25 years or so, and what changes are being made to make it more useful/applicable to today's data transmission methods?

Collect three pictures of old, current, and future Ethernet physical media and devices (focus on switches) – share these pictures with the class and discuss

- How have Ethernet physical media and intermediary devices changed?

- How have Ethernet physical media and intermediary devices stayed the same?

- How will Ethernet change in the future?

Ethernet is the most widely used LAN technology today. It is a family of networking technologies that are defined in the IEEE 802.2 and 802.3 standards. Ethernet standards define both the Layer 2 protocols and the Layer 1 technologies. For the Layer 2 protocols, as with all 802 IEEE standards, Ethernet relies on the two separate sublayers of the data link layer to operate, the Logical Link Control (LLC) and the MAC sublayers.

At the data link layer, the frame structure is nearly identical for all bandwidths of Ethernet. The Ethernet frame structure adds headers and trailers around the Layer 3 PDU to encapsulate the message being sent.

There are two styles of Ethernet framing: IEEE 802.3 Ethernet standard and the DIX Ethernet standard, which is now referred to Ethernet II. The most significant difference between the two standards is the addition of a Start Frame Delimiter (SFD) and the change of the Type field to a Length field in the 802.3. Ethernet II is the Ethernet frame format used in TCP/IP networks. As an implementation of the IEEE 802.2/3 standards, the Ethernet frame provides MAC addressing and error checking.

The Layer 2 addressing provided by Ethernet supports unicast, multicast, and broad-cast communications. Ethernet uses the Address Resolution Protocol to determine the MAC addresses of destinations and map them against known IPv4 addresses.

Each node on an IPv4 network has both a MAC address and an IPv4 address. The IP addresses are used to identify the original source and final destination of the packet. The Ethernet MAC addresses are used to send the packet from one Ethernet NIC to another Ethernet NIC on the same IP network. ARP is used to map a known IPv4 address to a MAC address, so the packet can be encapsulated in an Ethernet frame with the correct Layer 2 address.

ARP relies on certain types of Ethernet broadcast messages and Ethernet unicast messages, called ARP requests and ARP replies. The ARP protocol resolves IPv4 addresses to MAC addresses and maintains a table of mappings.

On most Ethernet networks, end devices are typically connected on a point-to-point basis to a Layer 2, full-duplex switch. A Layer 2 LAN switch performs switching and filtering based only on the OSI data link layer (Layer 2) MAC address. A Layer 2 switch builds a MAC address table that it uses to make forwarding decisions. Layer 2 switches depend on routers to pass data between independent IP subnetworks.

Practice

The following activities provide practice with the topics introduced in this chap-ter. The Labs and Class Activities are available in the companion Introduction to Networks v5.1 Lab Manual (ISBN 9781587133534). The Packet Tracer Activities PKA files are found in the online course.

Class Activities

Class Activity 5.0.1.2: Join My Social Circle!

Class Activity 5.4.1.1: MAC and Choose...

Labs

Lab 5.1.1.7: Using Wireshark to Examine Ethernet Frames

Lab 5.1.2.8: Viewing Network Device MAC Addresses

Lab 5.2.1.7: Viewing the Switch MAC Address Table

Packet Tracer
☐ Activity

Packet Tracer Activities

Packet Tracer 5.3.1.3: Identify MAC and IP Addresses

Packet Tracer 5.3.2.8: Examine the ARP Table

Check Your Understanding Questions

Complete all the review questions listed here to test your understanding of the topics and concepts in this chapter. The appendix "Answers to 'Check Your Understanding' Questions" lists the answers.

1. At which layers of the OSI model does Ethernet function? (Choose two.)

   A. Application

   B. Presentation

   C. Session

   D. Transport

   E. Network

   F. Data link

   G. Physical

2. Which standard specifies the Ethernet MAC sublayer functionality in a computer NIC?

   A. IEEE 802.2

   B. IEEE 802.3

   C. IEEE 802.6

   D. IEEE 802.11

   E. IEEE 802.15

3. What is the name given to the Ethernet MAC sublayer PDU?

   A. Segment

   B. Packet

   C. Frame

   D. Bit

4. What are the primary functions associated with data encapsulation at the Ethernet MAC sublayer? (Choose three.)

   A. Media recovery

   B. Frame delimiting

   C. Addressing

   D. Frame placement on the media

   E. Error detection

5. What happens when a data collision occurs on an Ethernet bus?

    A. The CRC value is used to repair the data frames.

    B. All devices stop transmitting and try again later.

    C. The device with the lower MAC address stops transmitting to give the device with the higher MAC address priority.

    D. The MAC sublayer prioritizes the frame with the lower MAC address.

6. What is true about the Ethernet MAC address? (Choose three.)

    A. A MAC address is 32 bits in length.

    B. The first 6 hexadecimal digits of a MAC address represent the OUI.

    C. The IEEE is responsible for assigning vendors a unique 6-byte code.

    D. The vendor is responsible for assigning the last 24 bits of the MAC address.

    E. The MAC address is also known as a burned-in address.

7. What is the minimum and maximum Ethernet frame size as defined by IEEE 802.3?

    A. 64 bytes – 1518 bytes

    B. 64 bytes – 1522 bytes

    C. 32 bytes – 1518 bytes

    D. 32 bytes – 1522 bytes

8. Which field in an Ethernet frame is used for error detection?

    A. Preamble

    B. Type

    C. Destination MAC Address

    D. Frame Check Sequence

9. Which address is used as a destination address on a broadcast Ethernet frame?

    A. 0.0.0.0

    B. 255.255.255.255

    C. FF-FF-FF-FF-FF-FF

    D. 0C-FA-94-24-EF-00

10. Which address is a multicast MAC address?

    A. 0-07-E9-00-00-D4

    B. 01-00-5E-00-00-C8

    C. FF-FF-FF-FF-FF-FF

    D. FF-FF-FF-01-00-5E

11. What functions are provided by the ARP process? (Choose two.)

    A. Resolving IPv4 addresses to MAC addresses

    B. Resolving host names to MAC addresses

    C. Maintaining a table of mappings

    D. Resolving host names to IP addresses

    E. Maintaining a table of active IP addresses

12. Which devices on a network will receive an ARP request?

    A. Only the device that has the IPv4 address that the request is looking for

    B. All devices in the L2 broadcast domain

    C. Only devices in the same collision domain

13. **Fill in the blanks.** When ARP receives a request to map an IPv4 address to a MAC address, it first looks in its _____. If no entry is found, ARP will send out an ARP_____.

14. **Fill in the blanks.** When a device receives an ARP request for a device with a different IP address, it will use the _____ information to update its ARP table and then it will _____ the packet.

15. **Fill in the blanks.** ARP _____ are sent to a broadcast MAC address, and ARP replies are sent to a _____ MAC address.

16. **Fill in the blanks.** When a switch receives a broadcast frame, it enters the source information in its _____ and then it _____ the frame to all ports except the one the frame was _____ on.

17. **Fill in the blanks.** The MAC address table is sometimes referred to as a _____ table because it is stored in _____ memory.

18. What type of switching is used on current L2 switches to allow QoS?

    A. Store-and-forward

    B. Cut-through

    C. Fragment-free

    D. Fast-forward

19. If the source and destination IPv4 addresses are on the same network, the destination MAC address will be that of which device?

    A. The same device as the destination IPv4 address

    B. The default gateway

    C. The Ethernet switch

20. If the source and destination IPv4 addresses are on different networks, the destination MAC address will be that of which device?

A. The same device as the destination IPv4 address

B. The default gateway

C. The Ethernet switch

CHAPTER 6

Network Layer

Objectives

Upon completion of this chapter, you will be able to answer the following questions:

- What is the purpose of the network layer in data communications?

- Why does the IPv4 protocol require services of other layers to provide reliability?

- What is the role of the major header fields in the IPv4 and IPv6 packets?

- How does a host device use routing tables to direct packets to itself, a local destination, or a default gateway?

- What are the similarities and differences between host routing tables and routing tables of a router?

- What are the common components and interfaces of a router?

- What are the steps in the bootup process of a Cisco IOS router?

- How do you configure the initials settings on a Cisco IOS router?

- How do you configure active interfaces on a Cisco IOS router?

- How do you configure the default gateway on network devices?

Key Terms

This chapter uses the following key terms. You can find the definitions in the Glossary.

Routing   Page 274

Connectionless   Page 278

Best-effort delivery   Page 278

Media independent   Page 278

Maximum transmission unit
 (MTU)   Page 280

Fragmentation   Page 281

Internet Control Message Protocol
 (ICMP)   Page 282

Network Address Translation
 (NAT)   Page 283

Loopback interface   Page 288

Default gateway   Page 289

Introduction (6.0)

Network applications and services on one end device can communicate with applications and services running on another end device. How is this data communicated across the network in an efficient way?

The protocols of the OSI model network layer specify addressing and processes that enable transport layer data to be packaged and transported. The network layer encapsulation enables data to be passed to a destination within a network (or on another network) with minimum overhead.

This chapter focuses on the role of the network layer. It examines how it divides networks into groups of hosts to manage the flow of data packets within a network. It also covers how communication between networks is facilitated. This communication between networks is called *routing*.

Class Activity 6.0.1.2: The Road Less Traveled...

During the upcoming weekend, you decide to visit a schoolmate who is currently at home sick. You know his street address, but you have never been to his town before. Instead of looking up the address on the map, you decide to ask town residents for directions after you arrive by train. The citizens you ask for directions are very helpful. However, they all have an interesting habit. Instead of explaining the entire route to your destination, they all tell you, "Take this road and as soon as you arrive at the nearest crossroad, ask somebody there again."

Somewhat bemused at this apparent oddity, you follow these instructions and finally arrive, crossroad by crossroad, and road by road, at your friend's house.

Answer the following questions:

- Would it have made a significant difference if you were told about the whole route or a larger part of the route instead of just being directed to the nearest crossroad?

- Would it have been more helpful to ask about the specific street address or just about the street name? What would happen if the person you asked for directions did not know where the destination street was, or directed you through an incorrect road?

- Assume that on your way back home, you again choose to ask residents for directions. Would it be guaranteed that you would be directed via the same route you took to get to your friend's home? Explain your answer.

- Is it necessary to explain where you depart from when asking directions to an intended destination?

Network Layer Protocols (6.1)

This section will introduce the protocols and functions of the network layer.

Network Layer in Communications (6.1.1)

Without network layer services, there would be no Internet. The function of the network layer is to facilitate the transport of data from one network to another. This topic will introduce elementary functions of the network layer.

The Network Layer (6.1.1.1)

The network layer, or OSI Layer 3, provides services to allow end devices to exchange data across the network. To accomplish this end-to-end transport, the network layer uses four basic processes:

- **Addressing end devices** – End devices must be configured with a unique IP address for identification on the network.

- **Encapsulation** – The network layer encapsulates the protocol data unit (PDU) from the transport layer into a packet, as shown in Figure 6-1. The encapsulation process adds IP header information, such as the IP address of the source (sending) and destination (receiving) hosts.

Network layer protocols forward transport layer PDUs between hosts.

Figure 6-1   Network Layer Encapsulates and De-Encapsulates Packets

- **Routing** – The network layer provides services to direct packets to a destination host on another network. To travel to other networks, the packet must be processed by a router. The role of the router is to select the best path and direct packets toward the destination host in a process known as routing. A packet may cross many intermediary devices before reaching the destination host. Each router a packet crosses to reach the destination host is called a hop.

- **De-encapsulation** – When the packet arrives at the network layer of the destination host, the host checks the IP header of the packet. If the destination IP address within the header matches its own IP address, the IP header is removed from the packet. After the packet is de-encapsulated by the network layer, the resulting Layer 4 PDU is passed up to the appropriate service at the transport layer.

Unlike the transport layer (OSI Layer 4), which manages the data transport between the processes running on each host, network layer protocols specify the packet structure and processing used to carry the data from one host to another host. Operating without regard to the data carried in each packet allows the network layer to carry packets for multiple types of communications between multiple hosts.

Network Layer Protocols (6.1.1.2)

There are several network layer protocols in existence. However, as shown in Figure 6-2, there are only two network layer protocols that are commonly implemented:

- Internet Protocol version 4 (IPv4)

- Internet Protocol version 6 (IPv6)

Legacy network layer protocols are not shown in the figure and are not discussed in this course.

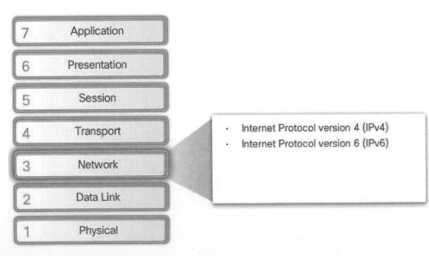

Figure 6-2   Network Layer Protocols

Characteristics of the IP Protocol (6.1.2)

IP is the premier network layer protocol. This topic will introduce the characteristics of IP.

Encapsulating IP (6.1.2.1)

IP encapsulates the transport layer segment or other data by adding an IP header. This header is used to deliver the packet to the destination host. The IP header remains the same from the time the packet leaves the source host until it arrives at the destination host.

Figure 6-3 shows the process to create the transport layer PDU and how the transport layer PDU is then encapsulated by the network layer PDU to create an IP packet.

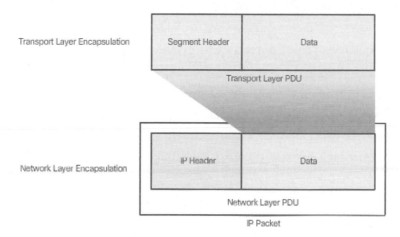

Figure 6-3   Network Layer PDU Is an IP Packet

The process of encapsulating data layer by layer enables the services at the different layers to develop and scale without affecting the other layers. This means the transport layer segments can be readily packaged by IPv4 or IPv6 or by any new protocol that might be developed in the future.

Routers can implement these different network layer protocols to operate concurrently over a network. The routing performed by these intermediate devices only considers the contents of the network layer packet header. In all cases, the data portion of the packet, that is, the encapsulated transport layer PDU, remains unchanged during the network layer processes.

Characteristics of IP (6.1.2.2)

IP was designed as a protocol with low overhead. It provides only the functions that are necessary to deliver a packet from a source to a destination over an interconnected system of networks. The protocol was not designed to track and manage the flow of packets. These functions, if required, are performed by other protocols at other layers, primarily TCP at Layer 4.

The basic characteristics of IP are as follows:

- *Connectionless* – No connection with the destination is established before sending data packets.

- *Best Effort* – IP is inherently unreliable because packet delivery is not guaranteed.

- *Media Independent* – Operation is independent of the medium (i.e., copper, fiber optic, or wireless) carrying the data.

IP – Connectionless (6.1.2.3)

IP is connectionless, meaning that no dedicated end-to-end connection is created before data is sent. Connectionless communication is conceptually similar to sending a letter to someone without notifying the recipient in advance, as shown in Figure 6-4. The sender doesn't know

- If the receiver is present

- If the letter arrived

- If the receiver can read the letter

The receiver doesn't know when the letter is coming.

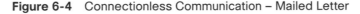

A letter is sent.

Figure 6-4   Connectionless Communication – Mailed Letter

Connectionless data communications work on the same principle. IP requires no initial exchange of control information to establish an end-to-end connection before packets are forwarded, as shown in Figure 6-5. Similar to a mailed letter, the sender of a packet doesn't know

- If the receiver is present

- If the packet arrived

- If the receiver can read the packet

The receiver doesn't know when the packet is coming.

A packet is sent.

Figure 6-5   Connectionless Communication – IP Packet

IP also does not require additional fields in the header to maintain an established connection.

This process greatly reduces the overhead of IP. However, with no pre-established end-to-end connection, senders are unaware whether destination devices are present and functional when sending packets, nor are they aware if the destination receives the packet, or if they are able to access and read the packet.

IP – Best Effort Delivery (6.1.2.4)

Figure 6-6 illustrates the unreliable or *best-effort delivery* characteristic of the IP protocol. The IP protocol does not guarantee that all packets that are delivered are, in fact, received.

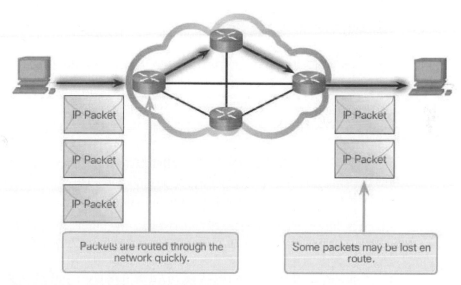

Figure 6-6   Best Effort Example

Unreliable means that IP does not have the capability to manage and recover from undelivered or corrupt packets. This is because while IP packets are sent with information about the location of delivery, they contain no information that can be processed to inform the sender whether delivery was successful. Packets may arrive at the destination corrupted, out of sequence, or not at all. IP provides no capability for packet retransmissions if errors occur.

If out-of-order packets are delivered, or packets are missing, then applications using the data, or upper layer services, must resolve these issues. This allows IP to function very efficiently. In the TCP/IP protocol suite, reliability is the role of the transport layer.

IP – Media Independent (6.1.2.5)

IP operates independently of the media that carry the data at lower layers of the protocol stack. As shown in Figure 6-7, IP packets can be communicated as electronic signals over copper cable, as optical signals over fiber, or wirelessly as radio signals.

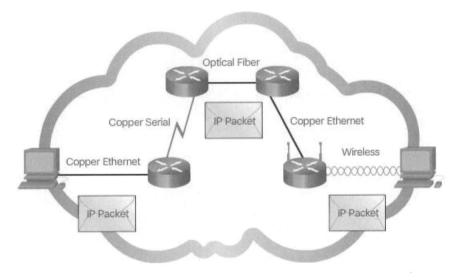

Figure 6-7 Media Independent Example

It is the responsibility of the OSI data link layer to take an IP packet and prepare it for transmission over the communications medium. This means that the transport of IP packets is not limited to any particular medium.

There is, however, one major characteristic of the media that the network layer considers: the maximum size of the PDU that each medium can transport. This characteristic is referred to as the *maximum transmission unit (MTU)*. Part of the control communication between the data link layer and the network layer is the establishment of a maximum size for the packet. The data link layer passes the MTU value up to the network layer. The network layer then determines how large packets can be.

In some cases, an intermediate device, usually a router, must split up a packet when forwarding it from one medium to another medium with a smaller MTU. This process is called fragmenting the packet or *fragmentation*.

Interactive Graphic

Activity 6.1.2.6: IP Characteristics

Go to the online course to perform this practice activity.

IPv4 Packet (6.1.3)

The ability to provide the end-to-end transfer of data by the network layer is based on the content and interpretation of the Layer 3 header. This topic will examine the structure and contents of the IPv4 header.

IPv4 Packet Header (6.1.3.1)

An IPv4 packet header consists of fields containing important information about the packet. These fields contain binary numbers that are examined by the Layer 3 process. The binary values of each field identify various settings of the IP packet. Protocol header diagrams, which are read left to right, and top down, provide a visual to refer to when discussing protocol fields. The IP protocol header diagram in Figure 6-8 identifies the fields of an IPv4 packet.

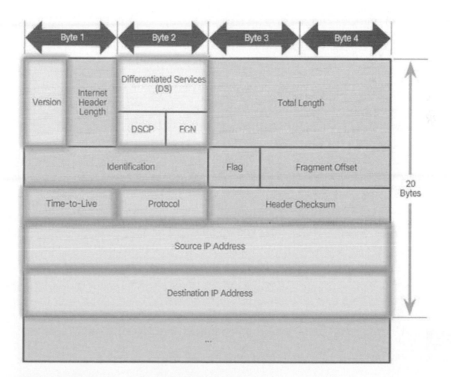

Figure 6-8   Details of the IPv4 Packet Header

Significant fields in the IPv4 header include

- **Version** – Contains a 4-bit binary value set to 0100 that identifies this as an IP version 4 packet.

- **Differentiated Services or DiffServ (DS)** – Formerly called the Type of Service (ToS) field, the DS field is an 8-bit field used to determine the priority of each packet. The six most significant bits of the DiffServ field is the Differentiated Services Code Point (DSCP) and the last two bits are the Explicit Congestion Notification (ECN) bits.

- **Time-to-Live (TTL)** – Contains an 8-bit binary value that is used to limit the lifetime of a packet. The packet sender sets the initial TTL value, and it is decreased by one each time the packet is processed by a router. If the TTL field decrements to zero, the router discards the packet and sends an *Internet Control Message Protocol (ICMP)* Time Exceeded message to the source IP address.

- **Protocol** – Field is used to identify the next level protocol. This 8-bit binary value indicates the data payload type that the packet is carrying, which enables the network layer to pass the data to the appropriate upper-layer protocol. Common values include ICMP (1), TCP (6), and UDP (17).

- **Source IPv4 Address** – Contains a 32-bit binary value that represents the source IPv4 address of the packet. The source IPv4 address is always a unicast address.

- **Destination IPv4 Address** – Contains a 32-bit binary value that represents the destination IPv4 address of the packet. The destination IPv4 address is a unicast, multicast, or broadcast address.

The two most commonly referenced fields are the source and destination IPv4 addresses. These fields identify where the packet is coming from and where it is going. Typically, these addresses do not change while traveling from the source to the destination.

The Internet Header Length (IHL), Total Length, and Header Checksum fields are used to identify and validate the packet.

Other fields are used to reorder a fragmented packet. Specifically, the IPv4 packet uses Identification, Flags, and Fragment Offset fields to keep track of the fragments. A router may have to fragment a packet when forwarding it from one medium to another with a smaller MTU.

The Options and Padding fields are rarely used and are beyond the scope of this chapter.

Video Demonstration 6.1.3.2: Sample IPv4 Headers in Wireshark

Video

Go to the online course to view this video.

Activity 6.1.3.3: IPv4 Header Fields

Go to the online course to perform this practice activity.

IPv6 Packet (6.1.4)

This topic introduces the successor of IPv4: IPv6.

Limitations of IPv4 (6.1.4.1)

Through the years, IPv4 has been updated to address new challenges. However, even with changes, IPv4 still has three major issues:

- **IP address depletion** – IPv4 has a limited number of unique public IPv4 addresses available. Although there are approximately 4 billion IPv4 addresses, the increasing number of new IP-enabled devices, always-on connections, and the potential growth of less-developed regions have increased the need for more addresses.

- **Internet routing table expansion** – A routing table is used by routers to make best path determinations. As the number of servers connected to the Internet increases, so too does the number of network routes. These IPv4 routes consume a great deal of memory and processor resources on Internet routers.

- **Lack of end-to-end connectivity** – *Network Address Translation (NAT)* is a technology commonly implemented within IPv4 networks. NAT provides a way for multiple devices to share a single public IPv4 address. However, because the public IPv4 address is shared, the IPv4 address of an internal network host is hidden. This can be problematic for technologies that require end-to-end connectivity.

Introducing IPv6 (6.1.4.2)

In the early 1990s, the Internet Engineering Task Force (IETF) grew concerned about the issues with IPv4 and began to look for a replacement. This activity led to the development of IP version 6 (IPv6). IPv6 overcomes the limitations of IPv4 and is a powerful enhancement with features that better suit current and foreseeable network demands.

Improvements that IPv6 provides include

- **Increased address space** – IPv6 addresses are based on 128-bit hierarchical addressing as opposed to IPv4 with 32 bits.

- **Improved packet handling** – The IPv6 header has been simplified with fewer fields.

- **Eliminates the need for NAT** – With such a large number of public IPv6 addresses, NAT between a private IPv4 address and a public IPv4 is not needed.

This avoids some of the NAT-induced application problems experienced by applications requiring end-to-end connectivity.

The 32-bit IPv4 address space provides approximately 4,294,967,296 unique addresses. IPv6 address space provides 340,282,366,920,938,463,463,374,607,431,7 68,211,456, or 340 undecillion addresses, which is roughly equivalent to every grain of sand on Earth.

Figure 6-9 provides a visual to compare the IPv4 and IPv6 address space.

Number Name	Scientific Notation	Number of Zeros
1 Thousand	10^3	1,000
1 Million	10^6	1,000,000
1 Billion	10^9	1,000,000,000
1 Trillion	10^12	1,000,000,000,000
1 Quadrillion	10^15	1,000,000,000,000,000
1 Quintillion	10^18	1,000,000,000,000,000,000
1 Sextillion	10^21	1,000,000,000,000,000,000,000
1 Septillion	10^24	1,000,000,000,000,000,000,000,000
1 Octillion	10^27	1,000,000,000,000,000,000,000,000,000
1 Nonillion	10^30	1,000,000,000,000,000,000,000,000,000,000
1 Decillion	10^33	1,000,000,000,000,000,000,000,000,000,000,000
1 Undecillion	10^36	1,000,000,000,000,000,000,000,000,000,000,000,000

Legend

 There are 4 billion IPv4 addresses

There are 340 undecillion IPv6 addresses

Figure 6-9   Comparison of the Number of IPv4 and IPv6 Addresses

Encapsulating IPv6 (6.1.4.3)

One of the major design improvements of IPv6 over IPv4 is the simplified IPv6 header.

For instance, the IPv4 header shown in Figure 6-10 consists of 20 octets (up to 60 bytes if the Options field is used) and 12 basic header fields, not including the Options field and Padding field.

Figure 6-10   IPv4 Header

As highlighted in Figure 6-10, for IPv6, some fields have remained the same, some fields have changed names and positions, and some IPv4 fields are no longer required.

In contrast, the simplified IPv6 header shown in Figure 6-11 consists of 40 octets (largely due to the length of the source and destination IPv6 addresses) and 8 header fields (3 IPv4 basic header fields and 5 additional header fields).

Figure 6-11   IPv6 Header

As highlighted in Figure 6-10, some fields have kept the same names as IPv4, some fields have changed names or positions, and a new field has been added.

The IPv6 simplified header offers several advantages over IPv4 including

- Better routing efficiency for performance and forwarding-rate scalability
- No requirement for processing checksums
- Simplified and more efficient extension header mechanisms (as opposed to the IPv4 Options field)
- A Flow Label field for per-flow processing with no need to open the transport inner packet to identify the various traffic flows

IPv6 Packet Header (6.1.4.4)

The IPv6 packet header is shown in Figure 6-12.

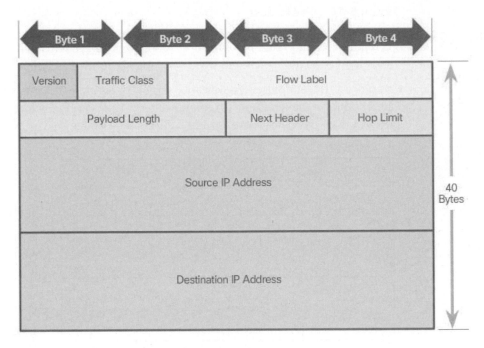

Figure 6-12   Details of the IPv6 Header

The fields in the IPv6 packet header include

- **Version –** This field contains a 4-bit binary value set to 0110 that identifies this as an IP version 6 packet.

- **Traffic Class** – This 8-bit field is equivalent to the IPv4 Differentiated Services (DS) field.

- **Flow Label** – This 20-bit field suggests that all packets with the same flow label receive the same type of handling by routers.

- **Payload Length** – This 16-bit field indicates the length of the data portion or payload of the IPv6 packet.

- **Next Header** – This 8-bit field is equivalent to the IPv4 Protocol field. It indicates the data payload type that the packet is carrying, enabling the network layer to pass the data to the appropriate upper-layer protocol.

- **Hop Limit** – This 8-bit field replaces the IPv4 TTL field. This value is decremented by a value of 1 by each router that forwards the packet. When the counter reaches 0, the packet is discarded, and an ICMPv6 Time Exceeded message is forwarded to the sending host, indicating that the packet did not reach its destination because the hop limit was exceeded.

- **Source IPv6 Address** – This 128-bit field identifies the IPv6 address of the sending host.

- **Destination IPv6 Address** – This 128-bit field identifies the IPv6 address of the receiving host.

An IPv6 packet may also contain extension headers (EH), which provide optional network layer information. Extension headers are optional and are placed between the IPv6 header and the payload. EHs are used for fragmentation, security, to support mobility, and more.

Unlike IPv4, routers do not fragment routed IPv6 packets.

Video

Video Demonstration 6.1.4.5: Sample IPv6 Headers and Wireshark

Go to the online course to view this video.

Interactive Graphic

Activity 6.1.4.6: IPv6 Header Fields

Go to the online course to perform this practice activity.

Routing (6.2)

The basic principle of internetworks is routing. This section introduces the routing between networks.

How a Host Routes (6.2.1)

Hosts need to communicate with hosts that might be on networks other than the local network. This topic examines how communication from hosts is able to reach hosts on remote networks.

Host Forwarding Decision (6.2.1.1)

Another role of the network layer is to direct packets between hosts. The three possible destinations for a packet are shown in Figure 6-13.

Figure 6-13 Three Types of Destinations

A host can send a packet to

- **Itself** – A host can ping itself by sending a packet to a special IPv4 address of 127.0.0.1, which is referred to as the *loopback interface*. Pinging the loopback interface tests the TCP/IP protocol stack on the host.

- **Local host** – This is a host on the same local network as the sending host. The hosts share the same network address.

- **Remote host** – This is a host on a remote network. The hosts do not share the same network address.

Whether a packet is destined for a local host or a remote host is determined by the IPv4 address and subnet mask combination of the source (or sending) device compared to the IPv4 address and subnet mask of the destination device.

In a home or business network, you may have several wired and wireless devices interconnected together using an intermediate device, such as a LAN switch and/or a wireless access point (WAP). This intermediate device provides interconnections between local hosts on the local network. Local hosts can reach each other and share information without the need for any additional devices. If a host is sending a packet to a device that is configured with the same IP network as the host device, the packet is simply forwarded out of the host interface, through the intermediate device, and to the destination device directly.

Of course, in most situations we want our devices to be able to connect beyond the local network segment, such as out to other homes, businesses, and the Internet. Devices that are beyond the local network segment are known as remote hosts. When a source device sends a packet to a remote destination device, then the help of routers and routing is needed. Routing is the process of identifying the best path to a destination. The router connected to the local network segment is referred to as the **default gateway**.

Default Gateway (6.2.1.2)

The *default gateway* is the network device that can route traffic to other networks. It is the router that can route traffic out of the local network.

If you use the analogy that a network is like a room, then the default gateway is like a doorway. If you want to get to another room or network you need to find the doorway.

Alternatively, a PC or computer that does not know the IP address of the default gateway is like a person, in a room, that does not know where the doorway is. They can talk to other people in the room or network, but if they do not know the default gateway address, or there is no default gateway, then there is no way out.

The functions provided by the default gateway are as follows:

- Routes traffic to other networks
- Has a local IP address in the same address range as other hosts on the network
- Can take data in and forward data out

Using the Default Gateway (6.2.1.3)

A host's routing table will typically include a default gateway. The host receives the IPv4 address of the default gateway either dynamically from Dynamic Host Configuration Protocol (DHCP) or configured manually. In Figure 6-14, PC1 and PC2 are configured with the default gateway's IPv4 address of 192.168.10.1.

Figure 6-14   Host Default Gateway

Having a default gateway configured creates a default route in the routing table of the PC. A default route is the route or pathway your computer will take when it tries to contact a remote network.

The default route is derived from the default gateway configuration and is placed in the host computer's routing table. Both PC1 and PC2 will have a default route to send all traffic destined to remote networks to R1.

Host Routing Tables (6.2.1.4)

On a Windows host, the **route print** or **netstat -r** command can be used to display the host routing table. Both commands generate the same output.

Figure 6-15 shows a sample topology of a host attached to network 192.168.10.0/24.

192.168.10.0/24

Figure 6-15   Host Routing Table Sample Topology

Example 6-1 shows the output of the host routing table.

Example 6-1 IPv4 Routing Table for PC1

```
C:\> netstat -r
<output omitted>


IPv4 Route Table
===========================================================================
Active Routes:
Network Destination        Netmask          Gateway       Interface   Metric
          0.0.0.0          0.0.0.0       10.10.10.1     10.10.10.12       10
       10.10.10.0    255.255.255.0        On-link      10.10.10.12      266
      10.10.10.12  255.255.255.255        On-link      10.10.10.12      266
     10.10.10.255  255.255.255.255        On-link      10.10.10.12      266
        127.0.0.0        255.0.0.0        On-link        127.0.0.1      306
        127.0.0.1  255.255.255.255        On-link        127.0.0.1      306
  127.255.255.255  255.255.255.255        On-link        127.0.0.1      306
        224.0.0.0        240.0.0.0        On-link        127.0.0.1      306
        224.0.0.0        240.0.0.0        On-link      10.10.10.12      266
  255.255.255.255  255.255.255.255        On-link        127.0.0.1      306
  255.255.255.255  255.255.255.255        On-link      10.10.10.12      266
===========================================================================
<output omitted>
```

The output may seem overwhelming at first, but is fairly simple to understand.

Entering the **netstat -r** command or the equivalent **route print** command displays three sections related to the current TCP/IP network connections:

- **Interface List** – Lists the Media Access Control (MAC) address and assigned interface number of every network-capable interface on the host, including Ethernet, Wi-Fi, and Bluetooth adapters.

- **IPv4 Route Table** – As displayed in Example 6-1, it lists all known IPv4 routes, including direct connections, local network, and local default routes.

- **IPv6 Route Table** – Lists all known IPv6 routes, including direct connections, local network, and local default routes.

Router Routing Tables (6.2.2)

This topic will introduce the role of the routing table in routing.

Router Packet Forwarding Decision (6.2.2.1)

When a host sends a packet to another host, it will use its routing table to determine where to send the packet. If the destination host is on a remote network, the packet is forwarded to the default gateway.

What happens when a packet arrives at the default gateway, which is usually a router? The router looks at its routing table to determine where to forward packets.

The routing table of a router can store information about

- **Directly-connected routes** – These routes come from the active router interfaces. Routers add a directly connected route when an interface is configured with an IP address and is activated. Each of the router's interfaces is connected to a different network segment.

- **Remote routes** – These routes come from remote networks connected to other routers. Routes to these networks can be manually configured on the local router by the network administrator or dynamically configured by enabling the local router to exchange routing information with other routers using a dynamic routing protocol.

- **Default route** – Like a host, routers also use a default route as a last resort if there is no other route to the desired network in the routing table.

Figure 6-16 identifies the directly connected networks and remote networks of router R1. R1 knows about its three directly connected networks: 192.168.10.0/24, 192.168.11.0/24, and 209.165.200.224/30. The topology also identifies two remote networks that R1 can learn about from R2: 10.1.1.0/24 and 10.1.2.0/24.

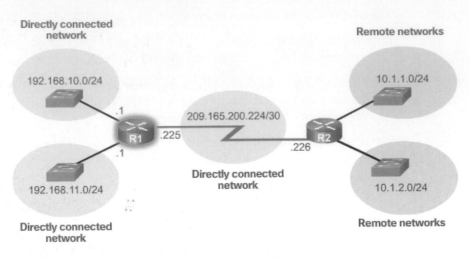

Figure 6-16   Directly Connected and Remote Network Routes

IPv4 Router Routing Table (6.2.2.2)

On a Cisco IOS router, the **show ip route** command can be used to display the router's IPv4 routing table, as shown in Example 6-2.

In addition to providing routing information for directly connected networks and remote networks, the routing table also has information on how the route was learned, the trustworthiness and rating of the route, when the route was last updated, and which interface to use to reach the requested destination.

When a packet arrives at the router interface, the router examines the packet header to determine the destination network. If the destination network matches a route in the routing table, the router forwards the packet using the information specified in the routing table. If there are two or more possible routes to the same destination, the metric is used to decide which route appears in the routing table.

Figure 6-17 shows the topology we will use for the rest of the chapter.

Figure 6-17   Chapter Topology

Example 6-2 shows the routing table for R1.

Example 6-2 R1 IPv4 Routing Table

```
R1# show ip route
<output omitted>
Gateway of last resort is not set

 10.0.0.0/24 is subnetted, 2 subnets
D 10.1.1.0/24 [90/2170112] via 209.165.200.226, 00:00:09, Serial0/0/0
D 10.1.2.0/24 [90/2170112] via 209.165.200.226, 00:00:09, Serial0/0/0
 192.168.10.0/24 is variably subnetted, 2 subnets, 2 masks
C 192.168.10.0/24 is directly connected, GigabitEthernet0/0
L 192.168.10.1/32 is directly connected, GigabitEthernet0/0
 192.168.11.0/24 is variably subnetted, 2 subnets, 2 masks
C 192.168.11.0/24 is directly connected, GigabitEthernet0/1
L 192.168.11.1/32 is directly connected, GigabitEthernet0/1
 209.165.200.0/24 is variably subnetted, 3 subnets, 3 masks
D 209.165.200.0/24 is a summary, 00:26:27, Null0
C 209.165.200.224/30 is directly connected, Serial0/0/0
L 209.165.200.225/32 is directly connected, Serial0/0/0
```

Video

Video Demonstration 6.2.2.3: Introducing the IPv4 Routing Table

Go to the online course to view this video.

Directly Connected Routing Table Entries (6.2.2.4)

When a router interface is configured with an IPv4 address, a subnet mask, and is activated, the following two routing table entries are automatically created:

- C – Identifies a directly connected network. Directly connected networks are automatically created when an interface is configured with an IP address and activated.

- L – Identifies that this is a local interface. This is the IPv4 address of the interface on the router.

The routing table entries on R1 for the directly connected network 192.168.10.0 are as follows:

```
C 192.168.10.0/24 is directly connected, GigabitEthernet0/0
L 192.168.10.1/32 is directly connected, GigabitEthernet0/0
```

These entries were automatically added to the routing table when the GigabitEthernet 0/0 interface was configured and activated. The details of directly connected routing table entries are explained in Table 6-1.

Table 6-1   Details of the Local Route Entry

Entry Part	Description
C L	Identifies how the network was learned by the router.
192.168.10.0/24 is directly connected 192.168.10.1/32 is directly connected	Identifies the destination network and how it was learned.
GigabitEthernet0/0	Identifies the exit interface to use to forward a packet toward the final destination.

Note

Local interface entries did not appear in routing tables prior to IOS Release 15.

Remote Network Routing Table Entries (6.2.2.5)

A router typically has multiple interfaces configured. The routing table stores information about both directly connected networks and remote networks.

The routing table entry on R1 for the remote network 10.1.1.0 is as follows:

```
D 10.1.1.0/24 [90/2170112] via 209.165.200.226, 00:00:09, Serial0/0/0
```

The details of the remote network routing table entry are explained in Table 6-2.

Table 6-2   Details of the Remote Network Entry

Entry Part	Entry Name	Description
D	Router Source	Identifies how the network was learned by the router. Common route sources include S (static route), D (Enhanced Interior Gateway Routing Protocol or EIGRP), and O (Open Shortest Path First or OSPF). Other route sources are beyond the scope of this chapter.
10.1.1.0/24	Destination Network	Identifies the destination network.
90	Administrative Distance	Identifies the administrative distance (i.e., trustworthiness) of the router source. Lower values indicate increased trustworthiness of the route source.
2170112	Metric	Identifies the metric value assigned to reach the remote network. Lower values indicate preferred routes.

Continued

Table 6-2 *Continued*

Entry Part	Entry Name	Description
209.165.200.226	Next-Hop	Identifies the IP address of the next router to forward the packet.
00:00:09	Route Timestamp	Specifies the last time the route was updated (in hours:minutes:seconds).
Serial0/0/0	Outgoing Interface	Identifies the exit interface to use to forward a packet toward the final destination.

Next-Hop Address (6.2.2.6)

When a packet destined for a remote network arrives at the router, the router matches the destination network to a route in the routing table. If a match is found, the router forwards the packet to the next hop address out of the identified interface.

For example, refer to the chapter topology in Figure 6-17. Assume that either PC1 or PC2 has sent a packet destined for either the 10.1.1.0 or 10.1.2.0 network. When the packet arrives on the R1 Gigabit interface, R1 will compare the packet's destination IPv4 address to entries in its routing table. The routing table is shown in Example 6-3. Based on the content of its routing, R1 will forward the packet out of its Serial 0/0/0 interface to the next hop address 209.165.200.226.

Example 6-3 R1 Routing Table Remote Network Entries

```
R1# show ip route
<output omitted>
Gateway of last resort is not set

 10.0.0.0/24 is subnetted, 2 subnets
D 10.1.1.0/24 [90/2170112] via 209.165.200.226, 00:00:09, Serial0/0/0
D 10.1.2.0/24 [90/2170112] via 209.165.200.226, 00:00:09, Serial0/0/0
 192.168.10.0/24 is variably subnetted, 2 subnets, 2 masks
C 192.168.10.0/24 is directly connected, GigabitEthernet0/0
L 192.168.10.1/32 is directly connected, GigabitEthernet0/0
 192.168.11.0/24 is variably subnetted, 2 subnets, 2 masks
C 192.168.11.0/24 is directly connected, GigabitEthernet0/1
L 192.168.11.1/32 is directly connected, GigabitEthernet0/1
 209.165.200.0/24 is variably subnetted, 3 subnets, 3 masks
D 209.165.200.0/24 is a summary, 00:26:27, Null0
C 209.165.200.224/30 is directly connected, Serial0/0/0
L 209.165.200.225/32 is directly connected, Serial0/0/0
```

Notice how directly connected networks with a route source of **C** and **L** have no next-hop address. This is because a router can forward packets directly to hosts on these networks using the designated interface.

It is also important to understand that packets cannot be forwarded by the router without a route for the destination network in the routing table. If a route representing the destination network is not in the routing table, the packet is dropped (that is, not forwarded). However, just as a host can use a default gateway to forward a packet to an unknown destination, a router can also include a default route to create a Gateway of Last Resort. The default route could be manually configured or dynamically obtained.

Video

Video Demonstration 6.2.2.7: Explaining the IPv4 Routing Table

Go to the online course to view this video.

Interactive Graphic

Activity 6.2.2.8: Identify Elements of a Router Routing Table Entry

Go to the online course to perform this practice activity.

Routers (6.3)

This section will introduce routers.

Anatomy of a Router (6.3.1)

The router is the fundamental network infrastructure device. This topic will introduce the structure and operation of routers.

A Router is a Computer (6.3.1.1)

There are many types of infrastructure routers available. In fact, Cisco routers are designed to address the needs of many different types of businesses and networks:

- **Branch** – Teleworkers, small businesses, and medium-size branch sites. Includes Cisco Integrated Services Routers (ISR) G2 (2nd generation).

- **WAN** – Large businesses, organizations, and enterprises. Includes the Cisco Catalyst Series Switches and the Cisco Aggregation Services Routers (ASR).

- **Service Provider** – Large service providers. Includes Cisco ASR, Cisco CRS-3 Carrier Routing System, and 7600 Series routers.

The focus of CCNA certification is on the branch family of routers. Figure 6-18 displays the Cisco 1900, 2900, and 3900 G2 Integrated Services Routers.

Figure 6-18   Cisco Integrated Service Routers

Regardless of their function, size, or complexity, all router models are essentially computers. Just like computers, tablets, and smart devices, routers also require

- Central processing units (CPU)

- Operating systems (OS)

- Memory consisting of random-access memory (RAM), read-only memory (ROM), nonvolatile random-access memory (NVRAM), and flash.

Router CPU and OS (6.3.1.2)

Like all computers, tablets, gaming consoles, and smart devices, Cisco devices require a CPU to execute OS instructions, such as system initialization, routing functions, and switching functions.

The highlighted component in Figure 6-19 is the CPU of a Cisco 1941 router with the heatsink attached. The heatsink helps dissipate the heat generated by the CPU.

Figure 6-19   Router CPU

The CPU requires an OS to provide routing and switching functions. The Cisco Internetwork Operating System (IOS) is the system software used for most Cisco devices regardless of the size and type of the device. It is used for routers, LAN switches, small wireless access points, large routers with dozens of interfaces, and many other devices.

Router Memory (6.3.1.3)

A router has access to volatile or non-volatile memory storage, as shown in Figure 6-20.

Figure 6-20 Router Memory

Volatile memory requires continual power to maintain its information. When the router is powered down or restarted, the content is erased and lost. Non-volatile memory retains its information even when a device is rebooted.

Specifically, a Cisco router uses four types of memory:

- **RAM** – This is volatile memory used in Cisco routers to store applications, processes, and data needed to be executed by the CPU. Cisco routers use a fast type of RAM called synchronous dynamic random access memory (SDRAM). RAM uses the following applications and processes:

  - The IOS image and running configuration file

  - The routing table used to determine the best path to use to forward packets

  - The ARP cache used to map IPv4 addresses to MAC addresses

  - The Packet buffer used to temporarily store packets before forwarding to the destination

- **ROM** – This non-volatile memory is used to store crucial operational instructions and a limited IOS. Specifically, ROM is firmware embedded on an integrated circuit inside the router that can only be altered by Cisco. ROM stores the following:

  - Bootup information that provides the startup instructions

  - Power-on self-test (POST) that tests all the hardware components

  - Limited IOS to provide a backup version of the IOS. It is used for loading a full-feature IOS when it has been deleted or corrupted.

- **NVRAM** – This non-volatile memory is used as the permanent storage for the startup configuration file (startup-config).

- **Flash** – This non-volatile computer memory used as permanent storage for the IOS and other system-related files such as log files, voice configuration files, HTML files, backup configurations, and more. When a router is rebooted, the IOS is copied from flash into RAM.

All router platforms have default settings and components. For instance, the Cisco 1941 comes with 512 MB of SDRAM but is upgradable up to 2.0 GB. The Cisco 1941 routers also come with 256 MB of flash but are upgradable using two external Compact Flash slots. Each slot can support high-speed storage cards upgradable to 4 GB.

Inside a Router (6.3.1.4)

Although there are several different types and models of routers, every router has the same general hardware components.

A Cisco 1841 first-generation ISR is shown in Figure 6-21 and has the following components:

1. Power Supply

2. Fan

3. Shields for WAN interface cards (WICs) or high-speed WICs (HWICs)

4. CPU

5. Nonvolatile RAM (NVRAM) and boot flash memory used for storing the ROMMON boot code as well as NVRAM data

6. Synchronous dynamic RAM (SDRAM) used for holding the running configuration and routing tables and for supporting packet buffering

7. Advanced Integration Module (AIM) option that offloads processor-intensive functions such as encryption from the main CPU.

Figure 6-21   Inside of a Router

Although shown and described, components such as the power supply, cooling fan, heat shields, and an advanced integration module (AIM) are beyond the scope of this chapter.

Note

A networking professional should be familiar with and understand the function of the main internal components of a router rather than the exact location of those components inside a specific router. Depending on the model, those components are located in different places inside the router.

Connect to a Router (6.3.1.5)

Cisco devices, routers, and switches typically interconnect many devices. For this reason, these devices have several types of ports and interfaces that are used to connect to the device. For example, a Cisco 1941 router backplane shown in Figure 6-22 includes the following connections and ports:

1. Compact Flash slots labeled CF0 and CF1 to provide increased storage flash space upgradable to 4 GB compact flash card per slot. By default, CF0 is populated with a 256 MB compact flash card and is the default boot location.

2. Console ports for the initial configuration and command-line interface (CLI) management access. Two ports are available; the commonly used regular RJ-45 port and a new USB Type-B (mini-B USB) connector. However, the console can only be accessed by one port at a time.

3. Gigabit Ethernet interfaces labeled GE0/0 and GE0/1. Typically used to provide LAN access by connecting to switches and users or to interconnect to another router.

4. USB ports labeled USB 0 and USB 1 to provide additional storage space similar to flash.

5. Auxiliary (AUX) RJ-45 port for remote management access similar to the Console port. Now considered a legacy port as it was used to provide support for dial-up modems.

6. Enhanced High-speed WAN Interface Card (eHWIC) slots labeled eHWIC 0 and eHWIC 1 to provide modularity and flexibility by enabling the router to support different types of interface modules, including serial, digital subscriber line (DSL), switch port, and wireless.

Figure 6-22 Cisco 1941 Backplane

Like many networking devices, Cisco devices use light-emitting diode (LED) indicators to provide status information. An interface LED indicates the activity of the corresponding interface. If an LED is off when the interface is active, and the interface is correctly connected, this may be an indication of a problem with that interface. If an interface is extremely busy, its LED is always on.

LAN and WAN Interfaces (6.3.1.6)

The connections on a Cisco router can be grouped into two categories: in-band router interfaces and management ports. Figure 6-23 shows the following management ports and interfaces:

1. In-band router interfaces are the LAN (i.e. Gigabit Ethernet) and WAN (i.e., eHWICs) interfaces configured with IP addressing to carry user traffic. Ethernet interfaces are the most common LAN connections, whereas common WAN connections include serial and DSL interfaces.

2. Management ports include the console and AUX ports, which are used to configure, manage, and troubleshoot the router. Unlike LAN and WAN interfaces, management ports are not used for packet forwarding user traffic.

Figure 6-23 Management Ports and Interfaces

Similar to a Cisco switch, there are several ways to access user EXEC mode in the CLI environment on a Cisco router. These are the most common:

- **Console** – This is a physical management port that provides out-of-band access to a Cisco device. Out-of-band access refers to access via a dedicated management channel that is used for device maintenance purposes only.

- **Secure Shell (SSH)** – SSH is a method for remotely establishing a secure CLI connection through a virtual interface, over a network. Unlike a console connection, SSH connections require active networking services on the device including an active interface configured with an address.

- **Telnet** – Telnet is an insecure method of remotely establishing a CLI session through a virtual interface, over a network. Unlike SSH, Telnet does not provide a securely encrypted connection. User authentication, passwords, and commands are sent over the network in plaintext.

Note

Some devices, such as routers, may also support a legacy auxiliary port that was used to establish a CLI session remotely using a modem. Similar to a console connection, the AUX port is out-of-band and does not require networking services to be configured or available.

Telnet and SSH require an in-band network connection, which means that an administrator must access the router through one of the WAN or LAN interfaces. Figure 6-24 shows the following in-band interfaces:

1. Serial WAN interfaces added to eHWIC0 and labeled Serial 0 (i.e., S0/0/0) and Serial 1 (i.e., S0/0/1). Serial interfaces are used for connecting routers to external WAN networks. Each serial WAN interface has its own IP address and subnet mask, which identifies it as a member of a specific network.

2. Ethernet LAN interfaces labeled GE 0/0 (i.e., G0/0) and GE 0/1 (i.e., G0/1). Ethernet interfaces are used for connecting to other Ethernet-enabled devices including switches, routers, firewalls, etc. Each LAN interface has its own IPv4 address and subnet mask and/or IPv6 address and prefix, which identifies it as a member of a specific network.

Figure 6-24 Inband Router Interfaces

In-band interfaces receive and forward IP packets. Every configured and active interface on the router is a member or host on a different IP network. Each interface must be configured with an IPv4 address and subnet mask of a different network. The Cisco IOS does not allow two active interfaces on the same router to belong to the same network.

Interactive Graphic

Activity 6.3.1.7: Identify Router Components

Go to the online course to perform this practice activity.

Packet Tracer ☐ Activity

Packet Tracer 6.3.1.8: Exploring Internetworking Devices

In this activity, you will explore the different options available on internetworking devices. You will also be required to determine which options provide the necessary connectivity when connecting multiple devices. Finally, you will add the correct modules and connect the devices.

Router Boot-up (6.3.2)

Understanding the bootup process of Cisco IOS and the associated messages is important when diagnosing a nonoperational device. This topic will provide an overview of the IOS boot process.

Bootset Files (6.3.2.1)

Both Cisco routers and switches load the IOS image and startup configuration file into RAM when they are booted, as shown in Figure 6-25.

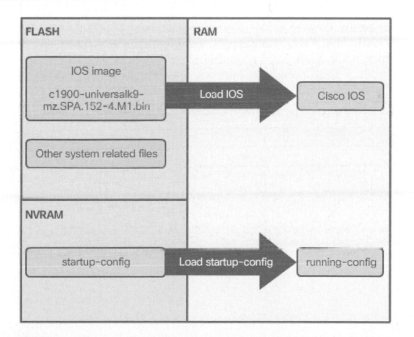

Figure 6-25   Files Copied to RAM During Bootup

The running configuration is modified when the network administrator performs device configurations. Changes made to the running-config file should be saved to the startup configuration file in NVRAM, in case the router is restarted or loses power.

Router Bootup Process (6.3.2.2)

There are three major phases to the bootup process, as shown in Figure 6-26.

Figure 6-26   How a Router Boots Up – Overview

1. Performing POST and Load Bootstrap Program (Figure 6-27)

During the Power-On Self-Test (POST), the router executes diagnostics from ROM on several hardware components, including the CPU, RAM, and NVRAM. After the POST, the bootstrap program is copied from ROM into RAM. The main task of the bootstrap program is to locate the Cisco IOS and load it into RAM.

Figure 6-27   How a Router Boots Up – POST and Bootstrap

Note

At this point, if you have a console connection to the router, you begin to see the output on the screen.

2. Locating and Loading Cisco IOS (Figure 6-28)

The IOS is typically stored in flash memory and is copied into RAM for execution by the CPU. If the IOS image is not located in flash, then the router may look for it using a Trivial File Transfer Protocol (TFTP) server. If a full IOS image cannot be located, a limited IOS is copied into RAM, which can be used to diagnose problems and transfer a full IOS into Flash memory.

Figure 6-28   How a Router Boots Up – Locate IOS

3. Locating and Loading the Configuration File (Figure 6-29)

The bootstrap program then copies the startup configuration file from NVRAM into RAM. This becomes the running configuration. If the startup configuration file does not exist in NVRAM, the router may be configured to search for a TFTP server. If a TFTP server is not found, then the router displays the setup mode prompt.

Figure 6-29   How a Router Boots Up – Locate Configuration

Note

Setup mode is not used in this course to configure the router. When prompted to enter setup mode, always answer **no**. If you answer yes and enter setup mode, press **Ctrl+C** at any time to terminate the setup process.

Video

Video Demonstration 6.3.2.3: Router Bootup Process

Go to the online course to view this video.

Show Version Output (6.3.2.4)

As highlighted in Example 6-4, the **show version** command displays information about the version of the Cisco IOS software currently running on the router, the version of the bootstrap program, and information about the hardware configuration, including the amount of system memory.

Example 6-4 The **show version** Command

```
R1# show version
Cisco IOS Software, C1900 Software (C1900-UNIVERSALK9-M), Version 15.4(3)M2,
RELEASE SOFTWARE (fc2)
Technical Support: http://www.cisco.com/techsupport
Copyright (c) 1986-2015 by Cisco Systems, Inc.
Compiled Fri 06-Feb-15 17:01 by prod_rel_team


ROM: System Bootstrap, Version 15.0(1r)M15, RELEASE SOFTWARE (fc1)


R1 uptime is 5 minutes
System returned to ROM by power-on
System image file is "flash0:c1900-universalk9-mz.SPA.1543-.M2.bin"
Last reload type: Normal Reload
Last reload reason: power-on


<output omitted>


Cisco CISCO1941/K9 (revision 1.0) with 446464K/77824K bytes of memory.
Processor board ID FTX1636848Z
2 Gigabit Ethernet interfaces
2 Serial(sync/async) interfaces
1 terminal line
1 Virtual Private Network (VPN) Module
DRAM configuration is 64 bits wide with parity disabled.
255K bytes of non-volatile configuration memory.
124400K bytes of USB Flash usbflash0 (Read/Write)
250880K bytes of ATA System CompactFlash 0 (Read/Write)


 <output omitted>
```

Video

Video Demonstration 6.3.2.5: The show version Command

Go to the online course to view this video.

Interactive Graphic

Activity 6.3.2.6: The Router Boot Process

Go to the online course to perform this practice activity.

Lab 6.3.2.7: Exploring Router Physical Characteristics

In this lab, you will complete the following objectives:

- Part 1: Examine Router External Characteristics
- Part 2: Examine Router Internal Characteristics Using Show Commands

Configure a Cisco Router (6.4)

This section will present the basic configuration needed for all IOS routers.

Configure Initial Settings (6.4.1)

Cisco routers require configuration before they are operational. This topic will introduce the basic CLI configuration of routers.

Basic Switch Configuration Steps (6.4.1.1)

Cisco routers and Cisco switches have many similarities. They support a similar operating system, support similar command structures, and support many of the same commands. In addition, both devices have identical initial configuration steps when implemented in a network.

Before we begin configuring a router, review the initial switch configuration tasks show in Table 6-3.

Table 6-3 Initial Switch Configuration Tasks

Task	Commands
Configure the device name	`Switch(config)# hostname name`
Secure user EXEC mode	`Switch(config)# line console 0`
	`Switch(config-line)# password password`
	`Switch(config-line)# login`
Secure remote Telnet/SSH access	`Switch(config)# line vty 0 15`
	`Switch(config-line)# password password`
	`Switch(config-line)# login`
Secure privilege EXEC mode	`Switch(config)# enable secret password`
Secure all passwords in the config file	`Switch(config)# service password-encryption`
Provide legal notification	`Switch(config)# banner motd delimiter message delimiter`
Configure the management SVI	`Switch(config)# interface vlan 1`
	`Switch(config-if)# ip address ip-address subnet-mask`
	`Switch(config-if)# no shutdown`
Save the configuration	`Switch# copy running-config startup-config`

Figure 6-30 highlights the switch in our chapter topology.

Figure 6-30   Switch Configuration Topology

Example 6-5 shows a sample configuration for S1.

Example 6-5 Basic Switch Configuration

```
Switch> enable
Switch# configure terminal
Switch(config)# hostname S1
S1(config)# enable secret class
S1(config)# line console 0
S1(config-line)# password cisco
S1(config-line)# login
S1(config-line)# line vty 0 15
S1(config-line)# password cisco
S1(config-line)# login
S1(config-line)# exit
S1(config)# service password-encryption
S1(config)# banner motd #No unauthorized access allowed!#
S1(config)# interface vlan1
S1(config-if)# ip address 192.168.10.50 255.255.255.0
S1(config-if)# no shutdown
S1(config-if)# end
S1# copy running-config startup-config
Destination filename [startup-config]?
Building configuration...
[OK]
S1#
```

Basic Router Configuration Steps (6.4.1.2)

The tasks used to configure a router are the same as those used to configure a switch, as shown in Table 6-4.

Table 6-4 Initial Router Configuration Tasks

Task	Commands
Configure the device name	Router(config)# **hostname** *name*
Secure user EXEC mode	Router(config)# **line console 0**
	Router(config-line)# **password** *password*
	Router(config-line)# **login**
Secure remote Telnet/SSH access	Router(config)# **line vty 0 4**
	Router(config-line)# **password** *password*
	Router(config-line)# **login**
Secure privilege EXEC mode	Router(config)# **enable secret** *password*
Secure all passwords in the config file	Router(config)# **service password-encryption**
Provide legal notification	Router(config)# **banner motd** *delimiter message delimiter*
Save the configuration	Router# **copy running-config startup-config**

In Example 6-6, the router is assigned a hostname.

Example 6-6 Configuring Hostname

```
Router> enable
Router# configure terminal
Enter configuration commands, one per line. End with CNTL/Z.
Router(config)# hostname R1
R1(config)#
```

In Example 6-7, the privileged EXEC, user EXEC, and remote access lines are secured with a password and all passwords in the configuration file are encrypted.

Example 6-7 Securing Management Access

```
R1(config)# enable secret class
R1(config)# line console 0
R1(config-line)# password cisco
R1(config-line)# login
R1(config-line)# exit
R1(config)# line vty 0 4
R1(config-line)# password cisco
R1(config-line)# login
R1(config-line)# exit
R1(config)# service password-encryption
R1(config)#
```

Providing legal notification is configured in Example 6-8.

Example 6-8 Providing Legal Notification

```
R1(config)# banner motd #
Enter TEXT message. End with the character '#'.
**************************************************
WARNING: Unauthorized access is prohibited!
**************************************************
#
R1(config)#
```

The configuration is saved in Example 6-9.

Example 6-9 Saving the Configuration

```
R1# copy running-config startup-config
Destination filename [startup-config]?
Building configuration...
[OK]
R1#
```

Packet Tracer
☐ Activity

Packet Tracer 6.4.1.3: Configure Initial Router Settings

In this activity, you will perform basic router configurations. You will secure access to the CLI and console port using encrypted and plaintext passwords. You will also configure messages for users logging into the router. These banners also warn unauthorized users that access is prohibited. Finally, you will verify and save your running configuration.

Configure Interfaces (6.4.2)

This topic introduces the basic router interface configuration.

Configure Router Interfaces (6.4.2.1)

For routers to be reachable, the in-band router interfaces must be configured. There are many different types of interfaces available on Cisco routers. In this example, the Cisco 1941 router is equipped with

- **Two Gigabit Ethernet interfaces** – GigabitEthernet 0/0 (G0/0) and GigabitEthernet 0/1 (G0/1)

- **A serial WAN interface card (WIC) consisting of two interfaces** – Serial 0/0/0 (S0/0/0) and Serial 0/0/1 (S0/0/1)

The tasks to configure a router interface are shown in Table 6-5. Notice how they are very similar to configuring a management SVI on a switch.

Table 6-5   Router Interface Configuration Tasks

Task	Commands
Configure the interface	`Router(config)# ` **`interface`** *`type number`*
	`Router(config-if)# ` **`ip address`** *`ip-address subnet-mask`*
	`Router(config-if)# ` **`description`** *`description-text`*
	`Router(config-if)# ` **`no shutdown`**

Although not required, it is good practice to configure a description on each interface to help document the network information. The description text is limited to 240 characters. On production networks, a description can be helpful in troubleshooting by providing information about the type of network that the interface is connected to and if there are any other routers on that network. If the interface connects to an ISP or service carrier, it is helpful to enter the third party connection and contact information.

Using the **no shutdown** command activates the interface and is similar to powering on the interface. The interface must also be connected to another device, such as a switch or a router, for the physical layer to be active.

Example 6-10 shows the configuration of the LAN interfaces connected to R1.

Example 6-10 Configuring Router Interfaces

```
R1# conf t
Enter configuration commands, one per line. End with CNTL/Z.
R1(config)# interface gigabitethernet 0/0
R1(config-if)# ip address 192.168.10.1 255.255.255.0
R1(config-if)# description Link to LAN-10
R1(config-if)# no shutdown
%LINK-3-UPDOWN: Interface GigabitEthernet0/0, changed state to up
%LINEPROTO-5-UPDOWN: Line protocol on Interface GigabitEthernet0/0, changed state
to up
R1(config-if)# exit
R1(config)#
```

Verify Interface Configuration (6.4.2.2)

There are several commands that can be used to verify interface configuration. The most useful of these is the **show ip interface brief** command. The output generated displays all interfaces, their IPv4 address, and their current status. The configured and connected interfaces should display a Status of "up" and Protocol of "up." Anything else would indicate a problem with either the configuration or the cabling.

You can verify connectivity from the interface using the **ping** command. Cisco routers send five consecutive pings and measure minimal, average, and maximum round trip times. Exclamation marks verify connectivity.

Example 6-11 displays the output of the **show ip interface brief** command, which reveals that the LAN interfaces and the WAN link are all activated and operational. Notice that the **ping** command generated five exclamation marks verifying connectivity to R2.

Example 6-11 Verifying Router Interface Configuration

```
R1# show ip interface brief
Interface IP-Address OK? Method Status Protocol
Embedded-Service-Engine0/0 unassigned YES unset administratively down down
GigabitEthernet0/0 192.168.10.1 YES manual up up
GigabitEthernet0/1 192.168.11.1 YES manual up up
Serial0/0/0 209.165.200.225 YES manual up up
Serial0/0/1 unassigned YES unset administratively down down
R1#
R1# ping 209.165.200.226
Type escape sequence to abort.
Sending 5, 100-byte ICMP Echos to 209.165.200.226, timeout is 2 seconds:
!!!!!
Success rate is 100 percent (5/5), round-trip min/avg/max = 1/1/4 ms
R1#
```

Other interface verification commands include

- **show ip route** – Displays the contents of the IPv4 routing table stored in RAM.

- **show interfaces** – Displays statistics for all interfaces on the device.

- **show ip interface** – Displays the IPv4 statistics for all interfaces on a router.

Example 6-12 displays the output of the **show ip route** command. Notice the three directly connected network entries with their local interface IPv4 addresses.

Example 6-12 Verifying the Routing Table

```
R1# show ip route
Codes: L - local, C - connected, S - static, R - RIP, M - mobile, B - BGP
 D - EIGRP, EX - EIGRP external, O - OSPF, IA - OSPF inter area
 N1 - OSPF NSSA external type 1, N2 - OSPF NSSA external type 2
 E1 - OSPF external type 1, E2 - OSPF external type 2
 i - IS-IS, su - IS-IS summary, L1 - IS-IS level-1, L2 - IS-IS level-2
 ia - IS-IS inter area, * - candidate default, U - per-user static route
 o - ODR, P - periodic downloaded static route, H - NHRP, l - LISP
 a - application route
 + - replicated route, % - next hop override

Gateway of last resort is not set

 192.168.10.0/24 is variably subnetted, 2 subnets, 2 masks
C 192.168.10.0/24 is directly connected, GigabitEthernet0/0
L 192.168.10.1/32 is directly connected, GigabitEthernet0/0
 192.168.11.0/24 is variably subnetted, 2 subnets, 2 masks
C 192.168.11.0/24 is directly connected, GigabitEthernet0/1
L 192.168.11.1/32 is directly connected, GigabitEthernet0/1
 209.165.200.0/24 is variably subnetted, 2 subnets, 2 masks
C 209.165.200.224/30 is directly connected, Serial0/0/0
L 209.165.200.225/32 is directly connected, Serial0/0/0
R1#
```

Remember to save the configuration using the **copy running-config startup-config** command.

Configure the Default Gateway (6.4.3)

To send a packet outside of the local network, a device needs to know where to forward the packet. For an end device, this generally called the default gateway. This topic will introduce the concept and use of the default gateway.

Default Gateway for a Host (6.4.3.1)

For an end device to communicate over the network, it must be configured with the correct IP address information, including the default gateway address. The default gateway is only used when the host wants to send a packet to a device on another network. The default gateway address is generally the router interface address attached to the local network of the host. The IP address of the host device and the router interface address must be in the same network.

The network topology in the next two figures consists of a router interconnecting two separate LANs. G0/0 is connected to network 192.168.10.0, whereas G0/1 is connected to network 192.168.11.0. Each host device is configured with the appropriate default gateway address.

In Figure 6-31, PC1 sends a packet to PC2. In this example, the default gateway is not used. Instead, PC1 addresses the packet with the IP address of PC2 and forwards the packet directly to PC2 through the switch.

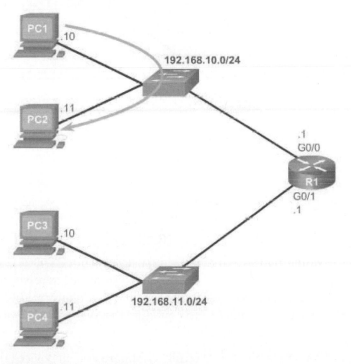

Figure 6-31   Pinging a Local Host

In Figure 6-32, PC1 sends a packet to PC3. In this example, PC1 addresses the packet with the IP address of PC3 but then forwards the packet to the router. The router accepts the packet, accesses its routing table to determine the appropriate exit interface based on the destination address, and then forwards the packet out of the appropriate interface to reach PC3.

Figure 6-32   Pinging a Remote Host

Default Gateway for a Switch (6.4.3.2)

Typically, a workgroup switch that interconnects client computers is a Layer 2 device. As such, a Layer 2 switch does not require an IP address to function properly. However, if you wish to connect to the switch and administratively manage it over multiple networks, you will need to configure the SVI with an IPv4 address, subnet mask, and default gateway address.

The default gateway address is typically configured on all devices that wish to communicate beyond just their local network. In other words, to remotely access the switch from another network using SSH or Telnet, the switch must have an SVI with an IPv4 address, subnet mask, and default gateway address configured. If the switch is accessed from a host within the local network, then the default gateway IPv4 address is not required.

To configure a default gateway on a switch, use the **ip default-gateway** global configuration command. The IP address configured is that of the router interface of the connected switch.

Figure 6-33 shows an administrator establishing a remote connection to switch S1 on another network. S1 must be configured with a default gateway to be able to reply and establish an SSH connection with the administrative host.

```
S1#show running-config
Building configuration...
!
<output omitted>
service password-encryption
!
hostname S1
!
Interface Vlan1
ip address 192.168.10.50
!
ip default-gateway 192.168.10.1
<output omitted>
```

Figure 6-33   Example of Configuring a Default Gateway on a Switch

A common misconception is that the switch uses its configured default gateway address to determine where to forward packets originating from hosts connected to the switch and destined for hosts on remote networks. Actually, the IP address and default gateway information are only used for packets that originate from the switch. Packets originating from host computers connected to the switch must already have the default gateway address configured on their host computer operating systems.

Packet Tracer 6.4.3.3: Connect a Router to a LAN

In this activity, you will use various show commands to display the current state of the router. You will then use the Addressing Table to configure router Ethernet interfaces. Finally, you will use commands to verify and test your configurations.

Packet Tracer
☐ **Activity**

Packet Tracer 6.4.3.4: Troubleshooting Default Gateway Issues

For a device to communicate across multiple networks, it must be configured with an IP address, subnet mask, and a default gateway. The default gateway is used when the host wants to send a packet to a device on another network. The default gateway address is generally the router interface address attached to the local network to which the host is connected. In this activity, you will finish documenting the network. You will then verify the network documentation by testing end-to-end connectivity and troubleshooting issues. The troubleshooting method you will use consists of the following steps:

Step 1. Verify the network documentation and use tests to isolate problems.

Step 2. Determine an appropriate solution for a given problem.

Step 3. Implement the solution.

Step 4. Test to verify the problem is resolved.

Step 5. Document the solution.

Summary (6.5)

Class Activity 6.5.1.1: Can You Read This Map?

Note

It is suggested that students work in pairs; however, if preferred, students can complete this activity individually.

Your instructor will provide you with output generated by a router's **show ip route** command. Use Packet Tracer to build a topology model using this routing information.

At a minimum, the following should be used in your topology model:

- 1 Catalyst 2960 switch
- 1 Cisco Series 1941 Router with one HWIC-4ESW switching port modular card and IOS version 15.1 or higher
- 3 PCs (can be servers, generic PCs, laptops, etc.)

Use the note tool in Packet Tracer to indicate the addresses of the router interfaces and possible addresses for the end devices you chose for your model. Label all end devices, ports, and addresses ascertained from the **show ip route** output/routing table information in your Packet Tracer file. Save your work in hard or soft copy to share with the class.

Lab 6.5.1.2: Building a Switch and Router Network

In this lab, you will complete the following objectives:

- Part 1: Set Up the Topology and Initialize Devices
- Part 2: Configure Devices and Verify Connectivity
- Part 3: Display Device Information

Packet Tracer
☐ Activity

Packet Tracer 6.5.1.3: Skills Integration Challenge

Your network manager is impressed with your performance in your job as a LAN technician. She would like you to now demonstrate your ability to configure a router connecting two LANs. Your tasks include configuring basic settings on a router and a switch using the Cisco IOS. You will then verify your configurations as well as configurations on existing devices by testing end-to-end connectivity.

The network layer, or OSI Layer 3, provides services to allow end devices to exchange data across the network. To accomplish this end-to-end transport, the network layer uses four basic processes: IP addressing for end devices, encapsulation, routing, and de-encapsulation.

The Internet is largely based on IPv4, which is still the most widely used network layer protocol. An IPv4 packet contains the IP header and the payload. However, IPv4 has a limited number of unique public IP addresses available. This led to the development of IP version 6 (IPv6). The IPv6 simplified header offers several advantages over IPv4, including better routing efficiency, simplified extension headers, and capability for per-flow processing. Plus, IPv6 addresses are based on 128-bit hierarchical addressing as opposed to IPv4 with 32 bits. This dramatically increases the number of available IP addresses.

In addition to hierarchical addressing, the network layer is also responsible for routing.

Hosts require a local routing table to ensure that packets are directed to the correct destination network. The local table of a host typically contains the direct connection, the local network route, and the local default route. The local default route is the route to the default gateway.

The default gateway is the IP address of a router interface connected to the local network. When a host needs to forward a packet to a destination address that is not on the same network as the host, the packet is sent to the default gateway for further processing.

When a router, such as the default gateway, receives a packet, it examines the destination IP address to determine the destination network. The routing table of a router stores information about directly connected routes and remote routes to IP networks. If the router has an entry in its routing table for the destination network, the router forwards the packet. If no routing entry exists, the router may forward the packet to its own default route if one is configured or it will drop the packet.

Routing table entries can be configured manually on each router to provide static routing, or the routers may communicate route information dynamically between each other using a routing protocol.

In order for routers to be reachable, the router interface must be configured. To enable a specific interface, enter interface configuration mode using the **interface** *type-and-number* global configuration mode command.

Practice

The following activities provide practice with the topics introduced in this chapter. The Labs and Class Activities are available in the companion Introduction to Networks v5.1 Lab Manual (ISBN 9781587133534). The Packet Tracer Activities PKA files are found in the online course.

Class Activities

Class Activity 6.0.1.2: The Road Less Traveled...

Class Activity 6.5.1.1: Can You Read This Map?

Labs

Lab 6.3.2.7: Exploring Router Physical Characteristics

Lab 6.5.1.2: Building a Switch and Router Network

Packet Tracer Activities

Packet Tracer 6.3.1.8: Exploring Internetworking Devices

Packet Tracer 6.4.1.3: Configure Initial Router Settings

Packet Tracer 6.4.3.3: Connect a Router to a LAN

Packet Tracer 6.4.3.4: Troubleshooting Default Gateway Issues

Packet Tracer 6.5.1.3: Skills Integration Challenge

Check Your Understanding Questions

Complete all the review questions listed here to test your understanding of the topics and concepts in this chapter. The appendix "Answers to 'Check Your Understanding' Questions" lists the answers.

1. Which layer of the OSI model is concerned with end-to-end communication over the network?

   A. Network

   B. Transport

   C. Data link

   D. Application

2. Which of the following is associated with the network layer?

   A. IP address

   B. Frames

   C. MAC address

   D. Physical addressing

3. Why was IPv4 designed as a connectionless protocol?

4. On a router, what field in an IPv4 header should be examined to determine that the maximum number of hops has been reached by the packet on its way from the source to this destination?

   A. Version

   B. DS

   C. TTL

   D. Protocol

   E. Source IPv4 Address

   F. Destination IPv4 Address

5. When configuring a host, the gateway was not configured. How will this affect communication to and from this device?

   A. Host communication will not be affected.

   B. The host will not be able to communicate with devices by name.

   C. Communication will be limited to hosts in the local network.

   D. No communication will be successful to or from the host.

6. In what part of a router is the running configuration being used located?

   A. ROM

   B. NVRAM

   C. Flash

   D. RAM

7. During the boot process of a Cisco router, you notice a series of hash symbols (#) appearing on the terminal emulator screen from the console session. In what phase is the boot process?

   A. Loading the startup configuration

   B. Loading the IOS

   C. POST

   D. Loading the bootstrap

8. What are the required steps for configuring an interface on a router? (Choose two.)

   A. Provide Layer 3 addressing information

   B. Add a description to the interface

   C. Turn on routing on the interface

   D. Activate the interface

9. The **ip default-gateway** command was not used when configuring a switch. How will this affect network communication? (Choose two.)

   A. Host communication through the switch will not be affected.

   B. The hosts communicating through the switch will not be able to communicate with devices by name.

   C. The host communication through the switch will be limited to hosts in the local network.

   D. No communication through the switch will be successful.

   E. Communication to and from the switch will be limited to hosts in the local network.

10. When using the **netstat -r** command on a host, you see a route 0.0.0.0 0.0.0.0. What does this route represent?

    A. The host has no routes available for forwarding packets.

    B. This is a route for testing local communication.

    C. Destinations without a specified route are forwarded to the gateway.

    D. The host does not have an IP address configured.

CHAPTER 7

IP Addressing

Objectives

Upon completion of this chapter, you will be able to answer the following questions:

- How do you convert between decimal and binary number systems?

- What is the structure of an IPv4 address?

- What are the characteristics and uses of unicast, broadcast, and multicast IPv4 addresses?

- What are the uses of public, private, and reserved addresses?

- What are the reasons for the development of IPv6 addressing?

- How are IPv6 addresses represented?

- What are the different types of IPv6 addresses?

- How are global unicast addresses configured?

- What are the purpose and uses of multicast addresses?

- How is ICMP used to test network connectivity?

- How are the ping and traceroute utilities used to test network connectivity?

Key Terms

This chapter uses the following key terms. You can find the definitions in the Glossary.

Introduction (7.0)

Addressing is a critical function of network layer protocols. Addressing enables data communication between hosts, regardless of whether the hosts are on the same network, or on different networks. Both Internet Protocol version 4 (IPv4) and Internet Protocol version 6 (IPv6) provide hierarchical addressing for packets that carry data.

Designing, implementing, and managing an effective IP addressing plan ensures that networks can operate effectively and efficiently.

This chapter examines in detail the structure of IP addresses and their application to the construction and testing of IP networks and subnetworks.

Class Activity 7.0.1.1: The Internet of Everything (IoE)

If nature, traffic, transportation, networking, and space exploration depend on digital information sharing, how will that information be identified from source to destination?

In this activity, you will begin to think about not only what will be identified in the IoE world, but how everything will be addressed in the same world!

- Navigate to the IoE main page located at http://www.cisco.com/c/r/en/us/internet-of-everything-ioe.

- Next, watch some videos or read through some content from the IoE main page that interests you.

- Write 5 comments or questions about what you saw or read. Be prepared to share with the class.

IPv4 Network Addresses (7.1)

For communication to take place between hosts, the appropriate addresses must be applied to these devices. Managing the addressing of the devices and understanding the IPv4 address structure and its representation are essential.

Binary and Decimal Conversion (7.1.1)

IPv4 addresses are 32-bit addresses expressed in decimal notation. This topic will discuss the binary number system along with the conversion between the binary and decimal number systems.

IPv4 Addresses (7.1.1.1)

Binary is a numbering system that consists of the numbers 0 and 1 called bits. In contrast, the decimal numbering system consists of 10 digits consisting of the numbers 0–9.

Binary is important for us to understand because hosts, servers, and network devices use binary addressing. Specifically, they use binary IPv4 addresses, as shown in Figure 7-1, to identify each other.

Figure 7-1   IPv4 Addresses Expressed in Binary

Each address consists of a string of 32 bits, divided into four sections called *octets*. Each octet contains 8 bits (or 1 byte) separated with a dot. For example, PC1 in the figure is assigned IPv4 address 11000000.10101000.00001010.00001010. Its default gateway address would be that of R1 Gigabit Ethernet interface 11000000.10101000. 00001010.00000001.

Working with binary numbers can be challenging. For ease of use by people, IPv4 addresses are commonly expressed in dotted decimal notation as shown in Figure 7-2. PC1 is assigned IPv4 address 192.168.10.10, and its default gateway address is 192.168.10.1.

Figure 7-2 IPv4 Addresses Expressed in Dotted Decimal

Figure 7-3 contrasts the dotted decimal address and 32-bit binary address of PC1.

192.168.10.10 is an IP address that is assigned to a computer.

This address is made up of four different octets.

The computer stores the address as the entire 32-bit data stream.

Figure 7-3 Contrasting an IPv4 Dotted Decimal and Binary Address

For a solid understanding of network addressing, it is necessary to know binary addressing and gain practical skills converting between binary and dotted decimal IPv4 addresses.

This topic will cover how to convert between base 2 and base 10 numbering systems.

Video

Video Demonstration 7.1.1.2: Converting Between Binary and Decimal Numbering Systems

Go to the online course to view this video.

Positional Notation (7.1.1.3)

Learning to convert binary to decimal requires an understanding of positional notation. Positional notation means that a digit represents different values depending on the "position" the digit occupies in the sequence of numbers. You already know the most common numbering system, the decimal (base 10) notation system.

The decimal positional notation system operates as described in Figure 7-4.

Radix	10	10	10	10
Position in #	3	2	1	0
Calculate	(10^3)	(10^2)	(10^1)	(10^0)
Positional Value	1000	100	10	1

Figure 7-4   Decimal Positional Notation

The row headings in Figure 7-4 identify

- **Radix** – The 1st row identifies the number base or radix. The decimal notation system is based on 10; therefore, the radix is 10.

- **Position in #** – The 2nd row considers the position of the decimal number starting with, from right to left, 0 (1st position), 1 (2nd position), 2 (3rd position), 3 (4th position). These numbers also represent the exponential value that will be used to calculate the positional value (4th row).

- **Calculate** – The 3rd row calculates the positional value by taking the radix and raising it by the exponential value of its position. Note: n^0 is always = 1.

- **Positional Value** – The first row identifies the number base or radix. Therefore, the value listed, from left to right, represents units of thousands, hundreds, tens, and ones.

To use the positional system, match a given number to its positional value. The example in Figure 7-5 illustrates how positional notation is used with the decimal number 1234.

1234

	Thousands	Hundreds	Tens	Ones
Positional Value	1000	100	10	1
Decimal Number	1	2	3	4
Calculate	1 x1000	2 x100	3 x10	4 x1
Add them up ...	1000	+ 200	+ 30	+ 4
Result	1,234			

Figure 7-5   Applying the Decimal Positional Notation

In contrast, the binary positional notation operates as described in Figure 7-6.

Radix	2	2	2	2	2	2	2	2
Position in #	7	6	5	4	3	2	1	0
Calculate	(2^7)	(2^6)	(2^5)	(2^4)	(2^3)	(2^2)	(2^1)	(2^0)
Positional Value	128	64	32	16	8	4	2	1

Figure 7-6   Binary Positional Notation

The example in Figure 7-7 illustrates how a binary number 11000000 corresponds to the number 192. If the binary number had been 10101000, then the corresponding decimal number would be 168.

11000000

	128	64	32	16	8	4	2	1
Positional Value	128	64	32	16	8	4	2	1
Binary number	1	1	0	0	0	0	0	0
Calculate	1 x 128	1 x 64	0 x 32	0 x 16	0 x 8	0 x 4	0 x 2	0 x 1
Add them up ...	128	+ 64	+ 0	+ 0	+ 0	+ 0	+ 0	+ 0
Result	192							

Figure 7-7   Applying the Binary Positional Notation

Binary to Decimal Conversion (7.1.1.4)

To convert a binary IPv4 address to its dotted decimal equivalent, divide the IPv4 address into four 8-bit octets. Next apply the binary positional value to the first octet binary number and calculate accordingly.

For example, consider that 11000000.10101000.00001011.00001010 is the binary IPv4 address of a host. To convert the binary address to decimal, start with the first octet as shown in Figure 7-8.

11000000.10101000.00001011.00001010

Positional Value	128	64	32	16	8	4	2	1
Binary number	1	1	0	0	0	0	0	0
Calculate	1 x 128	1 x 64	0 x 32	0 x 16	0 x 8	0 x 4	0 x 2	0 x 1
Add them up ...	128	+ 64	+ 0	+ 0	+ 0	+ 0	+ 0	+ 0
Result	192							

192.___.___.___
Dotted Decimal Notation

Figure 7-8   Converting the First Octet to Decimal

Enter the 8-bit binary number under the positional value of row 1 and then calculate to produce the decimal number 192. This number goes into the first octet of the dotted decimal notation.

Next convert the second octet as shown in Figure 7-9.

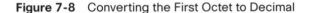

11000000.10101000.00001011.00001010

Positional Value	128	64	32	16	8	4	2	1
Binary number	1	0	1	0	1	0	0	0
Calculate	1 x 128	0 x 64	1 x 32	0 x 16	1 x 8	0 x 4	0 x 2	0 x 1
Add them up ...	128	+ 0	+ 32	+ 0	+ 8	+ 0	+ 0	+ 0
Result	168							

192.168.___.___
Dotted Decimal Notation

Figure 7-9   Converting the Second Octet to Decimal

The resulting decimal value is 168, and it goes into the second octet.

Convert the third octet as shown in Figure 7-10 and the fourth octet as shown in Figure 7-11, which completes the IP address and produces **192.168.11.10**.

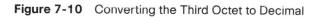

11000000.10101000.00001011.00001010

Positional Value	128	64	32	16	8	4	2	1
Binary number	0	0	0	0	1	0	1	1
Calculate	0 x 128	0 x 64	0 x 32	0 x 16	1 x 8	0 x 4	1 x 2	1 x 1
Add them up ...	0	+ 0	+ 0	+ 0	+ 8	+ 0	+ 2	+ 1
Result	11							

192.168.11.___
Dotted Decimal Notation

Figure 7-10   Converting the Third Octet to Decimal

11000000.10101000.00001011.00001010

Positional Value	128	64	32	16	8	4	2	1
Binary number	0	0	0	0	1	0	1	0
Calculate	0 x 128	0 x 64	0 x 32	0 x 16	1 x 8	0 x 4	1 x 2	0 x 1
Add them up ...	0	+ 0	+ 0	+ 0	+ 8	+ 0	+ 2	+ 0
Result	10							

192.168.11.10
Dotted Decimal Notation

Figure 7-11   Converting the Fourth Octet to Decimal

Interactive Graphic

Activity 7.1.1.5: Binary to Decimal Conversion

Go to the online course to perform this practice activity.

Decimal to Binary Conversion (7.1.1.6)

It is also necessary to understand how to convert a dotted decimal IPv4 address to binary. A useful tool is the binary positional value table. The following illustrates how to use the table to convert decimal to binary:

■ Figure 7-12 questions if the decimal number of the octet (n) is equal to or greater than the most-significant bit (128). If no, then enter binary 0 in the 128 positional value. If yes, then add a binary 1 in the 128 positional value and subtract 128 from the decimal number.

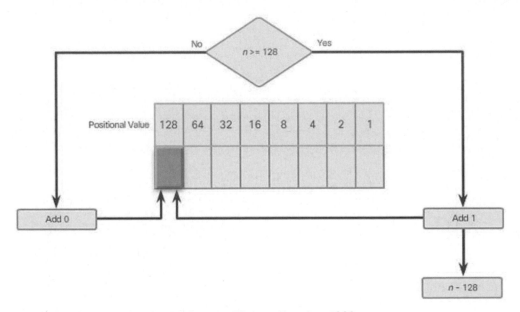

Figure 7-12   Is the Decimal *n* Greater Than or Equal to 128?

■ Figure 7-13 questions if the remainder (n) is equal to or greater than the next most-significant bit (64). If no, then add a binary 0 in the 64 positional value; otherwise, add binary 1 and subtract 64 from the decimal.

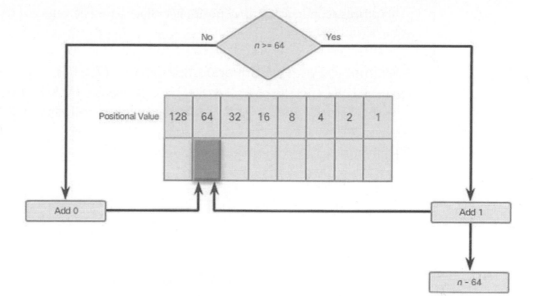

Figure 7-13   Is the Decimal *n* Greater Than or Equal to 64?

- Figure 7-14 questions if the remainder (*n*) is equal to or greater than the next most-significant bit (32). If no, then add a binary 0 in the 32 positional value; otherwise, add binary 1 and subtract 32 from the decimal.

Figure 7-14   Is the Decimal *n* Greater Than or Equal to 32?

This process continues until all positional values have been entered resulting in the equivalent binary value.

Decimal to Binary Conversion Examples (7.1.1.7)

To help understand the process, consider the IP address 192.168.11.10. Using the previously explained process, start with the binary positional value table and the first decimal number 192.

Figure 7-15 illustrates how 192 is converted into binary.

Example: 192.168.10.11

Figure 7-15   192 = 11000000

Because 192 is greater than 128, add a 1 to the high-order positional value to represent 128. Then subtract 128 from 192 to produce a remainder of 64. Because the remainder 64 is equal to the next bit position, add a 1. The result is the binary number 11000000.

Figure 7-16 shows the bit values required in the second octet to convert the decimal number 168 into the binary number 10101000.

Example: 192.168.10.11

Figure 7-16   168 = 10101000

Figure 7-17 shows the bit values required in the third octet to convert the decimal number 10 into the binary number 00001010.

Example: 192.168.10.11

Positional Value	128	64	32	16	8	4	2	1
	0	0	0	0	1	0	1	0

11000000 . 10101000 . 00001010 . _____

Figure 7-17   10 = 000001010

Figure 7-18 shows the bit values required in the fourth octet to convert the decimal number 11 into the binary number 00001011.

Example: 192.168.10.11

Positional Value	128	64	32	16	8	4	2	1
	0	0	0	0	1	0	1	1

11000000 . 10101000 . 00001010 . 00001011

Figure 7-18   11 = 000001011

Converting between binary and decimal may seem challenging at first, but with practice it should become easier over time. Search the Internet for "binary to decimal conversion games" to find some fun practice.

Interactive Graphic

Activity 7.1.1.8: Decimal to Binary Conversion Utility

Go to the online course to perform this practice activity.

Interactive Graphic

Activity 7.1.1.9: Binary Game

Go to the online course to perform this practice activity.

IPv4 Address Structure (7.1.2)

This topic will present the IPv4 address structure.

Network and Host Portions (7.1.2.1)

Understanding binary notation is important when determining if two hosts are in the same network. Recall that an IPv4 address is a hierarchical address that is made up of a network portion and a host portion. When determining the network portion versus the host portion, it is necessary to look at the 32-bit stream. Within the 32-bit stream, a portion of the bits identify the network, and a portion of the bits identify the host as shown in Figure 7-19.

Figure 7-19   Network and Host Position of an IPv4 Address

The bits within the network portion of the address must be identical for all devices that reside in the same network. The bits within the host portion of the address must be unique to identify a specific host within a network. If two hosts have the same bit-pattern in the specified network portion of the 32-bit stream, those two hosts will reside in the same network.

But how do hosts know which portion of the 32 bits identifies the network and which identifies the host? That is the job of the subnet mask.

The Subnet Mask (7.1.2.2)

As shown in Figure 7-20, three dotted decimal IPv4 addresses must be configured when assigning an IPv4 configuration to host:

- **IPv4 address** – Unique IPv4 address of the host
- **Subnet mask** – Used to identify the network/host portion of the IPv4 address
- **Default gateway** – Identifies the local gateway (i.e., local router interface IPv4 address) to reach remote networks

Figure 7-20   IPv4 Configuration of a Host

When an IPv4 address is assigned to a device, the subnet mask is used to determine the network address where the device belongs. The network address represents all the devices on the same network.

Figure 7-21 displays the dotted decimal address and the 32-bit subnet mask. Notice how the subnet mask is essentially a sequence of 1 bits followed by a sequence of 0 bits.

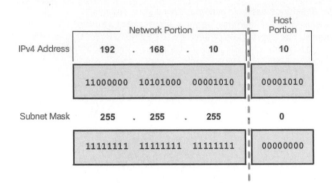

Figure 7-21   Comparing the IPv4 Address and Subnet Mask

To identify the network and host portions of an IPv4 address, the subnet mask is compared to the IPv4 address bit for bit, from left to right, as shown in Figure 7-21. The 1s in the subnet mask identify the network portion while the 0s identify the host portion. Note that the subnet mask does not actually contain the network or host portion of an IPv4 address; it just tells the computer where to look for these portions in a given IPv4 address.

The actual process used to identify the network portion and host portion is called ANDing.

Logical AND (7.1.2.3)

A *logical AND* is one of three basic binary operations used in digital logic. The other two are OR and NOT. Whereas all three are used in data networks, only AND is used in determining the network address. Therefore, our discussion here will be limited to the logical AND operation.

Logical AND is the comparison of two bits that produce the following results:

```
1 AND 1 = 1

0 AND 1 = 0

0 AND 0 = 0

1 AND 0 = 0
```

Note how only a 1 AND 1 produces a 1.

To identify the network address of an IPv4 host, the IPv4 address is logically ANDed, bit by bit, with the subnet mask. ANDing between the address and the subnet mask yields the network address.

To illustrate how AND is used to discover a network address, consider a host with IPv4 address 192.168.10.10 and subnet mask of 255.255.255.0. Figure 7-22 displays the host IPv4 address and subnet mask in dotted decimal and binary.

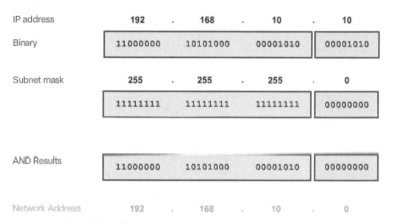

Figure 7-22   Resulting Network Address

The subnet mask is used to identify the AND bits that produce a binary 1 in the AND Results row. All other bit comparison produced binary 0s. Notice how the last octet no longer has any binary 1 bits.

The resulting network address is 192.168.10.0 255.255.255.0. Therefore, host 192.168.10.10 is on network 192.168.10.0 255.255.255.0.

Activity 7.1.2.4: ANDing to Determine the Network Address

Interactive Graphic

Go to the online course to perform this practice activity.

The Prefix Length (7.1.2.5)

Expressing network addresses and host addresses with the dotted decimal subnet mask address can become cumbersome. Fortunately, there is an alternate shorthand method of identifying a subnet mask called the *prefix length*.

Specifically, the prefix length is the number of bits set to 1 in the subnet mask. It is written in "*slash notation*," which is a "/" followed by the number of bits set to 1. Therefore, count the number of bits in the subnet mask and prepend it with a slash.

For example, refer to Table 7-1. The first column lists various subnet masks that can be used with a host address. The second column displays the converted 32-bit binary address. The last column displays the resulting prefix length.

Table 7-1   Subnet Mask in Dotted Decimal, Binary, and Prefix Length

Subnet Mask	32-bit Address	Prefix Length
255.0.0.0	11111111.00000000.00000000.00000000	/8
255.255.0.0	11111111.11111111.00000000.00000000	/16
255.255.255.0	11111111.11111111.11111111.00000000	/24
255.255.255.128	11111111.11111111.11111111.10000000	/25
255.255.255.192	11111111.11111111.11111111.11000000	/26
255.255.255.224	11111111.11111111.11111111.11100000	/27
255.255.255.240	11111111.11111111.11111111.11110000	/28
255.255.255.248	11111111.11111111.11111111.11111000	/29
255.255.255.252	11111111.11111111.11111111.11111100	/30

Using various types of prefix lengths will be discussed later. For now, the focus will be on the /24 (i.e., 255.255.255.0) subnet mask.

Network, Host, and Broadcast Addresses (7.1.2.6)

Each network address contains (or identifies) the following address, as shown in Figure 7-23:

Figure 7-23   Types of Addresses in a Network

- *Network Address* – Address and subnet mask refer to a network. All hosts within the network share the same network address. The host portion is all 0s.

- *Host Addresses* – Unique IP addresses assigned to hosts and devices. The host portion always contains assorted 0s and 1s but never all 0s or all 1s.

- **First Host Address** – First available host IP address in that network. The host portion always has all 0s and ends with a 1.

- **Last Host Address** – Last available host IP address in that network. The host portion always has all 1s and ends with a 0.

- *Broadcast Address* – A special address that communicates with all hosts in a network. For instance, when a host sends a packet to the network broadcast IPv4 address, all other hosts in the network receive the packet. The broadcast address uses the highest address in the network range. The host portion is all 1s.

To help understand network, host, and broadcast addresses, consider the example for network address 10.1.1.0 /24 in Figure 7-24.

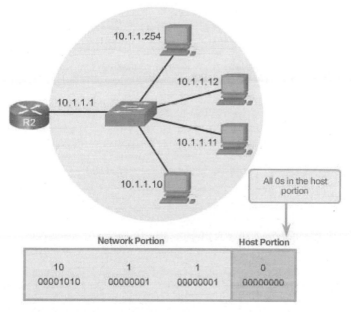

Figure 7-24   Network 10.1.1.0/24

Table 7-2 displays the main address types for the 10.1.1.0/24 network.

Table 7-2   Address Types for 10.1.1.0/24

Address Type	Network Portion	Host Portion
Network Address	10.1.1	0
First Host Address	10.1.1	1
Last Host Address	10.1.1	254
Broadcast Address	10.1.1	255

The concepts discussed in this topic form the basis for understanding IPv4 addressing. Make sure you understand how a network address identifies a network portion and host portion using the subnet mask or prefix length and the ANDing operation. Also make note of the various types of network addresses within a network.

Video Demonstration 7.1.2.7: Network, Host, and Broadcast Addresses

Go to the online course to view this video.

Lab 7.1.2.8: Using the Windows Calculator with Network Addresses

In this lab, you will complete the following objectives:

- Part 1: Access the Windows Calculator
- Part 2: Convert between Numbering Systems
- Part 3: Convert Host IPv4 Addresses and Subnet Masks into Binary
- Part 4: Determine the Number of Hosts in a Network Using Powers of 2
- Part 5: Convert MAC Addresses and IPv6 Addresses to Binary

Lab 7.1.2.9: Converting IPv4 Addresses to Binary

In this lab, you will complete the following objectives:

- Part 1: Convert IPv4 Addresses from Dotted Decimal to Binary
- Part 2: Use Bitwise ANDing Operation to Determine Network Addresses
- Part 3: Apply Network Address Calculations

IPv4 Unicast, Broadcast, and Multicast (7.1.3)

In IPv4 data networks, communication can take place as unicast, broadcast, or multicast. This topic will discuss these three methods of communication in IPv4.

Static IPv4 Address Assignment to a Host (7.1.3.1)

Devices can be assigned an IP address either statically or dynamically.

In networks, some devices require a fixed IP address. For instance, printers, servers, and networking devices need an IP address that does not change. For this reason, these devices are typically assigned static IP addresses.

A host can also be configured with a static IPv4 address such as shown in Figure 7-20 earlier in the chapter. Assigning hosts static IP addresses is acceptable in small networks. However, it would be time-consuming to enter static addresses on each host in a large network. It is important to maintain an accurate list of static IP addresses assigned to each device.

Dynamic IPv4 Address Assignment to a Host (7.1.3.2)

In most data networks, the largest population of hosts includes PCs, tablets, smart-phones, printers, and IP phones. It is also often the case that the user population and their devices change frequently. It would be impractical to statically assign IPv4 addresses for each device. Therefore, these devices are assigned IPv4 addresses dynamically using the Dynamic Host Configuration Protocol (DHCP).

As shown in Figure 7-25, a host can obtain IPv4 addressing information automatically. The host is a DHCP client and requests IPv4 address information from a DHCP server. The DHCP server provides an IPv4 address, subnet mask, default gateway, and other configuration information.

DHCP is generally the preferred method of assigning IPv4 addresses to hosts on large networks. An additional benefit of DHCP is the address is not permanently assigned to a host but is only "leased" for a period of time. If the host is powered down or taken off the network, the address is returned to the pool for reuse. This feature is especially helpful for mobile users that come and go on a network.

Figure 7-25 Dynamic IPv4 Address Assignment

IPv4 Communication (7.1.3.3)

A host successfully connected to a network can communicate with other devices in one of three ways:

- **Unicast** – The process of sending a packet from one host to an individual host.
- **Broadcast** – The process of sending a packet from one host to all hosts in the network.
- **Multicast** – The process of sending a packet from one host to a selected group of hosts, possibly in different networks.

These three types of communication are used for different purposes in data networks. In all three cases, the IPv4 address of the originating host is placed in the packet header as the source address.

Unicast Transmission (7.1.3.4)

Unicast communication is used for normal host-to-host communication in both a client/server and a peer-to-peer network, as shown in Figure 7-26. Unicast packets use the address of the destination device as the destination address and can be routed through an internetwork.

172.16.4.1

172.16.4.253

172.16.4.2   172.16.4.3

Figure 7-26   Unicast Communication

In an IPv4 network, the unicast address applied to an end device is referred to as the host address. For unicast communication, the addresses assigned to the two end devices are used as the source and destination IPv4 addresses. During the encapsulation process, the source host uses its IPv4 address as the source address and the IPv4 address of the destination host as the destination address. Regardless of whether the destination specified a packet as a unicast, broadcast, or multicast; the source address of any packet is always the unicast address of the originating host.

Note

In this course, all communication between devices is unicast unless otherwise noted.

IPv4 unicast host addresses are in the address range of 0.0.0.0 to 223.255.255.255. However, within this range are many addresses that are reserved for special purposes. These special purpose addresses will be discussed later in this chapter.

Broadcast Transmission (7.1.3.5)

Broadcast traffic is used to send packets to all hosts in the network using the broadcast address for the network, as shown in Figure 7-27.

172.16.4.1

172.16.4.253

172.16.4.2

172.16.4.3

Figure 7-27   Broadcast Communication

With a broadcast, the packet contains a destination IPv4 address with all ones (1s) in the host portion. This means that all hosts on that local network (broadcast domain) will receive and look at the packet. Many network protocols, such as DHCP, use broadcasts. When a host receives a packet sent to the network broadcast address, the host processes the packet as it would a packet addressed to its unicast address.

Broadcast may be directed or limited. A *directed broadcast* is sent to all hosts on a specific network. For example, a host on the 172.16.4.0/24 network sends a packet to 172.16.4.255. A *limited broadcast* is sent to 255.255.255.255. By default, routers do not forward broadcasts.

As an example, a host within the 172.16.4.0/24 network would broadcast to all hosts in its network using a packet with a destination address of 255.255.255.255.

When a packet is broadcast, it uses resources on the network and causes every receiving host on the network to process the packet. Therefore, broadcast traffic should be limited so that it does not adversely affect the performance of the network or devices. Because routers separate broadcast domains, subdividing networks can improve network performance by eliminating excessive broadcast traffic.

Multicast Transmission (7.1.3.6)

Multicast transmission reduces traffic by allowing a host to send a single packet to a selected set of hosts that subscribe to a multicast group, as shown in Figure 7-28.

172.16.4.1

172.16.4.2

172.16.4.3
224.10.10.5

172.16.4.4
224.10.10.5

172.16.4.253

Figure 7-28   Multicast Communication

IPv4 has reserved the 224.0.0.0 to 239.255.255.255 addresses as a multicast range. The IPv4 multicast addresses 224.0.0.0 to 224.0.0.255 are reserved for multicasting on the local network only. These addresses are to be used for multicast groups on a local network. A router connected to the local network recognizes that these packets are addressed to a local network multicast group and never forwards them further. A typical use of reserved local network multicast address is in routing protocols using multicast transmission to exchange routing information. For instance, 224.0.0.9 is the multicast address used by Routing Information Protocol (RIP) version 2 to communicate with other RIPv2 routers.

Hosts that receive particular multicast data are called multicast clients. The multicast clients use services requested by a client program to subscribe to the *multicast group*.

Each multicast group is represented by a single IPv4 multicast destination address. When an IPv4 host subscribes to a multicast group, the host processes packets addressed to this multicast address and packets addressed to its uniquely allocated unicast address.

Activity 7.1.3.7: Unicast, Broadcast, or Multicast

Go to the online course to perform this practice activity.

Packet Tracer 7.1.3.8: Investigate Unicast, Broadcast, and Multicast Traffic

This activity will examine unicast, broadcast, and multicast behavior. Most traffic in a network is unicast. When a PC sends an ICMP echo request to a remote router, the source address in the IPv4 packet header is the IPv4 address of the sending PC. The destination address in the IPv4 packet header is the IPv4 address of the interface on the remote router. The packet is sent only to the intended destination.

Using the ping command or the Add Complex PDU feature of Packet Tracer, you can directly ping broadcast addresses to view broadcast traffic.

For multicast traffic, you will view EIGRP traffic. EIGRP is used by Cisco routers to exchange routing information between routers. Routers using EIGRP send packets to the multicast address 224.0.0.10, which represents the group of EIGRP routers. Although these packets are received by other devices, they are dropped at Layer 3 by all devices except EIGRP routers, with no other processing required.

Types of IPv4 Addresses (7.1.4)

This topic will introduce the different types and uses of IPv4 addresses.

Public and Private IPv4 Addresses (7.1.4.1)

Public IPv4 addresses are addresses that are globally routed between ISP (Internet Service Provider) routers. However, not all available IPv4 addresses can be used on the Internet. There are blocks of addresses called private addresses that are used by most organizations to assign IPv4 addresses to internal hosts.

In the mid-1990s *private IPv4 addresses* were introduced because of the depletion of IPv4 address space. Private IPv4 addresses are not unique and can be used by an internal network.

Specifically, the private address blocks are

- **10.0.0.0 /8** or **10.0.0.0** to **10.255.255.255**
- **172.16.0.0 /12** or **172.16.0.0 to 172.31.255.255**
- **192.168.0.0 /16** or **192.168.0.0 to 192.168.255.255**

It is important to know that addresses within these address blocks are not allowed on the Internet and must be filtered (discarded) by Internet routers. For example, in Figure 7-29, users in networks 1, 2, or 3 are sending packets to remote destinations. The Internet Service Provider (ISP) routers would see that the source IPv4 addresses in the packets are from private addresses and would, therefore, discard the packets.

Note

Private addresses are defined in RFC 1918.

Figure 7-29 Private Address are not Routed on the Internet

Most organizations use private IPv4 addresses for their internal hosts. However, these RFC 1918 addresses are not routable in the Internet and must be translated to a public IPv4 address. Network Address Translation (NAT) is used to translate between private IPv4 and public IPv4 addresses. This is usually done on the router that connects the internal network to the ISP's network.

Home routers provide the same capability. For instance, most home routers assign IPv4 addresses to their wired and wireless hosts from the private address of 192.168.1.0 /24. The home router interface that connects to the Internet service provider (ISP) network is assigned a public IPv4 address to use on the Internet.

Interactive Graphic

Activity 7.1.4.2: Pass or Block IPv4 Addresses

Go to the online course to perform this practice activity.

Special User IPv4 Addresses (7.1.4.3)

There are certain addresses such as the network address and broadcast address that cannot be assigned to hosts. There are also special addresses that can be assigned to hosts but with restrictions on how those hosts can interact within the network.

- **Loopback addresses (127.0.0.0 /8 or 127.0.0.1 to 127.255.255.254)** – More commonly identified as only 127.0.0.1, these are special addresses used by a host to direct traffic to itself. For example, it can be used on a host to test if the TCP/IP configuration is operational, as shown in Example 7-1. Notice how the 127.0.0.1 loopback address replies to the ping command. Also note how any address within this block will loop back to the local host, such as shown with the second ping in Example 7-1.

Example 7-1 Ping the Loopback Interface on a PC

```
C:\> ping 127.0.0.1

Pinging 127.0.0.1 with 32 bytes of data:
Reply from 127.0.0.1: bytes=32 time<1ms TTL=128
Reply from 127.0.0.1: bytes=32 time<1ms TTL=128
Reply from 127.0.0.1: bytes=32 time<1ms TTL=128
Reply from 127.0.0.1: bytes=32 time<1ms TTL=128

Ping statistics for 127.0.0.1:
 Packets: Sent = 4, Received = 4, Lost = 0 (0% loss),
Approximate round trip times in milli-seconds:
 Minimum = 0ms, Maximum = 0ms, Average = 0ms

C:\> ping 127.1.1.1

Pinging 127.1.1.1 with 32 bytes of data:
Reply from 127.1.1.1: bytes=32 time<1ms TTL=128
Reply from 127.1.1.1: bytes=32 time<1ms TTL=128
Reply from 127.1.1.1: bytes=32 time<1ms TTL=128
Reply from 127.1.1.1: bytes=32 time<1ms TTL=128

Ping statistics for 127.1.1.1:
 Packets: Sent = 4, Received = 4, Lost = 0 (0% loss),
Approximate round trip times in milli-seconds:
 Minimum = 0ms, Maximum = 0ms, Average = 0ms

C:\>
```

- *Link-Local addresses* **(169.254.0.0 /16 or 169.254.0.1 to 169.254.255.254)** – More commonly known as the Automatic Private IP Addressing (APIPA) addresses, they are used by a Windows DCHP client to self-configure in the event that there are no DHCP servers available. Useful in a peer-to-peer connection.

- *TEST-NET addresses* **(192.0.2.0/24 or 192.0.2.0 to 192.0.2.255)** – These addresses are set aside for teaching and learning purposes and can be used in documentation and network examples.

Note

There are also Experimental Addresses in the block 240.0.0.0 to 255.255.255.254 that are reserved for future use (RFC 3330).

Legacy Classful Addressing (7.1.4.4)

In 1981, Internet IPv4 addresses were assigned using *classful addressing* as defined in RFC 790, Assigned Numbers. Customers were allocated a network address based on one of three classes, A, B, or C. The RFC divided the unicast ranges into specific classes called

- Class A **(0.0.0.0/8 to 127.0.0.0/8)** – Designed to support extremely large networks with more than 16 million host addresses. It used a fixed /8 prefix with the first octet to indicate the network address and the remaining three octets for host addresses. All class A addresses required that the most significant bit of the high-order octet be a zero creating a total of 128 possible class A networks. Figure 7-30 summarizes the class A.

Class A Specifics	
Address block	0.0.0.0 – 127.0.0.0*
Default Subnet Mask	/8 (255.0.0.0)
Maximum Number of Networks	128
Number of Host per Network	16,777,214
High order bit	0xxxxxxx.____.____.____

* 0.0.0.0 and 127.0.0.0 are reserved and cannot be assigned

Figure 7-30   Class A Specifics

■ **Class B (128.0.0.0 /16 to 191.255.0.0 /16)** – Designed to support the needs of moderate to large size networks with up to approximately 65,000 host addresses. It used a fixed /16 prefix with the two high-order octets to indicate the network address and the remaining two octets for host addresses. The most significant two bits of the high-order octet must be 10 creating over 16,000 networks. Figure 7-31 summarizes the class B.

Class B Specifics	
Address block	128.0.0.0 – 191.255.0.0
Default Subnet Mask	/16 (255.255.0.0)
Maximum Number of Networks	16,384
Number of Host per Network	65,534
High order bit	10xxxxxx.____.____.____

Figure 7-31   Class B Specifics

■ **Class C (192.0.0.0 /24 to 223.255.255.0 /24)** – Designed to support small networks with a maximum of 254 hosts. It used a fixed /24 prefix with the first three octets to indicate the network and the remaining octet for the host addresses. The most significant three bits of the high-order octet must be 110 creating over 2 million possible networks. Figure 7-32 summarizes the class C.

Class C Specifics	
Address block	192.0.0.0 – 223.255.255.0
Default Subnet Mask	/24 (255.255.255.0)
Maximum Number of Networks	2,097,152
Number of Host per Network	254
High order bit	110xxxxx.____.____.____

Figure 7-32   Class C Specifics

Note

There is also a Class D multicast block consisting of 224.0.0.0 to 239.0.0.0 and a Class E experimental address block consisting of 240.0.0.0 to 255.0.0.0.

Video

Video Demonstration 7.1.4.5: Classful IPv4 Addressing

Go to the online course to view this video.

Classless Addressing (7.1.4.6)

As shown in Figure 7-33, the classful system allocated 50% of the available IPv4 addresses to 128 Class A networks, 25% of the addresses to Class B, and then Class C shared the remaining 25% with Class D and E.

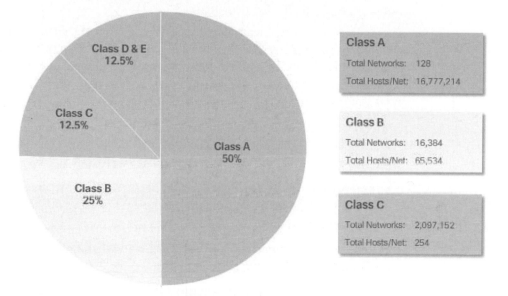

Figure 7-33   Summary of Classful Addressing

The problem is that this wasted a great deal of addresses and exhausted the availability of IPv4 addresses. Not all organizations' requirements fit well into one of these three classes. For example, a company that had a network with 260 hosts would need to be given a class B address with more than 65,000 addresses wasting 64,740 addresses.

Classful addressing was abandoned in the late 1990s for the newer and current classless addressing system. However, there are still classful remnants in networks today. For example, when you assign an IPv4 address to a computer, the operating system examines the address being assigned to determine if this address is a class A, class B, or class C. The operating system then assumes the prefix used by that class and makes the default subnet mask assignment.

The system in use today is referred to as *classless addressing*. The formal name is Classless Inter-Domain Routing (CIDR, pronounced "cider"). In 1993, the IETF created a new set of standards that allowed service providers to allocate IPv4 addresses on any address bit boundary (prefix length) instead of only by a class A, B, or C address. This was to help delay the depletion and eventual exhaustion of IPv4 addresses.

The IETF knew that CIDR was only a temporary solution and that a new IP protocol would have to be developed to accommodate the rapid growth in the number of

Internet users. In 1994, the IETF began its work to find a successor to IPv4, which eventually became IPv6.

So who manages and assigns these IP addresses?

Assignment of IP Addresses (7.1.4.7)

For a company or organization to support network hosts, such as web servers accessible from the Internet, that organization must have a block of public addresses assigned. Remember that public addresses must be unique, and use of these public addresses is regulated and allocated to each organization separately. This is true for IPv4 and IPv6 addresses.

Both IPv4 and IPv6 addresses are managed by the *Internet Assigned Numbers Authority (IANA)* (http://www.iana.org). The IANA manages and allocates blocks of IP addresses to the *Regional Internet Registries (RIRs)*. The RIRs are as follows:

- **American Registry for Internet Numbers** (ARIN) – manages and maintains IPv4 and IPv6 addresses for North America. For more information, go to http://www.arin.net

- **Réseaux IP Europeans** (RIPE) – manages and maintains IPv4 and IPv6 addresses for Europe, the Middle East, and Central Asia; http://www.ripe.net

- **Asia Pacific Network Information Centre** (APNIC) – manages and maintains IPv4 and IPv6 addresses for the Asia and Pacific regions including Australia. For more information, go to http://www.apnic.net

- **African Network Information Centre** (AfriNIC) – manages and maintains IPv4 and IPv6 addresses for Africa. For more information, go to http://www.afrinic.net

- **Regional Latin-American and Caribbean IP Address Registry** (LACNIC) – manages and maintains IPv4 and IPv6 addresses for Latin America and some Caribbean islands. For more information, go to http://www.lacnic.net

RIRs are responsible for allocating IP addresses to ISPs who in turn provide IPv4 address blocks to organizations and smaller ISPs. Organizations can get their addresses directly from an RIR subject to the policies of that RIR.

Interactive Graphic

Activity 7.1.4.8: Public or Private IPv4 Addresses

Go to the online course to perform this practice activity.

Lab 7.1.4.9: Identifying IPv4 Addresses

In this lab, you will complete the following objectives:

- Part 1: Identify IPv4 Addresses
- Part 2: Classify IPv4 Addresses

IPv6 Network Addresses (7.2)

This section will introduce IPv6.

IPv4 Issues (7.2.1)

This topic will examine the reasons for the migration to IPv6.

The Need for IPv6 (7.2.1.1)

IPv6 is designed to be the successor to IPv4. IPv6 has a larger 128-bit address space, providing for 340 undecillion addresses. (That is the number 340, followed by 36 zeroes.) However, IPv6 is more than just larger addresses. When the IETF began its development of a successor to IPv4, it used this opportunity to fix the limitations of IPv4 and include additional enhancements. One example is Internet Control Message Protocol version 6 (ICMPv6), which includes address resolution and address auto-configuration not found in ICMP for IPv4 (ICMPv4). ICMPv4 and ICMPv6 will be discussed later in this chapter.

Need for IPv6

The depletion of IPv4 address space has been the motivating factor for moving to IPv6. As Africa, Asia, and other areas of the world become more connected to the Internet, there are not enough IPv4 addresses to accommodate this growth. As shown in Figure 7-34, four out of the five RIRs have run out of IPv4 addresses.

Figure 7-34 RIR IPv4 Exhaustion Dates

IPv4 has a theoretical maximum of 4.3 billion addresses. Private addresses in combination with Network Address Translation (NAT) have been instrumental in slowing the depletion of IPv4 address space. However, NAT breaks many applications and has limitations that severely impede peer-to-peer communications.

Internet of Everything

The Internet of today is significantly different from the Internet of past decades. The Internet of today is more than email, web pages, and file transfer between computers. The evolving Internet is becoming an Internet of things. No longer will the only devices accessing the Internet be computers, tablets, and smartphones. The sensor-equipped, Internet-ready devices of tomorrow will include everything from automobiles and biomedical devices to household appliances and natural ecosystems.

With an increasing Internet population, a limited IPv4 address space, issues with NAT, and an Internet of Everything, the time has come to begin the transition to IPv6.

IPv4 and IPv6 Coexistence (7.2.1.2)

There is not a single date to move to IPv6. For the foreseeable future, both IPv4 and IPv6 will coexist. The transition is expected to take years. The IETF has created various protocols and tools to help network administrators migrate their networks to IPv6. The migration techniques can be divided into three categories:

- *Dual Stack* – As shown in Figure 7-35, dual stack allows IPv4 and IPv6 to coexist on the same network segment. Dual stack devices run both IPv4 and IPv6 protocol stacks simultaneously.

Figure 7-35   Dual Stack

■ *Tunneling* – As shown in Figure 7-36, tunneling is a method of transporting an IPv6 packet over an IPv4 network. The IPv6 packet is encapsulated inside an IPv4 packet, similar to other types of data.

Figure 7-36   Tunneling

■ **Translation** – As shown in Figure 7-37, *Network Address Translation 64 (NAT64)* allows IPv6-enabled devices to communicate with IPv4-enabled devices using a translation technique similar to NAT for IPv4. An IPv6 packet is translated to an IPv4 packet and vice versa.

Figure 7-37   Translation

Note

Tunneling and translation are only used where needed. The goal should be native IPv6 communications from source to destination.

Interactive Graphic

Activity 7.2.1.3: IPv4 Issues and Solutions

Go to the online course to perform this practice activity.

IPv6 Addressing (7.2.2)

This topic will discuss the representation of IPv6 addresses.

IPv6 Address Representation (7.2.2.1)

IPv6 addresses are 128 bits in length and written as a string of hexadecimal values. Every 4 bits is represented by a single hexadecimal digit, for a total of 32 hexadecimal values, as shown in Figure 7-38. IPv6 addresses are not case-sensitive and can be written in either lowercase or uppercase.

Figure 7-38   IPv6 Hextets

Preferred Format

As shown in Figure 7-38, the preferred format for writing an IPv6 address is x:x:x:x:x:x:x:x, with each "x" consisting of four hexadecimal values. When referring to 8 bits of an IPv4 address we use the term octet. In IPv6, a hextet is the unofficial term used to refer to a segment of 16 bits or four hexadecimal values. Each "x" is a single hextet, 16 bits or four hexadecimal digits.

Preferred format means the IPv6 address is written using all 32 hexadecimal digits. It does not necessarily mean it is the ideal method for representing the IPv6 address. In the following pages, we will see two rules to help reduce the number of digits needed to represent an IPv6 address.

Table 7-3 is a review of the relationship among decimal, binary, and hexadecimal.

Table 7-3   Decimal to Binary to Hexadecimal Conversion

Decimal	Binary	Hexadecimal
0	0000	0
1	0001	1
2	0010	2
3	0011	3
4	0100	4
5	0101	5
6	0110	6
7	0111	7
8	1000	8
9	1001	9
10	1010	A
11	1011	B
12	1100	C
13	1101	D
14	1110	E
15	1111	F

Figure 7-39 has examples of IPv6 addresses in the preferred format.

2001	:	0DB8	:	0000	:	1111	:	0000	:	0000	:	0000	:	0200
2001	:	0DB8	:	0000	:	00A3	:	ABCD	:	0000	:	0000	:	1234
2001	:	0DB8	:	000A	:	0001	:	0000	:	0000	:	0000	:	0100
2001	:	0DB8	:	AAAA	:	0001	:	0000	:	0000	:	0000	:	0200
FE80	:	0000	:	0000	:	0000	:	0123	:	4567	:	89AB	:	CDEF
FE80	:	0000	:	0000	:	0000	:	0000	:	0000	:	0000	:	0001
FF02	:	0000	:	0000	:	0000	:	0000	:	0000	:	0000	:	0001
FF02	:	0000	:	0000	:	0000	:	0000	:	0001	:	FF00	:	0200
0000	:	0000	:	0000	:	0000	:	0000	:	0000	:	0000	:	0001
0000	:	0000	:	0000	:	0000	:	0000	:	0000	:	0000	:	0000

Figure 7-39   Preferred Format Examples

Rule 1 – Omit Leading 0s (7.2.2.2)

The first rule to help reduce the notation of IPv6 addresses is to omit any leading 0s (zeros) in any 16-bit section or hextet. For example:

- 01AB can be represented as 1AB

- 09F0 can be represented as 9F0

- 0A00 can be represented as A00

- 00AB can be represented as AB

This rule only applies to leading 0s, NOT to trailing 0s; otherwise, the address would be ambiguous. For example, the hextet "ABC" could be either "0ABC" or "ABC0," but these do not represent the same value.

Rule 2 – Omit All 0 Segments (7.2.2.3)

The second rule to help reduce the notation of IPv6 addresses is that a double colon (::) can replace any single, contiguous string of one or more 16-bit segments (hextets) consisting of all 0s.

The double colon (::) can only be used once within an address; otherwise, there would be more than one possible resulting address. When used with the omitting leading 0s technique, the notation of IPv6 address can often be greatly reduced. This is commonly known as the compressed format.

Incorrect address:

- 2001:0DB8::ABCD::1234

Possible expansions of ambiguous compressed addresses:

- 2001:0DB8::ABCD:0000:0000:1234

- 2001:0DB8::ABCD:0000:0000:0000:1234

- 2001:0DB8:0000:ABCD::1234

- 2001:0DB8:0000:0000:ABCD::1234

Table 7-4 shows several examples of IPv6 addresses with Rule 1 and Rule 2 being applied.

Table 7-4   Examples of Compressing IPv6 Addresses

Example 1	
Preferred	`2001:0DB8:0000:1111:0000:0000:0000:0200`
Rule 1: Omit leading 0s	`2001: DB8: 0:1111: 0: 0: 0: 200`
Rule 2: Omit all 0 segments	`2001:DB8:0:1111::200`
Example 2	
Preferred	`2001:0DB8:0000:A300:ABCD:0000:0000:1234`
Rule 1: Omit leading 0s	`2001: DB8: 0:A300:ABCD: 0: 0:1234`
Rule 2: Omit all 0 segments	`2001:DB8::ABCD:0:0:100 or 2001:DB8:0:0:ABCD::100`
Example 3	
Preferred	`FE80:0000:0000:0000:0123:4567:89AB:CDEF`
Rule 1: Omit leading 0s	`FE80: 0: 0: 0: 123:4567:89AB:CDEF`
Rule 2: Omit all 0 segments	`FE80::123:4567:89AB:CDEF`
Example 4	
Preferred	`0000:0000:0000:0000:0000:0000:0000:0001`
Rule 1: Omit leading 0s	`0: 0: 0: 0: 0: 0: 0: 1`
Rule 2: Omit all 0 segments	`::1`

Activity 7.2.2.4: Practicing IPv6 Address Representations

Interactive Graphic

Go to the online course to perform this practice activity.

Types of IPv6 Addresses (7.2.3)

This topic will introduce the different types and uses of IPv6 addresses.

IPv6 Address Types (7.2.3.1)

There are three types of IPv6 addresses:

- **Unicast** – An IPv6 unicast address uniquely identifies an interface on an IPv6-enabled device. As shown in Figure 7-40, a source IPv6 address must be a unicast address.

- **Multicast** – An IPv6 multicast address is used to send a single IPv6 packet to multiple destinations.

- **Anycast** – An IPv6 anycast address is any IPv6 unicast address that can be assigned to multiple devices. A packet sent to an anycast address is routed to the nearest device having that address. Anycast addresses are beyond the scope of this course.

Figure 7-40   IPv6 Unicast Communications

Unlike IPv4, IPv6 does not have a broadcast address. However, there is an IPv6 all-nodes multicast address that essentially gives the same result.

IPv6 Prefix Length (7.2.3.2)

Recall that the prefix, or network portion, of an IPv4 address can be identified by a dotted-decimal subnet mask or prefix length (slash notation). For example, an IPv4 address of 192.168.1.10 with dotted-decimal subnet mask 255.255.255.0 is equivalent to 192.168.1.10/24.

IPv6 uses the prefix length to represent the prefix portion of the address. IPv6 does not use the dotted-decimal subnet mask notation. The prefix length is used to indicate the network portion of an IPv6 address using the IPv6 address/prefix length, as shown in Figure 7-41.

Figure 7-41   /64 Prefix

The prefix length can range from 0 to 128. A typical IPv6 prefix length for LANs and most other types of networks is /64. This means the prefix or network portion of the address is 64 bits in length, leaving another 64 bits for the interface ID (host portion) of the address.

IPv6 Unicast Addresses (7.2.3.3)

An IPv6 unicast address uniquely identifies an interface on an IPv6-enabled device. A packet sent to a unicast address is received by the interface that is assigned that address. Similar to IPv4, a source IPv6 address must be a unicast address. The destination IPv6 address can be either a unicast or a multicast address.

The IPv6 unicast address types are shown in Figure 7-42.

Figure 7-42   IPv6 Unicast Address Types

The most common types of IPv6 unicast addresses are global unicast addresses (GUA) and link-local unicast addresses.

Global unicast

A global unicast address is similar to a public IPv4 address. These are globally unique, Internet-routable addresses. Global unicast addresses can be configured statically or assigned dynamically.

Link-local

Link-local addresses are used to communicate with other devices on the same local link. With IPv6, the term link refers to a subnet. Link-local addresses are confined to a single link. Their uniqueness must only be confirmed on that link because they are not routable beyond the link. In other words, routers will not forward packets with a link-local source or destination address.

Unique local

Another type of unicast address is the unique local unicast address. IPv6 unique local addresses have some similarity to RFC 1918 private addresses for IPv4, but there are significant differences. Unique local addresses are used for local addressing within a site or between a limited number of sites. These addresses should not be routable in the global IPv6 and should not be translated to a global IPv6 address. Unique local addresses are in the range of FC00::/7 to FDFF::/7.

With IPv4, private addresses are combined with NAT/PAT to provide a many-to-one translation of private-to-public addresses. This is done because of the limited availability of IPv4 address space. Many sites also use the private nature of RFC 1918 addresses to help secure or hide their network from potential security risks. However, this was never the intended use of these technologies, and the IETF has always recommended that sites take the proper security precautions on their Internet-facing router. Unique local addresses can be used for devices that will never need or have access from another network.

IPv6 Link-Local Unicast Addresses (7.2.3.4)

An IPv6 link-local address enables a device to communicate with other IPv6-enabled devices on the same link and only on that link (subnet). Packets with a source or destination link-local address cannot be routed beyond the link from which the packet originated.

The global unicast address is not a requirement. However, every IPv6-enabled network interface is required to have a link-local address.

If a link-local address is not configured manually on an interface, the device will automatically create its own without communicating with a DHCP server. IPv6-enabled hosts create an IPv6 link-local address even if the device has not been assigned a global unicast IPv6 address. This allows IPv6-enabled devices to communicate with other IPv6-enabled devices on the same subnet. This includes communication with the default gateway (router).

IPv6 link-local addresses are in the FE80::/10 range. The /10 indicates that the first 10 bits are 1111 1110 10xx xxxx. The first hextet has a range of 1111 1110 1000 0000 (FE80) to 1111 1110 1011 1111 (FEBF).

Figure 7-43 shows an example of communication using IPv6 link-local addresses.

Figure 7-43   IPv6 Link-Local Communications

Figure 7-44 shows some of the uses for IPv6 link-local addresses.

Figure 7-44   Use of an IPv6 Link-Local Address

Note

Typically, it is the link-local address of the router, and not the global unicast address, that is used as the default gateway for other devices on the link.

Activity 7.1.2.5: Identify the EIGRP Packet Type

Go to the online course to perform this practice activity.

IPv6 Unicast Addresses (7.2.4)

This topic will introduce IPv6 unicast addressing.

Structure of an IPv6 Global Unicast Address (7.2.4.1)

IPv6 global unicast addresses (GUA) are globally unique and routable on the IPv6 Internet. These addresses are equivalent to public IPv4 addresses. The Internet Committee for Assigned Names and Numbers (ICANN), the operator for IANA, allocates IPv6 address blocks to the five RIRs. Currently, only global unicast addresses with the first three bits of 001 or 2000::/3 are being assigned. In other words, the first hexadecimal digit of a GUA address will begin with a 2 or a 3. This is only 1/8th of the total available IPv6 address space, excluding only a very small portion for other types of unicast and multicast addresses.

> **Note**
>
> The 2001:0DB8::/32 address has been reserved for documentation purposes, including use in examples.

Figure 7-45 shows the structure and range of a global unicast address.

Figure 7-45   IPv6 Global Unicast Address

A global unicast address has three parts:

- Global routing prefix
- Subnet ID
- Interface ID

Global Routing Prefix

The global routing prefix is the prefix, or network, portion of the address that is assigned by the provider, such as an ISP, to a customer or site. Typically, RIRs assign a /48 global routing prefix to customers. This can include everyone from enterprise business networks to individual households.

Figure 7-46 shows the structure of a global unicast address using a /48 global routing prefix. /48 prefixes are the most common global routing prefixes assigned and will be used in most of the examples throughout this course.

Figure 7-46   IPv6 /48 Global Routing Prefix

For example, the IPv6 address 2001:0DB8:ACAD::/48 has a prefix that indicates that the first 48 bits (3 hextets) (2001:0DB8:ACAD) is the prefix or network portion of the address. The double colon (::) prior to the /48 prefix length means the rest of the address contains all 0s.

The size of the global routing prefix determines the size of the subnet ID.

Subnet ID

The Subnet ID is used by an organization to identify subnets within its site. The larger the subnet ID, the more subnets available.

Interface ID

The IPv6 Interface ID is equivalent to the host portion of an IPv4 address. The term Interface ID is used because a single host may have multiple interfaces, each having one or more IPv6 addresses. It is highly recommended that in most cases /64 subnets should be used. In other words a 64-bit interface ID as shown in Figure 7-46.

Note

Unlike IPv4, in IPv6, the all-0s and all-1s host addresses can be assigned to a device. The all-1s address can be used due to the fact that broadcast addresses are not used within IPv6. The all-0s address can also be used but is reserved as a Subnet-Router anycast address, and should be assigned only to routers.

An easy way to read most IPv6 addresses is to count the number of hextets. As shown in Figure 7-47, in a /64 global unicast address the first four hextets are for the network portion of the address, with the fourth hextet indicating the Subnet ID. The remaining four hextets are for the Interface ID.

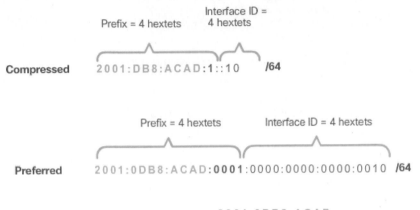

Figure 7-47   Reading a Global Unicast Address

Static Configuration of a Global Unicast Address (7.2.4.2)

Router Configuration

Most IPv6 configuration and verification commands in the Cisco IOS are similar to their IPv4 counterparts. In many cases, the only difference is the use of **ipv6** in place of **ip** within the commands.

The command to configure an IPv6 global unicast address on an interface is **ipv6 address** *ipv6-address/prefix-length*.

Notice that there is not a space between *ipv6-address* and *prefix-length*.

The topology shown in Figure 7-48 uses these IPv6 subnets:

- 2001:0DB8:ACAD:0001:/64 (or 2001:DB8:ACAD:1::/64)
- 2001:0DB8:ACAD:0002:/64 (or 2001:DB8:ACAD:2::/64)
- 2001:0DB8:ACAD:0003:/64 (or 2001:DB8:ACAD:3::/64)

Figure 7-48   IPv6 Configuration Topology

Example 7-2 shows the commands required to configure the IPv6 global unicast address on the GigabitEthernet 0/0, GigabitEthernet 0/1, and Serial 0/0/0 interface of R1.

Example 7-2 Configuring IPv6 on a Router

```
R1(config)# interface gigabitethernet 0/0
R1(config-if)# ipv6 address 2001:db8:acad:1::1/64
R1(config-if)# no shutdown
R1(config-if)# exit
R1(config)# interface gigabitethernet 0/1
R1(config-if)# ipv6 address 2001:db8:acad:2::1/64
R1(config-if)# no shutdown
R1(config-if)# exit
R1(config)# interface serial 0/0/0
R1(config-if)# ipv6 address 2001:db8:acad:3::1/64
R1(config-if)# no shutdown
R1(config-if)# end
R1#
```

Host Configuration

Manually configuring the IPv6 address on a host is similar to configuring an IPv4 address.

As shown in Figure 7-49, the default gateway address configured for PC1 is 2001:DB8:ACAD:1::1. This is the global unicast address of the R1 GigabitEthernet interface on the same network. Alternatively, the default gateway address can be configured to match the link-local address of the GigabitEthernet interface. Either configuration will work.

Figure 7-49   IPv6 Static Host Configuration

Just as with IPv4, configuring static addresses on clients does not scale to larger environments. For this reason, most network administrators in an IPv6 network will enable dynamic assignment of IPv6 addresses.

There are two ways in which a device can obtain an IPv6 global unicast address automatically:

- Stateless Address Autoconfiguration (SLAAC)

- Stateful DHCPv6

Note

When DHCPv6 or SLAAC is used, the local router's link-local address will automatically be specified as the default gateway address.

Dynamic Configuration – SLAAC (7.2.4.3)

Stateless Address Autoconfiguration (SLAAC) is a method that allows a device to obtain its prefix, prefix length, default gateway address, and other information from an *IPv6 router* without the use of a DHCPv6 server. Using SLAAC, devices rely on the local router's ICMPv6 Router Advertisement (RA) messages to obtain the necessary information.

IPv6 routers periodically send out ICMPv6 RA messages, every 200 seconds, to all IPv6-enabled devices on the network. An RA message will also be sent in response to a host sending an ICMPv6 Router Solicitation (RS) message.

IPv6 routing is not enabled by default. To enable a router as an IPv6 router, the **ipv6 unicast-routing** global configuration command must be used.

Note

IPv6 addresses can be configured on a router without it being an IPv6 router.

The ICMPv6 RA message is a suggestion to a device on how to obtain an IPv6 global unicast address. The ultimate decision is up to the device's operating system. The ICMPv6 RA message includes

- **Network prefix and prefix length** – Tells the device which network it belongs to.

- **Default gateway address** – This is an IPv6 link-local address, the source IPv6 address of the RA message.

- **DNS addresses and domain name** – Addresses of DNS servers and a domain name.

As shown in Figure 7-50, there are three options for RA messages:

- Option 1: SLAAC – "I'm everything you need (Prefix, Prefix-length, Default Gateway)"

- Option 2: SLAAC with a *stateless DHCPv6* server – "Here is my information but you need to get other information such as DNS addresses from a DHCPv6 server."

- Option 3: Stateful DHCPv6 (no SLAAC) – "I can't help you. Ask a DHCPv6 server for all your information, except for the default gateway address."

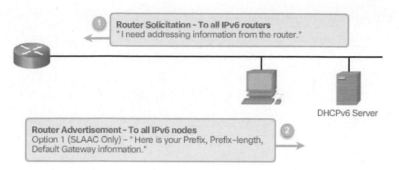

Figure 7-50   Router Solicitation and Router Advertisement Messages

RA Option 1: SLAAC

By default, the RA message suggests that the receiving device use the information in the RA message to create its own IPv6 global unicast address and for all other information. The services of a DHCPv6 server are not required.

SLAAC is stateless, which means there is no central server (for example, a stateful DHCPv6 server) allocating global unicast addresses and keeping a list of devices and their addresses. With SLAAC, the client device uses the information in the RA message to create its own global unicast address. As shown in Figure 7-51, the two parts of the address are created as follows:

- **Prefix** – Received in the RA message
- **Interface ID** – Uses the EUI-64 process or by generating a random 64-bit number

Figure 7-51   Global Unicast Address and SLAAC

Dynamic Configuration – DHCPv6 (7.2.4.4)

By default, the RA message is option 1, SLAAC only. The router's interface can be configured to send a router advertisement using SLAAC and stateless DHCPv6, or stateful DHCPv6 only.

RA Option 2: SLAAC and Stateless DHCPv6

With this option, shown in Figure 7-52, the RA message suggests devices use

- SLAAC to create its own IPv6 global unicast address
- The router's link-local address, the RA's source IPv6 address for the default gateway address.
- A stateless DHCPv6 server to obtain other information such as a DNS server address and a domain name.

Figure 7-52   Option 2: SLAAC and Stateless DHCP

A stateless DHCPv6 server distributes DNS server addresses and domain names. It does not allocate global unicast addresses.

RA Option 3: Stateful DHCPv6

An RA with option 3 (DHCPv6 Only) will require the client to obtain all the information from a DHCPv6 server except the default gateway address. The default gateway address is the RA's source IPv6 address. This *stateful DHCPv6* option is similar to DHCP for IPv4. A device can automatically receive its addressing information including a global unicast address, prefix length, and the addresses of DNS servers using the services of a stateful DHCPv6 server.

With this option the RA message suggests devices use

- The router's link-local address, the RA's source IPv6 address for the default gateway address.

- A stateful DHCPv6 server to obtain a global unicast address, DNS server address, domain name, and all other information.

A stateful DHCPv6 server allocates and maintains a list of which device receives which IPv6 address. DHCP for IPv4 is stateful.

Note

The default gateway address can only be obtained dynamically from the RA message. The stateless or stateful DHCPv6 server does not provide the default gateway address.

EUI-64 Process and Randomly Generated (7.2.4.5)

When the RA message is either SLAAC or SLAAC with stateless DHCPv6, the client must generate its own Interface ID. The client knows the prefix portion of the address from the RA message but must create its own Interface ID. The Interface ID can be created using the EUI-64 process or a randomly generated 64-bit number, as shown in Figure 7-53.

Figure 7-53   EUI-64 Example

EUI-64 Process

IEEE defined the *Extended Unique Identifier (EUI)* or modified *EUI-64* process. This process uses a client's 48-bit Ethernet MAC address and inserts another 16 bits in the middle of the 48-bit MAC address to create a 64-bit Interface ID.

Ethernet MAC addresses are usually represented in hexadecimal and are made up of two parts:

- **Organizationally Unique Identifier (OUI)** – The OUI is a 24-bit (6 hexadecimal digits) vendor code assigned by IEEE.

- **Device Identifier** – The device identifier is a unique 24-bit (6 hexadecimal digits) value within a common OUI.

An EUI-64 Interface ID is represented in binary and is made up of three parts:

- 24-bit OUI from the client MAC address, but the 7th bit (the Universally/Locally (U/L) bit) is reversed. This means that if the 7th bit is a 0, it becomes a 1, and vice versa.

- The inserted 16-bit value FFFE (in hexadecimal).

- 24-bit Device Identifier from the client MAC address.

The EUI-64 process is illustrated in Figure 7-54, using R1's GigabitEthernet MAC address of FC99:4775:CEE0.

Figure 7-54 EUI-64 Process

Step 1.   Divide the MAC address between the OUI and device identifier.

Step 2.   Insert the hexadecimal value FFFE, which in binary is: 1111 1111 1111 1110.

Step 3.   Convert the first 2 hexadecimal values of the OUI to binary and flip the U/L bit (bit 7). In this example, the 0 in bit 7 is changed to a 1.

The result is an EUI-64 generated Interface ID of FE99:47FF:FE75:CEE0.

Note

The use of the U/L bit, and the reasons for reversing its value, are discussed in RFC 5342.

Example 7-3 shows PCA's IPv6 global unicast address dynamically created using SLAAC and the EUI-64 process. An easy way to identify that an address was more than likely created using EUI-64 is the FFFE located in the middle of the Interface ID, as shown in Example 7-3.

Example 7-3 Verifying EUI-64 on a PC

```
PCA> ipconfig
Windows IP Configuration
Ethernet adapter Local Area Connection:
 Connection-specific DNS Suffix .
 IPv6 Address. . . . . . . . . . : 2001:db8:acad:1:fc99:47ff:fe75:cee0
 Link-local IPv6 Address . . . . : fe80::fc99:47ff:fe75:cee0
 Default Gateway . . . . . . . : fe80::1
```

The advantage of EUI-64 is the Ethernet MAC address can be used to determine the Interface ID. It also allows network administrators to easily track an IPv6 address to an end device using the unique MAC address. However, this has caused privacy concerns among many users. They are concerned that their packets can be traced to the actual physical computer. Due to these concerns, a randomly generated Interface ID may be used instead.

Randomly Generated Interface IDs

Depending upon the operating system, a device may use a randomly generated Interface ID instead of using the MAC address and the EUI-64 process. For example, beginning with Windows Vista, Windows uses a randomly generated Interface ID instead of one created with EUI-64. Windows XP and previous Windows operating systems used EUI-64.

After the Interface ID is established, either through the EUI-64 process or through random generation, it can be combined with an IPv6 prefix in the RA message to create a global unicast address, as shown in Example 7-4.

Example 7-4 Verifying Random 64-bit Number on a PC

```
PCB> ipconfig
Windows IP Configuration
Ethernet adapter Local Area Connection:
 Connection-specific DNS Suffix :
 IPv6 Address. . . . . . . . . : 2001:db8:acad:1:50a5:8a35:a5bb:66e1
 Link-local IPv6 Address . . . . : fe80::50a5:8a35:a5bb:66e1
 Default Gateway . . . . . . . : fe80::1
```

Note

To ensure the uniqueness of any IPv6 unicast address, the client may use a process known as Duplicate Address Detection (DAD). This is similar to an ARP request for its own address. If there isn't a reply, then the address is unique.

Dynamic Link-Local Addresses (7.2.4.6)

All IPv6 devices must have an IPv6 link-local address. A link-local address can be established dynamically or configured manually as a static link-local address.

Figure 7-55 shows the link-local address is dynamically created using the FE80::/10 prefix and the Interface ID using the EUI-64 process or a randomly generated 64-bit number.

Figure 7-55   IPv6 Link-Local Address

Operating systems will typically use the same method for both a SLAAC created global unicast address and a dynamically assigned link-local address (see the link-local addresses in Examples 7-3 and 7-4).

Cisco routers automatically create an IPv6 link-local address whenever a global unicast address is assigned to the interface. By default, Cisco IOS routers use EUI-64 to generate the Interface ID for all link-local address on IPv6 interfaces. For serial interfaces, the router will use the MAC address of an Ethernet interface. Recall that a link-local address must be unique only on that link or network. However, a drawback to using the dynamically assigned link-local address is its long interface ID, which makes it challenging to identify and remember assigned addresses. Example 7-5 displays the MAC address on router R1's GigabitEthernet 0/0 interface. This address is used to dynamically create the link-local address on the same interface, as shown in the output for the **show ipv6 interface brief** command.

Example 7-5 Router's EUI-64 Generated Link-Local Addresses

```
R1# show interface gigabitethernet 0/0
GigabitEthernet0/0 is up, line protocol is up
 Hardware is CN Gigabit Ethernet, address is fc99.4775.c3e0 (bia fc99.4775.c3e0)
<Output Omitted>


R1# show ipv6 interface brief
GigabitEthernet0/0 [up/up]
 FE80::FE99:47FF:FE75:C3E0
 2001:DB8:ACAD:1::1
GigabitEthernet0/1 [up/up]
 FE80::FE99:47FF:FE75:C3E1
 2001:DB8:ACAD:2::1
Serial0/0/0 [up/up]
 FE80::FE99:47FF:FE75:C3E0
 2001:DB8:ACAD:3::1
Serial0/0/1 [administratively down/down]
 unassigned
R1#
```

To make it easier to recognize and remember these addresses on routers, it is common to statically configure IPv6 link-local addresses on routers.

Static Link-Local Addresses (7.2.4.7)

Configuring the link-local address manually provides the ability to create an address that is recognizable and easier to remember. Typically, it is only necessary to create recognizable link-local addresses on routers. This is beneficial because router link-local addresses are used as default gateway addresses and in routing advertisement messages.

Link-local addresses can be configured manually using the same interface command used to create IPv6 global unicast addresses but with the additional **link-local** parameter. When an address begins with this hextet within the range of FE80 to FEBF, the link-local parameter must follow the address. The syntax to configure a link-local address is as follows:

```
Router(config-if)# ipv6 address link-local-address link-local
```

Example 7-6 shows the configuration of a link-local address using the **ipv6 address** interface command.

Example 7-6 Configuring Link-Local Addresses on R1

```
R1(config)# interface gigabitethernet 0/0
R1(config-if)# ipv6 address fe80::1 ?
 link-local Use link-local address

R1(config-if)# ipv6 address fe80::1 link-local
R1(config-if)# exit
R1(config)# interface gigabitethernet 0/1
R1(config-if)# ipv6 address fe80::1 link-local
R1(config-if)# exit
R1(config)# interface serial 0/0/0
R1(config-if)# ipv6 address fe80::1 link-local
R1(config-if)#
```

The link-local address FE80::1 is used to make it easily recognizable as belonging to router R1. The same IPv6 link-local address is configured on all of R1's interfaces. FE80::1 can be configured on each link because it only has to be unique on that link.

Similar to R1, router R2 would be configured with FE80::2 as the IPv6 link-local address on all of its interfaces.

Verifying IPv6 Address Configuration (7.2.4.8)

As shown in Example 7-7, the command to verify the IPv6 interface configuration is similar to the command used for IPv4.

Example 7-7 Verifying IPv6 Interface Configuration

```
R1# show ipv6 interface brief
GigabitEthernet0/0 [up/up]
 FE80::1
 2001:DB8:ACAD:1::1
GigabitEthernet0/1 [up/up]
 FE80::1
 2001:DB8:ACAD:2::1
Serial0/0/0 [up/up]
 FE80::1
 2001:DB8:ACAD:3::1
Serial0/0/1 [administratively down/down]
 unassigned
R1#
```

The **show interface** command displays the MAC address of the Ethernet interfaces. EUI-64 uses this MAC address to generate the Interface ID for the link-local address. Additionally, the **show ipv6 interface brief** command displays abbreviated output for each of the interfaces. The **[up/up]** output on the same line as the interface indicates the Layer 1/Layer 2 interface state. This is the same as the **Status** and **Protocol** columns in the equivalent IPv4 command.

Notice that each interface has two IPv6 addresses. The second address for each interface is the global unicast address that was configured. The first address, the one that begins with FE80, is the link-local unicast address for the interface. Recall that the link-local address is automatically added to the interface when a global unicast address is assigned.

Also, notice that R1's Serial 0/0/0 link-local address is the same as its GigabitEthernet 0/0 interface. Serial interfaces do not have Ethernet MAC addresses, so Cisco IOS uses the MAC address of the first available Ethernet interface. This is possible because link-local interfaces only have to be unique on that link.

The link-local address of the router interface is typically the default gateway address for devices on that link or network.

As shown in Example 7-8, the **show ipv6 route** command can be used to verify that IPv6 networks and specific IPv6 interface addresses have been installed in the IPv6 routing table. The **show ipv6 route** command will only display IPv6 networks, not IPv4 networks.

Example 7-8 Verifying IPv6 Routing Table

```
R1# show ipv6 route
IPv6 Routing Table - default - 7 entries
Codes: C - Connected, L - Local, S - Static, U - Per-user Static

<output omitted>

C 2001:DB8:ACAD:1::/64 [0/0]
 via GigabitEthernet0/0, directly connected
L 2001:DB8:ACAD:1::1/128 [0/0]
 via GigabitEthernet0/0, receive
C 2001:DB8:ACAD:2::/64 [0/0]
 via GigabitEthernet0/1, directly connected
L 2001:DB8:ACAD:2::1/128 [0/0]
 via GigabitEthernet0/1, receive
C 2001:DB8:ACAD:3::/64 [0/0]
 via Serial0/0/0, directly connected
L 2001:DB8:ACAD:3::1/128 [0/0]
 via Serial0/0/0, receive
L FF00::/8 [0/0]
 via Null0, receive
R1#
```

Within the route table, a C next to a route indicates that this is a directly connected network. When the router interface is configured with a global unicast address and is in the "up/up" state, the IPv6 prefix and prefix length are added to the IPv6 routing table as a connected route.

> **Note**
>
> The L indicates a Local route, the specific IPv6 address assigned to the interface. This is not a link-local address. Link-local addresses are not included in the router's routing table because they are not routable addresses.

The IPv6 global unicast address configured on the interface is also installed in the routing table as a local route. The local route has a /128 prefix. Local routes are used by the routing table to efficiently process packets with a destination address of the router's interface address.

The **ping** command for IPv6 is identical to the command used with IPv4, except that an IPv6 address is used. As shown in Example 7-9, the command is used to verify Layer 3 connectivity between R1 and PC1.

Example 7-9 Verifying IPv6 Connectivity

```
R1# ping 2001:db8:acad:1::10
Type escape sequence to abort.
Sending 5, 100-byte ICMP Echos to 2001:DB8:ACAD:1::10, timeout is 2 seconds:
!!!!!
Success rate is 100 percent (5/5)
R1#
```

When pinging a link-local address from a router, Cisco IOS will prompt the user for the exit interface. Because the destination link-local address can be on one or more of its links or networks, the router needs to know which interface to send the ping to.

Packet Tracer
☐ Activity

Packet Tracer 7.2.4.9: Configuring IPv6 Addressing

In this activity, you will practice configuring IPv6 addresses on a router, servers, and clients. You will also practice verifying your IPv6 addressing implementation.

IPv6 Multicast Addresses (7.2.5)

This topic will present IPv6 multicast addressing.

Assigned IPv6 Multicast Addresses (7.2.5.1)

IPv6 multicast addresses are similar to IPv4 multicast addresses. Recall that a multicast address is used to send a single packet to one or more destinations (multicast group). IPv6 multicast addresses have the prefix FF00::/8.

Note

Multicast addresses can only be destination addresses and not source addresses.

There are two types of IPv6 multicast addresses:

- Assigned multicast

- Solicited node multicast

Assigned Multicast

Assigned multicast addresses are reserved multicast addresses for predefined groups of devices. An assigned multicast address is a single address used to reach a group of devices running a common protocol or service. Assigned multicast addresses are used in context with specific protocols such as DHCPv6.

Two common IPv6 assigned multicast groups include

- FF02::1 All-nodes multicast group – This is a multicast group that all IPv6-enabled devices join. A packet sent to this group is received and processed by all IPv6 interfaces on the link or network. This has the same effect as a broadcast address in IPv4. Figure 7-56 shows an example of communication using the all-nodes multicast address. An IPv6 router sends Internet Control Message Protocol version 6 (ICMPv6) RA messages to the all-node multicast group. The RA message informs all IPv6-enabled devices on the network about addressing information, such as the prefix, prefix length, and default gateway.

Source IPv6 Address	Destination IPv6 Address
2001:0DB8:ACAD:1::1	FF02::1

2001:0DB8:ACAD:1::1/64

2001:0DB8:ACAD:1::10/64

2001:0DB8:ACAD:1::20/64

2001:0DB8:ACAD:1::8/64

2001:0DB8:ACAD:1::9/64

Figure 7-56   IPv6 All-Nodes Multicast Communications

- **FF02::2 All-routers multicast group** – This is a multicast group that all IPv6 routers join. A router becomes a member of this group when it is enabled as an IPv6 router with the **ipv6 unicast-routing** global configuration command. A packet sent to this group is received and processed by all IPv6 routers on the link or network.

IPv6-enabled devices send ICMPv6 Router Solicitation (RS) messages to the all-routers multicast address. The RS message requests an RA message from the IPv6 router to assist the device in its address configuration.

Solicited-Node IPv6 Multicast Addresses (7.2.5.2)

A *solicited-node multicast address*, shown in Figure 7-57, is similar to the all-nodes multicast address. The advantage of a solicited-node multicast address is that it is mapped to a special Ethernet multicast address. This allows the Ethernet NIC to filter the frame by examining the destination MAC address without sending it to the IPv6 process to see if the device is the intended target of the IPv6 packet.

Figure 7-57   IPv6 Solicited-Node Multicast Address

Lab 7.2.5.3: Identifying IPv6 Addresses

In this lab, you will complete the following objectives:

- Part 1: Identify the Different Types of IPv6 Addresses
- Part 2: Examine a Host IPv6 Network Interface and Address
- Part 3: Practice IPv6 Address Abbreviation

Lab 7.2.5.4: Configuring IPv6 Addresses on Network Devices

In this lab, you will complete the following objectives:

- Part 1: Set Up Topology and Configure Basic Router and Switch Settings
- Part 2: Configure IPv6 Addresses Manually
- Part 3: Verify End-to-End Connectivity

Connectivity Verification (7.3)

This section will introduce verifying IP connectivity.

ICMP (7.3.1)

Both IPv4 and IPv6 use the ICMP protocol for various purposes including verifying connectivity. This topic will introduce the use of ICMP in IPv4 and IPv6.

ICMPv4 and ICMPv6 (7.3.1.1)

Although IP is only a best-effort protocol, the TCP/IP suite does provide for messages to be sent in the event of certain errors. These messages are sent using the services of ICMP. The purpose of these messages is to provide feedback about issues related to the processing of IP packets under certain conditions, not to make IP reliable. ICMP messages are not required and are often not allowed within a network for security reasons.

ICMP is available for both IPv4 and IPv6. ICMPv4 is the messaging protocol for IPv4. ICMPv6 provides these same services for IPv6 but includes additional functionality. In this course, the term ICMP will be used when referring to both ICMPv4 and ICMPv6.

The types of ICMP messages, and the reasons why they are sent, are extensive. We will discuss some of the more common messages.

ICMP messages common to both ICMPv4 and ICMPv6 include

- Host confirmation
- Destination or Service Unreachable
- Time exceeded
- Route redirection

Host Confirmation

An ICMP Echo Message can be used to determine if a host is operational. The local host sends an ICMP Echo Request to a host. If the host is available, the destination host responds with an Echo Reply. This use of the ICMP Echo messages is the basis of the ping utility.

Destination or Service Unreachable

When a host or gateway receives a packet that it cannot deliver, it can use an ICMP Destination Unreachable message to notify the source that the destination or service is unreachable. The message will include a code that indicates why the packet could not be delivered.

Some of the Destination Unreachable codes for ICMPv4 are

- 0 – Net unreachable
- 1 – Host unreachable
- 2 – Protocol unreachable
- 3 – Port unreachable

Note

ICMPv6 has similar but slightly different codes for Destination Unreachable messages.

Time Exceeded

An ICMPv4 Time Exceeded message is used by a router to indicate that a packet cannot be forwarded because the Time to Live (TTL) field of the packet was decremented to 0. If a router receives a packet and decrements the TTL field in the IPv4 packet to zero, it discards the packet and sends a Time Exceeded message to the source host.

ICMPv6 also sends a Time Exceeded message if the router cannot forward an IPv6 packet because the packet has expired. IPv6 does not have a TTL field; it uses the hop limit field to determine if the packet has expired.

ICMPv6 Router Solicitation and Router Advertisement Messages (7.3.1.2)

The informational and error messages found in ICMPv6 are very similar to the control and error messages implemented by ICMPv4. However, ICMPv6 has new features and improved functionality not found in ICMPv4. ICMPv6 messages are encapsulated in IPv6.

ICMPv6 includes four new protocols as part of the Neighbor Discovery Protocol (ND or NDP).

Messaging between an IPv6 router and an IPv6 device:

- *Router Solicitation (RS) message*
- *Router Advertisement (RA) message*

Messaging between IPv6 devices:

- *Neighbor Solicitation (NS) message*
- *Neighbor Advertisement (NA) message*

Note

ICMPv6 ND also includes the redirect message, which has a similar function to the redirect message used in ICMPv4.

Figure 7-58 shows an example of a PC and router exchanging Solicitation and Router Advertisement messages.

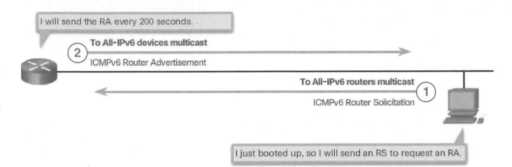

Figure 7-58   Messaging Between an IPv6 Router and an IPv6 Device

1. When a host is configured to obtain its addressing information automatically using Stateless Address Autoconfiguration (SLAAC), the host will send an RS message to the router requesting an RA message.

2. RA messages are sent by routers to provide addressing information to hosts using SLAAC. The RA message can include addressing information for the host such as the prefix, prefix length, DNS address, and domain name. A router will send an RA message periodically or in response to an RS message. A host using SLAAC will set its default gateway to the link-local address of the router that sent the RA.

Neighbor Solicitation and Neighbor Advertisement messages are used for Address resolution and Duplicate Address Detection (DAD).

Address Resolution

Address resolution is used when a device on the LAN knows the IPv6 unicast address of a destination but does not know its Ethernet MAC address. To determine the MAC address for the destination, the device will send an NS message to the solicited node address. The message will include the known (targeted) IPv6 address. The device that has the targeted IPv6 address will respond with an NA message containing its Ethernet MAC address. Figure 7-59 shows two PCs exchanging NS and NA messages.

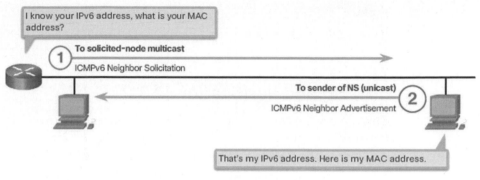

Figure 7-59 Messaging Between IPv6 Devices

1. NS messages are sent when a device knows the IPv6 address of a device but does not its MAC address. This is equivalent to an ARP Request for IPv4.

2. NA messages are sent in response to an NS message and matches the target IPv6 address in the NS. The NA message includes the device's Ethernet MAC address. This is equivalent to an ARP Reply for IPv4.

Duplicate Address Detection

When a device is assigned a global unicast or link-local unicast address, it is recommended that DAD is performed on the address to ensure that it is unique. To check the uniqueness of an address, the device will send an NS message with its own IPv6 address as the targeted IPv6 address, shown in Figure 7-60. If another device on the network has this address, it will respond with an NA message. This NA message will notify the sending device that the address is in use. If a corresponding NA message is not returned within a certain period of time, the unicast address is unique and acceptable for use.

Figure 7-60 Duplicate Address Detection (DAD)

Note

DAD is not required, but RFC 4861 recommends that DAD is performed on unicast addresses.

Testing and Verification (7.3.2)

This topic will introduce the use of the ping and traceroute utilities for testing networks.

Ping – Testing the Local Stack (7.3.2.1)

Ping is a testing utility that uses ICMP echo request and echo reply messages to test connectivity between hosts. Ping works with both IPv4 and IPv6 hosts.

To test connectivity to another host on a network, an echo request is sent to the host address using the ping command. If the host at the specified address receives the echo request, it responds with an echo reply. As each echo reply is received, ping provides feedback on the time between when the request was sent and when the reply was received. This can be a measure of network performance.

Ping has a timeout value for the reply. If a reply is not received within the timeout, ping provides a message indicating that a response was not received. This usually indicates that there is a problem, but could also indicate that security features blocking ping messages have been enabled on the network.

After all the requests are sent, the ping utility provides a summary that includes the success rate and average round-trip time to the destination.

Pinging the Local Loopback

There are some special testing and verification cases for which we can use ping. One case is for testing the internal configuration of IPv4 or IPv6 on the local host. To perform this test, we ping the local loopback address of 127.0.0.1 for IPv4 (::1 for IPv6). Testing the IPv4 loopback is shown in Figure 7-61.

Figure 7-61   Testing Local TCP/IP Stack

A response from 127.0.0.1 for IPv4, or ::1 for IPv6, indicates that IP is properly installed on the host. This response comes from the network layer. This response is not, however, an indication that the addresses, masks, or gateways are properly configured nor does it indicate anything about the status of the lower layer of the network stack. This simply tests IP down through the network layer of IP. An error message indicates that TCP/IP is not operational on the host.

Ping – Testing Connectivity to the Local LAN (7.3.2.2)

You can also use ping to test the ability of a host to communicate on the local network. This is generally done by pinging the IP address of the default gateway for the host, as shown in Figure 7-62. A ping to the gateway indicates that the host and the router interface serving as the gateway are both operational on the local network.

Figure 7-62   Testing IPv4 Connectivity to Local Network

For this test, the gateway address is most often used because the router is normally always operational. If the gateway address does not respond, a ping can be sent to the IP address of another host on the local network that is known to be operational.

If either the gateway or another host responds, then the local host can successfully communicate over the local network. If the gateway does not respond but another host does, this could indicate a problem with the router interface serving as the gateway.

One possibility is that the wrong gateway address has been configured on the host. Another possibility is that the router interface may be fully operational but have security applied to it that prevents it from processing or responding to ping requests.

Ping – Testing Connectivity to Remote (7.3.2.3)

Ping can also be used to test the ability of a local host to communicate across an internetwork. The local host can ping an operational IPv4 host of a remote network, as shown in Figure 7-63.

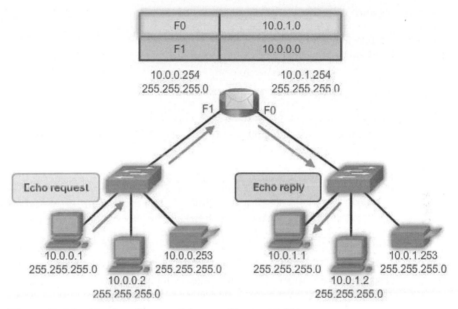

F0	10.0.1.0
F1	10.0.0.0

Figure 7-63 Testing Connectivity to a Remote LAN

If this ping is successful, the operation of a large piece of the internetwork can be verified. A successful ping across the internetwork confirms communication on the local network, the operation of the router serving as the gateway, and the operation of all other routers that might be in the path between the local network and the network of the remote host.

Additionally, the functionality of the remote host can be verified. If the remote host could not communicate outside of its local network, it would not have responded.

Note

Many network administrators limit or prohibit the entry of ICMP messages into the corporate network; therefore, the lack of a ping response could be due to security restrictions.

Traceroute – Testing the Path (7.3.2.4)

Ping is used to test connectivity between two hosts but does not provide information about the details of devices between the hosts. Traceroute (tracert) is a utility that generates a list of hops that were successfully reached along the path. This list can provide important verification and troubleshooting information. If the data reaches the destination, then the trace lists the interface of every router in the path between the hosts. If the data fails at some hop along the way, the address of the last router that responded to the trace can provide an indication of where the problem or security restrictions are found.

Round Trip Time (RTT)

Using traceroute provides round trip time for each hop along the path and indicates if a hop fails to respond. The round trip time is the time a packet takes to reach the remote host and for the response from the host to return. An asterisk (*) is used to indicate a lost or unreplied packet.

This information can be used to locate a problematic router in the path. If the display shows high response times or data losses from a particular hop, this is an indication that the resources of the router or its connections may be stressed.

IPv4 TTL and IPv6 Hop Limit

Traceroute makes use of a function of the TTL field in IPv4 and the Hop Limit field in IPv6 in the Layer 3 headers along with the ICMP time-exceeded message.

The first sequence of messages sent from traceroute will have a TTL field value of 1. This causes the TTL to timeout the IPv4 packet at the first router. This router then responds with an ICMPv4 message. Traceroute now has the address of the first hop.

Traceroute then progressively increments the TTL field (2, 3, 4...) for each sequence of messages. This provides the trace with the address of each hop as the packets timeout further down the path. The TTL field continues to be increased until the destination is reached or it is incremented to a predefined maximum.

After the final destination is reached, the host responds with either an ICMP port unreachable message or an ICMP echo reply message instead of the ICMP time exceeded message.

Interactive Graphic

Go to the online course to view an animation of how Traceroute takes advantage of TTL.

**Packet Tracer
☐ Activity**

Packet Tracer 7.3.2.5: Verifying IPv4 and IPv6 Addressing

IPv4 and IPv6 can coexist on the same network. From the command prompt of a PC, there are some differences in the way commands are issued and in the way output is displayed.

Packet Tracer 7.3.2.6: Pinging and Tracing to Test the Path

There are connectivity issues in this activity. In addition to gathering and documenting information about the network, you will locate the problems and implement acceptable solutions to restore connectivity.

Lab 7.3.2.7: Testing Network Connectivity with Ping and Traceroute

In this lab, you will complete the following objectives:

- Part 1: Build and Configure the Network
- Part 2: Use Ping Command for Basic Network Testing
- Part 3: Use Tracert and Traceroute Commands for Basic Network Testing
- Part 4: Troubleshoot the Topology

Lab 7.3.2.8: Mapping the Internet

In this lab, you will complete the following objectives:

- Part 1: Test Network Connectivity Using Ping
- Part 2: Trace a Route to a Remote Server Using Windows Tracert
- Part 3: Trace a Route to a Remote Server Using Web-Based and Software Tools
- Part 4: Compare Traceroute Results

Packet Tracer 7.3.2.9: Troubleshooting IPv4 and IPv6 Addressing

You are a network technician working for a company that has decided to migrate from IPv4 to IPv6. In the interim, they must support both protocols (dual stack). Three co-workers have called the help desk with problems and have received limited assistance. The help desk has escalated the matter to you, a Level 2 support technician.

Summary (7.4)

Class Activity 7.4.1.1: The Internet of Everything...Naturally!

In this chapter, you learned about how small- to medium-sized businesses are connected to networks in groups. The Internet of Everything was also introduced in the beginning modeling activity.

For this activity, choose one of the following:

- Online banking
- World news
- Weather forecasting/climate
- Traffic conditions

Devise an IPv6 addressing scheme for the area you chose. Include in your addressing scheme how you would plan for

- Subnetting
- Unicasts
- Multicasts
- Broadcasts

Keep a copy of your scheme to share with the class or learning community.
Be prepared to explain

- How subnetting, unicasts, multicasts, and broadcasts would be incorporated.
- Where your addressing scheme could be used.
- How small- to medium-size businesses would be impacted by using your plan.

Packet Tracer 7.4.1.2: Skills Integration Challenge

Your company has won a contract to set up a small network for a restaurant owner. There are two restaurants near each other, and they all share one connection. The equipment and cabling is installed, and the network administrator has designed the implementation plan. Your job is to implement the rest of the addressing scheme according to the abbreviated Addressing Table and verify connectivity.

IP addresses are hierarchical with network, subnetwork, and host portions. An IP address can represent a complete network, a specific host, or the broadcast address of the network.

Understanding binary notation is important when determining if two hosts are in the same network. The bits within the network portion of the IP address must be identical for all devices that reside in the same network. The subnet mask or prefix is used to determine the network portion of an IP address. IP addresses can be assigned either statically or dynamically. DHCP enables the automatic assignment of addressing information such as IP address, subnet mask, default gateway, and other configuration information.

IPv4 hosts can communicate one of three different ways: unicast, broadcast, or multicast. Also, blocks of addresses that are used in networks that require limited or no Internet access are called private addresses. The private IPv4 address blocks are 10.0.0.0/8, 172.16.0.0/12, and 192.168.0.0/16.

The depletion of IPv4 address space is the motivating factor for moving to IPv6. Each IPv6 address has 128 bits versus the 32 bits in an IPv4 address. IPv6 does not use the dotted-decimal subnet mask notation. The prefix length is used to indicate the network portion of an IPv6 address using the following format: IPv6 address/prefix length.

There are three types of IPv6 addresses: unicast, multicast, and anycast. An IPv6 link-local address enables a device to communicate with other IPv6-enabled devices on the same link and only on that link (subnet). Packets with a source or destination link-local address cannot be routed beyond the link from which the packet originated. IPv6 link-local addresses are in the FE80::/10 range.

ICMP is available for both IPv4 and IPv6. ICMPv4 is the messaging protocol for IPv4. ICMPv6 provides the same services for IPv6 but includes additional functionality.

After it is implemented, an IP network needs to be tested to verify its connectivity and operational performance.

Practice

The following activities provide practice with the topics introduced in this chapter. The Labs and Class Activities are available in the companion Introduction to Networks v5.1 Lab Manual (ISBN 9781587133534). The Packet Tracer Activities PKA files are found in the online course.

Class Activities

Class Activity 7.0.1.1: The Internet of Everything (IoE)

Class Activity 7.4.1.1: The Internet of Everything . . . Naturally!

Labs

Lab 7.1.2.8: Using the Windows Calculator with Network Addresses

Lab 7.1.2.9: Converting IPv4 Addresses to Binary

Lab 7.1.4.9: Identifying IPv4 Addresses

Lab 7.2.5.3: Identifying IPv6 Addresses

Lab 7.2.5.4: Configuring IPv6 Addresses on Network Devices

Lab 7.3.2.7: Testing Network Connectivity with Ping and Traceroute

Lab 7.3.2.8: Mapping the Internet

Packet Tracer Activities

Packet Tracer 7.1.3.8: Investigate Unicast, Broadcast, and Multicast Traffic

Packet Tracer 7.2.4.9: Configuring IPv6 Addressing

Packet Tracer 7.3.2.5: Verifying IPv4 and IPv6 Addressing

Packet Tracer 7.3.2.6: Pinging and Tracing to Test the Path

Packet Tracer 7.3.2.9: Troubleshooting IPv4 and IPv6 Addressing

Packet Tracer 7.4.1.2: Skills Integration Challenge

Check Your Understanding Questions

Complete all the review questions listed here to test your understanding of the topics and concepts in this chapter. The appendix "Answers to 'Check Your Understanding' Questions" lists the answers.

1. What are the parts of an IPv4 address? (Choose two.)

    A. Host

    B. Network

    C. Next hop

    D. Broadcast

    E. Subnet mask

2. What is the purpose of the network address?

    A. To support communication to all hosts within a subnet

    B. To refer to a network

    C. To provide a gate for hosts in the network

    D. To allow multicast

3. What are characteristics in common among unicast, broadcast, and multicast IPv4 communication? (Choose two.)

    A. The source address is always a unicast address.

    B. There is only one host that receives the packet.

    C. There are never multiple destination addresses in the header.

    D. There are equal numbers of addresses used for each.

    E. All are used for the same purpose.

4. Which of the following IPv4 addresses would be used in a private network?

    A. 240.23.56.12

    B. 192.0.1.12

    C. 127.27.20.10

    D. 192.168.1.1

    E. 169.254.72.6

5. What is the principal reason for the development of IPv6?

6. How are IPv6 addresses represented?

    A. 4 octets separated by periods

    B. 64 binary bits with no division

    C. 8 hextets separated by colons

    D. As an octal number

7. What type of IPv6 address should be used for communication that is limited to a single network segment?

    A. Global unicast

    B. Link-local

    C. Unspecified

    D. Unique local

8. What methods automatically provide IPv6 global unicast addresses? (Choose two.)

   A. SLAAC

   B. Stateful DHCPv6

   C. ICMP

   D. DAD

9. Which type of IPv4 address allows a host to send a message to a group of hosts?

   A. Unicast

   B. Link-local

   C. Multicast

   D. Broadcast

10. What protocol is used in IP networks to verify connectivity?

11. What utility is used to identify network path between hosts?

   A. DHCP

   B. Ping

   C. Multicast

   D. Traceroute

CHAPTER 8

Subnetting IP Networks

Objectives

Upon completion of this chapter, you will be able to answer the following questions:

- How can subnetting a network enable better communications?

- How do you calculate IPv4 subnets for a /24, 16, and /8 prefix?

- How would you calculate the number of host addresses available given a network and subnet mask?

- How would you calculate the required subnet mask to accommodate a given number of hosts?

- What are the benefits of variable-length subnet masking (VLSM)?

- How would you design and implement a hierarchical addressing scheme?

- How are IPv6 address assignments implemented in a business environment?

Key Terms

This chapter uses the following key terms. You can find the definitions in the Glossary.

Octet boundary   *Page 409*

Variable Length Subnet Masking (VLSM)   *Page 434*

Introduction (8.0)

Designing, implementing, and managing an effective IP addressing plan ensure that networks can operate effectively and efficiently. This is especially true as the number of host connections to a network increases. Understanding the hierarchical structure of the IP address and how to modify that hierarchy in order to more efficiently meet routing requirements is an important part of planning an IP addressing scheme.

In the original IPv4 address, there are two levels of hierarchy: a network and a host. These two levels of addressing allow for basic network groupings that facilitate in routing packets to a destination network. A router forwards packets based on the network portion of an IP address. When the network is located, the host portion of the address allows for identification of the destination device.

However, as networks grow, with many organizations adding hundreds, and even thousands of hosts to their network, the two-level hierarchy is insufficient.

Subdividing a network adds a level to the network hierarchy, creating, in essence, three levels: a network, a subnetwork, and a host. Introducing an additional level to the hierarchy creates additional sub-groups within an IP network that facilitates faster packet delivery and added filtration, by helping to minimize 'local' traffic.

This chapter examines, in detail, the creation and assignment of IP network and subnetwork addresses through the use of the subnet mask.

Class Activity 8.0.1.2: Call Me!

In this chapter, you will be learning how devices can be grouped into subnets, or smaller network groups, from a large network.

In this modeling activity, you are asked to think about a number you probably use every day, a number such as your telephone number. As you complete the activity, think about how your telephone number compares to strategies that network administrators might use to identify hosts for efficient data communication.

Complete the two questions listed below and record your answers. Save the two sections in either hard- or soft-copy format to use later for class discussion purposes.

- Explain how your smartphone or landline telephone number is divided into identifying groups of numbers. Does your telephone number use an area code? An ISP identifier? A city, state, or country code?

- In what ways does separating your telephone number into managed parts assist in contacting or communicating with others?

Subnetting an IPv4 Network (8.1)

Without subnetting an IPv4-based network, performance would quickly decrease as the number of hosts increased. Proper subnetting allows better control of network traffic and greatly improves network efficiency.

Network Segmentation (8.1.1)

Subnetting allows network segmentation, thus breaking a larger network into multiple smaller networks.

Broadcast Domains (8.1.1.1)

In an Ethernet LAN, devices use broadcasts to locate

- **Other devices** – A device uses Address Resolution Protocol (ARP) which sends Layer 2 broadcasts to a known IPv4 address on the local network to discover the associated MAC address.

- **Services** – A host typically acquires its IPv4 address configuration using the Dynamic Host Configuration Protocol (DHCP) which sends broadcasts on the local network to locate a DHCP server.

Switches propagate broadcasts out to all interfaces except the interface on which it was received. For example, if a switch in Figure 8-1 were to receive a broadcast, it would forward it to the other switches and other users connected in the network.

Figure 8-1   A Large Broadcast Domain

Routers do not propagate broadcasts. When a router receives a broadcast, it does not forward it out to other interfaces. For instance, when R1 receives a broadcast on its Gigabit Ethernet 0/0 interface, it does not forward it out to another interface.

Therefore, each router interface connects a *broadcast domain* and broadcasts are only propagated within its specific broadcast domain.

Problems with Large Broadcast Domains (8.1.1.2)

A large broadcast domain is a network that connects many hosts. A problem with a large broadcast domain is that these hosts can generate excessive broadcasts and negatively affect the network. In Figure 8-1, LAN 1 connects 400 users that could generate broadcast traffic resulting in

- Slow network operations due to the significant amount of traffic it can cause

- Slow device operations because a device must accept and process each broadcast packet

The solution is to reduce the size of the network to create smaller broadcast domains in a process called *subnetting*. These smaller network spaces are called *subnets*.

In Figure 8-2 for example, the 400 users in LAN 1 with network address 172.16.0.0 /16 have been divided into two subnets of 200 users each; 172.16.0.0 /24 and 172.16.1.0 /24. Broadcasts are only propagated within the smaller broadcast domains. Therefore a broadcast in LAN 1 would not propagate to LAN 2.

Figure 8-2   Communicating between Networks

Notice how the prefix length has changed from a /16 to a /24. This is the basis of subnetting; using host bits to create additional subnets.

Note

The terms *subnet* and *network* are often used interchangeably. Most networks are a subnet of some larger address block.

Reasons for Subnetting (8.1.1.3)

Subnetting reduces overall network traffic and improves network performance. It also enables an administrator to implement security policies such as which subnets are allowed or not allowed to communicate together.

There are various ways of using subnets to help manage network devices. Network administrators can group devices and services into subnets that are determined by

- Location, such as floors in a building (Figure 8-3)

Figure 8-3   Subnetting by Location

- Organizational unit (Figure 8-4)

Figure 8-4   Subnetting by Organization Unit

■ Device type (Figure 8-5)

Figure 8-5   Subnetting by Device Type

■ Any other division that makes sense for the network.

Notice in each figure, the subnets use longer prefix lengths to identify networks.

This chapter describes how subnetting is performed. Understanding how to subnet networks is a fundamental skill that all network administrators must develop. Various methods have been developed to help understand this process. This chapter will focus on looking at the binary method. Although a little overwhelming at first, focus and pay close attention to the detail and with practice, subnetting should become easier.

Subnetting an IPv4 Network (8.1.2)

IPv4 subnetting consists of borrowing host network bits to extend the network portion of the IPv4 address. The subnet mask is extended to divide a network into additional subnets.

Octet Boundaries (8.1.2.1)

Every interface on a router is connected to a network. The IPv4 address and subnet mask configured on the router interface are used to identify the specific broadcast domain. Recall that the prefix length and the subnet mask are different ways of identifying the network portion of an address.

IPv4 subnets are created by using one or more of the host bits as network bits. This is done by extending the subnet mask to borrow some of the bits from the host portion of the address to create additional network bits. The more host bits that are borrowed, the more subnets that can be defined.

Networks are most easily subnetted at the octet boundary of /8, /16, and /24. Table 8-1 identifies these prefix lengths, equivalent subnet masks, the network and host bits, and the number of hosts each subnet can connect. Notice that using longer prefix lengths decreases the number of hosts per subnet.

Table 8-1   Subnetting on the Octet Boundary

Prefix Length	Subnet Mask	Network Address (n = network, h = host)	# of Hosts
/8	255.0.0.0	nnnnnnnn.hhhhhhhh.hhhhhhhh.hhhhhhhh11111111. 00000000.00000000.00000000	16,777,214
/16	255.255.0.0	nnnnnnnn.nnnnnnnn.hhhhhhhh.hhhhhhhh 11111111.11111111.00000000.00000000	65,534
/24	255.255.255.0	nnnnnnnn.nnnnnnnn.nnnnnnnn.hhhhhhhh 11111111.11111111.11111111.00000000	254

Subnetting on the Octet Boundary (8.1.2.2)

To understand how subnetting on the *octet boundary* can be useful, consider the following example. Assume an enterprise has chosen the private address 10.0.0.0/8 as its internal network address. That network address can connect 16,777,214 hosts in one broadcast domain. Obviously, this is not ideal.

The enterprise could further subnet the 10.0.0.0/8 address at the octet boundary of /16, as shown in Table 8-2. This would provide the enterprise the ability to define up to 256 subnets (i.e., 10.0.0.0/16–10.255.0.0/16) with each subnet capable of connecting 65,534 hosts. Notice how the first two octets identify the network portion of the address while the last two octets are for host IP addresses.

Table 8-2   Subnetting Network 10.x.0.0/16

Subnet Address (256 Possible Subnets)	Host Range (65,534 Possible Hosts per Subnet)	Broadcast
10.0.0.0/16	10.0.0.1–10.0.255.254	10.0.255.255
10.1.0.0/16	10.1.0.1–10.1.255.254	10.1.255.255
10.2.0.0/16	10.2.0.1–10.2.255.254	10.2.255.255
10.3.0.0/16	10.3.0.1–10.3.255.254	10.3.255.255
10.4.0.0/16	10.4.0.1–10.4.255.254	10.4.255.255

Continued

Table 8-2 *Continued*

Subnet Address (256 Possible Subnets)	Host Range (65,534 Possible Hosts per Subnet)	Broadcast
10.5.0.0/16	10.5.0.1–10.5.255.254	10.5.255.255
10.6.0.0/16	10.6.0.1–10.6.255.254	10.6.255.255
10.7.0.0/16	10.7.0.1–10.7.255.254	10.7.255.255
. . .	. . .	. . .
10.255.0.0/16	10.255.0.1–10.255.255.254	10.255.255.255

Alternatively, the enterprise could choose to subnet at the /24 octet boundary as shown in Table 8-3. This would enable the enterprise to define 65,536 subnets, each capable of connecting 254 hosts. The /24 boundary is very popular in subnetting because it accommodates a reasonable number of hosts and conveniently subnets at the octet boundary.

Table 8-3 Subnetting Network 10.x.x.0/24

Subnet Address (65,536 Possible Subnets)	Host Range (254 Possible Hosts per Subnet)	Broadcast
10.0.0.0/24	10.0.0.1–10.0.0.254	10.0.0.255
10.0.1.0/24	10.0.1.1–10.0.1.254	10.0.1.255
10.0.2.0/24	10.0.2.1–10.0.2.254	10.0.2.255
. . .	. . .	. . .
10.0.255.0/24	10.0.255.1–10.0.255.254	10.0.255.255
10.1.0.0/24	10.1.0.1–10.1.0.254	10.1.0.255
10.1.1.0/24	10.1.1.1–10.1.1.254	10.1.1.0.255
10.1.2.0/24	10.1.2.1–10.1.2.254	10.1.2.0.255
. . .	. . .	. . .
10.100.0.0/24	10.100.0.1–10.100.0.254	10.100.0.255
. . .	. . .	. . .
10.255.255.0/24	10.255.255.1–10.255.255.254	10.255.255.255

Classless Subnetting (8.1.2.3)

The examples seen so far borrowed host bits from the common /8, /16, and /24 network prefixes. However, subnets can borrow bits from *any* host bit position to create other masks.

For instance, a /24 network address is commonly subnetted using longer prefix lengths by borrowing bits from the fourth octet. This provides the administrator with additional flexibility when assigning network addresses to a smaller number of end devices.

As shown in Table 8-4

- /25 row – Borrowing 1 bit from the fourth octet creates 2 subnets supporting 126 hosts each.

- /26 row – Borrowing 2 bits creates 4 subnets supporting 62 hosts each.

- /27 row – Borrowing 3 bits creates 8 subnets supporting 30 hosts each.

- /28 row – Borrowing 4 bits creates 16 subnets supporting 14 hosts each.

- /29 row – Borrowing 5 bits creates 32 subnets supporting 6 hosts each.

- /30 row – Borrowing 6 bits creates 64 subnets supporting 2 hosts each.

For each bit borrowed in the fourth octet, the number of subnetworks available is doubled while reducing the number of host addresses per subnet. Table 8-4 is a particularly useful tool for calculating subnets. It will be used again in this chapter.

Table 8-4   Subnetting a /24 Network

Prefix Length	Subnet Mask	Subnet Mask in Binary (n = network, h = host)	# of Subnets	# of Hosts
/25	255.255.255.128	nnnnnnnn.nnnnnnnn.nnnnnnnn.nhhhhhhh 11111111.11111111.11111111.10000000	2	126
/26	255.255.255.192	nnnnnnnn.nnnnnnnn.nnnnnnnn.nnhhhhhh 11111111.11111111.11111111.11000000	4	62
/27	255.255.255.224	nnnnnnnn.nnnnnnnn.nnnnnnnn.nnnhhhhh 11111111.11111111.11111111.11100000	8	30
/28	255.255.255.240	nnnnnnnn.nnnnnnnn.nnnnnnnn.nnnnhhhh 11111111.11111111.11111111.11110000	16	14
/29	255.255.255.248	nnnnnnnn.nnnnnnnn.nnnnnnnn.nnnnnhhh 11111111.11111111.11111111.11111000	32	6
/30	255.255.255.252	nnnnnnnn.nnnnnnnn.nnnnnnnn.nnnnnnhh 11111111.11111111.11111111.11111100	64	2

Video

Video Demonstration 8.1.2.4: The Subnet Mask

Go to the online course to view this video.

Video

Video Demonstration 8.1.2.5: Subnetting with the Magic Number

Go to the online course to view this video.

Classless Subnetting Example (8.1.2.6)

To understand how subnetting at a classless level can be useful, consider the following examples.

Consider the private network address 192.168.1.0/24 shown in Figure 8-6. The first three octets are displayed in decimal, while the last octet is displayed in binary. The reason for this is because we will be borrowing bits from the last octet to create subnets of the 192.168.1.0/24 network.

With no host bits borrowed, the host portion of both the network address and mask are all 0 bits.

Figure 8-6   The 192.168.1.0/24 Network

The subnet mask is 255.255.255.0 as indicated by the /24 prefix length. This identifies the first three octets as the network portion and the remaining 8 bits in the last octet as the host portion. Without subnetting, this network supports a single LAN interface providing 254 host IPv4 addresses. If an additional LAN is needed, the network would need to be subnetted.

In Figure 8-7, 1 bit is borrowed from the most significant bit (leftmost bit) in the host portion, thus extending the network portion to 25 bits or /25. This enables the creation of two subnets.

The two subnets created by borrowing 1 bit are 192.168.1.0/25 and 192.168.1.128/25. The two subnets are derived from changing the value of the bit borrowed to either 0 or 1. Because the bit borrowed is the 128 bit, the decimal value of the fourth octet for the 2nd subnet is 128.

The resulting subnet mask for both networks is 255.255.255.128. Notice how it uses a 1 in the borrowed bit position to indicate that this bit is now part of the network portion.

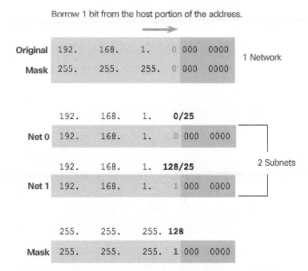

Figure 8-7 Results of Borrowing 1 Bit

Figure 8-8 displays the dotted decimal representation of the two subnet addresses and their common subnet mask. Because one bit has been borrowed, the subnet mask for each subnet is 255.255.255.128 or /25.

Figure 8-8 Dotted Decimal Addresses

Creating 2 Subnets (8.1.2.7)

To see how a /25 subnet is applied in a network, consider the topology in Figure 8-9. R1 has two LAN segments attached to its Gigabit Ethernet interfaces. Each LAN is assigned one of the subnets.

Figure 8-9   /25 Subnetting Topology

Figure 8-10 displays the important addresses of the first subnet, 192.168.1.0/25.

Network Address

| 192. | 168. | 1. | 0 | 000 0000 | = 192.168.1.0 |

First Host Address

| 192. | 168. | 1. | 0 | 000 0001 | = 192.168.1.1 |

Last Host Address

| 192. | 168. | 1. | 0 | 111 1110 | = 192.168.1.126 |

Broadcast Address

| 192. | 168. | 1. | 0 | 111 1111 | = 192.168.1.127 |

Figure 8-10   Address Range for the 192.168.1.0/25 Subnet

Notice how the

- **IPv4 Network address** is 192.168.1.0 and contains all 0 bits in the host portion of the address.

- **First IPv4 host address** is 192.168.1.1 and contains all 0 bits plus a rightmost 1 bit in the host portion of the address.

- **Last IPv4 host address** is 192.168.1.126 and contains all 1 bits plus a rightmost 0 bit in the host portion of the address.

- **IPv4 Broadcast address** is 192.168.1.127 and contains all 1 bits in the host portion of the address.

Figure 8-11 displays the important addresses of the second subnet, 192.168.1.128/25.

Network Address

| 192. | 168. | 1. | 1 | 000 0000 | = 192.168.1.128 |

First Host Address

| 192. | 168. | 1. | 1 | 000 0001 | = 192.168.1.129 |

Last Host Address

| 192. | 168. | 1. | 1 | 111 1110 | = 192.168.1.254 |

Broadcast Address

| 192. | 168. | 1. | 1 | 111 1111 | = 192.168.1.255 |

Figure 8-11   Address Range for the 192.168.1.128/25. Subnet

Router interfaces must be assigned an IP address within the valid host range for the assigned subnet. This is the address that hosts on that network will use as their default gateway. A very common practice is to use the first or last available address in a network range for the router interface address. Example 8-1 shows the configuration for R1's interfaces with the first IPv4 address for their respective subnets using the **ip address** interface configuration command.

Example 8-1 Configuring R1 Interfaces with /25 Addresses

```
R1(config)# interface gigabitethernet 0/0
R1(config-if)# ip address 192.168.1.1 255.255.255.128
R1(config-if)# exit
R1(contig)# interface gigabitethernet 0/1
R1(config-if)# ip address 192.168.1.129 255.255.255.128
```

Hosts on each subnet must be configured with an IPv4 address and default gateway. Figure 8-12 displays the IPv4 configuration for PC2 host on the 192.168.1.128/25 network. Notice that the default gateway IPv4 address is the address configured on the G0/1 interface of R1, 192.168.1.129, and the subnet mask is 255.255.255.128.

Internet Protocol Version 4 (TCP/IPv4) Properties

General

You can get IP settings assigned automatically if your network supports this capability. Otherwise, you need to ask your network administrator for the appropriate IP settings.

○ Obtain an IP address automatically

◉ Use the following IP address:

IP address: 192 . 168 . 1 . 130

Subnet mask: 255 . 255 . 255 . 128

Default gateway: 192 . 168 . 1 . 129

○ Obtain DNS server address automatically

◉ Use the following DNS server addresses

Preferred DNS server: . . .

Alternate DNS server: . . .

☐ Validate settings upon exit

Advanced...

OK   Cancel

Figure 8-12   Assign a Valid Host IP Address

Video

Video Demonstration 8.1.2.8: Creating Two Equal-Sized Subnets

Go to the online course to view this video.

Subnetting Formulas (8.1.2.9)

To calculate the number of subnets that can be created from the bits borrowed, use the formula displayed in Figure 8-13.

$$2\text{\textasciicircum}n$$

$n=$ bits borrowed

Figure 8-13   Calculate Number of Subnets Formula

Figure 8-14 displays the possible number of subnets that can be created when borrowing 1, 2, 3, 4, 5, or 6 bits.

```
192  .  168  .  1  .  0
nnnnnnnn.nnnnnnnn.nnnnnnnn.hhhhhhhh
```

Borrowing 1 bit:	2^1 = 2	
Borrowing 2 bits:	2^2 = 4	
Borrowing 3 bits:	2^3 = 8	
Borrowing 4 bits:	2^4 = 16	
Borrowing 5 bits:	2^5 = 32	
Borrowing 6 bits:	2^6 = 64	

Figure 8-14   Subnetting a /24 Network

To calculate the number of hosts that can be supported, use the formula displayed in Figure 8-15. There are two subnet addresses that cannot be assigned to a host, the network address and the broadcast address, so we must subtract 2.

$$2\textasciicircum n{-}2$$

$n=$ the number of bits remaining in the host field

Figure 8-15   Calculate Number of Hosts Formula

As shown in Figure 8-16, there are 7 host bits remaining, so the calculation is $2^7 = 128{-}2 = 126$. This means that each of the subnets has 126 valid host addresses.

192. 168.   1.   0 000 0000

7 bits remain in host field

2^7 = 128 hosts per subnet
2^7 - 2 = 126 valid hosts per subnet

Figure 8-16   Calculate Number of Hosts

Therefore, borrowing 1 host bit toward the network results in creating 2 subnets, and each subnet can have a total of 126 hosts assigned.

Creating 4 Subnets (8.1.2.10)

Now consider the network topology shown in Figure 8-17. The enterprise is using the private network address 192.168.1.0/24 range and requires three subnets.

Figure 8-17   /26 Subnetting Topology

Borrowing a single bit only provided 2 subnets; therefore, another host bit must be borrowed. Using the 2^n formula for two borrowed bits results in $2^2 = 4$ subnets. The specifics of the four subnets are shown in Figure 8-18. The resulting subnet mask of /26 or 255.255.255.192 is used by all four subnets.

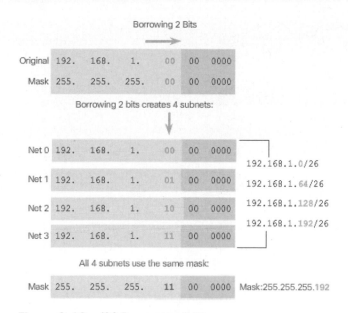

Figure 8-18   /26 Borrowing 2 Bits

To calculate the number of hosts, examine the last octet as shown in Figure 8-19.

Figure 8-19   Calculate Number of Hosts

After borrowing 2 bits for the subnet, there are 6 host bits remaining. Apply the host calculation formula $2^n - 2$ as shown to reveal that each subnet can support 62 host addresses. The significant addresses of the first subnet (i.e., Net 0) are displayed in Figure 8-20.

Figure 8-20 Address Range for 192.168.1.0/26 Subnet

Only the first three subnets are required because there are only three interfaces. Figure 8-21 displays the specifics of the first three subnets that will be used to satisfy the topology in Figure 8-17.

Figure 8-21 Address Ranges Nets 0–2

Finally, Example 8-2 shows the configuration to apply the first valid host address from each subnet to the respective R1 LAN interface.

Example 8-2 Configuring R1 Interfaces with /25 Addresses

```
R1(config)# interface gigabitethernet 0/0
R1(config-if)# ip address 192.168.1.1 255.255.255.192
R1(config-if)# exit
R1(config)# interface gigabitethernet 0/1
R1(config-if)# ip address 192.168.1.65 255.255.255.192
R1(config-if)# exit
R1(config)# interface serial 0/0/0
R1(config-if)# ip address 192.168.1.129 255.255.255.192
```

Video

Video Demonstration 8.1.2.11: Creating Four Equal-Sized Subnets

Go to the online course to view this video.

Video

Video Demonstration 8.1.2.12: Creating Eight Equal-Sized Subnets

Go to the online course to view this video.

Subnetting a /16 and /8 Prefix (8.1.3)

This topic explores subnetting a /16 and /8 network.

Creating Subnets with a /16 prefix (8.1.3.1)

In a situation requiring a larger number of subnets, an IPv4 network is required that has more hosts bits to borrow from. For example, the network address 172.16.0.0 has a default mask of 255.255.0.0, or /16. This address has 16 bits in the network portion and 16 bits in the host portion. The 16 bits in the host portion are available to borrow for creating subnets. Table 8-5 highlights all the possible scenarios for subnetting a /16 prefix.

Table 8-5   Subnetting a /16 Network

Prefix Length	Subnet Mask	Network Address (n = network, h = host)	# of Subnets	# of Hosts
/17	255.255.128.0	nnnnnnnn.nnnnnnnn.nhhhhhhh.hhhhhhhh 11111111.11111111.10000000.00000000	2	32564
/18	255.255.192.0	nnnnnnnn.nnnnnnnn.nnhhhhhh.hhhhhhhh 11111111.11111111.11000000.00000000	4	16282
/19	255.255.224.0	nnnnnnnn.nnnnnnnn.nnnhhhhh.hhhhhhhh 11111111.11111111.11100000.00000000	8	8190
/20	255.255.240.0	nnnnnnnn.nnnnnnnn.nnnnhhhh.hhhhhhhh 11111111.11111111.11110000.00000000	16	4094
/21	255.255.248.0	nnnnnnnn.nnnnnnnn.nnnnnhhh.hhhhhhhh 11111111.11111111.11111000.00000000	32	2046
/22	255.255.252.0	nnnnnnnn.nnnnnnnn.nnnnnnhh.hhhhhhhh 11111111.11111111.11111100.00000000	64	1022
/23	255.255.254.0	nnnnnnnn.nnnnnnnn.nnnnnnnh.hhhhhhhh 11111111.11111111.11111110.00000000	128	510
/24	255.255.255.0	nnnnnnnn.nnnnnnnn.nnnnnnnn.hhhhhhhh 11111111.11111111.11111111.00000000	256	254
/25	255.255.255.128	nnnnnnnn.nnnnnnnn.nnnnnnnn.nhhhhhhh 11111111.11111111.11111111.10000000	512	126
/26	255.255.255.192	nnnnnnnn.nnnnnnnn.nnnnnnnn.nnhhhhhh 11111111.11111111.11111111.11000000	1024	62
/27	255.255.255.224	nnnnnnnn.nnnnnnnn.nnnnnnnn.nnnhhhhh 11111111.11111111.11111111.11100000	2048	30
/28	255.255.255.240	nnnnnnnn.nnnnnnnn.nnnnnnnn.nnnnhhhh 11111111.11111111.11111111.11110000	4096	14
/29	255.255.255.248	nnnnnnnn.nnnnnnnn.nnnnnnnn.nnnnnhhh 11111111.11111111.11111111.11111000	8192	6
/30	255.255.255.252	nnnnnnnn.nnnnnnnn.nnnnnnnn.nnnnnnhh 11111111.11111111.11111111.11111100	16384	2

Although a complete memorization of the table is not required, it is suggested that you gain a good understanding of how each value in the table is generated. Do not let the size of the table intimidate you. The reason it is big is because it has 8 additional bits that can be borrowed, and, therefore, the number of subnets and hosts are simply larger.

Creating 100 Subnets with a /16 Network (8.1.3.2)

Consider a large enterprise that requires at least 100 subnets and has chosen the private address 172.16.0.0/16 as its internal network address.

When borrowing bits from a /16 address, start borrowing bits in the third octet, going from left to right. Borrow a single bit at a time until the number of bits necessary to create 100 subnets is reached.

Figure 8-22 displays the number of subnets that can be created when borrowing bits from the third octet and the fourth octet. Notice there is now up to 14 host bits that can be borrowed.

Figure 8-22   Number of Subnets for a /16 Network

To satisfy the requirements of the enterprise, 7 bits (i.e., $2^7 = 128$ subnets) would need to be borrowed. Recall that the subnet mask must change to reflect the borrowed bits. In this example, when 7 bits are borrowed, the mask is extended 7 bits into the third octet. In decimal, the mask is represented as 255.255.254.0, or a /23 prefix, because the third octet is 11111110 in binary and the fourth octet is 00000000 in binary.

Figure 8-23 displays the resulting subnets from 172.16.0.0 /23 up to 172.16.254.0 /23.

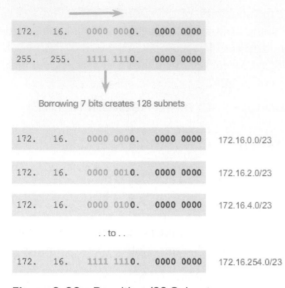

Figure 8-23 Resulting /23 Subnets

Calculating the Hosts (8.1.3.3)

To calculate the number of hosts each subnet can support, examine the third and fourth octet. After borrowing 7 bits for the subnet, there is one host bit remaining in the third octet and 8 host bits remaining in the fourth octet for a total of 9 bits that were not borrowed.

Apply the host calculation formula as shown in Figure 8-24. There are only 510 host addresses that are available for each /23 subnet.

Figure 8-24 Calculate Number of Hosts

As shown in Figure 8-25, the first host address for the first subnet is 172.16.0.1, and the last host address is 172.16.1.254.

Network Address

| 172. | 16. | 00 00 00 00. 0000 0000 | = 172.16.0.0/23 |

First Host Address

| 172. | 16. | 00 00 00 00. 0000 0001 | = 172.16.0.1/23 |

Last Host Address

| 172. | 16. | 00 00 00 01. 1111 1110 | = 172 16 1 254/23 |

Broadcast Address

| 172. | 16. | 00 00 00 01. 1111 1111 | = 172.16.1.255/23 |

Figure 8-25   Address Range for 172.16.0.0/23 Subnet

Video

Video Demonstration 8.1.3.4: Creating One Hundred Equal-Sized Subnets

Go to the online course to view this video.

Creating 1000 Subnets with a /8 Network (8.1.3.5)

Some organizations, such as small service providers or large enterprises, may need even more subnets. Take, for example, a small ISP that requires 1000 subnets for its clients. Each client will need plenty of space in the host portion to create their own subnets.

The network address 10.0.0.0 has a default subnet mask of 255.0.0.0 or /8. This means there are 8 bits in the network portion and 24 host bits available to borrow toward subnetting. Therefore, the small ISP will subnet the 10.0.0.0/8 network.

As always, in order to create subnets we must borrow bits from the host portion of the IP address of the existing internetwork. Starting from the left to the right with the first available host bit, we will borrow a single bit at a time until we reach the number of bits necessary to create 1000 subnets. As shown in Figure 8-26, we need to borrow 10 bits to create 1024 subnets. Specifically, we need to borrow the 8 bits in the second octet and 2 additional bits from the third octet.

Figure 8-26 displays the network address and the resulting subnet mask which converts to 255.255.192.0 or a /18 prefix as well as the resulting subnets from borrowing 10 bits creating subnets from 10.0.0.0 /18 to 10.255.255.128.0 /18.

Figure 8-26   Number of Subnets Created for a /8 Network

Figure 8-27 displays the network address and the resulting subnet mask which converts to 255.255.192.0 or a /18 prefix as well as the resulting subnets from borrowing 10 bits creating subnets from 10.0.0.0 /18 to 10.255.255.128.0 /18.

Figure 8-27   Resulting /18 Subnets

Figure 8-28 displays that 14 host bits were not borrowed, therefore, $2^{14} - 2 = 16{,}382$. This indicates that each of the 1000 subnets can support up to 16,382 hosts.

Figure 8-28   Calculate Number of Hosts

Figure 8-29 displays the specifics of the first subnet.

Figure 8-29   Address Range for 10.0.0.0/18 Subnet

Video Demonstration 8.1.3.6: Subnetting Across Multiple Octets

Go to the online course to view this video.

Subnetting to Meet Requirements (8.1.4)

Before any subnetting is carried out, it is important to understand the requirements of the network and to formulate a plan.

Subnetting Based on Host Requirements (8.1.4.1)

There are two considerations when planning subnets:

- the number of host addresses required for each network
- the number of individual subnets needed

Table 8-4 displayed the specifics for subnetting a /24 network. In that table, notice how there is an inverse relationship between the number of subnets and the number of hosts. The more bits borrowed to create subnets, the fewer host bits available. If more host addresses are needed, more host bits are required, resulting in fewer subnets.

The number of host addresses required in the largest subnet will determine how many bits must be left in the host portion. Recall that two of the addresses cannot be used, so the usable number of addresses can be calculated as 2^n-2.

Subnetting Based on Network Requirements (8.1.4.2)

Sometimes a certain number of subnets is required, with less emphasis on the number of host addresses per subnet. This may be the case if an organization chooses to separate their network traffic based on internal structure or department setup, as shown in Figure 8-30.

Figure 8-30   Subnets Based on Organizational Structure

For example, an organization may choose to put all host devices used by employees in the Engineering department in one network, and all host devices used by management in a separate network. In this case, the number of subnets is most important in determining how many bits to borrow.

Recall the number of subnets created when bits are borrowed can be calculated using the formula 2^n (where n is the number of bits borrowed). The key is to balance the number of subnets needed and the number of hosts required for the largest subnet. The more bits borrowed to create additional subnets means fewer hosts available per subnet.

Network Requirement Example (8.1.4.3)

Network administrators must devise the network addressing scheme to accommodate the maximum number of hosts for each network and the number of subnets. The addressing scheme should allow for growth in the both the number of host addresses per subnet and the total number of subnets.

In this example, corporate headquarters has allocated a private network address of 172.16.0.0/22 (10 host bits) to a branch location. As shown in Figure 8-31, this will provide 1,022 host addresses.

Figure 8-31   172.16.0.0/22 Network Address in Binary

The topology for the branch locations, shown in Figure 8-32, consists of 5 LAN segments and 4 internetwork connections between routers. Therefore, 9 subnets are required. The largest subnet requires 40 hosts.

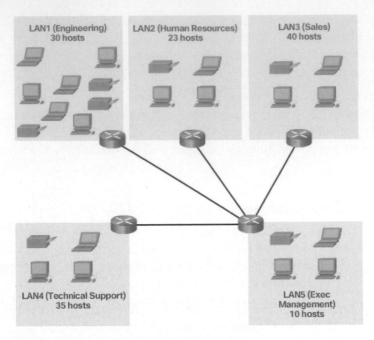

Figure 8-32   Branch Location Networks

The 172.16.0.0/22 network address has 10 host bits. Because the largest subnet requires 40 hosts, a minimum of 6 host bits are needed to provide addressing for 40 hosts. This is determined by using this formula: $2^6 - 2 = 62$ hosts.

Using the formula for determining subnets, results in 16 subnets: $2^4 = 16$. Because the example internetwork requires 9 subnets this will meet the requirement and allow for some additional growth.

Therefore, the first 4 host bits can be used to allocate subnets, as shown in Figure 8-33. When 4 bits are borrowed, the new prefix length is /26 with a subnet mask of 255.255.255.192.

	Network Portion	Host Portion	Dotted Decimal

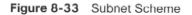

	10101100.00010000.000000	00.00	000000	172.16.0.0/22
0	10101100.00010000.000000	00.00	000000	172.16.0.0/26
1	10101100.00010000.000000	00.01	000000	172.16.0.64/26
2	10101100.00010000.000000	00.10	000000	172.16.0.128/26
3	10101100.00010000.000000	00.11	000000	172.16.0.192/26
4	10101100.00010000.000000	01.00	000000	172.16.1.0/26
5	10101100.00010000.000000	01.01	000000	172.16.1.64/26
6	10101100.00010000.000000	01.10	000000	172.16.1.128/26

Nets 7 – 13 not shown

14	10101100.00010000.000000	11.10	000000	172.16.3.128/26
15	10101100.00010000.000000	11.11	000000	172.16.3.192/26

4 bits borrowed from host portion to create subnets

Figure 8-33   Subnet Scheme

As shown in Figure 8-34, the subnets can be assigned to the LAN segments and router-to-router connections.

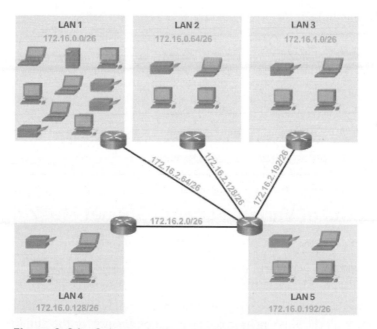

Figure 8-34   Subnets Assigned to Networks

This topic concludes with five activities to practice subnetting. The Chapter Appendix includes additional practice activities.

Interactive Graphic

Activity 8.1.4.4: Calculate the Subnet Mask

Go to the online course to perform this practice activity.

Interactive Graphic

Activity 8.1.4.5: Determining the Number of Bits to Borrow

Go to the online course to perform this practice activity.

Lab 8.1.4.6: Calculating IPv4 Subnets

In this lab, you will complete the following objectives:

- Part 1: Determine IPv4 Address Subnetting
- Part 2: Calculate IPv4 Address Subnetting

Packet Tracer ☐ Activity

Packet Tracer 8.1.4.7: Subnetting Scenario 1

In this activity, you are given the network address of 192.168.100.0/24 to subnet and provide the IP addressing for the network shown in the topology. Each LAN in the network requires enough space for, at least, 25 addresses for end devices, the switch and the router. The connection between R1 to R2 will require an IP address for each end of the link.

Lab 8.1.4.8: Designing and Implementing a Subnetted IPv4 Addressing Scheme

In this lab, you will complete the following objectives:

- Part 1: Design a Network Subnetting Scheme
- Part 2: Configure the Devices
- Part 3: Test and Troubleshoot the Network

Benefits of Variable Length Subnet Masking (8.1.5)

This topic discusses the benefits of implementing different size subnets.

Traditional Subnetting Wastes Addresses (8.1.5.1)

Using traditional subnetting, the same number of addresses is allocated for each subnet. If all the subnets have the same requirements for the number of hosts, these fixed size address blocks would be efficient. However, most often that is not the case.

For example, the topology shown in Figure 8-35 requires seven subnets, one for each of the four LANs, and one for each of the three WAN connections between routers.

Figure 8-35   Topology Example for Wasted Addresses

Using traditional subnetting with the given address of 192.168.20.0/24, 3 bits can be borrowed from the host portion in the last octet to meet the subnet requirement of seven subnets. As shown in Figure 8-36, borrowing 3 bits creates 8 subnets and leaves 5 host bits with 30 usable hosts per subnet. This scheme creates the needed subnets and meets the host requirement of the largest LAN.

```
          Network portion              Host portion

     11000000.10101000.00010100    .000  00000   192.168.20.0/24

  0  11000000.10101000.00010100    .000  00000   192.168.20.0/27
  1  11000000.10101000.00010100    .001  00000   192.168.20.32/27    Building LANs
  2  11000000.10101000.00010100    .010  00000   192.168.20.64/27    A, B, C, and D
  3  11000000.10101000.00010100    .011  00000   192.168.20.96/27
  4  11000000.10101000.00010100    .100  00000   192.168.20.128/27
  5  11000000.10101000.00010100    .101  00000   192.168.20.160/27   Site to Site
  6  11000000.10101000.00010100    .110  00000   192.168.20.192/27   WANs
  7  11000000.10101000.00010100    .111  00000   192.168.20.224/27   Unused /
                                                                     Available

    Subnet portion            Host portion
    2^3 = 8 subnets           2^5 - 2 = 30 hosts per subnet
```

Figure 8-36   Basic Subnet Scheme

Although this traditional subnetting meets the needs of the largest LAN and divides the address space into an adequate number of subnets, it results in significant waste of unused addresses.

For example, only two addresses are needed in each subnet for the three WAN links. Because each subnet has 30 usable addresses, there are 28 unused addresses in each of these subnets. As shown in Figure 8-37, this results in 84 unused addresses (28×3).

	Network portion	Host portion		Dotted Decimal
4	11000000.10101000.00010100	.100	00000	192.168.20.128/27
5	11000000.10101000.00010100	.101	00000	192.168.20.160/27
6	11000000.10101000.00010100	.110	00000	192.168.20.192/27

Host portion
2^5 – 2 = 30 hosts per subnet

30 – 2 = 28
Each WAN subnet wastes 28 addresses

28 x 3 = 84
84 addresses are unused

Figure 8-37 Unused Addresses on WAN Subnets

Further, this limits future growth by reducing the total number of subnets available. This inefficient use of addresses is characteristic of traditional subnetting. Applying a traditional subnetting scheme to this scenario is not very efficient and is wasteful.

Subnetting a subnet, or using *Variable Length Subnet Mask (VLSM)*, was designed to avoid wasting addresses.

Variable Length Subnet Masks (8.1.5.2)

In all of the previous examples of subnetting, notice that the same subnet mask was applied for all the subnets. This means that each subnet has the same number of available host addresses.

Traditional subnetting creates subnets of equal size. Each subnet in a traditional scheme uses the same subnet mask. As shown in Figure 8-38, VLSM allows a network space to be divided into unequal parts. With VLSM, the subnet mask will vary depending on how many bits have been borrowed for a particular subnet, thus the "variable" part of the VLSM.

One subnet was further divided to create 8
smaller subnets of 4 hosts each

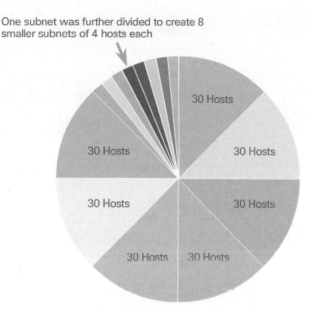

Figure 8-38   Subnets of Varying Sizes

VLSM subnetting is similar to traditional subnetting in that bits are borrowed to
create subnets. The formulas to calculate the number of hosts per subnet and the
number of subnets created still apply.

The difference is that subnetting is not a single pass activity. With VLSM, the
network is first subnetted, and then the subnets are subnetted again. This process can
be repeated multiple times to create subnets of various sizes.

Note

When using VLSM, always begin by satisfying the host requirements of the largest subnet.
Continue subnetting until the host requirements of the smallest subnet are satisfied.

Basic VLSM (8.1.5.3)

To better understand the VLSM process, go back to the previous example, shown in
Figure 8-39.

Figure 8-39   Choosing a Subnet to Subnet Further

The network 192.168.20.0/24 was subnetted into eight equal-sized subnets. Seven of the eight subnets were allocated. Four subnets were used for the LANs and three subnets for the WAN connections between the routers. Recall that the wasted address space was in the subnets used for the WAN connections, because those subnets required only two usable addresses: one for each router interface. To avoid this waste, VLSM can be used to create smaller subnets for the WAN connections.

To create smaller subnets for the WAN links, one of the subnets will be divided. In this example, the last subnet, 192.168.20.224/27, will be further subnetted.

Recall that when the number of needed host addresses is known, the formula $2^n - 2$ (where n equals the number of host bits remaining) can be used. To provide two usable addresses, 2 host bits must be left in the host portion.

Because there are 5 host bits in the subnetted 192.168.20.224/27 address space, 3 more bits can be borrowed, leaving 2 bits in the host portion, as shown in Figure 8-40. The calculations at this point are exactly the same as those used for traditional subnetting. The bits are borrowed, and the subnet ranges are determined.

Figure 8-40   VLSM Subnetting Scheme

This VLSM subnetting scheme reduces the number of addresses per subnet to a size appropriate for the WANs. Subnetting subnet 7 for WANs, allows subnets 4, 5, and 6 to be available for future networks, as well as 5 additional subnets available for WANs.

Video

Video Demonstration 8.1.5.4: Basic VLSM

Go to the online course to view this video.

VLSM in Practice (8.1.5.5)

Using the VLSM subnets, the LAN and WAN segments can be addressed without unnecessary waste.

As shown in Figure 8-41, the hosts in each of the LANs will be assigned a valid host address with the range for that subnet and /27 mask. Each of the four routers will have a LAN interface with a /27 subnet and a one or more serial interfaces with a /30 subnet.

Figure 8-41   VLSM Network Topology

Using a common addressing scheme, the first host IPv4 address for each subnet is assigned to the LAN interface of the router. The WAN interfaces of the routers are assigned the IP addresses and mask for the /30 subnets.

Example 8-3 shows the interface configuration for each of the routers.

Example 8-3   VLSM Configurations of Each Router

```
R1(config)# interface gigabitethernet 0/0
R1(config-if)# ip address 192.168.20.1 255.255.255.224
R1(config-if)# exit
R1(config)# interface serial 0/0/0
R1(config-if)# ip address 192.168.20.225 255.255.255.252
R1(config-if)# end
R1#
```

```
R2(config)# interface gigabitethernet 0/0
R2(config-if)# ip address 192.168.20.33 255.255.255.224
R2(config-if)# exit
R2(config)# interface serial 0/0/0
R2(config-if)# ip address 192.168.20.226 255.255.255.252
R2(config-if)# exit
R2(config)# interface serial 0/0/1
R2(config)# ip address 192.168.20.229 255.255.255.252
R2(config-if)# end
R2#
```

```
R3(config)# interface gigabitethernet 0/0
R3(config-if)# ip address 192.168.20.65 255.255.255.224
R3(config-if)# exit
R3(config)# interface serial 0/0/0
R3(config-if)# ip address 192.168.20.230 255.255.255.252
R3(config-if)# exit
R3(config)# interface serial 0/0/1
R3(config)# ip address 192.168.20.233 255.255.255.252
R3(config-if)# end
R3#
```

```
R4(config)# interface gigabitethernet 0/0
R4(config-if)# ip address 192.168.20.97 255.255.255.224
R4(config-if)# exit
R4(config)# interface serial 0/0/0
R4(config-if)# ip address 192.168.20.234 255.255.255.252
R4(config-if)# end
R4#
```

Hosts on each subnet will have a host IPv4 address from the range of host addresses for that subnet and an appropriate mask. Hosts will use the address of the attached router LAN interface as the default gateway address.

- Default gateway for Building A hosts (192.168.20.0/27) will be 192.168.20.1.

- Default gateway for Building B hosts (192.168.20.32/27) will be 192.168.20.33.

- Default gateway for Building C hosts (192.168.20.64/27) will be 192.168.20.65.

- Default gateway for Building D hosts (192.168.20.96/27) will be 192.168.20.97.

VLSM Chart (8.1.5.6)

An addressing chart can be used to identify which blocks of addresses are available for use and which ones are already assigned, as shown in Table 8-6. This method helps to prevent assigning addresses that have already been allocated.

Table 8-6 Basic Subnetting Chart for 192.168.20/24

Location	/27 Network	Hosts
Building A	.0	.1–.30
Building B	.32	.33–.62
Building C	.64	.65–.94
Building D	.96	.97–.126
WAN R1–R2	.128	.129 –.158
WAN R2–R3	.16	.161 –.190
WAN R3–R4	.192	.193 –.222
Unused	.224	.225 –.254

In order to use the address space more efficiently, /30 subnets are created for WAN links, as shown in the VLSM chart in Figure 8-42. To keep the unused blocks of addresses together in a block of contiguous address space, the last /27 subnet was further subnetted to create the /30 subnets. The first 3 subnets were assigned to WAN links.

	/27 Network	Hosts
Bldg A	.0	.1 - .30
Bldg B	.32	.33 - .62
Bldg C	.64	.65 - .94
Bldg D	.96	.97 - .126
Unused	.128	.129 - .158
Unused	.160	.161 - .190
Unused	.192	.193 - .222
	.224	.225 - .254

	/30 Network	Hosts
WAN R1–R2	.224	.225 - .226
WAN R2–R3	.228	.229 - .230
WAN R3–R4	.232	.233 - .234
Unused	.236	.237 - .238
Unused	.240	.241 - .242
Unused	.244	.245 - .246
Unused	.248	.249 - .250
Unused	.252	.253 - .254

Figure 8-42 Saving Addresses by Subnetting a Subnet for WAN Links

Designing the addressing scheme in this way leaves 3 unused, contiguous /27 subnets and 5 unused, contiguous /30 subnets.

Video

Video Demonstration 8.1.5.7: VLSM Example

Go to the online course to view this video.

Interactive Graphic

Activity 8.1.5.8: Practicing VLSM

Go to the online course to perform this practice activity.

Addressing Schemes (8.2)

Many different network devices require IP addresses. To accommodate all of these devices with the minimum amount of problems, it is necessary to develop a proper addressing scheme.

Structured Design (8.2.1)

The best addressing scheme is one based on the structure and function of the network devices that must be addressed.

IPv4 Network Address Planning (8.2.1.1)

As shown in Figure 8-43, the allocation of network layer address space within the corporate network needs to be well designed. Address assignment should not be random.

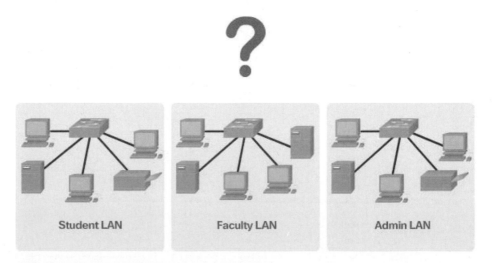

Figure 8-43   Planning IP Address Assignment

Planning network subnets requires examination of both the needs of an organization's network usage, and how the subnets will be structured. Performing a network requirement study is the starting point. This means looking at the entire network and determining the main sections of the network and how they will be segmented. The address plan includes determining the needs of each subnet in terms of size, how many hosts per subnet, how host addresses will be assigned, which hosts will require static IPv4 addresses, and which hosts can use DHCP for obtaining their addressing information.

The size of the subnet involves planning the number of hosts that will require IPv4 host addresses in each subnet of the subdivided private network. For example, in a campus network design, you might consider how many hosts are needed in the Administrative LAN, how many in the Faculty LAN, and how many in the Student LAN. In a home network, a consideration might be done by the number of hosts in the Main House LAN and the number of hosts in the Home Office LAN.

As discussed earlier, the private IPv4 address range used on a LAN is the choice of the network administrator and needs careful consideration to be sure that enough host addresses will be available for the currently known hosts and for future expansion. Remember the private IPv4 address ranges are

- 10.0.0.0 – 10.255.255.255 with a subnet mask of 255.0.0.0 or /8

- 172.16.0.0   172.31.255.255 with a subnet mask of 255.240.0.0 or /12

- 192.168.0.0 – 192.168.255.255 with a subnet mask of 255.255.0.0 or /16

Knowing your IPv4 address requirements will determine the range or ranges of host addresses you implement. Subnetting the selected private IPv4 address space will provide the host addresses to cover your network needs.

Public addresses used to connect to the Internet are typically allocated from a service provider. So, whereas the same principles for subnetting would apply, this is not generally the responsibility of the organization's network administrator.

Planning to Address the Network (8.2.1.2)

Three primary considerations for planning address allocation are as follows:

- Prevent duplication of addresses

- Provide and control access

- Monitor security and performance

Preventing the duplication of addresses refers to the fact that each host in an internetwork must have a unique address. Without the proper planning and documentation, an address could be assigned to more than one host, resulting in access issues for both hosts.

Providing and controlling access refers to the fact that some hosts, such as servers, provide resources to internal hosts as well as to external hosts. The Layer 3 address assigned to a server can be used to control access to that server. If, however, the address is randomly assigned and not well documented, controlling access is more difficult.

Monitoring security and performance of hosts means network traffic is examined for source IP addresses that are generating or receiving excessive packets. If there is proper planning and documentation of the network addressing, problematic network devices should easily be found.

Assigning Addresses to Devices (8.2.1.3)

Within a network, there are different types of devices that require addresses, including

- **End user clients** – Most networks allocate IPv4 addresses dynamically using Dynamic Host Configuration Protocol (DHCP). This reduces the burden on network support staff and virtually eliminates entry errors. As well, addresses are only leased for a period of time. Changing the subnetting scheme means that the DHCP server needs to be reconfigured, and the clients must renew their IPv4 addresses.

Note

IPv6 clients can obtain address information using DHCPv6 or SLAAC.

- **Servers and peripherals** – These should have a predictable static IP address. Use a consistent numbering system for these devices.

- **Servers that are accessible from the Internet** – In many networks, servers must be made available to the remote users. In most cases, these servers are assigned private addresses internally, and the router or firewall at the perimeter of the network must be configured to translate the internal address into a public address.

- **Intermediary devices** – These devices are assigned addresses for network management, monitoring, and security. Because we must know how to communicate with intermediary devices, they should have predictable, statically assigned addresses.

- **Gateway** – Routers and firewall devices have an IP address assigned to each interface which serves as the gateway for the hosts in that network. Typically, the router interface uses either the lowest or highest address in the network.

Table 8-7 provides a sample of address allocation for a small network.

Table 8-7 IPv4 Address Ranges

Use	First	Last
Host Devices	.1	.229
Servers	.230	.239
Printers	.240	.249
Intermediary Devices	.250	.253
Gateway (router LAN interface)	.254	

When developing an IP addressing scheme, it is generally recommended to have a set pattern of how addresses are allocated to each type of device. This benefits administrators when adding and removing devices, filtering traffic based on IP, as well as simplifying documentation.

Packet Tracer
☐ Activity

Packet Tracer 8.2.1.4: Designing and Implementing a VLSM Addressing Scheme

In this activity, you are given a /24 network address to use to design a VLSM addressing scheme. Based on a set of requirements, you will assign subnets and addresses, configure devices, and verify connectivity.

Lab 8.2.1.5: Designing and Implementing a VLSM Addressing Scheme

In this lab, you will complete the following objectives:

- Part 1: Examine Network Requirements
- Part 2: Design the VLSM Address Scheme
- Part 3: Cable and Configure the IPv4 Network

Design Considerations for IPv6 (8.3)

The current IPv4 address space is exhausted. Many network administrators are now incorporating IPv6 into their addressing plans.

Subnetting an IPv6 Network (8.3.1)

IPv6 global unicast address includes a subnet ID field which makes subnetting IPv6 relatively straightforward.

The IPv6 Global Unicast Address (8.3.1.1)

IPv6 subnetting requires a different approach than IPv4 subnetting. The same reasons for subnetting IPv4 address space in order to manage network traffic also apply to IPv6. However, due to the large number of IPv6 addresses, there is no longer the concern for conserving addresses. The IPv6 address plan can focus on the best hierarchical approach to manage and assign IPv6 subnets. Refer to Figure 8-44 for a quick review of the structure of an IPv6 global unicast address.

Figure 8-44   IPv6 Global Unicast Address Structure

The parts of a global IPv6 global unicast address are as follows:

- **Global Routing Prefix** – This is the prefix, or network, portion of the address that is assigned by the provider. Typically, Regional Internet Registries (RIRs) assign a /48 global routing prefix to ISPs and customers.

- **Subnet ID** – Used by an organization to identify subnets within its site.

- **Interface ID** – This is the equivalent to the host portion of an IPv4 address. The term interface ID is used because a single host may have multiple interfaces, each having one or more IPv6 addresses. It is recommended that a 64-bit interface ID should be used in most networks.

IPv4 subnetting is not only about limiting broadcast domains but also about managing address scarcity. Determining the subnet mask and the use of VLSM is done to help conserve IPv4 addresses. IPv6 subnetting is not concerned with conserving address space. The subnet ID includes more than enough subnets. IPv6 subnetting is about building an addressing hierarchy based on the number of subnetworks needed.

Recall that there are two types of assignable IPv6 addresses. An IPv6 link-local address is never subnetted because it exists only on the local link. However, an IPv6 global unicast address can be subnetted.

The IPv6 global unicast address normally consists of a /48 global routing prefix, a 16-bit subnet ID, and a 64-bit interface ID.

Subnetting Using the Subnet ID (8.3.1.2)

The 16-bit subnet ID section of the IPv6 global unicast address can be used by an organization to create internal subnets.

The subnet ID provides more than enough subnets and host support than will ever be needed in one subnet. For instance, the 16-bit section can:

- Create up to 65,536 /64 subnets. This does not include the possibility of borrowing any bits from the interface ID of the address.

- Support up to 18 quintillion host IPv6 addresses per subnet (i.e., 18,000,000,000,000,000,000).

> **Note**
>
> Subnetting into the 64-bit Interface ID (or host portion) is also possible, but it is rarely required.

IPv6 subnetting is also easier to implement than IPv4, because there is no conversion to binary required. To determine the next available subnet, just count up in hexadecimal.

For example, assume an organization has been assigned the 2001:0DB8:ACAD::/48 global routing prefix with a 16-bit subnet ID. This would allow the organization to create /64 subnets, as shown in Figure 8-45.

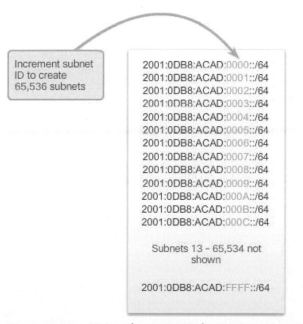

Figure 8-45   Using the 16-Bit Subnet ID to Create Subnets

Notice how the global routing prefix is the same for all subnets. Only the subnet ID hextet is incremented in hexadecimal for each subnet.

IPv6 Subnet Allocation (8.3.1.3)

With over 65,000 subnets to choose from, the task of the network administrator becomes one of designing a logical scheme to address the network.

As shown in Figure 8-46, the example topology will require subnets for each LAN as well as for the WAN link between R1 and R2. Unlike the example for IPv4, with IPv6 the WAN link subnet will not be subnetted further. Although this may "waste" addresses, that is not a concern when using IPv6.

Figure 8-46   Sample IPv6 Topology

As shown in Figure 8-47, the allocation of five IPv6 subnets, with the subnet ID field 0001 through 0005 will be used for this example. Each /64 subnet will provide more addresses than will ever be needed.

Address Block: 2001:0DB8:ACAD::/48

```
                    2001:0DB8:ACAD:0000::/64
                    2001:0DB8:ACAD:0001::/64
5 subnets allocated  2001:0DB8:ACAD:0002::/64
from 65,536          2001:0DB8:ACAD:0003::/64
available subnets    2001:0DB8:ACAD:0004::/64
                    2001:0DB8:ACAD:0005::/64
                    2001:0DB8:ACAD:0006::/64
                    2001:0DB8:ACAD:0007::/64
                    2001:0DB8:ACAD:0008::/64
                         .
                    2001:0DB8:ACAD:FFFF::/64
```

Figure 8-47   IPv6 Subnets

As shown in Figure 8-48, each LAN segment and the WAN link is assigned a /64 subnet.

Figure 8-48   Sample IPv6 Topology with Subnets

Similar to configuring IPv4, Example 8-4 shows that each of the router interfaces has been configured to be on a different IPv6 subnet.

Example 8-4   R1 IPv6 Address Configuration

```
R1(config)# interface gigabitethernet 0/0
R1(config-if)# ipv6 address 2001:db8:acad:1::1/64
R1(config-if)# exit
R1(config)# interface gigabitethernet 0/1
R1(config-if)# ipv6 address 2001:db8:acad:2::1/64
R1(config-if)# exit
R1(config)# interface serial 0/0/0
R1(config-if)# ipv6 address 2001:db8:acad:3::1/64
R1(config-if)# end
R1#
```

Packet Tracer
☐ Activity

Packet Tracer 8.3.1.4: Implementing a Subnetted IPv6 Addressing Scheme

Your network administrator wants you to assign five /64 IPv6 subnets to the network shown in the topology. Your job is to determine the IPv6 subnets, assign IPv6 addresses to the routers, and set the PCs to automatically receive IPv6 addressing. Your final step is to verify connectivity between IPv6 hosts.

Summary (8.4)

Class Activity 8.4.1.1: Can you call me now?

Note

This activity may be completed individually or in small/large groups using Packet Tracer software.

You are setting up a dedicated, computer addressing scheme for patient rooms in a hospital. The switch will be centrally located in the nurses' station, as each of the five rooms will be wired so that patients can just connect to a RJ-45 port built into the wall of their room. Devise a physical and logical topology for only one of the six floors using the following addressing scheme requirements:

- There are six floors, with five patient rooms on each floor, for a total of thirty connections. Each room needs a network connection.

- Subnetting must be incorporated into your scheme.

- Use one router, one switch, and five host stations for addressing purposes.

- Validate that all PCs can connect to the hospital's in-house services.

Keep a copy of your scheme to share later with the class or learning community. Be prepared to explain how subnetting, unicasts, multicasts, and broadcasts would be incorporated, and where your addressing scheme could be used.

Packet Tracer 8.4.1.2: Skills Integration Challenge

Packet Tracer
☐ Activity

As a network technician familiar with IPv4 and IPv6 addressing implementations, you are now ready to take an existing network infrastructure and apply your knowledge and skills to finalize the configuration. The network administrator has already configured some commands on the routers. Do not erase or modify those configurations. Your task is to complete the IPv4 and IPv6 addressing scheme, implement IPv4 and IPv6 addressing, and verify connectivity.

The process of segmenting a network by dividing it into multiple smaller network spaces is called subnetting.

Every network address has a valid range of host addresses. All devices attached to the same network will have an IPv4 host address for that network and a common subnet mask or network prefix. Traffic can be forwarded between hosts directly if they are on the same subnet. Traffic cannot be forwarded between subnets without the use of a router. To determine if traffic is local or remote, the router uses the subnet mask.

The prefix and the subnet mask are different ways of representing the same thing – the network portion of an address.

IPv4 subnets are created by using one or more of the host bits as network bits. Two very important factors that will lead to the determination of the IP address block with the subnet mask are the number of subnets required, and the maximum number of hosts needed per subnet. There is an inverse relationship between the number of subnets and the number of hosts. The more bits that are borrowed to create subnets, the fewer host bits that are available; therefore, there are fewer hosts per subnet.

The formula 2^n (where n is the number of host bits remaining) is used to calculate how many addresses will be available on each subnet. However, the network address and broadcast address within a range are not useable. Therefore, to calculate the useable number of addresses, the calculation $2^n - 2$ is required.

Subnetting a subnet, or using Variable Length Subnet Mask (VLSM), was designed to avoid wasting addresses.

IPv6 subnetting requires a different approach than IPv4 subnetting. An IPv6 address space is not subnetted to conserve addresses; rather it is subnetted to support a hierarchical, logical design of the network. So, whereas IPv4 subnetting is about managing address scarcity, IPv6 subnetting is about building an addressing hierarchy based on the number of routers and the networks they support.

Careful planning is required to make best use of the available address space. Size, location, use, and access requirements are all considerations in the address planning process.

After it is implemented, an IP network needs to be tested to verify its connectivity and operational performance.

Practice

The following activities provide practice with the topics introduced in this chapter. The Labs and Class Activities are available in the companion Introduction to Networks v5.1 Lab Manual (ISBN 9781587133534). The Packet Tracer Activities PKA files are found in the online course.

Class Activities

Class Activity 8.0.1.2: Call Me!

Class Activity 8.4.1.1: Can you call me now?

Labs

Lab 8.1.4.6: Calculating IPv4 Subnets

Lab 8.1.4.8: Designing and Implementing a Subnetted IPv4 Addressing Scheme

Lab 8.2.1.5: Designing and Implementing a VLSM Addressing Scheme

Packet Tracer Activities

Packet Tracer 8.1.4.7: Subnetting Scenario 1

Packet Tracer 8.2.1.4: Designing and Implementing a VLSM Addressing Scheme

Packet Tracer 8.3.1.4: Implementing a Subnetted IPv6 Addressing Scheme

Packet Tracer 8.4.1.2: Skills Integration Challenge

Check Your Understanding Questions

Complete all the review questions listed here to test your understanding of the topics and concepts in this chapter. The appendix "Answers to 'Check Your Understanding' Questions" lists the answers.

1. What are advantages of subnetting a large network? (Choose two.)

   A. More address space is created.

   B. Overall network traffic is reduced.

   C. IP addresses can be reused on the same subnetwork.

   D. Network performance is improved.

   E. Layer 3 devices are not required when a network is subnetted.

2. What device would permit hosts on different subnets to be able to communicate?

   A. Hub

   B. Layer 2 switch

   C. Router

3. Fill in the blank. To create subnets, bits are borrowed from the ____ portion of an IP address.

4. How many subnets can be created if 4 bits are borrowed to specify subnets?

   A. 4

   B. 8

   C. 14

   D. 16

5. What best describes a network broadcast address?

   A. All 0 bits in the host portion of the address

   B. All 0 bits plus a rightmost 1 bit in the host portion of the address

   C. All 1 bits plus a rightmost 0 bit in the host portion of the address

   D. All 1 bits in the host portion of the address

6. How many valid host addresses are created when 4 host bits are borrowed from the 10.20.20.0/24 network?

   A. 2

   B. 4

   C. 14

   D. 16

   E. 126

   F. 128

   G. 254

   H. 256

7. A junior network technician has subnetted the 10.20.30.0/24 address space by borrowing 3 bits. The technician decides to use the second subnet for the Accounting department computers. Which of the following addresses could the network technician assign to hosts? (Choose three.)

   A. 10.20.30.29/27

   B. 10.20.30.31/27

   C. 10.20.30.32/27

   D. 10.20.30.33/27

   E. 10.20.30.34/27

   F. 10.20.30.35/27

8. A junior network technician is assigning host addresses to devices in the 192.168.1.0/25 subnet. The departmental printer is assigned the address 192.168.1.131/25 with a 192.168.1.1/25 default gateway. No one in the department is able to print. What is the cause of the problem?

   A. The default gateway is not correct for the departmental subnet.

   B. The printer has been assigned a broadcast IP address.

   C. The printer has been assigned an address on another subnet.

   D. The printer has been assigned a network IP address.

9. A new department has been established with 511 hosts that require addresses. Currently the company uses the 10.20.0.0/16 address space. How many bits must the network administrator borrow to provide addresses for this subnet without wasting addresses?

   A. 5

   B. 6

   C. 7

   D. 8

   E. 9

10. A network technician borrows 5 bits from the 10.0.0.0/16 network to create subnets. What is the subnet mask that should be associated with each of the newly created subnets?

   A. 255.248.0.0

   B. 255.255.0.0

   C. 255.255.248.0

   D. 255.255.255.0

   E. 255.255.255.248

11. Fill in the blank. _____ provides a more efficient IP address allocation by allowing the use of different-size subnets in the same network.

12. A network administrator has borrowed 3 bits from the 10.20.0.0/25 network to create subnets. The administrator then decided to use the first subnet for point-to-point serial WAN connections each requiring two addresses. How many WAN connections can the administrator address using only the first subnet if he is using VLSM?

   A. 1

   B. 2

   C. 4

   D. 16

E. 32

F. 64

G. 128

13. A network administrator has decided to use VLSM to subnet the 10.11.0.0/20 network to provide addresses for two new departments and the point-to-point link that separates the two departments. The first department has 796 users and the second department has 31 users. The WAN link requires only two addresses. Which of the following subnets will provide the required contiguous space and waste the fewest addresses? (Choose three.)

A. 10.11.0.0/21

B. 10.11.0.0/22

C. 10.11.253.0/25

D. 10.11.253.0/26

E. 10.11.253.128/29

F. 10.11.253.64/30

14. What is the primary purpose of subnetting an IPv6 address space? (Choose two.)

A. Conservation of addresses

B. Support hierarchical network design

C. Manage network traffic

D. Support a classful addressing system

E. Simplify DHCP address assignment

15. What is the most common process to subnet an IPv6 network?

A. Use the range of hexadecimal values in the subnet ID

B. Borrow from the interface ID

C. Borrow from the host portion

CHAPTER 9

Transport Layer

Objectives

Upon completion of this chapter, you will be able to answer the following questions:

- What is the purpose of the transport layer in managing the transportation of data in end-to-end communications?

- What are the characteristics of TCP and UDP?

- What is a port number and what is it used for?

- How do the TCP session establishment and termination processes facilitate reliable communication?

- How are TCP protocol data units transmitted and acknowledged to guarantee delivery?

- How does UDP establish communications with a server?

- What factors determine whether high reliability TCP transmissions, or nonguaranteed UDP transmissions, are best suited for common applications?

Key Terms

This chapter uses the following key terms. You can find the definitions in the Glossary.

Introduction (9.0)

Data networks and the Internet support the human network by supplying reliable communication between people. On a single device, people can use multiple applications and services such as email, the web, and instant messaging to send messages or retrieve information. Data from each of these applications is packaged, transported, and delivered to the appropriate application on the destination device.

The processes described in the OSI transport layer accept data from the application layer and prepare it for addressing at the network layer. A source computer communicates with a receiving computer to decide how to break up data into segments, how to make sure none of the segments get lost, and how to verify all the segments arrived. When thinking about the transport layer, think of a shipping department preparing a single order of multiple packages for delivery.

Class Activity 9.0.1.2: We Need to Talk – Game

- Refer to Lab Activity for this chapter

- Note—This activity works best with medium-sized groups of 6 to 8 students per group.

- The instructor will whisper a complex message to the first student in a group. An example of the message might be "Our final exam will be given next Tuesday, February 5th, at 2 p.m. in Room 1151."

- That student whispers the message to the next student in the group. Each group follows this process until all members of each group have heard the whispered message. Here are the rules you are to follow:

- You can whisper the message only once to your neighbor.

- The message must keep moving from one person to the other with no skipping of participants.

- The instructor should ask a student to track how long it takes for the message to travel from the first person to the last. The first or last person is most likely the best to keep the time.

- The last student will say aloud exactly what he or she heard.

The instructor will then restate the original message so that the group can compare it to the message that was delivered by the last student in the group.

Transport Layer Protocols (9.1)

As previously discussed, for communication to occur between source and destination, a set of rules or protocols must be followed. This section focuses on the protocols at the transport layer.

Transportation of Data (9.1.1)

In the TCP/IP model, data that originates from application programs is passed to the application layer, which in turn passes the data to the transport layer.

Role of the Transport Layer (9.1.1.1)

The transport layer is responsible for establishing a temporary communication session between two applications and delivering data between them. An application generates data that is sent from an application on a source host to an application on a destination host. This is without regard to the destination host type, the type of media over which the data must travel, the path taken by the data, the congestion on a link, or the size of the network. As shown in Figure 9-1, the transport layer is the link between the application layer and the lower layers that are responsible for network transmission.

Figure 9-1   Enabling Applications on Devices to Communicate

Transport Layer Responsibilities (9.1.1.2)

Tracking Individual Conversations

At the transport layer, each set of data flowing between a source application and a destination application is known as a conversation (Figure 9-2). A host may have multiple applications that are communicating across the network simultaneously. Each of these applications communicates with one or more applications on one or more remote hosts. It is the responsibility of the transport layer to maintain and track these multiple conversations.

Figure 9-2   Tracking the Conversation

Segmenting Data and Reassembling Segments

Data must be prepared to be sent across the media in manageable pieces. Most networks have a limitation on the amount of data that can be included in a single packet. Transport layer protocols have services that segment the application data into blocks that are an appropriate size (Figure 9-3). This service includes the encapsulation required on each piece of data. A header, used for reassembly, is added to each block of data. This header is used to track the data stream.

Figure 9-3   Segmenting the Traffic

At the destination, the transport layer must be able to reconstruct the pieces of data into a complete data stream that is useful to the application layer. The protocols at the transport layer describe how the transport layer header information is used to reassemble the data pieces into streams to be passed to the application layer.

Identifying the Applications

To pass data streams to the proper applications, the transport layer must identify the target application (Figure 9-4). To accomplish this, the transport layer assigns each application an identifier called a *port number*. Each software process that needs to access the network is assigned a port number unique to that host.

Figure 9-4   Identifying the Application

Conversation Multiplexing (9.1.1.3)

Sending some types of data (for example, a streaming video) across a network, as one complete communication stream, can consume all of the available bandwidth. This will then prevent other communications from occurring at the same time. It would also make error recovery and retransmission of damaged data difficult.

As shown in Figure 9-5, *multiplexing* divides the data into smaller segments and enables communications from many different users to be interleaved (multiplexed) on the same network.

Figure 9-5 Multiplexing Conversations

To identify each segment of data, the transport layer adds a header containing binary data organized into several fields. It is the values in these fields that enable various transport layer protocols to perform different functions in managing data communication.

Transport Layer Reliability (9.1.1.4)

The transport layer is also responsible for managing reliability requirements of a conversation. Different applications have different transport reliability requirements.

IP is concerned only with the structure, addressing, and routing of packets. IP does not specify how the delivery or transportation of the packets takes place. Transport protocols specify how to transfer messages between hosts. TCP/IP provides two transport layer protocols, *Transmission Control Protocol (TCP)* and *User Datagram Protocol (UDP)*, as shown in Figure 9-6. IP uses these transport protocols to enable hosts to communicate and transfer data.

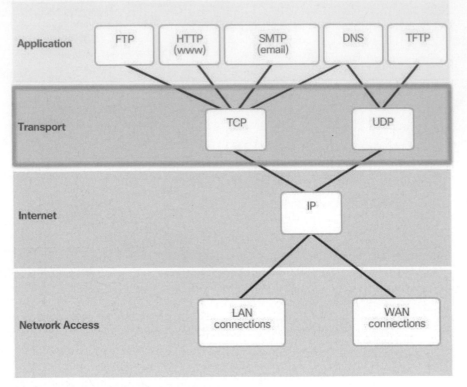

Figure 9-6   Transport Layer Protocols

TCP is considered a reliable, full-featured transport layer protocol, which ensures that all of the data arrives at the destination. However, this requires additional fields in the TCP header which increases the size of the packet and also increases delay. In contrast, UDP is a simpler transport layer protocol that does not provide for reliability. It therefore has fewer fields and is faster than TCP.

TCP (9.1.1.5)

TCP transport is analogous to sending packages that are tracked from source to destination. If a shipping order is broken up into several packages, a customer can check online to see the order of the delivery.

With TCP, there are three basic operations of reliability:

- Numbering and tracking data segments transmitted to a specific host from a specific application

- Acknowledging received data

- Retransmitting any unacknowledged data after a certain period of time

Video

Go to the online course to view an animation of TCP segments and acknowledgements being transmitted between sender and receiver.

UDP (9.1.1.6)

Whereas the TCP reliability functions provide more robust communication between applications, they also incur additional overhead and possible delays in transmission. There is a trade-off between the value of reliability and the burden it places on network resources. Adding overhead to ensure reliability for some applications could reduce the usefulness of the application and can even be detrimental. In such cases, UDP is a better transport protocol.

UDP provides the basic functions for delivering data segments between the appropriate applications, with very little overhead and data checking. UDP is known as a best-effort delivery protocol. In the context of networking, best-effort delivery is referred to as unreliable because there is no acknowledgement that the data is received at the destination. With UDP, there are no transport layer processes that inform the sender of a successful delivery.

UDP is similar to placing a regular, non-registered, letter in the mail. The sender of the letter is not aware of the availability of the receiver to receive the letter. Nor is the post office responsible for tracking the letter or informing the sender if the letter does not arrive at the final destination.

Video

Go to the online course to view an animation of UDP segments being transmitted from sender to receiver.

The Right Transport Layer Protocol for the Right Application (9.1.1.7)

For some applications, segments must arrive in a very specific sequence to be processed successfully. With other applications, all data must be fully received before any is considered useful. In both of these instances, TCP is used as the transport protocol. Application developers must choose which transport protocol type is appropriate based on the requirements of the applications, as shown in Figure 9-7.

Figure 9-7   Choosing a Transport Layer Protocol

For example, applications such as databases, web browsers, and email clients, require that all data that is sent arrives at the destination in its original condition. Any missing data could cause a corrupt communication that is either incomplete or unreadable. These applications are designed to use TCP.

In other cases, an application can tolerate some data loss during transmission over the network, but delays in transmission are unacceptable. UDP is the better choice for these applications because less network overhead is required. UDP is preferable for applications such as streaming live audio, live video, and Voice over IP (VoIP). Acknowledgements and retransmission would slow down delivery.

For example, if one or two segments of a live video stream fail to arrive, it creates a momentary disruption in the stream. This may appear as distortion in the image or sound, but may not be noticeable to the user. If the destination device had to account for lost data, the stream could be delayed while waiting for retransmissions, therefore causing the image or sound to be greatly degraded. In this case, it is better to render the best media possible with the segments received, and forego reliability.

> **Note**
>
> Applications that stream stored audio and video use TCP. For example, if your network suddenly cannot support the bandwidth needed to watch an on-demand movie, the application pauses the playback. During the pause, you might see a "buffering..." message whereas TCP works to re-establish the stream. Once all the segments are in order and a minimum level of bandwidth is restored, your TCP session resumes and the movie begins playing.

TCP and UDP Overview (9.1.2)

As previously mentioned, both TCP and UDP are transport layer protocols. It is up to the developer to determine which of these protocols best match the requirements of the application being developed. Regardless of the choice, a good understanding of both protocols is required by any networker.

TCP Features (9.1.2.1)

To understand the differences between TCP and UDP, it is important to understand how each protocol implements specific reliability features and how they track conversations. In addition to supporting the basic functions of data segmentation and reassembly, TCP, as shown in Figure 9-8, also provides other services.

Figure 9-8   TCP Services

Establishing a Session

TCP is a *connection-oriented* protocol. A connection-oriented protocol is one that negotiates and establishes a virtual connection (or session) between source and destination devices prior to forwarding any traffic. Through session establishment, the devices negotiate the amount of traffic that can be forwarded at a given time, and the communication data between the two can be closely managed.

Reliable Delivery

In networking terms, reliability means ensuring that each segment that the source sends arrives at the destination. For many reasons, it is possible for a segment to become corrupted or lost completely, as it is transmitted over the network.

Same-Order Delivery

Because networks may provide multiple routes that can have different transmission rates, data can arrive in the wrong order. By numbering and sequencing the segments, TCP can ensure that these segments are reassembled into the proper order.

Flow Control

Network hosts have limited resources, such as memory and processing power. When TCP is aware that these resources are overtaxed, it can request that the sending application reduce the rate of data flow. This is done by TCP regulating the amount of data the source transmits. Flow control can prevent the need for retransmission of the data when the receiving host's resources are overwhelmed.

For more information on TCP, search the Internet for RFC 793.

TCP Header (9.1.2.2)

TCP is a *stateful* protocol. A stateful protocol is a protocol that keeps track of the state of the communication session. To track the state of a session, TCP records which information it has sent and which information has been acknowledged. The stateful session begins with the session establishment and ends when closed with the session termination.

The TCP segment header is shown in Figure 9-9.

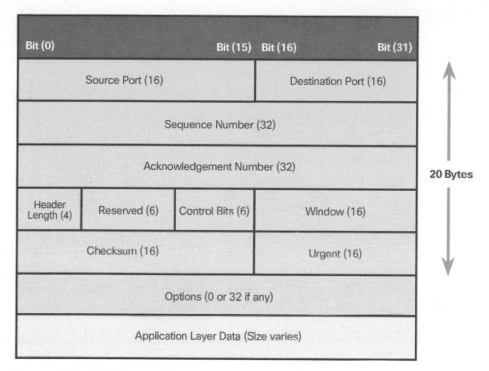

Figure 9-9   TCP Segment Header

Each TCP segment has 20 bytes of overhead in the header encapsulating the application layer data:

- **Source Port (16 bits) and Destination Port (16 bits)** – Used to identify a sending devices port number and the destination port number on the target device.

- **Sequence number (32 bits)** – Used for data reassembly purposes.

- **Acknowledgement number (32 bits)** – Indicates the data that has been received.

- **Header length (4 bits)** – Known as "data offset." Indicates the length of the TCP segment header.

- **Reserved (6 bits)** – This field is reserved for the future.

- **Control bits (6 bits)** – Known as flags, these identify bit codes that indicate the purpose and function of the TCP segment.

- **Window size (16 bits)** – Indicates the number of bytes that can be accepted at one time.

- **Checksum (16 bits)** – Used for error checking of the segment header and data.

- **Urgent (16 bits)** – Indicates if data is urgent.

UDP Features (9.1.2.3)

User Datagram Protocol (UDP) is considered a best-effort transport protocol. UDP is a lightweight transport protocol that offers the same data segmentation and reassembly as TCP, but without TCP reliability and flow control. UDP is such a simple protocol that it is usually described in terms of what it does not do compared to TCP.

The features of UDP are described in Figure 9-10.

Figure 9-10   UDP Services

For more information on UDP, search the Internet for RFC 768.

UDP Header (9.1.2.4)

UDP is a stateless protocol, meaning neither the client, nor the server, is obligated to keep track of the state of the communication session. If reliability is required when using UDP as the transport protocol, it must be handled by the application.

One of the most important requirements for delivering live video and voice over the network is that the data continues to flow quickly. Live video and voice applications can tolerate some data loss with minimal or no noticeable effect, and are perfectly suited to UDP.

The pieces of communication in UDP are called datagrams, as shown in Figure 9-11. These datagrams are sent as best-effort by the transport layer protocol. UDP has a low overhead of 8 bytes.

Figure 9-11   UDP Datagram Header

Multiple Separate Conversations (9.1.2.5)

The transport layer must be able to separate and manage multiple communications with different transport requirement needs. Users expect to be able to simultaneously receive and send email and instant messages, view websites, and conduct a VoIP phone call. Each of these applications is sending and receiving data over the network at the same time, despite different reliability requirements. Additionally, data from the phone call is not directed to the web browser, and text from an instant message does not appear in an email.

TCP and UDP manage these multiple simultaneous conversations by using header fields that can uniquely identify these applications. These unique identifiers are the port numbers, as shown in Figure 9-12.

Figure 9-12   Application Port Numbers

Port Numbers (9.1.2.6)

The source port number is associated with the originating application on the local host. The destination port number is associated with the destination application on the remote host.

Source Port

The source port number is dynamically generated by the sending device to identify a conversation between two devices. This process allows multiple conversations to occur simultaneously. It is common for a device to send multiple HTTP service requests to a web server at the same time. Each separate HTTP conversation is tracked based on the source ports.

Destination Port

The client places a destination port number in the segment to tell the destination server what service is being requested, as shown in Figure 9-13. For example, when a client specifies port 80 in the destination port, the server that receives the message knows that web services are being requested. A server can offer more than one service simultaneously such as web services on port 80 at the same time that it offers File Transfer Protocol (FTP) connection establishment on port 21.

Figure 9-13   Transport Layer Adds Port Numbers to Application Data

Socket Pairs (9.1.2.7)

The source and destination ports are placed within the segment. The segments are then encapsulated within an IP packet. The IP packet contains the IP address of the source and destination. The combination of the source IP address and source port number, or the destination IP address and destination port number is known as a *socket*. The socket is used to identify the server and service being requested by the client, as shown in Figure 9-14.

Figure 9-14   Examples of Socket Pairs

A client socket might look like this, with 1099 representing the source port number: 192.168.1.5:1099

The socket on a web server might be 192.168.1.7:80

Together, these two sockets combine to form a socket pair: 192.168.1.5:1099, 192.168.1.7:80

Sockets enable multiple processes, running on a client, to distinguish themselves from each other, and multiple connections to a server process to be distinguished from each other.

The source port number acts as a return address for the requesting application. The transport layer keeps track of this port and the application that initiated the request so that when a response is returned, it can be forwarded to the correct application.

Port Number Groups (9.1.2.8)

The Internet Assigned Numbers Authority (IANA) is the standards body responsible for assigning various addressing standards, including port numbers. There are different types of port numbers:

- **Well-known Ports (Numbers 0 to 1023)** – These numbers are reserved for services and applications. They are commonly used for applications such as web browsers, email clients, and remote access clients. By defining these well-known ports for server applications, client applications can be programmed to request a connection to that specific port and its associated service.

- **Registered Ports (Numbers 1024 to 49151)** – These port numbers are assigned by IANA to a requesting entity to use with specific processes or applications. These processes are primarily individual applications that a user has chosen to install, rather than common applications that would receive a well-known port number. For example, Cisco has registered port 1985 for its Hot Standby Routing Protocol (HSRP) process.

- **Dynamic or Private Ports (Numbers 49152 to 65535)** – Also known as ephemeral ports, these are usually assigned dynamically by the client's OS when a connection to a service is initiated. The dynamic port is then used to identify the client application during communication.

> **Note**
>
> Some client operating systems may use registered port numbers instead of dynamic port numbers for assigning source ports.

Table 9-1 displays some common well-known port numbers and their associated applications. Some applications may use both TCP and UDP. For example, DNS uses UDP when clients send requests to a DNS server. However, communication between two DNS servers always uses TCP.

Table 9-1   Well-Known Port Numbers

Port Number	Protocol	Application	Acronym
20	TCP	File Transfer Protocol (data)	FTP
21	TCP	File Transfer Protocol (control)	FTP
22	TCP	Secure Shell	SSH

Continued

Table 9-1 *Continued*

Port Number	Protocol	Application	Acronym
23	TCP	Telnet	–
25	TCP	Simple Mail Transfer Protocol	SMTP
53	UDP, TCP	Domain Name Service	DNS
67, 68	UDP	Dynamic Host Configuration Protocol	DHCP
69	UDP	Trivial File Transfer Protocol	TFTP
80	TCP	Hypertext Transfer Protocol	HTTP
110	TCP	Post Office Protocol version 3	POP3
143	TCP	Internet Message Access Protocol	IMAP
161	UDP	Simple Network Management Protocol	SNMP
443	TCP	Hypertext Transfer Protocol Secure	HTTPS

The netstat Command (9.1.2.9)

Unexplained TCP connections can pose a major security threat. They can indicate that something or someone is connected to the local host. Sometimes it is necessary to know which active TCP connections are open and running on a networked host. Netstat is an important network utility that can be used to verify those connections. As Example 9-1, enter the command **netstat** to list the protocols in use, the local address and port numbers, the foreign address and port numbers, and the connection state.

Example 9-1 Output from the **netstat** Command

```
C:\> netstat

Active Connections

 Proto Local Address Foreign Address State
 TCP kenpc:3126 192.168.0.2:netbios-ssn ESTABLISHED
 TCP kenpc:3158 207.138.126.152:http ESTABLISHED
 TCP kenpc:3159 207.138.126.169:http ESTABLISHED
 TCP kenpc:3160 66.163.36.181:https ESTABLISHED
 TCP kenpc:3161 sc.msn.com:http ESTABLISHED
 TCP kenpc:3166 www.cisco.com:http ESTABLISHED
<output omitted>
C:\>
```

By default, the **netstat** command will attempt to resolve IP addresses to domain names and port numbers to well-known applications. The **-n** option can be used to display IP addresses and port numbers in their numerical form.

Activity 9.1.2.10: Compare TCP and UDP Characteristics

Go to the online course to perform this practice activity.

Interactive Graphic

TCP and UDP (9.2)

We have seen that two different protocols exist at the transport layer, each with distinct characteristics. Both of these protocols support communication between source and destination, but the way this communication occurs is different between the two protocols.

TCP Communication Process (9.2.1)

Recall that TCP is considered a stateful protocol because it establishes a session between source and destination and keeps track of the data within that session. UDP is a stateless protocol and does not keep track of the data. So how does TCP establish this connection and track the data?

TCP Server Processes (9.2.1.1)

Each application process running on the server is configured to use a port number, either by default or manually, by a system administrator. An individual server cannot have two services assigned to the same port number within the same transport layer services.

For example, a host running a web server application and a file transfer application cannot have both configured to use the same port (for example, TCP port 80). An active server application assigned to a specific port is considered to be open, which means that the transport layer accepts and processes segments addressed to that port. Any incoming client request addressed to the correct socket is accepted, and the data is passed to the server application. There can be many ports open simultaneously on a server, one for each active server application.

Refer to Figures 9-15 through 9-19 to see the typical allocation of source and destination ports in TCP client/server operations.

Figure 9-15   Clients Sending TCP Requests

Figure 9-16   Request Destination Ports

Figure 9-17   Request Source Ports

Figure 9-18   Response Destination Ports

Figure 9-19   Response Source Ports

TCP Connection Establishment (9.2.1.2)

In some cultures, when two persons meet, they often greet each other by shaking hands. The act of shaking hands is understood by both parties as a signal for a friendly greeting. Connections on the network are similar. In TCP connections, the host client establishes the connection with the server.

A TCP connection is established in three steps:

Step 1.   The initiating client requests a client-to-server communication session with the server (Figure 9-20).

Figure 9-20   Step 1: A Sends SYN to B

Step 2.   The server acknowledges the client-to-server communication session and requests a server-to-client communication session (Figure 9-21).

Figure 9-21   Step 2: B Sends SYN and ACK to A

Step 3.   The initiating client acknowledges the server-to-client communication session (Figure 9-22).

Figure 9-22   Step 3: A Sends ACK to B

TCP Session Termination (9.2.1.3)

To close a connection, the Finish (FIN) control flag must be set in the segment header. To end each one-way TCP session, a two-way handshake, consisting of a FIN segment and an Acknowledgement (ACK) segment, is used. Therefore, to terminate a single conversation supported by TCP, four exchanges are needed to end both sessions.

Note

In this explanation, the terms client and server are used as a reference for simplicity, but the termination process can be initiated by any two hosts that have an open session:

Step 1. When the client has no more data to send in the stream, it sends a segment with the FIN flag set (Figure 9-23).

A sends FIN request to B.

Figure 9-23 Step 1: A Sends FIN to B

Step 2. The server sends an ACK to acknowledge the receipt of the FIN to terminate the session from client to server (Figure 9-24).

B sends ACK response to A.

Figure 9-24 Step 2: B Sends ACK to A

Step 3. The server sends a FIN to the client to terminate the server-to-client session (Figure 9-25).

Figure 9-25 Step 3: B Sends FIN to A

Step 4. The client responds with an ACK to acknowledge the FIN from the server (Figure 9-26).

Figure 9-26 Step 4: A Sends ACK to B

When all segments have been acknowledged, the session is closed (Figure 9-27).

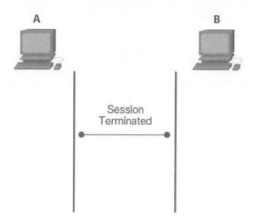

Figure 9-27 Session Is Terminated

TCP Three-way Handshake Analysis (9.2.1.4)

Hosts track each data segment within a session and exchange information about what data is received using the information in the TCP header. TCP is a full-duplex protocol, where each connection represents two one-way communication streams or sessions. To establish the connection, the hosts perform a *three-way handshake*. Control bits in the TCP header indicate the progress and status of the connection.

The three-way handshake

- Establishes that the destination device is present on the network

- Verifies that the destination device has an active service and is accepting requests on the destination port number that the initiating client intends to use

- Informs the destination device that the source client intends to establish a communication session on that port number

After the communication is completed, the sessions are closed, and the connection is terminated. The connection and session mechanisms enable TCP's reliability function.

The six bits in the Control Bits field of the TCP segment header are also known as flags. A flag is a bit that is either set to on or off. The Control Bits field is highlighted in Figure 9-28. We have discussed SYN, ACK, and FIN. The RST flag is used to reset a connection when an error or timeout occurs.

Figure 9-28   The Control Bits Field

Video

Video Demonstration 9.2.1.5: TCP 3-Way Handshake

Go to the online course to view this video.

Lab 9.2.1.6: Using Wireshark to Observe the TCP 3-Way Handshake

In this lab, you will complete the following objectives:

- Part 1: Prepare Wireshark to Capture Packets
- Part 2: Capture, Locate, and Examine Packets

Interactive
Graphic

Activity 9.2.1.7: TCP Connection and Termination Process

Go to the online course to perform this practice activity.

Reliability and Flow Control (9.2.2)

Reliability and flow control are two of the main features of TCP, not present in UDP.

TCP Reliability – Ordered Delivery (9.2.2.1)

Ordered Delivery

TCP segments may arrive at their destination out of order. For the original message to be understood by the recipient, the data in these segments is reassembled into the original order. Sequence numbers are assigned in the header of each packet to achieve this goal. The sequence number represents the first data byte of the TCP segment.

During session setup, an *initial sequence number (ISN)* is set. This ISN represents the starting value of the bytes for this session that is transmitted to the receiving application. As data is transmitted during the session, the sequence number is incremented by the number of bytes that have been transmitted. This data byte tracking enables each segment to be uniquely identified and acknowledged. Missing segments can then be identified.

Note

The ISN does not begin at one but is effectively a random number. This is to prevent certain types of malicious attacks. For simplicity, we will use an ISN of 1 for the examples in this chapter.

Segment sequence numbers indicate how to reassemble and reorder received segments, as shown in Figure 9-29.

Figure 9-29   TCP Segments Are Reordered at the Destination

The receiving TCP process places the data from a segment into a receiving buffer. Segments are placed in the proper sequence order and passed to the application layer when reassembled. Any segments that arrive with sequence numbers that are out of order are held for later processing. Then, when the segments with the missing bytes arrive, these segments are processed in order.

Reliability

Along with the ability to reorder segments, a mechanism is required to ensure that all segments are delivered.

One of the functions of TCP is ensuring that each segment reaches its destination. The TCP services on the destination host acknowledge the data that it has received by the source application.

The sequence (SEQ) number and acknowledgement (ACK) number are used together to confirm receipt of the bytes of data contained in the transmitted segments. The SEQ number identifies the first byte of data in the segment being transmitted. TCP uses the ACK number sent back to the source to indicate the next byte that the receiver expects to receive. This is called *expectational acknowledgement*.

The source is informed that the destination has received all bytes in this data stream up to, but not including, the byte indicated by the ACK number. The sending host is expected to send a segment with the first byte equal to the ACK number.

For example, the receiving host receives the segment at Layer 4 and determines that the sequence number is 1 and that it has 10 bytes of data. The host then sends a segment back to the host on the left to acknowledge the receipt of this data. In this segment, the host sets the ACK number to 11 to indicate that the next byte of data it expects to receive in this session is byte number 11. When the sending host receives this acknowledgement, it can now send the next segment containing data for this session starting with byte number 11.

No matter how well designed a network is, data loss occasionally occurs; therefore, TCP provides methods of managing these segment losses. Among these is a mechanism to retransmit segments with unacknowledged data.

A destination host service using TCP acknowledges data for contiguous sequence bytes. If one or more segments are missing, only the data in the first contiguous sequence of bytes is acknowledged. For example, if segments with sequence numbers 1500 to 3000 and 3400 to 3500 were received, the ACK number would be 3001. This is because there are segments with the SEQ numbers 3001 to 3399 that have not been received.

When TCP at the source host has not received an acknowledgement after a predetermined amount of time, it returns to the last ACK number received and retransmits the data from that point forward. The retransmission process is not specified by the Request for Comments (RFC), but is left up to the particular implementation of TCP.

For a typical TCP implementation, a host can transmit a segment, put a copy of the segment in a retransmission queue, and start a timer. When the data acknowledgement is received, the segment is deleted from the queue. If the acknowledgement is not received before the timer expires, the segment is retransmitted.

Note

TCP employs several algorithms for handling data loss, retransmission, congestion, and congestion avoidance. These algorithms and processes are beyond the scope of this course.

Hosts today typically employ an optional feature called *selective acknowledgements (SACK)*. If both hosts support SACKs, it is possible for the destination to acknowledge bytes in discontinuous segments and the host would only need to retransmit the missing data.

Video Demonstration 9.2.2.2: Sequence Numbers and Acknowledgements

One of the functions of TCP is ensuring that each segment reaches its destination. The TCP services on the destination host acknowledge the data that it has received by the source application.

Go to the online course to view this video.

Video Demonstration 9.2.2.3: Data Loss and Retransmission

No matter how well designed a network is, data loss occasionally occurs; therefore, TCP provides methods of managing these segment losses. Among these is a mechanism to retransmit segments for unacknowledged data.

Go to the online course to view this video.

TCP Flow Control – Window Size and Acknowledgements (9.2.2.4)

TCP also provides mechanisms for flow control, the amount of data that the destination can receive and process reliably. Flow control helps maintain the reliability of TCP transmission by adjusting the rate of data flow between source and destination for a given session. To accomplish this, the TCP header includes a 16-bit field called the *window size*.

Figure 9-30 shows an example of window size and acknowledgements.

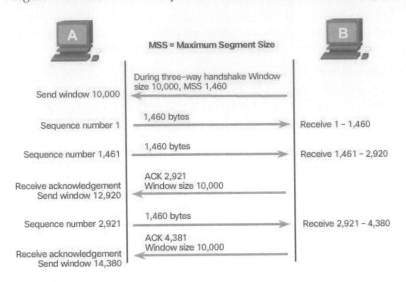

Figure 9-30   TCP Window Size Example

The window size is the number of bytes that the destination device of a TCP session can accept and process at one time. In this example, PC B's initial window size for the TCP session is 10,000 bytes. Starting with the first byte, byte number 1, the last byte PC A can send without receiving an acknowledgement is byte 10,000. This is known as PC A's send window. The window size is included in every TCP segment, so the destination can modify the window size at any time depending on buffer availability.

Note

In the figure, the source is transmitting 1,460 bytes of data within each TCP segment. This is known as the Maximum Segment Size (MSS).

The initial window size is agreed upon when the TCP session is established during the three-way handshake. The source device must limit the number of bytes sent to the destination device based on the destination's window size. Only after the source device receives an acknowledgement that the bytes have been received, can it continue sending more data for the session. Typically, the destination will not wait for all the bytes for its window size to be received before replying with an acknowledgement. As the bytes are received and processed, the destination will send acknowledgements to inform the source that it can continue to send additional bytes.

Typically, PC B will not wait until all 10,000 bytes have been received before sending an acknowledgement. This means PC A can adjust its send window as it receives acknowledgements from PC B. As shown in the figure, when PC A receives an acknowledgement with the acknowledgement number 2,921, PC A's send window will increment another 10,000 bytes (the size of PC B's current window size) to 12,920.

PC A can now continue to send up to another 10,000 bytes to PC B as long as it does not send past its new send window at 12,920. The process of the destination sending acknowledgements as it processes bytes received and the continual adjustment of the source's send window is known as sliding windows.

> **Note**
>
> Devices typically use the sliding windows protocol. With sliding windows, the receiver does not wait for the number of bytes in its window size to be reached before sending an acknowledgement. The receiver typically sends an acknowledgement after every two segments it receives. The number of segments received before being acknowledged may vary. The advantage of sliding windows is that it allows the sender to continuously transmit segments as long as the receiver is acknowledging previous segments. The details of sliding windows are beyond the scope of this course.

If the availability of the destination's buffer space decreases, it may reduce its window size to inform the source to reduce the number of bytes it should send without receiving an acknowledgement.

TCP Flow Control – Congestion Avoidance (9.2.2.5)

When congestion occurs on a network, it results in packets being discarded by the overloaded router. When packets containing TCP segments don't reach their destination, they are left unacknowledged. By determining the rate at which TCP segments are sent but not acknowledged, the source can assume a certain level of network congestion.

Whenever there is congestion, retransmission of lost TCP segments from the source will occur, as shown in Figure 9-31.

Figure 9-31   TCP Congestion Control

If the retransmission is not properly controlled, the additional retransmission of the TCP segments can make the congestion even worse. Not only are new packets with TCP segments introduced into the network, but the feedback effect of the retransmitted TCP segments that were lost will also add to the congestion. To avoid and control congestion, TCP employs several congestion handling mechanisms, timers, and algorithms.

If the source determines that the TCP segments are either not being acknowledged or not acknowledged in a timely manner, then it can reduce the number of bytes it sends before receiving an acknowledgement. Notice that it is the source that is reducing the number of unacknowledged bytes it sends and not the window size determined by the destination.

Note

Explanation of actual congestion handling mechanisms, timers, and algorithms are beyond the scope of this course.

UDP Communication (9.2.3)

Sometimes the reliability associated with TCP is not required or the overhead associated with providing this reliability is not suitable for the application. This is where UDP is used.

UDP Low Overhead versus Reliability (9.2.3.1)

UDP is a simple protocol that provides the basic transport layer functions. As shown in Figure 9-32, UDP has much lower overhead than TCP because it is not connection-oriented and does not offer the sophisticated retransmission, sequencing, and flow control mechanisms that provide reliability.

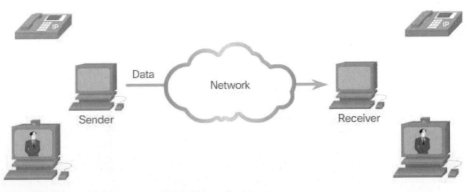

Figure 9-32 UDP Low Overhead Data Transport

This does not mean that applications that use UDP are always unreliable, nor does it mean that UDP is an inferior protocol. It simply means that these functions are not provided by the transport layer protocol and must be implemented elsewhere if required.

The low overhead of UDP makes it very desirable for protocols that make simple request and reply transactions. For example, using TCP for DHCP would introduce unnecessary network traffic. If there is a problem with a request or a reply, the device simply sends the request again if no response is received.

UDP Datagram Reassembly (9.2.3.2)

Like segments with TCP, when UDP datagrams are sent to a destination, they often take different paths and arrive in the wrong order. UDP does not track sequence numbers the way TCP does. UDP has no way to reorder the datagrams into their transmission order, as shown in Figure 9-33.

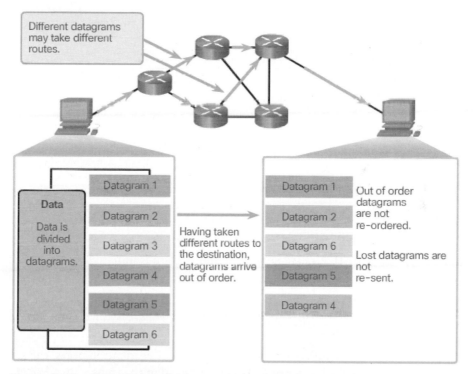

Figure 9-33   UDP: Connectionless and Unreliable

Therefore, UDP simply reassembles the data in the order that it was received and forwards it to the application. If the data sequence is important to the application, the application must identify the proper sequence and determine how the data should be processed.

UDP Server Processes and Requests (9.2.3.3)

Like TCP-based applications, UDP-based server applications are assigned well-known or registered port numbers, as shown in Figure 9-34. When these applications or processes are running on a server, they accept the data matched with the assigned port number. When UDP receives a datagram destined for one of these ports, it forwards the application data to the appropriate application based on its port number.

Figure 9-34   UDP Server Listening for Requests

Note

The Remote Authentication Dial-in User Service (RADIUS) server shown in the figure provides authentication, authorization, and accounting services to manage user access. The operation of RADIUS is beyond the scope of this course.

UDP Client Processes (9.2.3.4)

As with TCP, client-server communication is initiated by a client application that requests data from a server process. The UDP client process dynamically selects a port number from the range of port numbers and uses this as the source port for the conversation. The destination port is usually the well-known or registered port number assigned to the server process.

After a client has selected the source and destination ports, the same pair of ports is used in the header of all datagrams used in the transaction. For the data returning to the client from the server, the source and destination port numbers in the datagram header are reversed. This is essentially the same process as illustrated for TCP in Figure 9-15 through 9-19.

Lab 9.2.3.5: Using Wireshark to Examine a UDP DNS Capture

In this lab, you will complete the following objectives:

- Part 1: Record a PC's IP Configuration Information
- Part 2: Use Wireshark to Capture DNS Queries and Responses
- Part 3: Analyze Captured DNS or UDP Packets

TCP or UDP (9.2.4)

As previously stated, the decision to use TCP or UDP as a transport layer protocol rests with the application developer. Each protocol has unique characteristics that must be matched to the specific application.

Applications that Use TCP (9.2.4.1)

TCP is a great example of how the different layers of the TCP/IP protocol suite have specific roles. TCP handles all tasks associated with dividing the data stream into segments, providing reliability, controlling data flow, and the reordering of segments. TCP frees the application from having to manage any of these tasks. Applications, like those shown in Figure 9-35, can simply send the data stream to the transport layer and use the services of TCP.

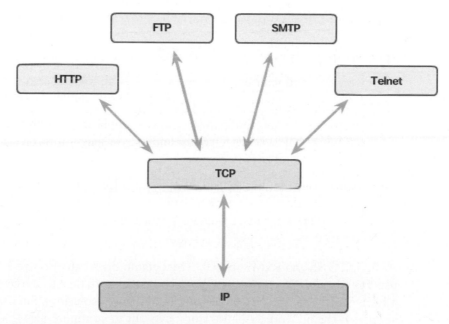

Figure 9-35   TCP Applications

Applications that Use UDP (9.2.4.2)

Common UDP applications are shown in Figure 9-36.

Figure 9-36   UDP Applications

There are three types of applications that are best suited for UDP:

- **Live video and multimedia applications** – Can tolerate some data loss, but require little or no delay. Examples include VoIP and live streaming video.

- **Simple request and reply applications** – Applications with simple transactions where a host sends a request and may or may not receive a reply. Examples include DNS and DHCP.

- **Applications that handle reliability themselves** – Unidirectional communications where flow control, error detection, acknowledgements, and error recovery is not required or can be handled by the application. Examples include SNMP and TFTP.

Although DNS and SNMP use UDP by default, both can also use TCP. DNS will use TCP if the DNS request or DNS response is more than 512 bytes, such as when a DNS response includes a large number of name resolutions. Similarly, under some situations the network administrator may want to configure SNMP to use TCP.

Lab 9.2.4.3: Using Wireshark to Examine FTP and TFTP Captures

In this lab, you will complete the following objectives:

- Part 1: Identify TCP Header Fields and Operation Using a Wireshark FTP Session Capture

- Part 2: Identify UDP Header Fields and Operation Using a Wireshark TFTP Session Capture

---

Interactive
Graphic

Activity 9.2.4.4: TCP, UDP, or Both

Go to the online course to perform this practice activity.

Summary (9.3)

Class Activity 9.3.1.1: We Need to Talk, Again – Game

Note

It is important that the students have completed the Introductory Modeling Activity for this chapter. This activity works best in medium-sized groups of 6 to 8 students.

The instructor will whisper a complex message to the first student in a group. An example of the message might be "We are expecting a blizzard tomorrow. It should be arriving in the morning, and school will be delayed two hours, so bring your homework."

That student whispers the message to the next student in the group. The last student of each group whispers the message to a student in the following group. Each group follows this process until all members of each group have heard the whispered message.

Here are the rules you are to follow:

- You can whisper the message in short parts to your neighbor AND you can repeat the message parts after verifying your neighbor heard the correct message.

- Small parts of the message may be checked and repeated (clockwise OR counter-clockwise to ensure accuracy of the message parts) by whispering. A student will be assigned to time the entire activity.

- When the message has reached the end of the group, the last student will say aloud what she or he heard. Small parts of the message may be repeated (i.e., re-sent), and the process can be restarted to ensure that ALL parts of the message are fully delivered and correct.

- The Instructor will restate the original message to check for quality delivery.

Packet Tracer 9.3.1.2: TCP and UDP Communications

This simulation activity is intended to provide a foundation for understanding the TCP and UDP in detail. Simulation mode provides the ability to view the functionality of the different protocols.

As data moves through the network, it is broken down into smaller pieces and identified in some fashion so that the pieces can be put back together. Each of these pieces is assigned a specific name (PDU) and associated with a specific layer. Packet Tracer Simulation mode enables the user to view each of the protocols and the associated PDU.

This activity provides an opportunity to explore the functionality of the TCP and UDP protocols, multiplexing, and the function of port numbers in determining which local application requested the data or is sending the data.

The transport layer provides transport-related services by

- Dividing data received from an application into segments

- Adding a header to identify and manage each segment

- Using the header information to reassemble the segments back into application data

- Passing the assembled data to the correct application

UDP and TCP are common transport layer protocols.

UDP datagrams and TCP segments have headers added in front of the data that include a source port number and destination port number. These port numbers enable data to be directed to the correct application running on the destination computer.

TCP does not pass any data to the network until it knows that the destination is ready to receive it. TCP then manages the flow of the data and resends any data segments that are not acknowledged as being received at the destination. TCP uses mechanisms of handshaking, timers, acknowledgement messages, and dynamic windowing to achieve reliability. The reliability process, however, imposes overhead on the network in terms of much larger segment headers and more network traffic between the source and destination.

If the application data needs to be delivered across the network quickly, or if network bandwidth cannot support the overhead of control messages being exchanged between the source and the destination systems, UDP would be the developer's preferred transport layer protocol. UDP provides none of the TCP reliability features. However, this does not necessarily mean that the communication itself is unreliable; there may be mechanisms in the application layer protocols and services that process lost or delayed datagrams if the application has these requirements.

The application developer decides the transport layer protocol that best meets the requirements for the application. It is important to remember that the other layers all play a part in data network communications and influences its performance.

Practice

The following activities provide practice with the topics introduced in this chapter. The Labs and Class Activities are available in the companion Introduction to Networks v5.1 Lab Manual (ISBN 9781587133534). The Packet Tracer Activities PKA files are found in the online course.

Class Activities

Class Activity 9.0.1.2: We Need to Talk – Game

Class Activity 9.3.1.1: We Need to Talk, Again – Game

Labs

Lab 9.2.1.6: Using Wireshark to Observe the TCP 3-Way Handshake

Lab 9.2.3.5: Using Wireshark to Examine a UDP DNS Capture

Lab 9.2.4.3: Using Wireshark to Examine FTP and TFTP Captures

Packet Tracer Activities

Packet Tracer 9.3.1.2: TCP and UDP Communications

Check Your Understanding Questions

Complete all the review questions listed here to test your understanding of the topics and concepts in this chapter. The appendix "Answers to 'Check Your Understanding' Questions" lists the answers.

1. What are the primary purposes of the transport layer? (Choose three.)

    A. Determining the best route between source and destination

    B. Adding the source and destination MAC address to frames

    C. Tracking the individual communication between applications on the source and destination hosts

    D. Adding the source and destination IP address

    E. Segmenting data for and reassembling segmented data into streams of application data at the destination

    F. Identifying the proper application for each communication stream

2. What is assigned by the transport layer to identify an application or service?

    A. Segment

    B. Packet

    C. Port

    D. MAC address

    E. IP address

3. Fill in the blank. _____ is the term used to describe the interleaving of data from multiple users on the same network.

4. What is a characteristic of UDP?

   A. Reliable delivery

   B. Connectionless

   C. Windowing

   D. Expectational acknowledgements

   E. Flow control

5. Which of the following types of applications would use UDP? (Choose three.)

   A. Telnet

   B. VoIP

   C. FTP

   D. HTTP

   E. DHCP

   F. TFTP

6. Which TCP header field specifies the number of bytes that can be accepted before an acknowledgement is required?

   A. Acknowledgement number

   B. Header length

   C. Window size

   D. Checksum

7. Fill in the blank. Both TCP and UDP use ____ to separate multiple communications on the same channel.

8. What is an advantage that UDP has over TCP?

   A. Advanced flow control

   B. Low overhead

   C. Reordering of segments

   D. Reliable delivery

9. What range of ports can either be used by TCP or UDP to identify the requested service on the destination device or as a client source port?

   A. 0 to 1023

   B. 0 to 49151

   C. 1024 to 49151

   D. 49152 to 65535

10. Fill in the blank. A dynamic port in the range of 49152 to 65535 is also known as a(n) _____ port.

11. What does UDP do when receiving messages that are more than one datagram in length?

    A. UDP places the datagrams into the correct order before passing them to the application.

    B. UDP reassembles that data in the order it was received and passes it to the application.

    C. UDP requests retransmission of the datagrams in the correct order before passing to the application.

    D. UDP transmissions are limited to a single datagram.

12. Which TCP header control bit is set on to terminate a TCP conversation?

    A. URG

    B. ACK

    D. PSH

    D. RST

    E. SYN

    F. FIN

13. If a client sends an ISN of 2 to a server and a server responds with an ISN of 1 to the client, what is the final stage of the TCP three-way handshake?

    A. Client sends an acknowledgement of 2.

    B. Server sends an acknowledgement of 2.

    C. Client sends an acknowledgement of 3.

    D. Server sends an acknowledgement of 3.

    E. Client sends a new ISN of 3.

    F. Server sends a new ISN of 2.

14. A client is downloading a large file from a server using FTP. Many of the segments are lost during transit. What will most likely happen?

    A. The FTP session is immediately terminated.

    B. The FTP client responds to the server with a smaller window size in the TCP header.

    C. The FTP client responds to the client with an increased window size in the TCP header.

    D. The FTP server responds to the client with a smaller window size in the TCP header.

E. The FTP server responds to the client with an increased window size in the TCP header.

F. The FTP session continues, but the result is a corrupt file that must be downloaded again.

G. The FTP session continues with no alteration in window size, and the missing segment is requested again after the rest of the file is downloaded.

15. Fill in the blank. TCP will normally retransmit lost data from the last successful acknowledgement. To allow the destination to acknowledge bytes in discontinuous segments and request retransmission of only the missing data, both hosts must be able to support an optional feature called _____.

CHAPTER 10

Application Layer

Objectives

Upon completion of this chapter, you will be able to answer the following questions:

- How do the functions of the application layer, session layer, and presentation layer work together to provide network services to end-user applications?

- How do common application layer protocols interact with end-user applications?

- How do common application layer protocols provide Internet services to end users, including WWW services and email?

- What application layer protocols provide IP addressing services, including DNS and DHCP?

- What are the features and operation of well-known application layer protocols that allow file-sharing services, including FTP, File Sharing Services, and SMB protocol?

Key Terms

This chapter uses the following key terms. You can find the definitions in the Glossary.

Bootstrap Protocol (BOOTP)   Page 505

Simple Mail Transfer Protocol (SMTP)
  Page 505

Post Office Protocol (POP)   Page 505

*Internet Message Access Protocol
  (IMAP)*   Page 505

File Transfer Protocol (FTP)   Page 505

Trivial File Transfer Protocol (TFTP)
  Page 505

Client-server   Page 506

Server Message Block (SMB)   Page 527

Introduction (10.0)

Applications, such as web browsers, online gaming, and chatting with and emailing friends, enable us to send and receive data with relative ease. Typically we can access and use these applications without knowing how they work. However, for network professionals, it is important to know how an application is able to format, transmit, and interpret messages that are sent and received across the network.

Visualizing the mechanisms that enable communication across the network is made easier if we use the layered framework of the OSI model.

In this chapter, we will explore the role of the application layer and how the applications, services, and protocols within the application layer make robust communication across data networks possible.

Class Activity 10.0.1.2: Application Investigation

In this activity, you will envision what it would be like not to have network applications available to use in the workplace. You may also estimate what it would cost to not use networked applications for a short period of time.

Application Layer Protocols (10.1)

This section will describe the protocols, applications, and services of the TCP/IP model.

Application, Presentation, and Session (10.1.1)

This topic will introduce some protocols of the TCP/IP application layer, which also relates to the top three layers of the OSI model.

Application Layer (10.1.1.1)

The application layer is closest to the end user. As shown in Figure 10-1, it is the layer that provides the interface between the applications used to communicate and the underlying network over which messages are transmitted. Application layer protocols are used to exchange data between programs running on the source and destination hosts.

Figure 10-1   Applications of the TCP/IP and OSI Models

The upper three layers of the OSI model (application, presentation, and session) define functions of the single TCP/IP application layer.

There are many application layer protocols, and new protocols are always being developed. Some of the most widely known application layer protocols include Hypertext Transfer Protocol (HTTP), File Transfer Protocol (FTP), Trivial File Transfer Protocol (TFTP), Internet Message Access Protocol (IMAP), and Domain Name System (DNS) protocol.

Presentation and Session Layer (10.1.1.2)

The presentation layer has three primary functions:

- Formatting, or presenting, data at the source device into a compatible form for receipt by the destination device

- Compressing data in a way that can be decompressed by the destination device

- Encrypting data for transmission and decrypting data upon receipt

As shown in Figure 10-2, the presentation layer formats data for the application layer, and it sets standards for file formats.

Figure 10-2   Presentation Layer Standards

Some well-known standards for video include QuickTime and Motion Picture Experts Group (MPEG). Some well-known graphic image formats that are used on networks are Graphics Interchange Format (GIF), Joint Photographic Experts Group (JPEG), and Portable Network Graphics (PNG) format.

As the name implies, functions at the session layer create and maintain dialogs between source and destination applications. The session layer handles the exchange of information to initiate dialogs, keep them active, and to restart sessions that are disrupted or idle for a long period of time.

TCP/IP Application Layer Protocols (10.1.1.3)

The TCP/IP application protocols specify the format and control information necessary for many common Internet communication functions. Table 10-1 list so of the more common applications.

Table 10-1   Application Layer Protocols

Name	TCP/UDP Port #	Description
Web Related Protocols		
Hypertext Transfer Protocol (HTTP)	TCP 80	Set of rules for exchanging text, graphic images, sound, video, and other multimedia files on the World Wide Web.
Hypertext Transfer Protocol Secure (HTTPS)	TCP 443	The browser uses encryption to secure HTTP communications. Authenticates the website to which you are connecting your browser.
Email Related Protocols		
Simple Mail Transfer Protocol (SMTP)	TCP 25	Enables clients to send email to a mail server. Enables servers to send email to other servers
Post Office Protocol (POP)	TCP 110	Enables clients to retrieve email from a mail server. Downloads email from the mail server to the desktop
Internet Message Access Protocol (IMAP)	TCP 143	Enables clients to access email stored on a mail server. Maintains email on the server.
Naming System Protocol		
Domain Name System (DNS)	TCP/UDP 53	Translates domain names, such as cisco.com, into IP addresses
Host Configuration Related Protocols		
Bootstrap Protocol (BOOTP)	UDP 67, 68	Enables a diskless workstation to discover its own IP address, the IP address of a BOOTP server on the network, and a file to be loaded into memory to boot the machine. BOOTP is superseded by DHCP.
Dynamic Host Configuration Protocol (DHCP)	UDP 67, 68	Dynamically assigns IP addresses to client stations at start-up. Allows the addresses to be re-used when no longer needed.
File Transfer Related Protocols		
File Transfer Protocol (FTP)	TCP 20, 21	Sets rules that enable a user on one host to access and transfer files to and from another host over a network. A reliable, connection-oriented, and acknowledged file delivery protocol.
Trivial File Transfer Protocol (TFTP)	UDP 69	A simple, connectionless file transfer protocol. A best-effort, unacknowledged file delivery protocol. Utilizes less overhead than FTP.

Application layer protocols are used by both the source and destination devices during a communication session. For the communications to be successful the application layer protocols implemented on the source and destination host must be compatible.

Activity 10.1.1.4: Application and Presentation (Protocols and Standards)

Go to the online course to perform this practice activity.

Interactive Graphic

How Application Protocols Interact with End-User Applications (10.1.2)

This topic introduces peer-to-peer and client-server environments.

Client-Server Model (10.1.2.1)

In the *client-server* model, the device requesting the information is called a client and the device responding to the request is called a server. Client and server processes are considered to be in the application layer. The client begins the exchange by requesting data from the server, which responds by sending one or more streams of data to the client. Application layer protocols describe the format of the requests and responses between clients and servers. In addition to the actual data transfer, this exchange may also require user authentication and the identification of a data file to be transferred.

One example of a client-server network is using an ISP's email service to send, receive, and store email. The email client on a home computer issues a request to the ISP's email server for any unread mail. The server responds by sending the requested email to the client. As shown in Figure 10-3, data transfer from a client to a server is referred to as an upload and data from a server to a client as a download.

Figure 10-3   Client-Server Model

Peer-to-Peer Networks (10.1.2.2)

In the peer-to-peer (P2P) networking model, the data is accessed from a peer device without the use of a dedicated server.

The P2P network model involves two parts: P2P networks and P2P applications. Both parts have similar features, but in practice work quite differently.

In a P2P network, two or more computers are connected via a network and can share resources (such as printers and files) without having a dedicated server. Every connected end device (known as a peer) can function as both a server and a client. One computer might assume the role of server for one transaction while simultaneously serving as a client for another. The roles of client and server are set on a per request basis.

A simple example of P2P networking is shown in Figure 10-4. In addition to sharing files, a network such as this one would allow users to enable networked games, or share an Internet connection.

Figure 10-4   Peer-to-Peer Networking

Peer-to-Peer Applications (10.1.2.3)

A P2P application allows a device to act as both a client and a server within the same communication, as shown in Figure 10-5. In this model, every client is a server and every server is a client. P2P applications require that each end device provides a user interface and runs a background service.

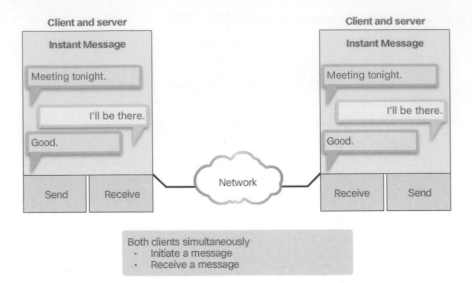

Figure 10-5   Peer-to-Peer Applications

Some P2P applications use a hybrid system where resource sharing is decentralized, but the indexes that point to resource locations are stored in a centralized directory. In a hybrid system, each peer accesses an index server to get the location of a resource stored on another peer.

Common P2P Applications (10.1.2.4)

With P2P applications, each computer in the network running the application can act as a client or a server for the other computers in the network running the application. Common P2P networks include

- eDonkey
- G2
- BitTorrent
- Bitcoin

Some P2P applications are based on the Gnutella protocol, where each user shares whole files with other users. As shown in Figure 10-6, Gnutella-compatible client software allows users to connect to Gnutella services over the Internet and to locate and access resources shared by other Gnutella peers. Many Gnutella client applications are available, including gtk-gnutella, WireShare, Shareaza, and Bearshare.

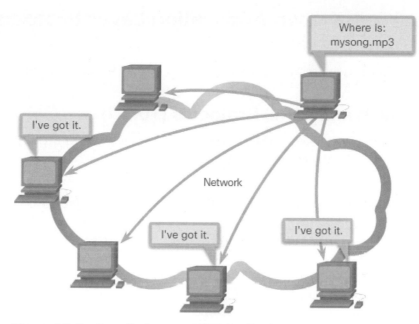

Figure 10-6   Gnutella Supports P2P Applications

Many P2P applications allow users to share pieces of many files with each other at the same time. Clients use a small file called a torrent file to locate other users who have pieces that they need so that they can connect directly to them. This file also contains information about tracker computers that keep track of which users have what files. Clients ask for pieces from multiple users at the same time, known as a swarm. This technology is called BitTorrent. There are many BitTorrent clients including BitTorrent, uTorrent, Frostwire, and qBittorrent.

Note

Any type of file can be shared between users. Many of these files are copyrighted, meaning that only the creator has the right to use and distribute them. It is against the law to download or distribute copyrighted files without permission from the copyright holder. Copyright violation can result in criminal charges and civil lawsuits. Complete the lab on the following page to find out more about these legal issues.

Lab 10.1.2.5: Researching Peer-to-Peer File Sharing

In this lab, you will complete the following objectives:

- Part 1: Identify P2P Networks, File Sharing Protocols, and Applications

- Part 2: Research P2P File Sharing Issues

- Part 3: Research P2P Copyright Litigations

Well-Known Application Layer Protocols and Services (10.2)

This section describes the OSI presentation and session layers in more detail.

Web and Email Protocols (10.2.1)

This topic focuses on three common application layer protocols that support users' everyday Internet services.

Hypertext Transfer Protocol and Hypertext Markup Language (10.2.1.1)

When a web address or uniform resource locator (URL) is typed into a web browser, the web browser establishes a connection to the web service running on the server using the HTTP protocol. URLs and Uniform Resource Identifier (URIs) are the names most people associate with web addresses.

To better understand how the web browser and web server interact, we can examine how a web page is opened in a browser. For this example, use the http://www.cisco.com/index.html URL.

The browser interprets the three parts of the URL:

1. **http** (the protocol or scheme)

2. **www.cisco.com** (the server name)

3. **index.html** (the specific filename requested)

As shown in Figure 10-7, the browser then checks with a name server to convert www.cisco.com into a numeric IP address, which it uses to connect to the server.

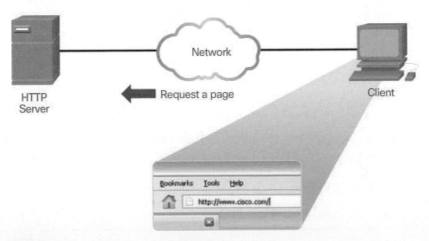

Figure 10-7   HTTP Protocol Step 1

Using HTTP requirements, the browser sends a GET request to the server and asks for the **index.html** file. The server, as shown in Figure 10-8, sends the HTML code for this web page to the browser.

```
HTTP/1.1 200 OK
Date: Mon, 23 May 2005 22:38:34 GMT
Server: Apache/1.3.27 (unix) (Red-Hat/Linux)
Last-Modified: wed, 08 Jan 2003 23:11:55 GMT
Etag: "3f80f-1b6-3elcb03b"
Accept-Ranges: bytes
Content-Length: 438
connection: close
content-Type: text/html; charset-UTF-8
<html>
<head>
<title>Cisco Systems Inc, Home Page</title>
</head>
<body>
...CONTENTS OF HTML PAGE...
</body>
```

Figure 10-8   HTTP Protocol Step 2

Finally, as shown in Figure 10-9, the browser deciphers the HTML code and formats the page for the browser window.

Figure 10-9   HTTP Protocol Step 3

HTTP and HTTPS (10.2.1.2)

HTTP is a request/response protocol. When a client, typically a web browser, sends a request to a web server, HTTP specifies the message types used for that communication. The three common message types are GET, POST, and PUT:

- **GET** – A client request for data. A client (web browser) sends the GET message to the web server to request HTML pages, as shown in Figure 10-10.

- **POST** – Uploads data files to the web server such as form data.

- **PUT** – Uploads resources or content to the web server such as an image.

Figure 10-10   The HTTP GET Process

Although HTTP is remarkably flexible, it is not a secure protocol. The request messages send information to the server in plain text that can be intercepted and read. The server responses, typically HTML pages, are also unencrypted.

For secure communication across the Internet, the HTTP Secure (HTTPS) protocol is used. HTTPS uses authentication and encryption to secure data as it travels between the client and server. HTTPS uses the same client request-server response process as HTTP, but the data stream is encrypted with Secure Socket Layer (SSL) before being transported across the network.

Email Protocols (10.2.1.3)

One of the primary services offered by an ISP is email hosting. To run on a computer or other end device, email requires several applications and services, as shown in Figure 10-11. Email is a store-and-forward method of sending, storing, and retrieving electronic messages across a network. Email messages are stored in databases on mail servers.

Figure 10-11   SMTP, POP, and IMAP Operation

Email clients communicate with mail servers to send and receive email. Mail servers communicate with other mail servers to transport messages from one domain to another. An email client does not communicate directly with another email client when sending email. Instead, both clients rely on the mail server to transport messages.

Email supports three separate protocols for operation: Simple Mail Transfer Protocol (SMTP), Post Office Protocol (POP), and IMAP. The application layer process that sends mail uses SMTP. A client retrieves email, however, using one of the two application layer protocols: POP or IMAP.

SMTP Operation (10.2.1.4)

SMTP message formats require a message header and a message body. Whereas the message body can contain any amount of text, the message header must have a properly formatted recipient email address and a sender address.

When a client sends email, the client SMTP process connects with a server SMTP process on well-known port 25. After the connection is made, the client attempts to send the email to the server across the connection. When the server receives the message, it either places the message in a local account, if the recipient is local, or forwards the message to another mail server for delivery, as shown in Figure 10-12.

Figure 10-12   SMTP

The destination email server may not be online or may be busy when email messages are sent. Therefore, SMTP spools messages to be sent at a later time. Periodically, the server checks the queue for messages and attempts to send them again. If the message is still not delivered after a predetermined expiration time, it is returned to the sender as undeliverable.

POP Operation (10.2.1.5)

POP is used by an application to retrieve mail from a mail server. With POP, mail is downloaded from the server to the client and then deleted on the server. This is how POP operates, by default, as shown in Figure 10-13.

Figure 10-13   POP3

The server starts the POP service by passively listening on TCP port 110 for client connection requests. When a client wants to make use of the service, it sends a request to establish a TCP connection with the server. When the connection is established, the POP server sends a greeting. The client and POP server then exchange commands and responses until the connection is closed or aborted.

With POP, email messages are downloaded to the client and removed from the server, so there is no centralized location where email messages are kept. Because POP does not store messages, it is undesirable for a small business that needs a centralized backup solution.

IMAP Operation (10.2.1.6)

IMAP is another protocol that describes a method to retrieve email messages. Unlike POP, when the user connects to an IMAP-capable server, copies of the messages are downloaded to the client application, as shown in Figure 10-14. The original messages are kept on the server until manually deleted. Users view copies of the messages in their email client software.

Figure 10-14   IMAP

Users can create a file hierarchy on the server to organize and store mail. That file structure is duplicated on the email client as well. When a user decides to delete a message, the server synchronizes that action and deletes the message from the server.

Click here to learn more about email protocols.

Packet Tracer 10.2.1.7: Web and Email

In this activity, you will configure HTTP and email services using the simulated server in Packet Tracer. You will then configure clients to access the HTTP and email services.

IP Addressing Services (10.2.2)

This topic presents addressing services including DNS and DHCP.

Domain Name Service (10.2.2.1)

In data networks, devices are labeled with numeric IP addresses to send and receive data over networks. Domain names were created to convert the numeric address into a simple, recognizable name.

On the Internet, these domain names, such as http://www.cisco.com, are much easier for people to remember than 198.133.219.25, which is the actual numeric address for this server. If Cisco decides to change the numeric address of www.cisco.com, it is transparent to the user because the domain name remains the same. The new address is simply linked to the existing domain name and connectivity is maintained.

The DNS protocol defines an automated service that matches resource names with the required numeric network address. It includes the format for queries, responses, and data. The DNS protocol communications use a single format called a message. This message format is used for all types of client queries and server responses, error messages, and the transfer of resource record information between servers.

The steps involved in DNS resolution are as follows:

Step 1:   User enters a fully qualified domain name (FQDN), as shown in Figure 10-15.

Resolving DNS Addresses Step 1

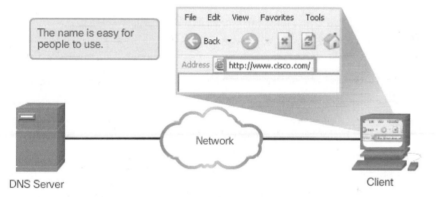

Figure 10-15   Resolving DNS Addresses Step 1

Step 2:   The client computer sends a DNS query to the DNS server requesting an IP address to match the FQDN, as shown in Figure 10-16.

Figure 10-16   Resolving DNS Addresses Step 2

Step 3:   The DNS server resolve the FQDN to an IP address in the DNS server database, as shown in Figure 10-17.

Figure 10-17   Resolving DNS Addresses Step 3

Step 4:   The DNS server sends back a response to the client with the IP address for the FQDN, as shown in Figure 10-18.

Figure 10-18   Resolving DNS Addresses Step 4

Step 5:   The client can now send an HTTP GET message with the destination IP address inserted in the packet, as shown in Figure 10-19.

Figure 10-19   Resolving DNS Addresses Step 5

DNS Message Format (10.2.2.2)

The DNS message format is shown in Figure 10-20.

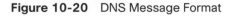

Header	
Question	The question for the name server
Answer	Resource Records answering the question
Authority	Resource Records pointing toward an authority
Additional	Resource Records holding additional information

Figure 10-20   DNS Message Format

DNS uses the same message format for

- all types of client queries and server responses
- error messages
- the transfer of resource record information between servers

The DNS server stores different types of resource records used to resolve names. These records contain the name, address, and type of record. Some of these record types are

- **A** – An end device IPv4 address
- **NS** – An authoritative name server
- **AAAA** – An end device IPv6 address (pronounced quad-A)
- **MX** – A mail exchange record

When a client makes a query, the server's DNS process first looks at its own records to resolve the name. If it is unable to resolve the name using its stored records, it contacts other servers to resolve the name. After a match is found and returned to the original requesting server, the server temporarily stores the numbered address in the event that the same name is requested again.

The DNS Client service on Windows PCs also stores previously resolved names in memory. The **ipconfig /displaydns** command displays all of the cached DNS entries.

DNS Hierarchy (10.2.2.3)

The DNS protocol uses a hierarchical system to create a database to provide name resolution. The hierarchy looks like an inverted tree with the root at the top and branches below, as shown in Figure 10-21. DNS uses domain names to form the hierarchy.

Figure 10-21 DNS Server Hierarchy

The naming structure is broken down into small, manageable zones. Each DNS server maintains a specific database file and is only responsible for managing name-to-IP mappings for that small portion of the entire DNS structure. When a DNS server receives a request for a name translation that is not within its DNS zone, the DNS server forwards the request to another DNS server within the proper zone for translation.

Note

DNS is scalable because hostname resolution is spread across multiple servers.

The different top-level domains represent either the type of organization or the vcountry of origin. Examples of top-level domains are

- .com – a business or industry
- .org – a non-profit organization
- .au – Australia
- .co – Colombia

The nslookup Command (10.2.2.4)

When configuring a network device, one or more DNS server addresses are provided that the DNS client can use for name resolution. Usually the Internet service provider (ISP) provides the addresses to use for the DNS servers. When a user's application requests to connect to a remote device by name, the requesting DNS client queries the name server to resolve the name to a numeric address.

Computer operating systems also have a utility called nslookup that allows the user to manually query the name servers to resolve a given host name. This utility can also be used to troubleshoot name resolution issues and to verify the current status of the name servers.

When the **nslookup** command is issued, the default DNS server configured for your host is displayed. The name of a host or domain can be entered at the **nslookup** prompt. The nslookup utility has many options available for extensive testing and verification of the DNS process. Enter the command quit to exit the nslookup process, as shown in Example 10-1.

Example 10-1 The nslookup Command

```
C:\> nslookup
Default Server: dns-rch1.cisco.com
Address: 173.37.87.157

> www.cisco.com
Server: dns-rch1.cisco.com
Addv : 173.37.87.157

Name: origin-www.cisco.com
Addresses: 2001:420:1101:1::a
 72.163.4.161
Aliases: www.cisco.com
 www.cisco.com.akadns.net

> www.netacad.com
Server: dns-rch1.cisco.com
Address: 173.37.87.157

Non-authoritative answer:
Name: Liferay-Prod-1009279580.us-east-1.elb.amazonaws.com
Addresses: 52.70.250.119
 52.1.15.10
Aliases: www.netacad.com

> quit

C:\>
```

Dynamic Host Configuration Protocol (10.2.2.5)

The Dynamic Host Configuration Protocol (DHCP) for IPv4 service automates the assignment of IPv4 addresses, subnet masks, gateways, and other IPv4 networking parameters. This is referred to as dynamic addressing. The alternative to dynamic addressing is static addressing. When using static addressing, the network administrator manually enters IP address information on hosts.

When a host connects to the network, the DHCP server is contacted, and an address is requested. The DHCP server chooses an address from a configured range of addresses called a pool and assigns (leases) it to the host.

On larger networks, or where the user population changes frequently, DHCP is preferred for address assignment. New users may arrive and need connections; others may have new computers that must be connected. Rather than use static addressing for each connection, it is more efficient to have IPv4 addresses assigned automatically using DHCP.

DHCP-distributed addresses are leased for a set period of time. When the lease is expired, the address is returned to the pool for reuse if the host has been powered down or taken off the network. Users can freely move from location to location and easily re-establish network connections through DHCP.

As shown in Figure 10-22, various types of devices can be DHCP servers.

Figure 10-22   DHCP Is Used in Many Networks

The DHCP server in most medium-to-large networks is usually a local, dedicated PC-based server. With home networks, the DHCP server is usually located on the local router that connects the home network to the ISP.

Many networks use both DHCP and static addressing. DHCP is used for general purpose hosts, such as end-user devices. Static addressing is used for network devices, such as gateways, switches, servers, and printers.

DHCPv6 (DHCP for IPv6) provides similar services for IPv6 clients. One important difference is that DHCPv6 does not provide a default gateway address. This can only be obtained dynamically from the router's Router Advertisement message.

DHCP Operation (10.2.2.6)

The DHCP messages used during DHCP operation are shown in Figure 10-23.

Figure 10-23   DHCP Messages

When an IPv4, DHCP-configured device boots up or connects to the network, the client broadcasts a DHCP discover (DHCPDISCOVER) message to identify any available DHCP servers on the network. A DHCP server replies with a DHCP offer (DHCPOFFER) message, which offers a lease to the client. The offer message contains the IPv4 address and subnet mask to be assigned, the IPv4 address of the DNS server, and the IPv4 address of the default gateway. The lease offer also includes the duration of the lease.

The client may receive multiple DHCPOFFER messages if there is more than one DHCP server on the local network. Therefore, it must choose between them, and sends a DHCP request (DHCPREQUEST) message that identifies the explicit server and lease offer that the client is accepting. A client may also choose to request an address that it had previously been allocated by the server.

Assuming that the IPv4 address requested by the client, or offered by the server, is still available, the server returns a DHCP acknowledgment (DHCPACK) message that acknowledges to the client that the lease has been finalized. If the offer is no longer valid, then the selected server responds with a DHCP negative acknowledgment (DHCPNAK) message. If a DHCPNAK message is returned, then the selection process must begin again with a new DHCPDISCOVER message being transmitted. After the client has the lease, it must be renewed prior to the lease expiration through another DHCPREQUEST message.

The DHCP server ensures that all IP addresses are unique (the same IP address cannot be assigned to two different network devices simultaneously). Most Internet providers use DHCP to allocate addresses to their customers.

DHCPv6 has similar set of messages to those shown in the figure for DHCP for IPv4. The DHCPv6 messages are SOLICIT, ADVERTISE, INFORMATION REQUEST, and REPLY.

Packet Tracer
☐ Activity

Packet Tracer 10.2.2.7: DHCP and DNS Servers

In this activity, you will configure and verify static IP addressing and DHCP addressing. You will then configure a DNS server to map IP addresses to the website names.

Lab 10.2.2.8: Observing DNS Servers

In this lab, you will complete the following objectives:

- Part 1: Observe the DNS Conversion of a URL to an IP Address
- Part 2: Observe DNS Lookup Using the nslookup Command on a Website
- Part 3: Observe DNS Lookup Using the nslookup Command on Mail Servers

File Sharing Services (10.2.3)

Transferring files from one computer to another is a common process. This topic will introduce protocols that support file transfers.

File Transfer Protocol (10.2.3.1)

FTP is another commonly used application layer protocol. FTP was developed to allow for data transfers between a client and a server. An FTP client is an application that runs on a computer that is used to push and pull data from an FTP server.

The FTP process is shown in Figure 10-24.

Figure 10-24 FTP Process

To successfully transfer data, FTP requires two connections between the client and the server, one for commands and replies, the other for the actual file transfer:

■ The client establishes the first connection to the server for control traffic using TCP port 21, consisting of client commands and server replies.

■ The client establishes the second connection to the server for the actual data transfer using TCP port 20. This connection is created every time there is data to be transferred.

The data transfer can happen in either direction. The client can download (pull) data from the server, or the client can upload (push) data to the server.

Server Message Block (10.2.3.2)

The *Server Message Block (SMB)* is a client/server file sharing protocol that describes the structure of shared network resources, such as directories, files, printers, and serial ports. It is a request-response protocol. All SMB messages share a common format. This format uses a fixed-sized header, followed by a variable-sized parameter and data component.

SMB messages can

- Start, authenticate, and terminate sessions

- Control file and printer access

- Allow an application to send or receive messages to or from another device

SMB file-sharing and print services have become the mainstay of Microsoft networking. With the introduction of the Windows 2000 software series, Microsoft changed the underlying structure for using SMB. In previous versions of Microsoft products, the SMB services used a non-TCP/IP protocol to implement name resolution. Beginning with Windows2000, all subsequent Microsoft products use DNS naming, which allows TCP/IP protocols to directly support SMB resource sharing, as shown in Figure 10-25.

Figure 10-25   SMB Protocol

The SMB file exchange process between Windows PCs is shown in Figure 10-26.

Figure 10-26   SMB File Sharing

Unlike the file sharing supported by FTP, clients establish a long-term connection to servers. After the connection is established, the user of the client can access the resources on the server as if the resource is local to the client host.

The LINUX and UNIX operating systems also provide a method of sharing resources with Microsoft networks using a version of SMB called SAMBA. The Apple Macintosh operating systems also support resource sharing using the SMB protocol.

Packet Tracer
☐ Activity

Packet Tracer 10.2.3.3: FTP

In this activity, you will configure FTP services. You will then use the FTP services to transfer files between clients and the server.

Lab 10.2.3.4: Exploring FTP

In this lab, you will complete the following objectives:

- Part 1: Use FTP from a Command Prompt
- Part 2: Download an FTP File Using WS_FTP LE
- Part 3: Use FTP in a Browser

Summary (10.3)

Class Activity 10.3.1.1: Make it happen!

In this activity, you will apply new knowledge of application layer protocols and methods of the TCP/IP layer in streamlining data/network communication.

Packet Tracer 10.3.1.2: Explore a Network

This simulation activity is intended to help you understand the flow of traffic and the contents of data packets as they traverse a complex network. Communications will be examined at three different locations simulating typical business and home networks.

Packet Tracer 10.3.1.3: Multiuser - Tutorial

The multiuser feature in Packet Tracer allows multiple point-to-point connections between multiple instances of Packet Tracer. This first Packet Tracer Multiuser (PTMU) activity is a quick tutorial demonstrating the steps to establish and verify a multiuser connection to another instance of Packet Tracer within the same LAN. Ideally, this activity is meant for two students. However, it can also be completed as a solo activity simply by opening the two separate files to create two separate instances of Packet Tracer on your local machine.

Packet Tracer Multiuser 10.3.1.4: Implement Services

In this multiuser activity, two students (players) cooperate to implement and verify services including DHCP, HTTP, Email, DNS, and FTP. The server side player will implement and verify services on one server. The client side player will configure two clients and verify access to services.

The application layer is responsible for directly accessing the underlying processes that manage and deliver communication to the human network. This layer serves as the source and destination of communications across data networks. The application layer applications, services, and protocols enable users to interact with the data network in a way that is meaningful and effective.

- Applications are computer programs with which the user interacts and which initiate the data transfer process at the user's request.

- Services are background programs that provide the connection between the application layer and the lower layers of the networking model.

- Protocols provide a structure of agreed-upon rules and processes that ensure services running on one particular device can send and receive data from a range of different network devices.

Delivery of data over the network can be requested from a server by a client, or between devices that operate in a P2P arrangement. In P2P, the client/server relationship is established according to which device is the source and destination at that time. Messages are exchanged between the application layer services at each end device in accordance with the protocol specifications to establish and use these relationships.

Protocols like HTTP, for example, support the delivery of web pages to end devices. SMTP, IMAP, and POP support sending and receiving email. SMB and FTP enable users to share files. P2P applications make it easier for consumers to seamlessly share media in a distributed fashion. DNS resolves the human-legible names, used to refer to network resources, into numeric addresses usable by the network. Clouds are remote upstream locations that store data and host applications so that users do not require as many local resources, and so that users can seamlessly access content on different devices from any location.

All of these elements work together, at the application layer. The application layer enables users to work and play over the Internet.

Practice

The following activities provide practice with the topics introduced in this chapter. The Labs and Class Activities are available in the companion Introduction to Networks v5.1 Lab Manual (ISBN 9781587133534). The Packet Tracer Activities PKA files are found in the online course.

Class Activities

Class Activity 10.0.1.2: Application Investigation

Class Activity 10.3.1.1: Make it happen!

Labs

Lab 10.1.2.5: Researching Peer-to-Peer File Sharing

Lab 10.2.2.8: Observing DNS Servers

Lab 10.2.3.4: Exploring FTP

Packet Tracer Activities

Packet Tracer 10.2.1.7: Web and Email

Packet Tracer 10.2.2.7: DHCP and DNS Servers

Packet Tracer 10.2.3.3: FTP

Packet Tracer 10.3.1.2: Explore a Network

Packet Tracer 10.3.1.3: Multiuser - Tutorial

Packet Tracer Multiuser 10.3.1.4: Implement Services

Check Your Understanding Questions

Complete all the review questions listed here to test your understanding of the topics and concepts in this chapter. The appendix "Answers to 'Check Your Understanding' Questions" lists the answers.

1. The TCP/IP application layer effectively consists of which three OSI layers?

    A. Application, session, transport

    B. Application, presentation, session

    C. Application, transport, network

    D. Application, network, data link

2. What three protocols do email users and servers use to process email? (Choose three.)

    A. DHCP

    B. SMTP

    C. IMAP4

    D. DNS

    E. POP3

3. DHCP enables clients on a network to do which of the following?

    A. Have unlimited telephone conversations

    B. Play back video streams

    C. Obtain IP addresses

    D. Track intermittent denial of service attacks

4. What TCP/IP layer supports the exchange of data between programs running on the source and destination hosts?

   A. Application

   B. Transport

   C. Internetwork

   D. Network

5. What is the purpose of DNS?

CHAPTER 11

Build a Small Network

Objectives

Upon completion of this chapter, you will be able to answer the following questions:

- What devices and protocols are used in a small network?

- What are the protocols used in a small network?

- How does a small network serve as the basis for a larger network?

- Why are basic security measures required on network devices?

- What security vulnerabilities and common mitigation techniques exist to protect against these vulnerabilities?

- How are network devices configured with hardening features to mitigate security threats?

- How can the **ping** and **tracert** commands be used to establish relative network performance?

- How can **show** commands be used to verify the configuration and status of device interfaces?

- How can basic host and IOS commands be used to acquire information about devices in the network?

- How are debug commands used to monitor and gather information about devices in a network?

- What are common network troubleshooting methodologies?

- What is the process for troubleshooting cable and interface problems?

- What is the process for troubleshooting problems with devices such as IP addressing, DNS and default gateway issues?

Key Terms

This chapter uses the following key terms. You can find the definitions in the Glossary.

Redundancy   Page 536

Real-time traffic   Page 539

Protocol analyzer   Page 544

Introduction (11.0)

Note

The chapter includes new content to cover the additional on the CCNA Routing & Switching Exam (need exam number here).

Up to this point in the course, we have considered the services that a data network can provide to the human network, examined the features of each layer of the OSI model and the operations of TCP/IP protocols, and looked in detail at Ethernet, a universal LAN technology. The next step is to learn how to assemble these elements together in a functioning network that can be maintained.

Class Activity 11.0.1.2: Did You Notice...?

Note

Students can work singularly, in pairs, or the full classroom can complete this activity together.

Take a look at the two networks in the diagram. Visually compare and contrast the two networks. Make note of the devices used in each network design. Since the devices are labeled, you already know what types of end devices and intermediate devices are on each network.

How are the two networks different? Is it just that there are more devices present on Network B than on Network A?

Select the network you would use if you owned a small to medium-sized business. Be able to justify your selected network based on cost, speed, ports, expandability, and manageability.

Network Design (11.1)

Small networks become the building blocks of larger networks. To ensure that networks can grow without problems, they must be properly designed and understood.

Devices in a Small Network (11.1.1)

The number and type of network devices in a small network often differ from those found in larger networks, but they must still provide many of the same services.

Small Network Topologies (11.1.1.1)

The majority of businesses are small. It is not surprising then that the majority of networks are also small. A typical small-business network is shown in Figure 11-1.

Figure 11-1   Typical Small Business Network

With small networks, the design of the network is usually simple. The number and type of devices included are significantly reduced compared to that of a larger network. The network topologies typically involve a single router and one or more switches. Small networks may also have wireless access points (possibly built into the router) and IP phones. As for connection to the Internet, normally a small network has a single WAN connection provided by DSL, cable, or an Ethernet connection.

Managing a small network requires many of the same skills as those required for managing a larger one. The majority of work is focused on maintenance and troubleshooting of existing equipment, as well as securing devices and information on the network. The management of a small network is either done by an employee of the company or a person contracted by the company, depending on the size and type of the business.

Device Selection for a Small Network (11.1.1.2)

In order to meet user requirements, even small networks require planning and design. Planning ensures that all requirements, cost factors, and deployment options are given due consideration.

When implementing a small network, one of the first design considerations is the type of intermediate devices to use to support the network. When selecting the type of intermediate devices, the following factors need to be considered:

Cost

The cost of a switch or router is determined by its capacity and features. The device capacity includes the number and types of ports available and the backplane speed.

Other factors that impact the cost are network management capabilities, embedded security technologies, and optional advanced switching technologies. The expense of cable runs required to connect every device on the network must also be considered. Another key element affecting cost considerations is the amount of *redundancy* to incorporate into the network.

Speed and Types of Ports/Interfaces

Choosing the number and type of ports on a router or switch is a critical decision. Newer computers have built-in 1 Gb/s NICs. 10 Gb/s ports are already included with some workstations and servers. Although it is more expensive, choosing Layer 2 devices that can accommodate increased speeds allows the network to evolve without replacing central devices.

Expandability

Networking devices come in both fixed and modular physical configurations. Fixed configurations have a specific number and type of ports or interfaces. Modular devices have expansion slots that provide the flexibility to add new modules as requirements evolve. Switches are available with additional ports for high-speed uplinks. Routers can be used to connect different types of networks. Care must be taken to select the appropriate modules and interfaces for the specific media.

Operating System Features and Services

Depending on the version of the operating system, a network device can support certain features and services, such as

- Security
- Quality of Service (QoS)
- Voice over IP (VoIP)
- Layer 3 switching
- Network Address Translation (NAT)
- Dynamic Host Configuration Protocol (DHCP)

IP Addressing for a Small Network (11.1.1.3)

When implementing a small network, it is necessary to plan the IP addressing space. All hosts within an internetwork must have a unique address. The IP addressing scheme should be planned, documented and maintained based on the type of device receiving the address, as shown in Figure 11-2.

Figure 11-2   IPv4 Address Planning and Assignment Options

Examples of different types of devices that will factor into the IP design are

- End devices for users

- Servers and peripherals

- Hosts that are accessible from the Internet

- Intermediary devices

Planning and documenting the IP addressing scheme helps the administrator track device types. For example, if all servers are assigned a host address between the range of 50–100, it is easy to identify server traffic by IP address. This can be very useful when troubleshooting network traffic issues using a protocol analyzer.

Additionally, administrators are better able to control access to resources on the network based on IP address when a deterministic IP addressing scheme is used. This can be especially important for hosts that provide resources to the internal network as well, as to the external network. Web servers or e-commerce servers play such a role. If the addresses for these resources are not planned and documented, the security and accessibility of the devices are not easily controlled. If a server has a random address assigned, blocking access to this address is difficult, and clients may not be able to locate this resource.

Each of these different device types should be allocated to a logical block of addresses within the address range of the network.

Redundancy in a Small Network (11.1.1.4)

Another important part of network design is reliability. Even small businesses often rely heavily on their network for business operation. A failure of the network can be very costly. In order to maintain a high degree of reliability, redundancy is required in the network design. Redundancy helps to eliminate single points of failure. There are many ways to accomplish redundancy in a network. Redundancy can be accomplished by installing duplicate equipment, but it can also be accomplished by supplying duplicate network links for critical areas, as shown in Figure 11-3.

Figure 11-3   Sample Redundant Topology

The redundancies shown in Figure 11-3 are as follows:

- **Data Center –** If one server fails, another is there to handle customer requests.

- **Links –** If the link to one switch fails, the link to the second switch is still available.

- **Switches –** Redundant switches are present to avoid a switching failure.

- **Routers –** Router redundancy can help to ensure that application transactions received from external traffic can be handled in the event of a router or route failure.

Small networks typically provide a single exit point toward the Internet via one or more default gateways. If the router fails, the entire network loses connectivity to the Internet. For this reason, it may be advisable for a small business to pay for a second service provider as backup.

Traffic Management (11.1.1.5)

The network administrator should consider the various types of traffic and their treatment in the network design. The routers and switches in a small network should be configured to support *real-time traffic*, such as voice and video, in a distinct manner relative to other data traffic. In fact, a good network design will classify traffic carefully according to priority, as shown in Figure 11-4. In the end, the goal for a good network design, even for a small network, is to enhance the productivity of the employees and minimize network downtime.

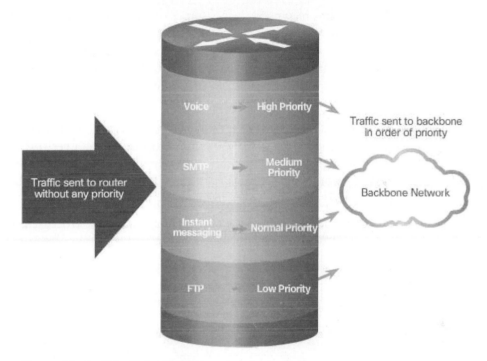

Figure 11-4   Prioritizing Traffic

Small Network Applications and Protocols (11.1.2)

Along with the network devices found in a small network, it is important to examine the applications and services that it must support.

Common Applications (11.1.2.1)

The network is only as useful as the applications that are on it. There are two forms of software programs or processes that provide access to the network: network applications and application layer services.

Network Applications

Applications are the software programs used to communicate over the network. Some end-user applications are network-aware, meaning that they implement application layer protocols and are able to communicate directly with the lower layers of the protocol stack. Email clients and web browsers are examples of this type of application.

Application Layer Services

Other programs may need the assistance of application layer services to use network resources like file transfer or network print spooling. Though transparent to an employee, these services are the programs that interface with the network and prepare the data for transfer. Different types of data, whether text, graphics or video, require different network services to ensure that they are properly prepared for processing by the functions occurring at the lower layers of the OSI model.

Each application or network service uses protocols, which define the standards and data formats to be used. Without protocols, the data network would not have a common way to format and direct data. In order to understand the function of various network services, it is necessary to become familiar with the underlying protocols that govern their operation.

Use the Task Manager to view the current applications, processes, and services running on a Windows PC, as shown in Figure 11-5.

Image Name	User Name	CPU	Memory (P...	Description
ibmpmsvc.exe	SYSTEM	00	528 K	Lenovo Power Management Service
igfxpers.exe	alljohns	00	384 K	persistence Module
igfxsrvc.exe	alljohns	00	244 K	igfxsrvc Module
lsass.exe	SYSTEM	00	6,028 K	Local Security Authority Process
lsm.exe	SYSTEM	00	1,280 K	Local Session Manager Service
MBAMAgent.exe	SYSTEM	00	2,480 K	MBAMAgent
mcshield.exe	SYSTEM	00	75,920 K	McAfee On-Access Scanner service
McTray.exe *32	alljohns	00	1,536 K	McTray Application
mfeann.exe *32	SYSTEM	00	460 K	VSCore Announcer
mfefire.exe	SYSTEM	00	928 K	McAfee Core Firewall Service
mfevtps.exe	SYSTEM	00	4,256 K	McAfee Process Validation Service
micmute.exe *32	SYSTEM	00	660 K	Microphone Mute Controll Service for ThinkPad
msid.exe *32	SYSTEM	00	1,568 K	Cisco Media Services Interface Windows Service
msirest.exe *32	SYSTEM	00	804 K	Cisco MSI Management Windows Service
naPrdMgr.exe *32	SYSTEM	00	1,732 K	NAI Product Manager
nvvsvc.exe	SYSTEM	00	696 K	NVIDIA Driver Helper Service, Version 327.68
nvvsvc.exe	SYSTEM	00	456 K	NVIDIA Driver Helper Service, Version 327.68
nvxdsync.exe	SYSTEM	00	768 K	NVIDIA User Experience Driver Component
o2flash.exe *32	SYSTEM	00	512 K	O2 Flash Memory Service
OSPPSVC.EXE	NETWOR...	00	2,032 K	Microsoft Office Software Protection Platform Ser...
OUTLOOK.EXE *32	alljohns	00	78,416 K	Microsoft Outlook
policyHost.exe	SYSTEM	00	6,280 K	Microsoft(R) Policy PlatformService Host
POWERPNT.EXE *32	alljohns	00	11,640 K	Microsoft PowerPoint
PresentationFontCache.exe	LOCAL S...	00	952 K	PresentationFontCache.exe
PrintClientMessenger.exe *...	alljohns	00	9,788 K	PrintClientMessenger
ptoneclk.exe *32	alljohns	00	1,608 K	WebEx One-Click Application
ptSrv.exe *32	alljohns	00	996 K	ptService Module
PWMDBSVC.exe *32	SYSTEM	00	720 K	Power Manager Dynamic Brightness Control Service
RAVBg64.exe	alljohns	00	968 K	HD Audio Background Process
RAVBg64.exe	alljohns	00	996 K	HD Audio Background Process
RAVCpl64.exe	alljohns	00	1,148 K	Realtek HD Audio Manager
rundll32.exe	alljohns	00	1,424 K	Windows host process (Rundll32)

☑ Show processes from all users

End Process

Processes: 147   CPU Usage: 9%   Physical Memory: 35%

Figure 11-5   Common Applications in a Small Network

Common Protocols (11.1.2.2)

Most of a technician's work, in either a small or a large network, will in some way be involved with network protocols. Network protocols support the applications and services used by employees in a small network. Common network protocols are shown in Figure 11-6.

Figure 11-6   Network Services

These network protocols comprise the fundamental toolset of a network professional. Each of these network protocols define

- Processes on either end of a communication session

- Types of messages

- Syntax of the messages

- Meaning of informational fields

- How messages are sent and the expected response

- Interaction with the next lower layer

Many companies have established a policy of using secure versions of these protocols whenever possible. These protocols are HTTPS, SFTP, and SSH.

Voice and Video Applications (11.1.2.3)

Businesses today are increasingly using IP telephony and streaming media to communicate with customers and business partners. The network administrator must ensure the proper equipment is installed in the network and that the network devices are configured to ensure priority delivery. Figure 11-7 shows elements of a small network that support real-time applications.

Cable and switch   IP phones

Cisco Unified Communications 500 Series

Figure 11-7   Support for Real-Time Traffic

Infrastructure

To support the existing and proposed real-time applications, the infrastructure must accommodate the characteristics of each type of traffic. The network designer must determine whether the existing switches and cabling can support the traffic that will be added to the network.

VoIP

VoIP devices convert analog into digital IP packets. The device could be an analog telephone adapter (ATA) that is attached between a traditional analog phone and the Ethernet switch. After the signals are converted into IP packets, the router sends those packets between corresponding locations. VoIP is much less expensive than an integrated IP telephony solution, but the quality of communications does not meet the same standards. Voice and video over IP solutions for small businesses can be realized, for example, with Skype and non-enterprise versions of Cisco WebEx.

IP Telephony

In IP telephony, the IP phone itself performs voice-to-IP conversion. Voice-enabled routers are not required within a network with an integrated IP telephony solution. IP phones use a dedicated server for call control and signaling. There are now many vendors with dedicated IP telephony solutions for small networks.

Real-Time Applications

To transport streaming media effectively, the network must be able to support applications that require delay-sensitive delivery. Real-Time Transport Protocol (RTP) and Real-Time Transport Control Protocol (RTCP) are two protocols that support this requirement. RTP and RTCP enable control and scalability of the network resources by allowing Quality of Service (QoS) mechanisms to be incorporated. These QoS mechanisms provide valuable tools for minimizing latency issues for real-time streaming applications.

Scale to Larger Networks (11.1.3)

Networks support the business and must be able to grow as the business grows.

Small Network Growth (11.1.3.1)

Growth is a natural process for many small businesses, and their networks must grow accordingly. Ideally, the network administrator has enough lead time to make intelligent decisions about growing the network in-line with the growth of the company.

To scale a network, several elements are required:

- **Network documentation** – physical and logical topology

- **Device inventory** – list of devices that use or comprise the network

- **Budget** – itemized IT budget, including fiscal year equipment purchasing budget

- **Traffic analysis** – protocols, applications, and services and their respective traffic requirements, should be documented

These elements are used to inform the decision-making that accompanies the scaling of a small network.

Protocol Analysis (11.1.3.2)

When trying to determine how to manage network traffic, especially as the network grows, it is important to understand the type of traffic that is crossing the network as well as the current traffic flow. If the types of traffic are unknown, a *protocol analyzer*, such as Wireshark shown in Figure 11-8, will help identify the traffic and its source.

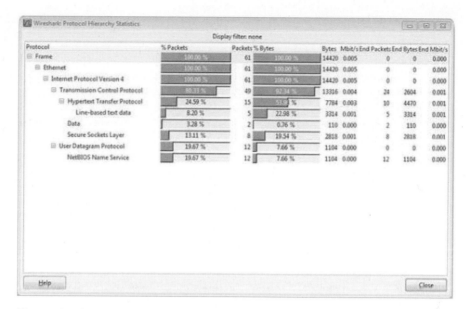

Figure 11-8   Wireshark Statistics

To determine traffic flow patterns, it is important to

- Capture traffic during peak utilization times to get a good representation of the different traffic types.

- Perform the capture on different network segments; some traffic will be local to a particular segment.

Information gathered by the protocol analyzer is evaluated based on the source and destination of the traffic, as well as the type of traffic being sent. This analysis can be used to make decisions on how to manage the traffic more efficiently. This can be done by reducing unnecessary traffic flows or changing flow patterns altogether by moving a server, for example.

Sometimes, simply relocating a server or service to another network segment improves network performance and accommodates the growing traffic needs. At other times, optimizing the network performance requires major network redesign and intervention.

Employee Network Utilization (11.1.3.3)

In addition to understanding changing traffic trends, a network administrator must also be aware of how network use is changing. As shown in Figure 11-9, a small network administrator has the ability to obtain in-person IT "snapshots" of employee application utilization for a significant portion of the employee workforce over time.

Figure 11-9   Software Processes

These snapshots typically include information such as

- OS and OS Version

- Non-Network Applications

- Network Applications

- CPU Utilization

- Drive Utilization

- RAM Utilization

Documenting snapshots for employees in a small network over a period of time will go a long way toward informing the network administrator of evolving protocol requirements and associated traffic flows. A shift in resource utilization may require the network administrator to adjust network resource allocations accordingly.

Network Security (11.2)

We have come to expect that the information we move on a network is safe from tampering and unauthorized access. Without this assumption, such routine events as e-business and online banking would not occur. As networks grow and offer new services, the threats to their continued integrity increase and measures must be taken to ensure the security of network devices and information.

Security Threats and Vulnerabilities (11.2.1)

Before we can properly secure the network, it is important to understand the threats that we must secure against.

Types of Threats (11.2.1.1)

Whether wired or wireless, computer networks are essential to everyday activities. Individuals and organizations alike depend on their computers and networks. Intrusion by an unauthorized person can result in costly network outages and loss of work. Attacks on a network can be devastating and can result in a loss of time and money due to damage or theft of important information or assets.

Intruders can gain access to a network through software vulnerabilities, hardware attacks or through guessing someone's username and password. Intruders who gain access by modifying software or exploiting software vulnerabilities are often called hackers.

After the hacker gains access to the network, one or more of the following threats may occur:

- **Information Theft** – This is breaking into a computer to obtain confidential information. Information can be used or sold for various purposes. Example: stealing an organization's proprietary information, such as research and development information.

- **Data Loss and Manipulation** – This is breaking into a computer to destroy or alter data records. Examples of data loss: sending a virus that reformats a computer's hard drive. Examples of data manipulation include breaking into a records system to change information, such as the price of an item.

- **Identity Theft** – This is a form of information theft where personal information is stolen for the purpose of taking over someone's identity. Using this information, an individual can obtain legal documents, apply for credit, and make unauthorized online purchases. Identity theft is a growing problem costing billions of dollars per year.

- **Disruption of Service** – This is preventing legitimate users from accessing services to which they should be entitled. Examples include Denial of Service (DoS) attacks on servers, network devices, or network communications links.

Physical Security (11.2.1.2)

An equally important vulnerability is the physical security of devices. An attacker can deny the use of network resources if those resources can be physically compromised.

The four classes of physical threats are

- **Hardware threats** – physical damage to servers, routers, switches, cabling plant, and workstations

- **Environmental threats** – temperature extremes (too hot or too cold) or humidity extremes (too wet or too dry)

- **Electrical threats** – voltage spikes, insufficient supply voltage (brownouts), unconditioned power (noise), and total power loss

- **Maintenance threats** – poor handling of key electrical components (electrostatic discharge), lack of critical spare parts, poor cabling, and poor labeling

These issues must be dealt with in an organizational policy.

Types of Vulnerabilities (11.2.1.3)

Vulnerability is the degree of weakness which is inherent in every network and device. This includes routers, switches, desktops, servers, and even security devices. Typically, the network devices under attack are the endpoints, such as servers and desktop computers. There are three primary vulnerabilities or weaknesses. All three of the following vulnerabilities or weaknesses can lead to various attacks, including malicious code attacks and network attacks.

Technological Vulnerabilities

Examples of technological vulnerabilities include the following:

- TCP/IP protocol weakness
  - HTTP, FTP, and ICMP are inherently insecure
  - SNMP and SMTP are related to the inherently insecure structure upon which TCP was designed

- Operating system weakness

    o Each operating system has security problems that must be addressed

    o UNIX, Linux, Mac OS, Mac OS X, Windows Server 2012, Windows 7, Windows 8, Windows 10

    o They are documented in the Computer Emergency Response Team (CERT) archives at http://www.cert.org

- Network equipment weakness – Various types of network equipment, such as routers, firewall, and switches have security weaknesses that must be recognized and protected against. Their weaknesses include password protection, lack of authentication, routing protocols, and firewall holes.

Configuration Vulnerabilities

Examples of configuration vulnerabilities are shown in Table 11-1.

Table 11-1   Examples of Configuration Vulnerabilities

Configuration Weakness	How the Weakness Is Exploited
Unsecured user accounts	User account information may be transmitted insecurely across the network, exposing usernames and passwords to snoopers.
System accounts with easily guessed passwords	This common problem is the result of poorly selected and easily guessed user passwords.
Misconfigured Internet services	A common problem is to turn on JavaScript in Web browsers, enabling attacks by way of hostile JavaScript when accessing untrusted sites. Other potential sources of weaknesses include misconfigured terminal services, FTP, or Web servers (e.g., Microsoft Internet Information Services (IIS), Apache HTTP Server).
Unsecured default settings within products	Many products have default settings that enable security holes.
Misconfigured network equipment	Misconfigurations of the equipment itself can cause significant security problems. For example, misconfigured access lists, routing protocols, or SNMP community strings can open up large security holes.

Policy Vulnerabilities

Examples of configuration vulnerabilities are shown in Table 11-2.

Table 11-2 Examples of Policy Vulnerabilities

Policy Weakness	How the Weakness Is Exploited
Lack of written security policy	An unwritten policy cannot be consistently applied or enforced.
Politics	Political battles and turf wars can make it difficult to implement a consistent security policy.
Lack of authentication continuity	Poorly chosen, easily cracked, or default passwords can allow unauthorized access to the network.
Logical access controls not applied	Inadequate monitoring and auditing allow attacks and unauthorized use to continue, wasting company resources. This could result in legal action or termination against IT technicians, IT management, or even company leadership that allows these unsafe conditions to persist.
Software and hardware installation and changes do not follow policy	Unauthorized changes to the network topology or installation of unapproved applications create security holes.
Disaster recovery plan is nonexistent	The lack of a disaster recovery plan allows chaos, panic, and confusion to occur when someone attacks the enterprise.

Interactive Graphic

Activity 11.2.1.4: Security Threats and Vulnerabilities

Go to the online course to perform this practice activity.

Network Attacks (11.2.2)

There are many different types of attacks against networks. To secure the network, these attacks must be understood and countermeasures taken.

Types of Malware (11.2.2.1)

Malware or malicious code (malcode) is short for malicious software. It is code or software that is specifically designed to damage, disrupt, steal, or inflict "bad" or illegitimate action on data, hosts, or networks. Viruses, worms, and Trojan horses are types of malware.

Viruses

A computer virus is a type of malware that propagates by inserting a copy of itself into, and becoming part of, another program. It spreads from one computer to another, leaving infections as it travels. Viruses can range in severity from causing mildly annoying effects to damaging data or software and causing denial-of-service (DoS) conditions. Almost all viruses are attached to an executable file, which means the virus may exist on a system but will not be active or able to spread until a user runs or opens the malicious host file or program. When the host code is executed, the viral code is executed as well. Normally, the host program keeps functioning after it is infected by the virus. However, some viruses overwrite other programs with copies of themselves, which destroys the host program altogether. Viruses spread when the software or document they are attached to is transferred from one computer to another using the network, a disk, file sharing, or infected e-mail attachments.

Worms

Computer worms are similar to viruses in that they replicate functional copies of themselves and can cause the same type of damage. In contrast to viruses, which require the spreading of an infected host file, worms are standalone software and do not require a host program or human help to propagate. A worm does not need to attach to a program to infect a host and enter a computer through a vulnerability in the system. Worms take advantage of system features to travel through the network unaided.

Trojan Horses

A Trojan horse is another type of malware named after the wooden horse the Greeks used to infiltrate Troy. It is a harmful piece of software that looks legitimate. Users are typically tricked into loading and executing it on their systems. After it is activated, it can achieve any number of attacks on the host, from irritating the user (popping up windows or changing desktops) to damaging the host (deleting files, stealing data, or activating and spreading other malware, such as viruses). Trojan horses are also known to create back doors to give malicious users access to the system.

Unlike viruses and worms, Trojan horses do not reproduce by infecting other files, nor do they self-replicate. Trojan horses must spread through user interaction such as opening an e-mail attachment or downloading and running a file from the Internet.

Reconnaissance Attacks (11.2.2.2)

In addition to malicious code attacks, it is also possible for networks to fall prey to various network attacks. Network attacks can be classified into three major categories:

- **Reconnaissance attacks** – the discovery and mapping of systems, services, or vulnerabilities

- **Access attacks** – the unauthorized manipulation of data, system access, or user privileges

- **Denial of service** – the disabling or corruption of networks, systems, or services

For reconnaissance attacks, external attackers can use Internet tools, such as the **nslookup** and **whois** utilities, to easily determine the IP address space assigned to a given corporation or entity. After the IP address space is determined, an attacker can then ping the publicly available IP addresses to identify the addresses that are active. To help automate this step, an attacker may use a ping sweep tool, such as *fping* or *gping*, which systematically pings all network addresses in a given range or subnet. This is similar to going through a section of a telephone book and calling each number to see who answers.

Access Attacks (11.2.2.3)

Access attacks exploit known vulnerabilities in authentication services, FTP services, and web services to gain entry to web accounts, confidential databases, and other sensitive information. An access attack allows an individual to gain unauthorized access to information that they have no right to view. Access attacks can be classified into four types:

- Password attacks – Attackers can implement password attacks using several different methods:

  o Brute-force attacks

  o Trojan horse programs

  o Packet sniffers

- Trust Exploitation (Figure 11-10)

Network OS	Trust Models
Windows	Domains Active Directory (AD)
Linux and UNIX	Network File System (NFS) Network Information Service Plus (NIS+)

Figure 11-10   Example of a Trust Exploitation

■ Port Redirection (Figure 11-11)

Figure 11-11   Example of Port Redirection

■ Man-in-the-Middle (Figure 11-12)

Figure 11-12   Example of Man-in-the-Middle

Denial of Service Attacks (11.2.2.4)

Denial of Service (DoS) attacks are the most publicized form of attack and also among the most difficult to eliminate. Even within the attacker community, DoS attacks are regarded as trivial and considered bad form because they require so little effort to execute. But because of their ease of implementation and potentially significant damage, DoS attacks deserve special attention from security administrators.

DoS attacks take many forms. Ultimately, they prevent authorized people from using a service by consuming system resources.

Figure 11-13 shows an example a DoS attack.

Resource overloads	Malformed data
Disk space, bandwidth, buffers	Oversized packets such as ping of death
Ping floods such as smurf	Overlapping packet such as winuke
Packet storms such as UDP bombs and fraggle	Unhandled data such as teardrop

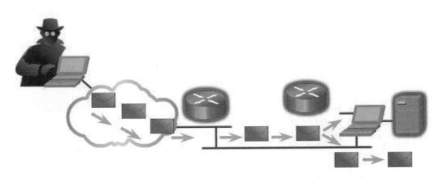

Figure 11-13   DoS Attack

Figure 11-14 shows an example of a distributed DoS (DDoS) attack.

Figure 11-14   DDoS Attack

Figure 11-15 shows an example of a Smurf attack.

Figure 11-15   Smurf Attack

To help prevent DoS attacks it is important to stay up to date with the latest security updates for operating systems and applications. For example, the *ping of death* is no longer a threat because updates to operating systems have fixed the vulnerability that it exploited.

Activity 11.2.2.5: Types of Attack

Go to the online course to perform this practice activity.

Lab 11.2.2.6: Researching Network Security Threats

In this lab, you will complete the following objectives:

- Part 1: Explore the SANS Website

- Part 2: Identify Recent Network Security Threats

- Part 3: Detail a Specific Network Security Threat

Network Attack Mitigation (11.2.3)

To keep network resources and data safe, measures have to be taken to mitigate the risks associated with these attacks on network vulnerabilities. It is necessary to take a proactive stance to network security.

Backup, Upgrade, Update, and Patch (11.2.3.1)

Keeping up-to-date with the latest developments can lead to a more effective defense against network attacks. As new malware is released, enterprises need to keep current with the latest versions of antivirus software.

The most effective way to mitigate a worm attack is to download security updates from the operating system vendor and patch all vulnerable systems. Administering numerous systems involves the creation of a standard software image (operating system and accredited applications that are authorized for use on client systems) that is deployed on new or upgraded systems. However, security requirements change and already deployed systems may need to have updated security patches installed.

One solution to the management of critical security patches is to create a central patch server that all systems must communicate with after a set period of time, as shown in Figure 11-16. Any patches that are not applied to a host are automatically downloaded from the patch server and installed without user intervention.

Figure 11-16   Windows Update

Authentication, Authorization, and Accounting (11.2.3.2)

Authentication, authorization, and accounting (AAA, or "triple A") network security services provide the primary framework to set up access control on a network device. AAA is a way to control who is permitted to access a network (authenticate), what they can do while they are there (authorize), and what actions they perform while accessing the network (accounting).

The concept of AAA is similar to the use of a credit card. The credit card identifies who can use it, how much that user can spend, and keeps account of what items the user spent money on, as shown in Figure 11-17.

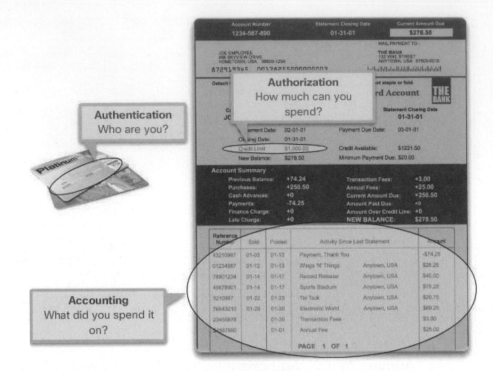

Figure 11-17 AAA is Similar to Using a Credit Card

Firewalls (11.2.3.3)

A firewall is one of the most effective security tools available for protecting users from external threats. Network firewalls reside between two or more networks, control the traffic between them, and help prevent unauthorized access. Host-based firewalls or personal firewalls are installed on end systems. Firewall products use various techniques for determining what is permitted or denied access to a network. These techniques are

- **Packet filtering** – Prevents or allows access based on IP or MAC addresses.

- **Application filtering** – Prevents or allows access by specific application types based on port numbers.

- **URL filtering** – Prevents or allows access to websites based on specific URLs or keywords.

- **Stateful packet inspection (SPI)** – Incoming packets must be legitimate responses to requests from internal hosts. Unsolicited packets are blocked unless permitted specifically. SPI can also include the capability to recognize and filter out specific types of attacks, such as denial of service (DoS).

Firewall products may support one or more of these filtering capabilities. Firewall products come packaged in various forms, such as the following:

- **Cisco Security Appliances** – Dedicated firewall devices are specialized computers that do not have peripherals or hard drives. Appliance-based firewalls can inspect traffic faster and are less prone to failure.

- **Server-Based Firewall** – Firewall applications that generally provide a solution that combines an SPI firewall and access control based on IP address or application. Server-based firewalls can be less secure than dedicated, appliance-based firewalls because of the security weaknesses of the general purpose OS.

- **Wireless Router with Integrated Firewall** – Most home integrated routers have built-in basic firewall capabilities that support packet, application, and web site filtering. Higher-end routers that run special operating systems like Cisco Internetwork Operating System (IOS) also have firewall capabilities that can be configured.

- **Personal Firewall** – Client-side firewalls that typically filter using SPI. The user may be prompted to allow certain applications to connect or may define a list of automatic exceptions. Personal firewalls are often used when a host device is connected directly to an ISP modem. It may interfere with Internet access if not properly configured. It is not recommended to use more than one personal firewall at a time since they can conflict with one another.

Endpoint Security (11.2.3.4)

An endpoint, or host, is an individual computer system or device that acts as a network client. Common endpoints include laptops, desktops, servers, smartphones, and tablets. Securing endpoint devices is one of the most challenging jobs of a network administrator because it involves human nature. A company must have well-documented policies in place and employees must be aware of these rules. Employees need to be trained on proper use of the network. Policies often include the use of antivirus software and host intrusion prevention. More comprehensive endpoint security solutions rely on network access control.

Device Security (11.2.4)

Part of network security is securing actual devices, including end devices and intermediate devices such as network devices.

Device Security Overview (11.2.4.1)

When a new operating system is installed on a device, the security settings are set to the default values. In most cases, this level of security is inadequate. For Cisco routers, the Cisco AutoSecure feature can be used to assist securing the system, as shown in Figure 11-18.

```
R2# auto secure

--- AutoSecure Configuration ---
*** AutoSecure configuration enhances
the security of the router, but it will
not make it absolutely resistant to all
security attacks ***
<output omitted>
```

Figure 11-18   Locking Down Your Router

In addition, there are some simple steps that should be taken that apply to most operating systems:

- Default usernames and passwords should be changed immediately.

- Access to system resources should be restricted to only the individuals that are authorized to use those resources.

- Any unnecessary services and applications should be turned off and uninstalled when possible.

Often, devices shipped from the manufacturer have been sitting in a warehouse for a period of time and do not have the most up-to-date patches installed. It is important to update any software and install any security patches prior to implementation.

Passwords (11.2.4.2)

To protect network devices, it is important to use strong passwords. Here are standard guidelines to follow:

- Use a password length of at least 8 characters, preferably 10 or more characters. A longer password is a better password.

- Make passwords complex. Include a mix of uppercase and lowercase letters, numbers, symbols, and spaces, if allowed.

- Avoid passwords based on repetition, common dictionary words, letter or number sequences, usernames, relative or pet names, biographical information, such as birthdates, ID numbers, ancestor names, or other easily identifiable pieces of information.

- Deliberately misspell a password. For example, Smith = Smyth = 5mYth or Security = 5ecur1ty.

- Change passwords often. If a password is unknowingly compromised, the window of opportunity for the attacker to use the password is limited.

- Do not write passwords down and leave them in obvious places such as on the desk or monitor.

Table 11-3 shows examples of strong and weak passwords.

Table 11-3   Weak and Strong Passwords

Weak Password	Why It Is Weak
secret	Simple dictionary password
smith	Mother's maiden name
toyota	Make of a car
bob1967	Name and birthday of user
Blueleaf23	Simple words and numbers
Strong Password	**Why It Is Strong**
b67n42d39c	Combines alphanumeric characters
12^h u4@1p7	Combines alphanumeric characters, symbols, and also includes a space

On Cisco routers, leading spaces are ignored for passwords, but spaces after the first character are not. Therefore, one method to create a strong password is to use the space bar and create a phrase made of many words. This is called a passphrase. A pass phrase is often easier to remember than a simple password. It is also longer and harder to guess.

Basic Security Practices (11.2.4.3)

Additional Password Security

Strong passwords are only as useful as they are secret. There are several steps that can be taken to help ensure that passwords remain secret. Using the global configuration command **service password-encryption** prevents unauthorized individuals from viewing passwords in plain text in the configuration file, as shown in Example 11-1. This command causes the encryption of all passwords that are unencrypted.

Example 11-1 Configuring Password Security

```
Router(config)# service password-encryption
Router(config)# security password min-length 8
Router(config)# login block-for 120 attempts 3 within 60
Router(config)# line vty 0 4
Router(config-line)# exec-timeout 10
Router(config-line)# end
Router# show running-config
<output omitted>
!
line vty 0 4
 password 7 0822455D0A16544541
 exec-timeout 10
 login
!
<output omitted>
```

Additionally, to ensure that all configured passwords are a minimum of a specified length, use the **security passwords min-length** command in global configuration mode.

Another way hackers learn passwords is simply by brute-force attacks, trying multiple passwords until one works. It is possible to prevent this type of attack by blocking login attempts to the device if a set number of failures occur within a specific amount of time.

```
Router(config)# login block-for 120 attempts 3 within 60
```

This command will block login attempts for 120 seconds if there are three failed login attempts within 60 seconds.

Exec Timeout

Another recommendation is setting executive timeouts. By setting the exec timeout, you are telling the Cisco device to automatically disconnect users on a line after they have been idle for the duration of the exec timeout value. Exec timeouts can be configured on console, VTY, and aux ports using the **exec-timeout** command in line configuration mode.

```
Router(config)# line vty 0 4
```

```
Router(config-line)# exec-timeout 10
```

This command configures the device to disconnect idle users after 10 minutes.

Enable SSH (11.2.4.4)

Telnet is not secure. Data contained within a Telnet packet is transmitted unencrypted. For this reason, it is highly recommended to enable SSH on devices for secure remote access. It is possible to configure a Cisco device to support SSH using the following four steps:

Step 1.   Ensure that the router has a unique hostname, and then configure the IP domain name of the network using the **ip domain-name** command in global configuration mode.

Step 2.   One-way secret keys must be generated for a router to encrypt SSH traffic. To generate the SSH key, use the **crypto key generate rsa general-keys** command in global configuration mode. The specific meaning of the various parts of this command are complex and out of scope for this course. Just note that the modulus determines the size of the key and can be configured from 360 bits to 2048 bits. The larger the modulus, the more secure the key, but the longer it takes to encrypt and decrypt information. The minimum recommended modulus length is 1024 bits.

Step 3.   Create a local database username entry using the **username** global configuration command.

Step 4.   Enable inbound SSH sessions using the line vty commands **login local** and **transport input ssh.**

Example 11-2 demonstrates an SSH configuration on R1.

Example 11-2 Configuring SSH

```
R1# conf t
Enter configuration commands, one per line.  End with CNTL/Z.
R1(config)# ip domain-name span.com
R1(config)# crypto key generate rsa general-keys modulus 1024
The name for the keys will be: R1.span.com

% The key modulus size is 1024 bits
% Generating 1024 bit RSA keys, keys will be non-exportable...
[OK] (elapsed time was 3 seconds)

R1(config)#
*Jan  9 15:02:22.043: %SSH-5-ENABLED: SSH 1.99 has been enabled
R1(config)# username Bob secret cisco
R1(config)# line vty 0 4
R1(config-line)# transport input ssh
R1(config-line)# exit
```

The router can now be remotely accessed only by using SSH.

Packet Tracer
□ Activity

Packet Tracer 11.2.4.5: Configuring Secure Passwords and SSH

The network administrator has asked you to prepare a router for deployment. Before it can be connected to the network, security measures must be enabled.

Lab 11.2.4.6: Accessing Network Devices with SS

In this lab, you will complete the following objectives:

- Part 1: Configure Basic Device Settings
- Part 2: Configure the Router for SSH Access

Lab 11.2.4.7: Examining Telnet and SSH in Wireshark

In this lab, you will complete the following objectives:

- Part 1: Examine a Telnet Session with Wireshark
- Part 2: Examine an SSH Session with Wireshark

Lab 11.2.4.8: Securing Network Devices

In this lab, you will complete the following objectives:

- Part 1: Configure Basic Device Settings
- Part 2: Configure Basic Security Measures on the Router
- Part 3: Configure Basic Security Measures on the Switch

Backup and Restore Configuration Files (11.2.5)

In addition to implementing and securing a small network, it is also the job of the network administrator to manage configuration files. Managing the configuration files is important for purposes of backup and retrieval in the event of a device failure.

Router File Systems (11.2.5.1)

The Cisco IOS File System (IFS) allows the administrator to navigate to different directories and list the files in a directory, and to create subdirectories in flash memory or on a disk. The directories available depend on the device.

Example 11-3 displays the output of the **show file systems** command, which lists all of the available file systems on a Cisco 1941 router.

Example 11-3 File Systems

```
Router# show file systems
File Systems:

        Size(b)        Free(b)         Type    Flags   Prefixes
              -              -        opaque       rw   archive:
              -              -        opaque       rw   system:
              -              -        opaque       rw   tmpsys:
              -              -        opaque       rw   null:
              -              -       network       rw   tftp:
*     256487424      173817856          disk       rw   flash0: flash:#
              -              -          disk       rw   flash1:
         262136         249494         nvram       rw   nvram:
              -              -        opaque       wo   syslog:
              -              -        opaque       rw   xmodem:
              -              -        opaque       rw   ymodem:
              -              -       network       rw   rcp:
              -              -       network       rw   http:
              -              -       network       rw   ftp:
              -              -       network       rw   scp:
              -              -        opaque       ro   tar:
              -              -       network       rw   https:
              -              -        opaque       ro   cns:
      127090688       59348992      usbflash       rw   usbflash0:
```

This command provides useful information such as the amount of available and free memory, the type of file system, and its permissions. Permissions include read only (ro), write only (wo), and read and write (rw), shown in the Flags column of the command output.

Although there are several file systems listed, of interest to us will be the tftp, flash, nvram, and usbflash file systems.

Notice that the flash file system also has an asterisk preceding it. This indicates that flash is the current default file system. The bootable IOS is located in flash; therefore, the pound symbol (#) is appended to the flash listing, indicating that it is a bootable disk.

The Flash File System

Example 11-4 displays the output from the **dir** command.

Example 11-4 Flash

```
Router# dir
Directory of flash0:/


    1  -rw-         1248   Mar 29 2013 18:17:58 +00:00  R1-running-config-backup
    2  -rw-         2903   Sep  7 2012 06:58:26 +00:00  cpconfig-19xx.cfg
    3  -rw-      3000320   Sep  7 2012 06:58:40 +00:00  cpexpress.tar
    4  -rw-         1038   Sep  7 2012 06:58:52 +00:00  home.shtml
    5  -rw-       122880   Sep  7 2012 06:59:02 +00:00  home.tar
    6  -rw-      1697952   Sep  7 2012 06:59:20 +00:00  securedesktop-ios-3.1.1.
45-k9.pkg
    7  -rw-       415956   Sep  7 2012 06:59:34 +00:00  sslclient-win-1.1.4.176.pkg
    8  -rw-         1153   Apr 26 2013 02:24:30 +00:00  all_licenses.lic
   11  -rw-         1673   Aug 16 2013 20:38:26 +00:00  FrameRelay
   12  -rw-     75551300   Feb 16 2015 16:18:40 +00:00  c1900-universalk9-mz.
SPA.154-3.M2.bin
   13  -rw-         2182   Feb 18 2015 19:12:02 +00:00  rescue-cfg
   14  -rw-         1381   Feb 18 2015 20:37:14 +00:00  R2backup.cfg
   15  drw-            0   Feb 28 2015 01:14:12 +00:00  ipsdir
   22  -rw-         2234   Jun  5 2015 16:46:48 +00:00  R1-Config


256487424 bytes total (173817856 bytes free)
```

Because flash is the default file system, the **dir** command lists the contents of flash. Several files are located in flash, but of specific interest is the last listing. This is the name of the current Cisco IOS file image that is running in RAM.

The NVRAM File System

To view the contents of NVRAM, you must change the current default file system using the **cd** (change directory) command, as shown in Example 11-5.

Example 11-5 NVRAM

```
Router# cd nvram:
Router# pwd
nvram:/
Router# dir
Directory of nvram:/


  253  -rw-         1321                       <no date>  startup-config
  254  ----            5                       <no date>  private-config
  255  -rw-         1321                       <no date>  underlying-config
    1  -rw-         2945                       <no date>  cwmp_inventory
    4  ----          439                       <no date>  persistent-data
```

```
     5    -rw-              17                  <no date>   ecfm_ieee_mib
     6    -rw-             559                  <no date>   IOS-Self-Sig#1.cer
     7    -rw-             559                  <no date>   IOS-Self-Sig#2.cer
     8    -rw-             559                  <no date>   IOS-Self-Sig#3.cer
     9    -rw-               0                  <no date>   ifIndex-table
    10    -rw-             559                  <no date>   IOS-Self-Sig#4.cer
    11    -rw-             559                  <no date>   IOS-Self-Sig#5.cer


262136 bytes total (249494 bytes free)
```

The **pwd** (present working directory) command verifies that we are viewing the NVRAM directory. Finally, the **dir** (directory) command lists the contents of NVRAM. Although there are several configuration files listed, of specific interest is the startup-configuration file.

Switch File Systems (11.2.5.2)

With the Cisco 2960 switch flash file system, you can copy configuration files, and archive (upload and download) software images.

The command to view the file systems on a Catalyst switch is the same as on a Cisco router: **show file systems**, as shown in Example 11-6.

Example 11-6 Cisco 2960 Switch

```
Switch# show file systems
File Systems:

       Size(b)        Free(b)      Type   Flags   Prefixes
*      32514048     20650496      flash      rw     flash:
              -             -     opaque     rw     vb:
              -             -     opaque     ro     bs:
              -             -     opaque     rw     system:
              -             -     opaque     rw     tmpsys:
         65536          2817       nvram     rw     nvram:
              -             -     opaque     ro     xmodem:
              -             -     opaque     ro     ymodem:
              -             -     opaque     rw     null:
              -             -     opaque     ro     tar:
              -             -    network     rw     tftp:
              -             -    network     rw     rcp:
              -             -    network     rw     http:
              -             -    network     rw     ftp:
              -             -    network     rw     scp:
              -             -    network     rw     https:
              -             -     opaque     ro     cns:
```

Backing Up and Restoring Using Text Files (11.2.5.3)

Backup Configurations with Text Capture (Tera Term)

Configuration files can be saved/archived to a text file using Tera Term, as shown in Figure 11-19.

Figure 11-19   Saving to a Text File in Tera Term

The steps to capture the configuration to a text file are as follows:

Step 1.   On the File menu, click **Log**.

Step 2.   Choose the location to save the file. Tera Term will begin capturing text.

Step 3.   After capture has been started, execute the **show running-config** or **show startup-config** command at the privileged EXEC prompt. Text displayed in the terminal window will be directed to the chosen file.

Step 4.   When the capture is complete, select **Close** in the Tera Term: Log window.

Step 5.   View the file to verify that it was not corrupted.

Restoring Text Configurations

A configuration can be copied from a file to a device. When copied from a text file and pasted into a terminal window, the IOS executes each line of the configuration text as a command. This means that the file will require editing to ensure that encrypted passwords are in plain text and that non-command text such as "—More—" and IOS messages are removed. This process is discussed in the lab.

Further, at the CLI, the device must be set at the global configuration mode to receive the commands from the text file being pasted into the terminal window.

When using Tera Term, the steps are

Step 1.   On the File menu, click **Send** file.

Step 2.   Locate the file to be copied into the device and click **Open**.

Step 3.   Tera Term will paste the file into the device.

The text in the file will be applied as commands in the CLI and become the running configuration on the device. This is a convenient method for manually configuring a router.

Backing up and Restoring TFTP (11.2.5.4)

Backup Configurations with TFTP

Copies of configuration files should be stored as backup files in the event of a problem. Configuration files can be stored on a Trivial File Transfer Protocol (TFTP) server or a USB drive. A configuration file should also be included in the network documentation.

To save the running configuration or the startup configuration to a TFTP server, use either the **copy running-config tftp** or **copy startup-config tftp** command as shown in Example 11-7.

Example 11-7 Backing Up the Running-Config File

```
R1# copy running-config tftp
Remote host []? 192.168.10.254
Name of the configuration file to write[R1-config]? R1-Jan-2016
Write file R1-Jan-2016 to 192.168.10.254? [confirm]
Writing R1-Jan-2016 !!!!!! [OK]
```

Follow these steps to backup the running configuration to a TFTP server:

Step 1.   Enter the **copy running-config tftp** command.

Step 2.   Enter the IP address of the host where the configuration file will be stored.

Step 3.   Enter the name to assign to the configuration file.

Step 4.   Press Enter to confirm each choice.

Restoring Configurations with TFTP

To restore the running configuration or the startup configuration from a TFTP server, use either the **copy tftp running-config** or **copy tftp startup-config** command. Use these steps to restore the running configuration from a TFTP server:

Step 1.   Enter the **copy tftp running-config** command.

Step 2.   Enter the IP address of the host where the configuration file is stored.

Step 3.   Enter the name to assign to the configuration file.

Step 4.   Press **Enter** to confirm each choice.

Using USB Ports on a Cisco Router (11.2.5.5)

The Universal Serial Bus (USB) storage feature enables certain models of Cisco routers to support USB flash drives. For example, as shown in Figure 11-20, the 1941 ISR has two USB ports. The USB flash feature provides an optional secondary storage capability and an additional boot device. Images, configurations, and other files can be copied to or from the Cisco USB flash memory with the same reliability as storing and retrieving files using the Compact Flash card. In addition, modular integrated services routers can boot any Cisco IOS Software image saved on USB flash memory. Ideally, USB flash can hold multiple copies of the Cisco IOS and multiple router configurations.

Use the **dir** command to view the contents of the USB flash drive, as shown in Figure 11-20.

Figure 11-20   Cisco 1941 Router USB Port

Backing Up and Restoring Using a USB (11.2.5.6)

Backup Configurations with a USB Flash Drive

When backing up to a USB port, it is a good idea to issue the **show file systems** command to verify that the USB drive is there and confirm the name.

Next, use the **copy run usbflash0:/** command to copy the configuration file to the USB flash drive. Be sure to use the name of the flash drive, as indicated in the file system. The slash is optional but indicates the root directory of the USB flash drive.

The IOS will prompt for the filename. If the file already exists on the USB flash drive, the router will prompt to overwrite.

Use the **dir** command to see the file on the USB drive and use the **more** command to see the contents, as shown in Example 11-8.

Example 11-8 Backing Up Config to a USB Drive

```
R1# dir usbflash0:/
Directory of usbflash0:/


    4  -rw-          1393    Jan 9 2016 15:31:34 +00:00   R1-Config
<output omitted>


127090688 bytes total (59346944 bytes free)
R1# more usbflash0:/R1-Config
!
! Last configuration change at 15:30:42 UTC Sat Jan 9 2016
!
version 15 4
service timestamps debug datetime msec
service timestamps log datetime msec
no service password-encryption
!
hostname R1
!
boot-start-marker
boot-end-marker
!
!
<output omitted>
```

Restore Configurations with a USB Flash Drive

In order to copy the file back, it will be necessary to edit the USB R1-Config file with a text editor. Assuming the file name is **R1-Config**, use the command **copy usbflash0:/R1-Config** *running-config* to restore a running configuration.

Packet Tracer
☐ Activity

Packet Tracer 11.2.5.7: Backing Up Configuration Files

This activity is designed to show how to restore a configuration from a backup and then perform a new backup. Due to an equipment failure, a new router has been put in place. Fortunately, backup configuration files have been saved to a Trivial File

Transfer Protocol (TFTP) Server. You are required to restore the files from the TFTP Server to get the router back online with as little downtime as possible.

Lab 11.2.5.8: Managing Router Configuration Files with Tera Term

In this lab, you will complete the following objectives:

- Part 1: Configure Basic Device Settings

- Part 2: Use Terminal Emulation Software to Create a Backup Configuration File

- Part 3: Use a Backup Configuration File to Restore a Router

Lab 11.2.5.9: Managing Device Configuration Files Using TFTP, Flash, and USB

In this lab, you will complete the following objectives:

- Part 1: Build the Network and Configure Basic Device Settings

- Part 2: (Optional) Download TFTP Server Software

- Part 3: Use TFTP to Back Up and Restore the Switch Running Configuration

- Part 4: Use TFTP to Back Up and Restore the Router Running Configuration

- Part 5: Back Up and Restore Running Configurations Using Router Flash Memory

- Part 6: (Optional) Use a USB Drive to Back Up and Restore the Running Configuration

Lab 11.2.5.10: Researching Password Recovery Procedures

In this lab, you will complete the following objectives:

- Part 1: Research the Configuration Register

- Part 2: Document the Password Recovery Procedure for a Specific Cisco Router

Network Testing and Verification (11.3)

After the network has been implemented, a network administrator must be able to test the network connectivity to ensure that it is operating appropriately. Additionally, it is a good idea for the network administrator to document the network.

The ping Command (11.3.1)

Using the **ping** command is an effective way to test connectivity. The test is often referred to as testing the protocol stack, because the **ping** command moves from

Layer 3 of the OSI model to Layer 2 and then Layer 1. Ping uses the ICMP protocol to check for connectivity.

Interpreting Ping Results (11.3.1.1)

Using the **ping** command is an effective way to test connectivity. The **ping** command uses the Internet Control Message Protocol (ICMP) and verifies Layer 3 connectivity. The **ping** command will not always pinpoint the nature of a problem, but it can help to identify the source of the problem, an important first step in troubleshooting a network failure.

IOS Ping Indicators

A ping issued from the IOS will yield one of several indications for each ICMP echo request that was sent, such as the ! shown in Figure 11-21.

Figure 11-21   IOS Ping Indicators

The most common indicators are

- ! – indicates receipt of an ICMP echo reply message, as shown in Figure 11-21
- . – indicates a time expired while waiting for an ICMP echo reply message
- U – an ICMP unreachable message was received

The "." (period) may indicate that a connectivity problem occurred somewhere along the path. It may also indicate that a router along the path did not have a route to the destination and did not send an ICMP destination unreachable message. It also may indicate that the ping was blocked by device security. When sending a ping on an Ethernet LAN it is common for the first echo request to timeout if the ARP process is required.

The "U" indicates that a router along the path responded with an ICMP unreachable message. The router either did not have a route to the destination address or that the ping request was blocked.

Testing the Loopback

The ping command can also be used to verify the internal IP configuration on the local host by pinging the loopback address, 127.0.0.1, as shown in Figure 11-22. This verifies the proper operation of the protocol stack from the network layer to the physical layer – and back – without actually putting a signal on the media.

```
C:\> ping 127.0.0.1
Pinging 127.0.0.1 with 32 bytes of data:
Reply from 127.0.0.1: bytes=32 time=0ms TTL=128
Reply from 127.0.0.1: bytes=32 time=4ms TTL=128
Reply from 127.0.0.1: bytes=32 time=3ms TTL=128
Reply from 127.0.0.1: bytes=32 time=3ms TTL=128

Ping statistics for 127.0.0.1:
Packets: Sent = 4, Received = 4, Lost = 0 (0% loss),
Approximate round trip times in milli-seconds:
Minimum = 0ms, Maximum = 4ms, Average = 2ms
```

Figure 11-22   Testing the Loopback

Extended Ping (11.3.1.2)

The Cisco IOS offers an "extended" mode of the **ping** command. This mode is entered by typing **ping** in privileged EXEC mode, without a destination IPv4 address.

As shown in the figure, a series of prompts are then presented. Pressing **Enter** accepts the indicated default values. The example illustrates how to force the source address for a ping to be 10.1.1.1 (see R2 in Figure 11-23); the source address for a standard ping would be 209.165.200.226. By doing this, the network administrator can verify from R2 that R1 has a route to 10.1.1.0/24.

```
R2# ping
Protocol [ip]:
Target IP address: 192.168.10.1
Repeat count [5]:
Datagram size [100]:
Timeout in seconds [2]:
Extended commands [n]: y
Source address or interface: 10.1.1.1
Type of service [0]:
Set DF bit in IP header? [no]:
Validate reply data? [no]:
Data pattern [0xABCD]:
Loose, Strict, Record, Timestamp, Verbose[none]:
Sweep range of sizes [n]:
Type escape sequence to abort.
Sending 5, 100-byte ICMP Echos to 192.168.10.1, timeout is 2 seconds:
```

Figure 11-23   Extended Ping

Note

The **ping ipv6** command is used for extended ping for IPv6.

Network Baseline (11.3.1.3)

One of the most effective tools for monitoring and troubleshooting network performance is to establish a network baseline. Creating an effective network performance baseline is accomplished over a period of time. Measuring performance at varying times (Figures 11-24 and 11-25) and loads will assist in creating a better picture of overall network performance.

FEB 8, 2013 08:14:43

```
C:\>ping 10.66.254.159

Pinging 10.66.254.159 with 32 bytes of data:

Reply from 10.66.234.159: bytes=32 time<1ms TTL=128
Reply from 10.66.234.159: bytes=32 time<1ms TTL=128
Reply from 10.66.234.159: bytes=32 time<1ms TTL=128
Reply from 10.66.234.159: bytes=32 time<1ms TTL=128

Ping statistics for 10.66.254.159:
    Packets: Sent = 4, Received = 4, Lost = 0 (0% loss),
Approximate round trip times in milli-seconds:
    Minimum = 0ms, Maximum = 0ms, Average = 0ms
```

MAR 17, 2013 14:41:06

```
C:\>ping 10.66.254.159

Pinging 10.66.254.159 with 32 bytes of data:

Reply from 10.66.234.159: bytes=32 time<6ms TTL=128
Reply from 10.66.234.159: bytes=32 time<6ms TTL=128
Reply from 10.66.234.159: bytes=32 time<6ms TTL=128
Reply from 10.66.234.159: bytes=32 time<6ms TTL=128

Ping statistics for 10.66.254.159:
    Packets: Sent = 4, Received = 4, Lost = 0 (0% loss),
Approximate round trip times in milli-seconds:
    Minimum = 6ms, Maximum = 6ms, Average = 6ms
```

Figure 11-24   Run the Same Test

FEB 8, 2013 08:14:43

```
C:\>ping 10.66.254.159

Pinging 10.66.254.159 with 32 bytes of data:

Reply from 10.66.234.159: bytes=32 time<1ms TTL=128
Reply from 10.66.234.159: bytes=32 time<1ms TTL=128
Reply from 10.66.234.159: bytes=32 time<1ms TTL=128
Reply from 10.66.234.159: bytes=32 time<1ms TTL=128

Ping statistics for 10.66.254.159:
    Packets: Sent = 4, Received = 4, Lost = 0 (0% loss),
Approximate round trip times in milli-seconds:
    Minimum = 0ms, Maximum = 0ms, Average = 0ms
```

MAR 17, 2013 14:41:06

```
C:\>ping 10.66.254.159

Pinging 10.66.254.159 with 32 bytes of data:

Reply from 10.66.234.159: bytes=32 time<6ms TTL=128
Reply from 10.66.234.159: bytes=32 time<6ms TTL=128
Reply from 10.66.234.159: bytes=32 time<6ms TTL=128
Reply from 10.66.234.159: bytes=32 time<6ms TTL=128

Ping statistics for 10.66.254.159:
    Packets: Sent = 4, Received = 4, Lost = 0 (0% loss),
Approximate round trip times in milli-seconds:
    Minimum = 0ms, Maximum = 0ms, Average = 0ms
```

Figure 11-25   At Different Times

The output derived from network commands can contribute data to the network baseline.

One method for starting a baseline is to copy and paste the results from an executed **ping, traceroute or tracert,** or other relevant commands into a text file. These text files can be time stamped with the date and saved into an archive for later retrieval and comparison (Figure 11-26). Among items to consider are error messages and the response times from host to host. If there is a considerable increase in response times, there may be a latency issue to address.

FEB 8, 2013 08:14:43

```
C:\>ping 10.66.254.159

Pinging 10.66.254.159 with 32 bytes of data:

Reply from 10.66.234.159: bytes=32 time<1ms TTL=128
Reply from 10.66.234.159: bytes=32 time<1ms TTL=128
Reply from 10.66.234.159: bytes=32 time<1ms TTL=128
Reply from 10.66.234.159: bytes=32 time<1ms TTL=128

Ping statistics for 10.66.254.159:
    Packets: Sent = 4, Received = 4, Lost = 0 (0% loss),
Approximate round trip times in milli-seconds:
    Minimum = 0ms, Maximum = 0ms, Average = 0ms
```

MAR 17, 2013 14:41:06

```
C:\>ping 10.66.254.159

Pinging 10.66.254.159 with 32 bytes of data:

Reply from 10.66.234.159: bytes=32 time<6ms TTL=128
Reply from 10.66.234.159: bytes=32 time<6ms TTL=128
Reply from 10.66.234.159: bytes=32 time<6ms TTL=128
Reply from 10.66.234.159: bytes=32 time<6ms TTL=128

Ping statistics for 10.66.254.159:
    Packets: Sent = 4, Received = 4, Lost = 0 (0% loss),
Approximate round trip times in milli-seconds:
    Minimum = 0ms, Maximum = 0ms, Average = 0ms
```

Figure 11-26 Compare Values

Corporate networks should have extensive baselines; more extensive than we can describe in this course. Professional-grade software tools are available for storing and maintaining baseline information. In this course, we only cover some basic techniques and discuss the purpose of baselines.

The traceroute and tracert Command (11.3.2)

Sometimes more information is required then a simple end-to-end connectivity test can provide. Running a packet trace from source to destination can alert the user to where problems actually exist.

Interpreting Trace Messages (11.3.2.1)

A trace returns a list of hops as a packet is routed through a network. The form of the command depends on where the command is issued. When performing the trace from a Windows computer, use **tracert**. When performing the trace from a router CLI, use **traceroute**, as shown in Figure 11-27.

Figure 11-27　Testing the Path to a Remote Host

Example 11-9 shows output of the **tracert** command entered on Host 1 to trace the route to Host 2.

Example 11-9　Tracing the Route from Host 1 to Host 2

```
c:\> tracert 10.1.0.2
tracing route to 10.1.0.2 over a maximum of 30 hops
1 2 ms 2 ms 2 ms 10.0.0.254
2 * * * Request timed out.
3 * * * Request timed out.
4 ^C
C:\>
```

The only successful response was from the gateway on Router A. Trace requests to the next hop timed out, meaning that the next hop router did not respond. The trace results indicate that there is either a failure in the internetwork beyond the LAN or that these routers have been configured not to respond to echo requests used in the trace.

Extended traceroute (11.3.2.2)

Designed as a variation of the **traceroute** command, the extended **traceroute** command allows the administrator to adjust minor parameters related to the command operation. This is helpful when troubleshooting routing loops, determining the exact next-hop router, or to help determine where packets are getting dropped by a router or denied by a firewall. Whereas the extended **ping** command can be used to determine the type of connectivity problem, the extended **traceroute** command is useful in locating the problem.

An ICMP "time exceeded" error message indicates that a router in the path has seen and discarded the packet. An ICMP "destination unreachable" error message indicates that a router has received the packet, but discarded it because it could not be delivered. Traceroute uses ICMP echo requests and echo replies. If the ICMP timer expires before an ICMP echo reply is received, **traceroute** command output displays an asterisk (*).

In IOS, the extended **traceroute** command terminates when any of the following occur:

- The destination responds with an ICMP echo reply

- The user interrupts the trace with the escape sequence

Note

In IOS, you can invoke this escape sequence by pressing Ctrl+Shift+6. In Windows, the escape sequence is invoked by pressing Ctrl+C.

To use extended **traceroute**, simply type **traceroute**, without providing any parameters, and press **ENTER**. IOS will guide you through the command, by presenting a number of prompts related to the setting of all the different parameters. Table 11-4 shows the IOS extended **traceroute** options and the respective descriptions.

Table 11-4   IOS Extended traceroute Options

Option	Description
Protocol [ip]:	Prompts for a supported protocol. The default is IPv4.
Target IP address:	You must enter a host name or an IPv4 address. There is no default.
Source address:	The interface or IPv4 address of the router to use as a source address for the probes. The router normally picks the IP address of the outbound interface to use.
Numeric display [n]:	The default is to have both a symbolic and numeric display; however, you can suppress the symbolic display.
Timeout in seconds [3]:	The number of seconds to wait for a response to a probe packet. The default is 3 seconds.

Continued

Table 11-4   *Continued*

Option	Description
Probe count [3]:	The number of probes to be sent at each TTL level. The default count is 3.
Minimum Time to Live [1]:	The TTL value for the first probes. The default is 1, but it can be set to a higher value to suppress the display of known hops.
Maximum Time to Live [30]:	The largest TTL value that can be used. The default is 30. The **traceroute** command terminates when the destination is reached or when this value is reached.
Port Number [33434]:	The destination port used by the UDP probe messages. The default is 33434.
Loose, Strict, Record, Timestamp, Verbose [none]:	IP header options. You can specify any combination. The **traceroute** command issues prompts for the required fields. Note that the **traceroute** command will place the requested options in each probe; however, there is no guarantee that all routers (or end nodes) will process the options.

Whereas the Windows **tracert** command allows the input of several parameters, it is not guided and must be performed through options in the command line. Example 11-10 shows the available options for **tracert** in Windows.

Example 11-10 Available options for tracert in Windows.

```
C:\> tracert
Usage: tracert [-d] [-h maximum_hops] [-j host-list] [-w timeout]
               [-R] [-S srcaddr] [-4] [-6] target_name
Options:
    -d                 Do not resolve addresses to hostnames.
    -h maximum_hops    Maximum number of hops to search for target.
    -j host-list       Loose source route along host-list (IPv4-only).
    -w timeout         Wait timeout milliseconds for each reply.
    -R                 Trace round-trip path (IPv6-only).
    -S srcaddr         Source address to use (IPv6-only).
    -4                 Force using IPv4.
    -6                 Force using IPv6.
C:\>
```

Packet Tracer
☐ Activity

Packet Tracer 11.3.2.3: Test Connectivity with Traceroute

This activity is designed to help you troubleshoot network connectivity issues using commands to trace the route from source to destination. You are required to examine the output of **tracert** (the Windows command) and **traceroute** (the IOS command) as packets traverse the network and determine the cause of a network issue. After the issue is corrected, use the **tracert** and **traceroute** commands to verify the completion.

Lab 11.3.2.4: Testing Network Latency with Ping and Traceroute

In this lab, you will complete the following objectives:

- Part 1: Use Ping to Document Network Latency
- Part 2: Use Traceroute to Document Network Latency

Show Commands (11.3.3)

Show commands allow the network technician to look at a static snapshot of a configuration or process.

Common show Commands Revisited (11.3.3.1)

The Cisco IOS CLI **show** commands display relevant information about the configuration and operation of the device.

Network technicians use **show** commands extensively for viewing configuration files, checking the status of device interfaces and processes, and verifying the device operational status. The **show** commands are available whether the device was configured using the CLI or Cisco Configuration Professional.

The status of nearly every process or function of the router can be displayed using a **show** command. Some of the more popular **show** commands are shown in Examples 11-11 through 11-16.

Example 11-11 The **show running-config** Command

```
R1# show running-config
Building configuration...


Current configuration : 1484 bytes
!
! Last configuration change at 16:00:05 UTC Sat Jan 9 2016
!
version 15.4
service timestamps debug datetime msec
service timestamps log datetime msec
no service password-encryption
!
hostname R1
!
<output omitted>
!
interface GigabitEthernet0/0
```

```
 ip address 192.168.10.1 255.255.255.0
 duplex auto
 speed auto
!
interface GigabitEthernet0/1
 no ip address
 shutdown
 duplex auto
 speed auto
!
interface Serial0/0/0
 ip address 209.165.200.225 255.255.255.252
 clock rate 2000000
!
interface Serial0/0/1
 no ip address
 shutdown
!
router rip
 network 192.168.10.0
 network 209.165.200.0
!
<output omitted>
```

Example 11-12 The **show interfaces** command

```
R1# show interfaces
<output omitted>
GigabitEthernet0/0 is up, line protocol is up
  Hardware is CN GigabitEthernet, address is fc99.4775.c3e0 (bia fc99.4775.c3e0)
  Internet address is 192.168.10.1/24
  MTU 1500 bytes, BW 1000000 Kbit/sec, DLY 10 usec,
      reliability 255/255, txload 1/255, rxload 1/255
  Encapsulation ARPA, loopback not set
  Keepalive set (10 sec)
  Full Duplex, 1000Mbps, media type is RJ45
  output flow-control is unsupported, input flow-control is unsupported
  ARP type: ARPA, ARP Timeout 04:00:00
  Last input 00:00:07, output 00:00:07, output hang never
  Last clearing of "show interface" counters never
 Input queue: 0/75/0/0 (size/max/drops/flushes); Total output drops: 0
  Queueing strategy: fifo
  Output queue: 0/40 (size/max)
 5 minute input rate 0 bits/sec, 0 packets/sec
```

```
        5 minute output rate 0 bits/sec, 0 packets/sec
            24 packets input, 1996 bytes, 0 no buffer
            Received 21 broadcasts (0 IP multicasts)
            0 runts, 0 giants, 0 throttles
            0 input errors, 0 CRC, 0 frame, 0 overrun, 0 ignored
            0 watchdog, 0 multicast, 0 pause input
            117 packets output, 12592 bytes, 0 underruns
            0 output errors, 0 collisions, 1 interface resets
            0 unknown protocol drops
            0 babbles, 0 late collision, 0 deferred
            0 lost carrier, 0 no carrier, 0 pause output
            0 output buffer failures, 0 output buffers swapped out
<output omitted>
```

Example 11-13 The **show arp** Command

```
R1# show arp
Protocol   Address           Age (min)   Hardware Addr   Type   Interface
Internet   192.168.10.1           -      fc99.4775.c3e0  ARPA   GigabitEthernet0/0
R1#
```

Example 11-14 The **show ip route** Command

```
R1# show ip route
Codes: L - local, C - connected, S - static, R - RIP, M - mobile, B - BGP
       D - EIGRP, EX - EIGRP external, O - OSPF, IA - OSPF inter area
       N1 - OSPF NSSA external type 1, N2 - OSPF NSSA external type 2
       E1 - OSPF external type 1, E2 - OSPF external type 2
       i - IS-IS, su - IS-IS summary, L1 - IS-IS level-1, L2 - IS-IS level-2
       ia - IS-IS inter area, * - candidate default, U - per-user static route
       o - ODR, P - periodic downloaded static route, H - NHRP, l - LISP
       a - application route
       + - replicated route, % - next hop override

Gateway of last resort is not set

R     10.0.0.0/8 [120/1] via 209.165.200.226, 00:00:26, Serial0/0/0
      192.168.10.0/24 is variably subnetted, 2 subnets, 2 masks
C        192.168.10.0/24 is directly connected, GigabitEthernet0/0
L        192.168.10.1/32 is directly connected, GigabitEthernet0/0
      209.165.200.0/24 is variably subnetted, 2 subnets, 2 masks
C        209.165.200.224/30 is directly connected, Serial0/0/0
L        209.165.200.225/32 is directly connected, Serial0/0/0
R1#
```

Example 11-15 The **show protocols** Command

```
R1# show protocols
Global values:
  Internet Protocol routing is enabled
Embedded-Service-Engine0/0 is administratively down, line protocol is down
GigabitEthernet0/0 is up, line protocol is up
  Internet address is 192.168.10.1/24
GigabitEthernet0/1 is administratively down, line protocol is down
Serial0/0/0 is up, line protocol is up
  Internet address is 209.165.200.225/30
Serial0/0/1 is administratively down, line protocol is down
R1#
```

Example 11-16 The **show version** Command

```
R1# show version
Cisco IOS Software, C1900 Software (C1900-UNIVERSALK9-M), Version 15.4(3)M2,
  RELEASE SOFTWARE (fc2)
Technical Support: http://www.cisco.com/techsupport
Copyright (c) 1986-2015 by Cisco Systems, Inc.
Compiled Fri 06-Feb-15 17:01 by prod_rel_team


ROM: System Bootstrap, Version 15.0(1r)M15, RELEASE SOFTWARE (fc1)


R1 uptime is 1 hour, 20 minutes
System returned to ROM by power-on
System image file is "flash0:c1900-universalk9-mz.SPA.154-3.M2.bin"
Last reload type: Normal Reload
Last reload reason: power-on


<output omitted>


Cisco CISCO1941/K9 (revision 1.0) with 446464K/77824K bytes of memory.
Processor board ID FTX1636848Z
2 Gigabit Ethernet interfaces
2 Serial(sync/async) interfaces
1 terminal line
1 Virtual Private Network (VPN) Module
DRAM configuration is 64 bits wide with parity disabled.
255K bytes of non-volatile configuration memory.
124400K bytes of USB Flash usbflash0 (Read/Write)
250880K bytes of ATA System CompactFlash 0 (Read/Write)

  License Info:

License UDI:
```

```
-----------------------------------------------------
Device#     PID                  SN
-----------------------------------------------------
*1          CISCO1941/K9         FTX1636848Z




Technology Package License Information for Module:'c1900'


------------------   -------------------------------------------
Technology   Technology-package                Technology-package
             Current              Type         Next reboot
------------------   -------------------------------------------
ipbase       ipbasek9             Permanent    ipbasek9
security     securityk9           EvalRightToUse  securityk9
data         disable              None         disable
NtwkEss      None                 None         None

Configuration register is 0x2142 (will be 0x2102 at next reload)
```

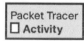

Video Demonstration 11.3.3.2: The show version Command

Go to the online course to view this video.

Packet Tracer 11.3.3.3: Using Show Commands

This activity is designed to reinforce the use of router **show commands**. You are not required to configure, but rather examine, the output of several show commands.

Host and IOS Commands (11.3.4)

In addition to the **show** commands, a number of additional commands are available on hosts and network devices.

The ipconfig Command (11.3.4.1)

As shown in Example 11-17, the IP address of the default gateway of a host can be viewed by issuing the **ipconfig** command at the command line of a Windows computer.

Example 11-17 The **ipconfig** Command

```
C:\> ipconfig

Windows IP Configuration


Ethernet adapter Local Area Connection 2:

   Connection-specific DNS Suffix   . : cisco.com
   IPv4 Address. . . . . . . . . . . : 192.168.10.10
   Subnet Mask . . . . . . . . . . . : 255.255.255.0
   Default Gateway . . . . . . . . . : 192.168.10.1

<output omitted>
```

As shown in Example 11-18, use the **ipconfig /all** command to view the MAC address as well as a number of details regarding the Layer 3 addressing of the device.

Example 11-18 The **ipconfig /all** Command

```
C:\> ipconfig /all
Ethernet adapter Local Area Connection:

   Connection-specific DNS Suffix   . :
   Description . . . . . . . . . . . : Intel(R) Ethernet Connection I217-LM
   Physical Address. . . . . . . . . : 54-EE-75-37-00-69
   DHCP Enabled. . . . . . . . . . . : Yes
   Autoconfiguration Enabled . . . . : Yes
   Link-local IPv6 Address . . . . . : fe80::487a:32ba:8937:f07b%11(Preferred)
   IPv4 Address. . . . . . . . . . . : 192.168.10.10
   Subnet Mask . . . . . . . . . . . : 255.255.255.0
   Lease Obtained. . . . . . . . . . : Thursday, January 07, 2016 9:40:57 PM
   Lease Expires . . . . . . . . . . : Sunday, January 10, 2016 12:47:58 PM
   Default Gateway . . . . . . . . . : 192.168.10.1
<output omitted>
```

The DNS Client service on Windows PCs optimizes the performance of DNS name resolution by storing previously resolved names in memory, as well. As shown if Example 11-19, the **ipconfig /displaydns** command displays all of the cached DNS entries on a Windows computer system.

Example 11-19 The **ipconfig /displaydns** Command

```
C:\> ipconfig /displaydns


Windows IP Configuration


    dm-dm-aln-a03-p.cisco.com
    ----------------------------------------
    Record Name . . . . . : dm-dm-aln-a03-p.cisco.com
    Record Type . . . . . : 1
    Time To Live  . . . . : 457
    Data Length . . . . . : 4
    Section . . . . . . . : Answer
    A (Host) Record . . . : 173.36.32.145


    Record Name . . . . . : ns1.cisco.com
    Record Type . . . . . : 1
    Time To Live  . . . . : 457
    Data Length . . . . . : 4
    Section . . . . . . . : Additional
    A (Host) Record . . . : 72.163.5.201


    Record Name . . . . . : ns1.cisco.com
    Record Type . . . . . : 28
    Time To Live  . . . . : 457
    Data Length . . . . . : 16
    Section . . . . . . . : Additional
    AAAA Record . . . . . : 2001:420:1101:6::a
```

The arp Command (11.3.4.2)

The **arp** command is executed from the Windows command prompt, as shown in Figure 11-28.

Figure 11-28   The arp Command

The **arp -a** command lists all devices currently in the ARP cache of the host, which includes the IPv4 address, physical address, and the type of addressing (static/dynamic), for each device.

The cache can be cleared by using the **arp -d*** command in the event the network administrator wants to repopulate the cache with updated information.

Note

The ARP cache only contains information from devices that have been recently accessed. To ensure that the ARP cache is populated, ping a device so that it will have an entry in the ARP table.

The show cdp neighbors Command (11.3.4.3)

There are several other IOS commands that are useful. For example, the Cisco Discovery Protocol (CDP) is a Cisco-proprietary protocol that runs at the data link layer. Because CDP operates at the data link layer, two or more Cisco network devices, such as routers that support different network layer protocols, can learn about each other even if Layer 3 connectivity does not exist.

Compare the topology in Figure 11-29 with the output from the **show cdp neighbors** commands in Example 11-20. Notice that R3 has gathered some detailed information about R2 and the switch connected to the Fast Ethernet interface on R3.

Figure 11-29   CDP Neighbors Topology

Example 11-20 Examining the CDP Neighbors

```
R3# show cdp neighbors
Capability Codes: R - Router, T - Trans Bridge, B - Source Route Bridge
                  S - Switch, H - Host, I - IGMP, r - Repeater, P - Phone
Device ID       Local Intrfce   Holdtme   Capability   Platform    Port ID
R2              Ser 0/0/1       178          R          C1900       Ser 0/0/1
S3              Gig 0/0         147          S          2960        Gig 0/1
R3# show cdp neighbors detail

Device ID: R2
Entry address(es):
  IP address : 192.168.1.2
Platform: cisco C1900, Capabilities: Router
Interface: Serial0/0/1, Port ID (outgoing port): Serial0/0/1
Holdtime: 168

Version :
Cisco IOS Software, C1900 Software (C1900-UNIVERSALK9-M), Version 15.1(4)M4,
  RELEASE SOFTWARE (fc2)
Technical Support: http://www.cisco.com/techsupport
Copyright (c) 1986-2012 by Cisco Systems, Inc.
Compiled Thurs 5-Jan-12 15:41 by pt_team

advertisement version: 2
Duplex: full
--------------------------
```

```
Device ID: S3
Entry address(es):
  IP address : 192.168.2.10
Platform: cisco 2960, Capabilities: Switch
Interface: GigabitEthernet0/0, Port ID (outgoing port): GigabitEthernet0/1
Holdtime: 137

Version :
Cisco IOS Software, C2960 Software (C2960-LANBASE-M), Version 12.2(25)FX, RELEASE
  SOFTWARE (fc1)
Copyright (c) 1986-2005 by Cisco Systems, Inc.
Compiled Wed 12-Oct-05 22:05 by pt_team

advertisement version: 2
Duplex: full
```

When a Cisco device boots, CDP starts by default. CDP automatically discovers neighboring Cisco devices running CDP, regardless of which Layer 3 protocol or suites are running. CDP exchanges hardware and software device information with its directly connected CDP neighbors.

As shown in Example 11-20, the **show cdp neighbors detail** command reveals the IP address of a neighboring device. CDP will reveal the neighbor's IP address regardless of whether or not you can ping the neighbor. This command is very helpful when two Cisco routers cannot route across their shared data link. The **show cdp neighbors detail** command will help determine if one of the CDP neighbors has an IP configuration error.

CDP provides the following information about each CDP neighbor device:

- **Device identifiers** – For example, the configured host name of a switch

- **Address list** – Up to one network layer address for each protocol supported

- **Port identifier** – The name of the local and remote port in the form of an ASCII character string, such as GigabitEthernet0/0

- **Capabilities list** – For example, whether this device is a router or a switch

- **Platform** – The hardware platform of the device; for example, a Cisco 1900 ISR series router

As helpful as CDP is, it can also be a security risk since it can provide useful network infrastructure information to attackers. For example, by default many IOS versions send out CDP advertisements out all enabled ports. However, best practices suggest that CDP should be enabled only on interfaces connecting to other infrastructure Cisco devices. CDP advertisements should be disabled on user-facing ports.

Because some IOS versions send out CDP advertisements by default, it is important to know how to disable CDP. To disable CDP globally, use the global configuration command **no cdp run**. To disable CDP on an interface, use the interface command **no cdp enable**.

The show ip interface brief Command (11.3.4.4)

In the same way that commands and utilities are used to verify a host configuration, commands can be used to verify the interfaces of intermediate devices. The Cisco IOS provides commands to verify the operation of router and switch interfaces.

Verifying Router Interfaces

One of the most frequently used commands is the **show ip interface brief** command. This command provides a more abbreviated output than the **show ip interface** command. It provides a summary of the key information for all the network interfaces on a router.

Figure 11-30 shows the topology that is being used in this example.

Figure 11-30   Interface Configuration Topology

The **show ip interface brief** command in Example 11-21 displays all interfaces on the router, the IPv4 address assigned to each interface, if any, and the operational status of the interface.

Example 11-21 R1 Interface Verification

```
R1# show ip interface brief
Interface              IP-Address      OK? Method Status                 Protocol
GigabitEthernet0/0     192.168.254.254 YES manual up                     up
GigabitEthernet0/1     unassigned      YES NVRAM  administratively down  down
Serial0/0/0            172.16.0.254    YES manual up                     up
Serial0/0/1            unassigned      YES NVRAM  administratively down  down
Vlan1                  unassigned      YES NVRAM  administratively down  down
R1#
```

Verifying the Switch Interfaces

The **show ip interface brief** command can also be used to verify the status of the switch interfaces, as shown in Example 11-22. The Vlan1 interface is assigned an IPv4 address of 192.168.254.250 and has been enabled and is operational.

Example 11-22 S1 Interface Verification

```
S1# show ip interface brief
Interface              IP-Address       OK? Method Status           Protocol
Vlan1                  192.168.254.250  YES manual up               up
FastEthernet0/1        unassigned       YES unset  down             down
FastEthernet0/2        unassigned       YES unset  up               up
FastEthernet0/3        unassigned       YES unset  up               up
<output omitted>
```

The output also shows that the FastEthernet0/1 interface is down. This indicates that either no device is connected to the interface or the device that is connected has a network interface that is not operational.

In contrast, the output shows that the FastEthernet0/2 and FastEthernet0/3 interfaces are operational. This is indicated by both the Status and Protocol being shown as up.

Activity 11.3.4.5: Show Commands

Go to the online course to perform this practice activity.

Lab 11.3.4.6: Using the CLI to Gather Network Device Information

SIn this lab, you will complete the following objectives:

- Part 1: Set Up Topology and Initialize Devices

- Part 2: Configure Devices and Verify Connectivity

- Part 3: Gather Network Device Information

Debugging (11.3.5)

Understand how to interpret debug output is an important skill for a network administrator.

The debug Command (11.3.5.1)

IOS processes, protocols, mechanisms and events generate messages to communicate their status. These messages can provide valuable information when troubleshooting or verifying system operations. The IOS **debug** command allows the administrator to display these messages in real-time for analysis. It is a very important tool for monitoring events in a Cisco IOS device.

All **debug** commands are entered in privileged EXEC mode. The Cisco IOS allows for narrowing the output of **debug** to include only the relevant feature or sub-feature. This is important because debugging output is assigned high priority in the CPU process and it can render the system unusable. For this reason, use **debug** commands only to troubleshoot specific problems. To monitor the status of ICMP messages in a Cisco router for example, use **debug ip icmp**. Example 11-23 shows the output of **debug ip icmp**.

Example 11-23 Output of **debug ip icmp** Command

```
R1# debug ip icmp
ICMP packet debugging is on
R1# ping 10.0.0.10
Type escape sequence to abort.
Sending 5, 100-byte ICMP Echos to 10.0.0.10, timeout is 2 seconds:
!!!!!
Success rate is 100 percent (5/5), round-trip min/avg/max = 1/1/4 ms
*Nov 13 12:56:08.147: ICMP: echo reply rcvd, src 10.0.0.10, dst 10.0.0.1,
  topology BASE, dscp 0 topoid 0
*Nov 13 12:56:08.151: ICMP: echo reply rcvd, src 10.0.0.10, dst 10.0.0.1,
  topology BASE, dscp 0 topoid 0
*Nov 13 12:56:08.151: ICMP: echo reply rcvd, src 10.0.0.10, dst 10.0.0.1,
  topology BASE, dscp 0 topoid 0
*Nov 13 12:56:08.151: ICMP: echo reply rcvd, src 10.0.0.10, dst 10.0.0.1,
  topology BASE, dscp 0 topoid 0
*Nov 13 12:56:08.151: ICMP: echo reply rcvd, src 10.0.0.10, dst 10.0.0.1,
  topology BASE, dscp 0 topoid 0
R1# undebug all
All possible debugging has been turned off
R1#
```

To list a brief description of all the debugging command options, use the **debug ?** command in privileged EXEC mode at the command line.

To turn off a specific debugging feature, add the no keyword in front of the **debug** command:

```
Router# no debug ip icmp
```

Alternatively, you can enter the **undebug** form of the command in privileged EXEC mode:

```
Router# undebug ip icmp
```

To turn off all active debug commands at once, use the **undebug all** command:

```
Router# undebug all
```

Some debug commands such as **debug all** and **debug ip packet** generate a substantial amount of output and use a large portion of system resources. The router would get so busy displaying debug messages that it would not have enough processing power to perform its network functions, or even listen to commands to turn off debugging. For this reason, using these command options is not recommended and should be avoided.

The terminal monitor Command (11.3.5.2)

Connections to grant access to the IOS command line interface can be established locally or remotely.

Local connections require physical access to the router or switch, therefore; a cable connection is required. This connection is usually established by connecting a PC to the router or switch console port using a rollover cable. In this course, we refer to a local connection as a console connection.

Remote connections are established over the network, and therefore; require a network protocol such as IP. No physical access is required for remote sessions. SSH and Telnet are two common connection protocols used for remote sessions. In this course, we use the protocol when discussing a specific remote connection, such as a Telnet connection or an SSH connection.

Whereas IOS log messages are sent to the console by default, these same log messages are not sent to the virtual lines by default. Because debug messages are log messages, this behavior prevents any debug-related messages from being displayed on VTY lines.

To display log messages on a terminal (virtual console), use the **terminal monitor** privileged EXEC command.

To stop logging messages on a terminal, use the **terminal no monitor** privileged EXEC command.

Network Troubleshooting (11.4)

Network troubleshooting is a critical skill for any network professional.

Troubleshooting Methodologies (11.4.1)

Network troubleshooting usually involves using a methodical process to identify and resolve the problem.

Basic Troubleshooting Approaches (11.4.1.1)

Network problems can be simple or complex, and can result from a combination of hardware, software, and connectivity issues. Technicians must be able to analyze the problem and determine the cause of the error before they can resolve the network issue. This process is called troubleshooting.

A common and efficient troubleshooting methodology is based on the scientific method and can be broken into the six main steps in Table 11-5.

Table 11-5   Six Steps of Troubleshooting Methodology

Step	Title	Description
1	Identify the Problem	The first step in the troubleshooting process is to identify the problem. Whereas tools can be used in this step, a conversation with the user is often very helpful.
2	Establish a Theory of Probable Causes	After you have talked to the user and identified the problem, you can try and establish a theory of probable causes. This step often yields more than a few probably causes to the problem.
3	Test the Theory to Determine Cause	Based on the probable causes, test your theories to determine which one is the cause of the problem. A technician will often apply a quick procedure to test and see if it solves the problem. If a quick procedure does not correct the problem, you might need to research the problem further to establish the exact cause.
4	Establish a Plan of Action to Resolve the Problem and Implement the Solution	After you have determined the exact cause of the problem, establish a plan of action to resolve the problem and implement the solution.
5	Verify Full System Functionality and Implement the Solution	After you have corrected the problem, verify full functionality and, if applicable, implement preventive measures.
6	Document Findings, Actions, and Outcomes	In the final step of the troubleshooting process, document your findings, actions, and outcomes. This is very important for future reference.

To assess the problem, determine how many devices on the network are experiencing the problem. If there is a problem with one device on the network, start the troubleshooting process at that device. If there is a problem with all devices on the network, start the troubleshooting process at the device where all other devices are connected. You should develop a logical and consistent method for diagnosing network problems by eliminating one problem at a time.

Resolve or Escalate? (11.4.1.2)

In some situations, it may not be possible to resolve the problem immediately. A problem should be escalated when it requires a manager's decision, some specific expertise, or access level unavailable to the troubleshooting technician.

For example, after troubleshooting, the technician concludes a router module should be replaced. This problem should be escalated for manager approval. The manager may have to escalate the problem again as it may require the financial department's approval before a new module can be purchased.

A company's policy should clearly state when and how a technician should escalate a problem.

Verify and Monitor Solution (11.4.1.3)

Cisco IOS includes powerful tools to help troubleshooting and verification. When a problem has been solved and a solution implemented, it is important to verify the system operation. Verification tools include the **ping**, **traceroute** and **show** commands. The **ping** command can be used to verify if network connectivity has been achieved.

All command output in the following examples are based on the topology shown in Figure 11-31.

10.0.0.10   10.0.0.0/24   10.1.0.0/24   10.2.0.0/24   10.3.0.0/24

Figure 11-31   Verification and Troubleshooting Topology

If a ping is successful, as shown in Example 11-24, it is safe to conclude packets are being routed from source to destination.

Example 11-24 Successful Connectivity Test Using the **ping** Command

```
R1# ping 10.0.0.10
Type escape sequence to abort.
Sending 5, 100-byte ICMP Echos to 10.0.0.10, timeout is 2 seconds:
!!!!!
Success rate is 100 percent (5/5), round-trip min/avg/max = 1/1/4 ms
R1#
```

Note

A failed ping usually does not provide enough information to draw any conclusions. It could be the result of an ACL or firewall blocking ICMP packets, or the destination device may be configured to not respond to pings. A failed ping is usually indication that further investigation is required.

The **traceroute** command, as shown in Example 11-25, is useful for displaying the path that packets are using to reach a destination. Although output from the **ping** command shows whether a packet has arrived at the destination, output from the **traceroute** command shows what path it took to get there, or where the packet was stopped along the path.

Example 11-25 Tracing a path to the Destination with the **traceroute** Command

```
R1# traceroute 10.3.0.1
Type escape sequence to abort.
Tracing the route to 10.3.0.1
VRF info: (vrf in name/id, vrf out name/id)
  1 10.1.0.2 12 msec 12 msec 16 msec
  2 10.2.0.2 24 msec *  24 msec
R1#
```

The Cisco IOS **show** commands are some of the most useful troubleshooting and verification tools included the Cisco IOS. Taking advantage of a large variety of options and sub-options, the **show** command can be used to narrow down and display information about practically any specific aspect of IOS.

Example 11-26 displays the output of a **show ip interface brief** command. Notice that the two interfaces configured with IPv4 addresses are both "up" and "up." These interfaces can send and receive traffic. The other three interfaces have no IPv4 addressing and are administratively down.

Example 11-26 The **show ip interface brief** Command

```
R1# show ip interface brief
Interface                    IP-Address      OK? Method Status                Protocol
Embedded-Service-Engine0/0   unassigned      YES unset  administratively down down
GigabitEthernet0/0           10.0.0.1        YES manual up                    up
GigabitEthernet0/1           unassigned      YES unset  administratively down down
Serial0/0/0                  10.1.0.1        YES manual up                    up
Serial0/0/1                  unassigned      YES unset  administratively down down
R1#
```

Interactive Graphic

Activity 11.4.1.4: Order the Troubleshooting Steps

Go to the online course to perform this practice activity.

Troubleshoot Cables and Interfaces (11.4.2)

Cabling and interface issues can be difficult to troubleshoot because many times the problems are intermittent. This section discusses troubleshooting duplex mismatch issues.

Duplex Operation (11.4.2.1)

In data communications, duplex refers to the direction of data transmission between two devices. If the communications are restricted to the exchange of data in one direction at a time, this connection is called half-duplex. Full-duplex allows the sending and receiving of data to happen simultaneously.

For best communication performance, two connected Ethernet network interfaces must operate in the same duplex mode to avoid inefficiency and latency on the link.

Ethernet autonegotiation was designed to facilitate configuration, minimize problems and maximize link performance. The connected devices first announce their supported capabilities and then choose the highest performance mode supported by both ends. For example, the switch and router in Figure 11-32 successfully autonegotiated full-duplex mode.

Figure 11-32   Successful Full-Duplex Autonegotiation

If one of the two connected devices is operating in full-duplex and the other is operating in half-duplex, a duplex mismatch occurs. Whereas data communication will occur through a link with a duplex mismatch, link performance will be very poor. Duplex mismatch may be caused by incorrect manual configuration, which is manually setting the two connected devices to different duplex modes. Duplex mismatch can also occur by connecting a device performing auto-negotiation to another that is manually set to full-duplex. Although rare, duplex mismatch can also occur due to failed autonegotiation.

Duplex Mismatch (11.4.2.2)

Duplex mismatch conditions may be difficult to troubleshoot as the communication between devices still occurs. A duplex mismatch may not become apparent even when using tools such as **ping**. Single small packets may fail to reveal a duplex mismatch problem. A terminal session which sends data slowly (in very short bursts) could also communicate successfully under a duplex mismatch situation. Even when either end of the connection attempts to send any significant amount of data and the link performance drops considerably, the cause may not be readily apparent because the network is otherwise operational.

CDP, the Cisco proprietary protocol, can easily detect a duplex mismatch situation between two Cisco devices. Consider the topology in Figure 11-33 where the G0/0 interface on R1 has been erroneously configured to operate in half duplex mode.

Figure 11-33   Duplex Mismatch Topology

CDP will display log messages about the link with the duplex mismatch. The messages also contain the device name and ports involved in the duplex mismatch, which makes it much easier to identify and fix the problem. Example 11-27 shows the CDP duplex mismatch log messages.

Example 11-27 Duplex Mismatch Log Messages

```
S1#
*Mar  1 01:01:03.858: %CDP-4-DUPLEX_MISMATCH: duplex mismatch discovered on
  FastEthernet0/5 (not half duplex), with R1 GigabitEthernet0/0 (half duplex).
*Mar  1 01:01:04.856: %CDP-4-DUPLEX_MISMATCH: duplex mismatch discovered on
  FastEthernet0/5 (not half duplex), with R1 GigabitEthernet0/0 (half duplex).
*Mar  1 01:01:05.855: %CDP-4-DUPLEX_MISMATCH: duplex mismatch discovered on
  FastEthernet0/5 (not half duplex), with R1 GigabitEthernet0/0 (half duplex).
S1#
```

Note

Because these are log messages, they are only displayed on a console session by default. You would only see these messages on a remote connection if the terminal monitor command is enabled.

Example 11-28 shows the duplex configuration that caused the problem.

Example 11-28 Duplex Configuration Comparison

```
S1# show interfaces fastethernet 0/5
FastEthernet0/5 is up, line protocol is up (connected)
 Hardware is Fast Ethernet, address is 0cd9.96e2.3d05 (bia 0cd9.96e2.3d05)
  MTU 1500 bytes, BW 100000 Kbit/sec, DLY 100 usec,
     reliability 255/255, txload 1/255, rxload 1/255
  Encapsulation ARPA, loopback not set
  Keepalive set (10 sec)
  Full-duplex, Auto-speed, media type is 10/100BaseTX
  input flow-control is off, output flow-control is unsupported
 <output omitted>
S1#
!----------------------------------------------------------------
R1# show interfaces gigabitethernet 0/0
GigabitEthernet0/0 is up, line protocol is up
  Hardware is CN Gigabit Ethernet, address is fc99.4775.c3e0 (bia fc99.4775.c3e0)
  Internet address is 10.0.0.1/24
  MTU 1500 bytes, BW 100000 Kbit/sec, DLY 100 usec,
     reliability 255/255, txload 1/255, rxload 1/255
  Encapsulation ARPA, loopback not set
  Keepalive set (10 sec)
  Half Duplex, 100Mbps, media type is RJ45
  output flow-control is unsupported, input flow-control is unsupported
 <output omitted>
R1#
```

Troubleshooting Scenarios (11.4.3)

The following topic focuses on different troubleshooting scenarios.

IP Addressing Issues on IOS Devices (11.4.3.1)

IP address-related problems will likely keep remote network devices from communicating. Because IP addresses are hierarchical, any IP address assigned to a network device must conform to that network's range of addresses. Wrongly assigned IP addresses create a variety of issues, including IP address conflicts and routing problems.

Two common causes of incorrect IPv4 assignment are manual assignment mistakes or DHCP-related issues.

Network administrators often have to manually assign IP addresses to devices such as servers and routers. If a mistake is made during the assignment, then communications issues with the device are very likely to occur.

On an IOS device, use the **show ip interface** or **show ip interface brief** commands to verify what IPv4 addresses are assigned to the network interfaces for R1 shown in Example 11-29.

Example 11-29 displays the output of **show ip interface** issued on a R1.

Example 11-29 The **show ip interface** Command

```
R1# show ip interface gigabitethernet 0/0
GigabitEthernet0/0 is up, line protocol is up
  Internet address is 10.0.0.1/24
  Broadcast address is 255.255.255.255
  Address determined by setup command
  MTU is 1500 bytes
  Helper address is not set
  Directed broadcast forwarding is disabled
  Outgoing access list is not set
  Inbound  access list is not set
<output omitted>
```

Notice that the **show ip interface** command displays IPv4 information (OSI Layer 3), whereas the previously mentioned **show interface** command displays the physical and data link details of an interface.

IP Addressing Issues on End Devices (11.4.3.2)

Most end devices are configured to rely on a DHCP server for automatic IPv4 address assignment. If the device is unable to communicate with the DHCP server, then the server cannot assign an IPv4 address for the specific network and the device will not be able to communicate.

In Windows-based machines, when the device cannot contact a DHCP server, Windows will automatically assign an address belonging to the 169.254.0.0/16 range. Designed to facilitate communication within the local network, this behavior can be seen as a backup plan. Think of it as Windows saying "I will use this address from the 169.254.0.0/16 range because I could not get any other address." More often than not, a computer with a 169.254.0.0/16 will not be able to communicate with other devices in the network and indicates an automatic IPv4 address assignment problem that should be fixed.

Other operating systems, such Linux and OS X, will simply not assign an IPv4 address to the network interface, if communication with a DHCP server fails.

To verify the IP addresses assigned to a Windows-based computer, use the **ipconfig** command, as shown in Example 11-30.

Example 11-30 The **ipconfig** Command

```
C:\> ipconfig

Windows IP Configuration

Ethernet adapter Local Area Connection:

   Connection-specific DNS Suffix   . :
   Link-local IPv6 Address . . . . . : fe80::fd4c:6609:6733:c5cc%11
   IPv4 Address. . . . . . . . . . . : 10.0.0.10
   Subnet Mask . . . . . . . . . . . : 255.255.255.0
   Default Gateway . . . . . . . . . : 10.0.0.1

C:\>
```

Default Gateway Issues (11.4.3.3)

The default gateway for an end device is the closest networking device that can forward traffic to other networks. If a device has an incorrect or nonexistent default gateway address, it will not be able to communicate with devices in remote networks. Because the default gateway is the path to remote networks, its address must belong to the same network as the end device.

The address of the default gateway can be manually set or obtained from a DHCP server. Similar to IPv4 addressing issues, default gateway problems can be related to misconfiguration (in the case of manual assignment) or DHCP problems (if automatic assignment is in use).

To solve misconfigured default gateway issues, ensure that the device has the correct default gateway configured. If the default address was manually set but is incorrect, simply replace it with the proper address. If the default gateway address was automatically set, ensure the device can properly communicate with the DHCP server. It is also important to verify that the proper IPv4 address and subnet mask were configured on the router's interface and that the interface is active.

To verify the default gateway on Windows-based computers, use the **ipconfig** command, as shown in Example 11-31.

Example 11-31 Verify the Default Gateway on a Windows PC

```
C:\> ipconfig

Windows IP Configuration

Ethernet adapter Local Area Connection:

   Connection-specific DNS Suffix . . . :
   Link-local IPv6 Address . . . . . : fe80::fd4c:6609:6733:c5cc%11
   IPv4 Address. . . . . . . . . . . : 10.0.0.10
   Subnet Mask . . . . . . . . . . . : 255.255.255.0
   Default Gateway . . . . . . . . . : 10.0.0.1

C:\>
```

On a router, use the **show ip route** command to list the routing table and verify that the default gateway, known as a default route, has been set. This route is used when the destination address of the packet does not match any other routes in its routing table. Figure 11-34 shows that R2 is the default route for R1.

Figure 11-34 Default Route for R1

Example 11-32 shows that the default gateway has been set with at default route of 10.1.0.2.

Example 11-32 Default Gateway Displayed in Output of **show ip route** Command

```
R1# show ip route
<output omitted>

Gateway of last resort is 10.1.0.2 to network 0.0.0.0

S*    0.0.0.0/0 [1/0] via 10.1.0.2
      10.0.0.0/8 is variably subnetted, 4 subnets, 2 masks
C        10.0.0.0/24 is directly connected, GigabitEthernet0/0
L        10.0.0.1/32 is directly connected, GigabitEthernet0/0
C        10.1.0.0/24 is directly connected, Serial0/0/0
L        10.1.0.1/32 is directly connected, Serial0/0/0
R1#
```

Troubleshooting DNS Issues (11.4.3.4)

Domain Name Service (DNS) defines an automated service that matches names, such as www.cisco.com, with the IP address. Although DNS resolution is not crucial to device communication, it is very important to the end user.

It is common for users to mistakenly relate the operation of an Internet link to the availability of the DNS service. User complaints such as "the network is down" or "the Internet is down" are often caused by an unreachable DNS server. Whereas packet routing and all other network services are still operational, DNS failures often lead the user to the wrong conclusion. If a user types in a domain name such as www. cisco.com in a web browser and the DNS server is unreachable, the name will not be translated into an IP address and the website will not display.

DNS server addresses can be manually or automatically assigned. Network administrators are often responsible for manually assigning DNS server addresses on servers and other devices, whereas DHCP is used to automatically assign DNS server addresses to clients.

Although it is common for companies and organizations to manage their own DNS servers, any reachable DNS server can be used to resolve names. Small office and home office (SOHO) users often rely on the DNS server maintained by their ISP for name resolution. ISP-maintained DNS servers are assigned to SOHO customers via DHCP. For example, Google maintains a public DNS server that can be used by anyone and it is very useful for testing. The IPv4 address of Google's public DNS server is 8.8.8.8 and 2001:4860:4860::8888 for its IPv6 DNS address.

Use the **ipconfig /all**, as shown in Example 11-33, to verify which DNS server is in use by the Windows computer. The **nslookup** command is another useful DNS troubleshooting tool for PCs. With **nslookup** a user can manually place DNS queries and analyze the DNS response.

Example 11-33 DNS Server Information Available in the Output of the **ipconfig /all** Command

```
C:\> ipconfig /all
<some output omitted>


Ethernet adapter Local Area Connection:

   Connection-specific DNS Suffix  . :
   Description . . . . . . . . . . . : Realtek PCIe GBE Family Controller
   Physical Address. . . . . . . . . : F0-4D-A2-DD-A7-B2
   DHCP Enabled. . . . . . . . . . . : Yes
   Autoconfiguration Enabled . . . . : Yes
   Link-local IPv6 Address . . . . . : fe80::449f:c2:de06:ebad%10(Preferred)
   IPv4 Address. . . . . . . . . . . : 10.0.0.10(Preferred)
```

```
Subnet Mask . . . . . . . . . . . : 255.255.255.0
Lease Obtained. . . . . . . . . . : Monday, November 09, 2015 7:49:48 PM
Lease Expires . . . . . . . . . . : Thursday, November 19, 2015 7:49:51 AM
Default Gateway . . . . . . . . . : 10.0.0.1
DHCP Server . . . . . . . . . . . : 10.0.0.1
DNS Servers . . . . . . . . . . . : 8.8.8.8
NetBIOS over Tcpip. . . . . . . . : Enabled
```

Example 11-34 shows the output of **nslookup** when placing a query for |
www.cisco.com.

Example 11-34 Output from **nslookup** Command

```
C:\> nslookup
Default Server:  dns-cac-lb-01 rr.com
Address:  209.18.47.61
> cisco.com
Server:  dns-cac-lb-01.rr.com
Address:  209.18.47.61
Non-authoritative answer:
Name:    cisco.com
Addresses:  2001:420:1101:1::a
            72.163 4 161
> quit
C:\>
```

Lab 11.4.3.5: Troubleshooting Connectivity Issues

In this lab, you will complete the following objectives:

- Identify the Problem
- Implement Network Changes
- Verify Full Functionality
- Document Findings and Configuration Changes

Packet Tracer 11.4.3.6: Troubleshooting Connectivity Issues

Packet Tracer
☐ Activity

This activity is designed to help you troubleshoot network connectivity issues using commands to trace the route from source to destination. You are required to examine the output of **tracert** (the Windows command) and **traceroute** (the IOS command) as packets traverse the network and determine the cause of a network issue. After the issue is corrected, use the **tracert** and **traceroute** commands to verify the completion.

Summary (11.5)

Class Activity 11.5.1.1: Design and Build a Small Business Network

- Use Packet Tracer and a word processing application to complete this activity – 2–3 students per group.

- Design and build a network from scratch.

- Your design must include a minimum of one router, one switch, and one PC.

- Fully configure the network – use IPv4 or IPv6 (subnetting must be included as a part of your addressing scheme).

- Verify the network using at least five show commands.

- Secure the network using SSH, secure passwords, and console passwords (minimum).

Create a rubric to use for peer grading – or your instructor may choose to use the rubric provided with this activity.

Present your capstone project to the class – be able to answer questions from your peers and instructor!

Packet Tracer 11.5.1.2: Skill Integration Challenge

Packet Tracer
☐ Activity

In this activity, you will design and implement an addressing scheme in a two router, three switch topology. You will configure basic device settings including line access, banners, passwords, and SSH. You will then verify that all devices can access network resources.

Packet Tracer 11.5.1.3: Troubleshooting Challenge

Packet Tracer
☐ Activity

In this activity, you will troubleshoot the configurations in a two router, three switch topology. Once all issues are resolved, all devices should be able to access network resources.

In order to meet user requirements, even small networks require planning and design. Planning ensures that all requirements, cost factors, and deployment options are given due consideration. An important part of network design is reliability, scalability, and availability.

Supporting and growing a small network requires being familiar with the protocols and network applications running over the network. Protocol analyzers enable a network professional to quickly compile statistical information about traffic flows on a network. Information gathered by the protocol analyzer is evaluated based on the source and destination of the traffic as well as the type of traffic being sent. This analysis can be used by a network technician to make decisions on how to manage the traffic more efficiently. Common network protocols include DNS, Telnet, SMTP, POP, DHCP, HTTP, and FTP.

It is a necessity to consider security threats and vulnerabilities when planning a network implementation. All network devices must be secured. This includes routers, switches, end-user devices, and even security devices. Networks need to be protected from malicious software such as viruses, Trojan horses, and worms. Antivirus software can detect most viruses and many Trojan horse applications and prevent them from spreading in the network. The most effective way to mitigate a worm attack is to download security updates from the operating system vendor and patch all vulnerable systems.

Networks must also be protected from network attacks. Network attacks can be classified into three major categories: reconnaissance, access attacks, and denial of service. There are several ways to protect a network from attacks.

- Authentication, authorization, and accounting (AAA, or "triple A") network security services provide the primary framework to set up access control on a network device. AAA is a way to control who is permitted to access a network (authenticate), what they can do while they are there (authorize), and to watch the actions they perform while accessing the network (accounting).

- A firewall is one of the most effective security tools available for protecting internal network users from external threats. A firewall resides between two or more networks and controls the traffic between them and also helps prevent unauthorized access.

- To protect network devices, it is important to use strong passwords. Also, when accessing network devices remotely, it is highly recommended to enable SSH instead of the unsecured telnet.

After the network has been implemented, a network administrator must be able to monitor and maintain network connectivity. There are several commands available toward this end. For testing network connectivity to local and remote destinations, commands such as **ping**, **telnet**, and **traceroute** are commonly used.

On Cisco IOS devices, the **show version** command can be used to verify and troubleshoot some of the basic hardware and software components used during the boot process. To view information for all network interfaces on a router, the **show ip interface** command is used. The **show ip interface brief** can also be used to view a more abbreviated output than the **show ip interface** command. Cisco Discovery Protocol (CDP) is a Cisco-proprietary protocol that runs at the data link layer. Because CDP operates at the data link layer, two or more Cisco network devices, such as routers that support different network layer protocols, can learn about each other even if Layer 3 connectivity does not exist.

Cisco IOS configuration files such as startup-config or running-config should be archived. These files can be saved to a text file or stored on a TFTP server. Some models of routers also have a USB port, and a file can be backed up to a USB drive. If needed, these files can be copied to the router and or switch from the TFTP server or USB drive.

Practice

The following activities provide practice with the topics introduced in this chapter. The Labs and Class Activities are available in the companion Introduction to Networks v5.1 Lab Manual (ISBN 9781587133534). The Packet Tracer Activities PKA files are found in the online course.

Class Activities

Class Activity 11.0.1.2: Did You Notice...?

Class Activity 11.4.1.1: Design and Build a Small Business Network

Labs

Lab 11.2.2.6: Researching Network Security Threats

Lab 11.2.4.6: Accessing Network Devices with SS

Lab 11.2.4.7: Examining Telnet and SSH in Wireshark

Lab 11.2.4.8: Securing Network Devices

Lab 11.2.5.8: Managing Router Configuration Files with Tera Term

Lab 11.2.5.9: Managing Device Configuration Files Using TFTP, Flash, and USB

Lab 11.2.5.10: Researching Password Recovery Procedures

Lab 11.3.2.3: Testing Network Latency with Ping and Traceroute

Lab 11.3.4.6: Using the CLI to Gather Network Device Information

Lab 11.4.3.5: Troubleshooting Connectivity Issues

Packet Tracer
☐ Activity

Packet Tracer Activities

Packet Tracer 11.2.4.5: Configuring Secure Passwords and SSH

Packet Tracer 11.2.5.7: Backing Up Configuration Files

Packet Tracer 11.3.2.2: Test Connectivity with Traceroute

Packet Tracer 11.3.3.3: Using show Commands

Packet Tracer 11.4.3.6: Troubleshooting Connectivity Issues

Packet Tracer 11.5.1.2: Skill Integration Challenge

Packet Tracer 11.5.1.3: Troubleshooting Challenge

Check Your Understanding Questions

Complete all the review questions listed here to test your understanding of the topics and concepts in this chapter. The appendix "Answers to 'Check Your Understanding' Questions" lists the answers.

1. Why should the IP addressing scheme be carefully planned and documented? (Choose two.)

   A. Improved network performance

   B. Easier control of security

   C. Easier troubleshooting

   D. Reduction in network traffic

   E. Elimination of requirement for subnetting

2. What would be considered an example of redundancy in network design? (Choose three.)

   A. Installation of a switch that functions at both Layer 2 and Layer 3.

   B. Installation of duplicate switches in a company network.

   C. Keeping a spare router that has already been properly configured.

   D. Installation of multiple high-speed links to the company server farm.

3. Which type of traffic should be given the highest priority on a network?

   A. Voice

   B. SMTP

   C. Instant messaging

   D. FTP

4. Which planning and design factors would be considered as part of manageability focus when implementing a small network? (Choose two.)

A. Types of cable runs

B. Prioritization of data traffic

C. Upgrades to network devices

D. Number of interfaces required

E. IP addressing scheme

F. Bandwidth requirement

5. What is true of an application layer service?

A. Application layer services provide the human interface.

B. Application layer services interface with the network and prepare the data for transfer.

C. Application layer services include such things as email and web clients.

D. Application layer services are dependent on the OS vendor.

6. Which network protocol should a network administrator use to remotely configure a network device?

A. FTP

B. HTTP

C. Telnet

D. SSH

7. Fill in the blank. ____ allows users of analog phones to take advantage of the IP network.

8. What factors should be taken into account when using a protocol analyzer to determine traffic flow on a network? (Choose two.)

A. Always capture the traffic on the same network segment.

B. Capture traffic during peak utilization times.

C. Capture traffic on different network segments.

D. Capture traffic only during off-peak times.

E. Capture traffic during both peak and off-peak times.

9. A key network switch has failed because of excessive humidity. What type of physical threat caused the problem?

    A. Hardware threat

    B. Environmental threat

    C. Electrical threat

    D. Maintenance threat

10. What is a network vulnerability?

    A. The degree of weakness inherent in a network

    B. Tools used to launch attacks against a network

    C. Individuals interested and qualified in taking advantage of security weaknesses

    D. Ping of death

11. The network administrator set the admin password on a new router to pa55w0rd. The security of the router was later compromised. What type of vulnerability allowed the attack?

    A. Technology

    B. Configuration

    C. Policy

12. Making illegal online purchases is what type of security threat?

    A. Information theft

    B. Identity theft

    C. Data loss/manipulation

    D. Disruption of service

13. What name is given to a program that is disguised as another program to attack a system?

    A. Virus

    B. Trojan horse

    C. Worm

14. An attacker runs a ping sweep against a network. What type of attack is this?

    A. Reconnaissance

    B. Access

    C. Denial of service

15. What type of attack is a smurf attack?

    A. Reconnaissance

    B. Access

    C. Denial of service

16. With regard to firewall technology, what is stateful packet inspection?

    A. Incoming packets must be legitimate responses from internal requests.

    B. The incoming packet must have been initiated from a trusted source.

    C. The incoming packet must be in an active state before being admitted to the network.

    D. Only secure traffic, such as SSH and HTTPS, is permitted through the firewall.

17. Which of the following is an example of a strong password?

    A. Champion

    B. Cisco123

    C. 2#4@Tpg%

    D. Eruces

    E. Pa55w0rd

18. How is an extended **ping** entered on a Cisco router?

    A. Type **ping/e** and press Enter

    B. Type **ping** followed by a destination IP address

    C. Type **ping** followed by a source IP address

    D. Type **ping** and press Enter

19. What **show** command can be issued on a Cisco router to view the configuration register value?

    A. show ip route

    B. show running-config

    C. show protocols

    D. show version

    E. show cdp neighbors detail

Answers to the "Check Your Understanding" Questions

Chapter 1

1. **B.** Podcasting and blogs allow the one-way dissemination of information. Instant messaging allows the synchronous communication between individuals. A wiki allows groups of individuals to view and edit web pages collaboratively.

2. **B, D.** Peer-to-peer networks are inexpensive and easy to configure but lack any centralized management and do not scale well.

3. **B, C, D, E.** End devices form the interface between users and the underlying communication network.

4. **C.** Logical topology diagrams identify devices, ports, and IP addressing schemes. Physical topology diagrams identify the physical location of intermediate devices, configured ports, and cable installations.

5. **D.** A wide-area network (WAN) provides access to other networks over a wide geographic area. A metropolitan-area network (MAN) spans an area larger than a local-area network (LAN) and is typically operated by a single entity. A wireless LAN (WLAN) is similar to a LAN, and a storage-area network (SAN) is designed to provide data storage, retrieval, and replication.

6. **A, C.** Leased lines and Metro Ethernet are considered business-class Internet connection technologies. Mobile services and broadband cable are considered technologies to connect remote users.

7. **B.** DSL is an always-on technology that offers good bandwidth at reasonable cost. Dial-up and cellular connections are not always-on technology and do not offer the same bandwidth capabilities as DSL. Satellite and cellular connections are also relatively expensive.

8. **B.** A converged network is where voice, video, and data move over the same infrastructure. The underlying infrastructure can be wired or wireless.

9. **C.** A fault-tolerant network is one that can continue to function if an intermediate device or path fails. A fault-tolerant network can fail if a sufficient number of intermediate devices and/or paths fail.

10. **C.** Quality of service (QoS) prioritizes data based on many factors including the traffic's sensitivity to network delay. Voice over IP (VoIP) is very sensitive to network delay and must be given priority treatment.

11. **A, B, C.** Information security includes ensuring that only the intended recipient can access the data (confidentiality), ensuring that the data has not been altered in transmission (integrity), and that the information is available in a timely manner (availability). Quality of service is not a primary requirement of information security.

12. **B.** A WISP connects subscribers to a designated access point or hot spot using similar wireless technologies found in home wireless local area networks (WLANs). WISPs are more commonly found in rural environments where DSL or cable services are not available.

13. The ready availability of network resources continues to change the way we work, play, and learn. Some of the current trends include the increased use of video, the use of client end-user-supplied devices on corporate networks (BYOD), the increased use of collaborative technologies, and a migration to cloud computing.

14. Networks have changed the way we live our everyday lives. Some examples of ways that networks are used include

- Checking the weather forecast
- Watching movies
- Sharing photographs and movies
- Playing games
- Checking your bank balance
- Taking an online class

15. Networks extend the learning environment into the virtual world by providing tools for collaboration and mobility, thus creating a global classroom. Some of the ways that the learning environment has been transformed by networks include

- Creates virtual classrooms
- Enables mobile learning
- Creates collaborative learning spaces
- Provides enhanced tracking of student performance
- Provides a global learning environment

Chapter 2

1. **C.** The Cisco IOS (Internetwork Operating System) is the operating system used in most Cisco network devices.

2. **B.** The initial configuration of Cisco IOS devices is accomplished through the CLI on the console connection.

3. **C.** Entering a question mark (?) after a command will show all additional commands and keywords to be used in the command sequence.

4. **A.** While there are some GUI interfaces available on Cisco IOS-based devices, the current practice is to use the CLI for device configuration and troubleshooting.

5. **C.** The IOS command parser inspects the first entries of a command sequence, expecting to identify a known command.

6. **C.** When the device's host name is configured, this name is used verbatim in the CLI prompt.

7. **C.** Forcing authentication for remote access by requiring a password to remotely connect to a network is a basic security measure. Option C provides the configuration to require authentication of users for remote access. In practice, stronger authentication should be required.

8. **C.** The startup config provides the configuration for the operation of the IOS device during startup.

9. **A.** This configuration provides connectivity to the switch. Option B is incorrect as a switch will forward traffic without any configuration. The other two options, C and D, have no relation to this configuration.

10. **D.** This provides a ping to a remote host. Option A does not verify connectivity. Option B verifies that the logical IP stack has been configured. Option C verifies the configuration of the local host.

Chapter 3

1. **A, C, E.** All communication, human or machine, requires three elements: a source or sender, a receiver, and a channel to carry the message.

2. **B.** The format and contents of a frame are determined by the type of message being sent and the channel being used. Frames that are not correctly formatted are not delivered. Also frames that are too long or too short are dropped.

3. **C.** The access method determines when a message can be sent, flow control affects how much information can be sent and at what speed, and response timeout is how long the device will wait for a response before taking action.

4. **B.** A unicast message is one-to-one, multicast is one-to-many, and broadcast is one-to-all.

5. **C.** A protocol suite is a group of interrelated protocols designed to carry out the communication function. A protocol stack is the implementation of the protocol suite.

6. **D.** Network access protocols control the hardware devices and the media that make up the network.

7. **C, D.** A proprietary protocol is one in which a single vendor controls the definition of a protocol and how it functions. Both AppleTalk and Novell NetWare fall into this category.

8. **D.** The Institute of Electrical and Electronics Engineers (IEEE) 802 family of standards deals with LAN and MAN networks, both wired and wireless. The 802.3 working group deals specifically with Media Access Control for wired Ethernet.

9. **A.** The Internet Society (ISOC) oversees the Internet Architecture Board (IAB), which is responsible for the overall management and development of Internet standards.

10. **B.** The Telecommunications Industry Association (TIA) is responsible for developing communication standards in a variety of areas, including radio equipment, cellular towers, VoIP devices, and satellite communications.

11. **C, E.** User Datagram Protocol (UDP) and Transmission Control Protocol (TCP) exist at the transport layer. Hypertext Transfer Protocol (HTTP), File Transfer Protocol (FTP), and Domain Name System (DNS) are all application layer protocols.

12. **D, F.** The TCP/IP model consists of four layers but has all the functionality of the seven layers found in the OSI model. The TCP/IP network access layer has the functionality of both the physical and data link layers in the OSI model. The TCP/IP application layer has the functionality of the OSI application, presentation, and session layers.

13. **E.** Data representation is the responsibility of the OSI presentation layer. In the TCP/IP model, the application layer has this functionality as it combines the functionality of the OSI application, presentation, and session layers.

14. **C.** Address in best path is the responsibility of the TCP/IP Internet layer. In the OSI model, this equates to the OSI network layer.

15. **B.** TFTP uses UDP but FTP makes use of TCP, providing reliability in file transfer.

16. **B.** A PDU is a protocol data unit in the form that the data takes at that specific layer. Data is segmented at the transport layer; thus, the PDU is named a segment.

17. **C.** De-encapsulation is the process used by the receiving device to remove control information and reassemble the bit stream into a data message. The bits arrive at the physical layer and are passed to the data link layer (PDU = frame), then the network layer (PDU = packet, then the transport layer (PDU = segment), and then up to the upper layer in the form of data.

18. **A, B, C.** To access local resources, a device must know the source and destination physical addresses, the source and destination logical addresses, and the source and destination port numbers. The default gateway address is only required to access resources on a remote network. Names are not used on a network. Host names are resolved into addresses by DNS.

19. **A, B, C, D.** To access remote resources, a device must know the source and destination physical addresses, the source and destination logical addresses, and the source and destination port numbers. The default gateway address is also required to access resources on a remote network as it specifies the way out of the local network. Names are not used on a network. Host names are resolved into addresses by DNS.

20. Protocols are responsible for many different aspects of communication. This includes such things as encoding, formatting, encapsulation, and timing.

Chapter 4

1. **A, B.** The physical layer controls data transmitted onto the media and provides encoding of the bits. Logical addressing is provided by Layer 3. The packaging of bits and Media Access Control is provided by the data link layer.

2. **B, E.** Even though the twists provide some measure of rejection of stray electrical/magnetic signals, it is still subject to EMI and RFI. Because of its relatively low cost and good performance, UDP is still the most common networking media in use.

3. **C.** Cladding is the glass that surrounds the core and acts as a mirror. The light pulses propagate down the core, while the cladding reflects the light pulses. This keeps the light pulses contained in the fiber core in a phenomenon known as total internal reflection.

4. **C.** The actual fields associated with a data link header will depend on the layer 2 protocol.

5. **B, D, F.** Unlike copper wires, fiber-optic cable can transmit signals with less attenuation and is immune to EMI and RFI. Fiber-optic cables can also be operated at much greater lengths than copper media and with higher bandwidth.

6. **B.** All wireless devices must share access to the airwaves connecting to the wireless access point. This means that slower network performance might occur as more wireless devices access the network simultaneously.

7. **C.** The LLC identifies which network layer protocol is being used for the frame.

8. **B.** The Layer 3 PDU is wrapped with a header and trailer to form the Layer 2 frame.

9. D. Logical topology refers to the way a network transfers frames from one node to the next.

10. B. In contention-based access, all nodes compete for the use of the medium but have a plan if there are collisions.

Chapter 5

1. F, G. Ethernet standards define both the data link layer protocols and the physical layer technologies.

2. B. IEEE 802.3 specifies the Ethernet MAC sublayer functionality

3. C. The MAC sublayer is part of the OSI data link layer. The frame is the data link layer PDU. Segments are associated with the transport layer, packets with the network layer, and bits with the physical layer.

4. B, C, E. The Ethernet MAC layer has two primary responsibilities: data encapsulation and media access control. Frame delimiting, addressing, and error detection are part of data encapsulation. Media recovery and media access are part of CSMA/CD.

5. B. Ethernet uses CSMA/CD. When a collision is detected on the media, all devices stop transmitting to allow the collision to clear. After the collision has cleared, devices will again attempt to transmit.

6. B, D, E. The Ethernet MAC address is 48 bits in length with the first 3 bytes (6 hexadecimal digits) assigned by the IEEE. The vendor is responsible for assigning the last 24 bits in the address. Because this address was permanently configured on a device, it is also known as a burned-in address, or BIA.

7. A. The IEEE 802.3 standard defines a minimum frame size of 64 bytes and a maximum frame size of 1518 bytes. The IEEE 802.3ac standard released in 1998 extended the maximum size to 1522 bytes to allow the inclusion of an 802.1q VLAN tag in the Ethernet frame.

8. D. The Frame Check Sequence field is used to detect frames that might have been damaged in transit.

9. C. The broadcast MAC address is when all 48 bits are turned on and is represented by FF-FF-FF-FF-FF-FF.

10. B. All multicast MAC addresses start with 01-00-5E.

11. A, C. The ARP process resolves IPv4 address to MAC addresses and maintains a table of these mappings.

12. **B.** RP requests are sent out with a broadcast MAC address. All devices in the L2 broadcast domain will hear the request and use the information it contains to update their ARP tables with information for the source device.

13. ARP table or ARP cache, request

14. source, drop

15. requests, unicast

16. MAC address table, floods, received

17. CAM, content addressable

18. **A, C.** The ARP process resolves IPv4 address to MAC addresses and maintains a table of these mappings.

19. **A.** When the source and destination IPv4 addresses are on the same network, the Ethernet frame can be sent directly to the destination device.

20. **B.** When the source and destination IPv4 addresses are on different networks, the Ethernet frame cannot be sent directly to the destination device and must be sent to the default gateway (router).

Chapter 6

1. **A.** The network layer, or OSI Layer 3, provides services to allow end-to-end communication across a network.

2. **A.** The network layer uses Layer 3 addressing such as IPv4 and IPv6 to identify end hosts.

3. IP is connectionless, which greatly reduces the overhead of IP. Therefore, there is no initial exchange of control information before packets are forwarded, and no additional fields exist in the header to maintain an established connection.

4. **C.** Time-to-Live (TTL) contains an 8-bit binary value that is used to limit the lifetime of a packet. It is specified in seconds but is commonly referred to as hop count.

5. **C.** Without a proper default gateway, the host will not be able to communicate with devices on another network.

6. **D.** The running configuration file is located in RAM and is the configuration file that stores the configuration commands that the router IOS is currently using. It is also known as the running config.

7. **B.** During self-decompression of the IOS image file, a string of hash (pound) signs will be displayed.

8. **A, D.** The requirement for router interface configuration is to provide Layer 3 (IPv4, IPv6, and so on) addressing information and to enable the interface.

9. **A, E.** A common misconception is that the switch uses its configured default gateway address to determine where to forward packets originating from hosts connected to the switch and destined for hosts on a remote network. Actually, the IP address and default gateway information are only used for packets that originate from the switch.

10. **C.** The local default route (0.0.0.0) — that is, all packets with destinations that do not match other specified addresses in the routing table — are forwarded to the gateway.

Chapter 7

1. **A, B.** An IPv4 address is a hierarchical address that is made up of two parts: a network portion and a host portion.

2. **B.** The network address is a standard way to refer to a network.

3. **A, C.** For all three types of communication, the IPv4 address of the originating host is placed in the packet header as the source address, and there is only one IP source and destination address.

4. **D.** The private address blocks are 10.0.0.0 to 10.255.255.255 (10.0.0.0/8), 172.16.0.0 to 172.31.255.255 (172.16.0.0/12), and 192.168.0.0 to 192.168.255.255 (192.168.0.0/16).

5. The need for more address space is because of the exhaustion of the IPv4 addresses.

6. **C.** Hextet is the unofficial term used to refer to a segment of 16 bits or four hexadecimal values. An IPv6 address requires 8 hextets to represent the 128 bits.

7. **B.** An IPv6 link-local address enables a device to communicate with other IPv6-enabled devices on the same link and only on that link (subnet).

8. **A, B.** Two ways in which a device can obtain an IPv6 global unicast address automatically are Stateless Address Autoconfiguration (SLAAC) and stateful DHCPv6.

9. **C.** Multicast is used to send a single IP packet to multiple destinations.

10. Both IPv4 and IPv6 use an ICMP protocol as the principal means to verify connectivity.

11. **D.** Traceroute (tracert) is a utility that generates a list of hops that were successfully reached along the path.

Chapter 8

1. **B, D.** Subnetting a large address space into smaller subnetworks helps to contain network traffic and thus improve network performance.

2. **C.** A router or Layer 3 switch is required for devices on different networks or subnets to be able to communicate.

3. host. Subnets are created by borrowing bits from the host portion of an IP address to create additional network bits. The more bits borrowed, the more subnets created.

4. **D.** Every bit borrowed can have one of two values, 0 or 1. The number of subnets created is 2^n, where n is the number of bits borrowed. In this case, we have borrowed 4 bits, so 2^4, or 16, subnets are created, all of which can be used.

5. **D.** A network broadcast address has all host bits turned on.

6. **C.** The number of valid host addresses created by borrowing 4 bits is $2^4 - 2$, or 14. It is necessary to subtract 2 because the network address and the broadcast address for each subnet cannot be used as host addresses.

7. **D, E, F.** By borrowing 3 bits, the technician created nine subnets, each with 30 usable hosts. The second subnet is 10.20.30.32/27 and consists of addresses from 10.20.30.32 to 10.20.30.63. The first and last addresses in this range are not usable, but all others are.

8. **C.** The assigned subnet has the address range from 192.168.1.0/25 to 192.168.1.127/25. The departmental printer has been placed in another subnet and will be unreachable without a router.

9. **B.** The new department requires 511 hosts, but in any subnet, two addresses (network and broadcast) are unusable, so a subnet must be created that can accommodate 513 addresses. The closest matching number would be a network with 1024 hosts. To create 1024 hosts requires 10 host bits ($2^{10} - 1024$). Currently there are 16 host bits available, so the administrator must borrow 6 bits to create 64 subnets, each with 1022 available hosts.

10. **C.** Currently 16 bits are assigned to the network. If the network administrator borrows an additional 5 bits from the host field, 21 bits are now assigned to the network field. For the subnet mask, the first 21 bits (network) would be turned on and the last 11 (host) bits would be turned off. This creates a mask of 111111 11.11111111.11111000.00000000 (255.255.248.0).

11. VLSM. With traditional subnetting, all subnets must be of the same size, wasting a lot of addresses. With VLSM, different subnet masks can be used on different portions of the network, thus providing a more efficient allocation of available address space.

12. C. By borrowing 3 bits from the network portion of the original network, the administrator has now assigned 28 bits to the network, leaving only 4 host bits. Each WAN link requires two addresses, but each subnet has two unusable addresses, meaning that each created subnet must have four available hosts. To create subnets with four hosts means that 2 host bits must be available, allowing the administrator to borrow 2 additional bits, creating four subnets each with four hosts.

13. B, D, F. To produce a subnet that could accommodate 796 users would require 10 bits (1024 hosts). To accommodate 31 users would require 6 bits (64 hosts). The WAN links require 2 bits (four hosts). Starting with the largest subnet would require borrowing 2 bits, leaving the 10 bits for hosts. This creates a 10.11.0.0/22 network, which includes the range 10.11.0.0/22–10.11.251.255/22. The second network requires 6 bits, can start at 10.11.253.0/26, and would run to 10.11.253.63/24. The third network would start at the next available address (10.11.253.64/30) and run until 10.11.253.67/30.

14. B, C. Due to the extremely large IPv6 address space, the conservation of addresses does not apply.

15. A. The most common method to subnet an IPv6 network is to simply modify the subnet ID.

Chapter 9

1. C, E, F. The transport layer is responsible for segmenting data, adding the port number to identify the proper application, and keeping track of individual conversations. MAC addresses are added by the data link layer, and IP addresses and routing are handled by the network layer.

2. C. Source port addresses are assigned by the transport layer to identify the individual conversation and destination port addresses to identify the service being looked for.

3. Multiplexing

4. B. TCP uses acknowledgements and windowing to offer flow control and reliable delivery. UDP is connectionless and does not resend lost datagrams.

5. B, E, F. Applications that are simple request and reply transactions, those sensitive to delay, and those that are unidirectional in nature make use of UDP. Applications requiring reliable delivery and that can tolerate delay associated with protocol overhead make use of TCP. In this question, Telnet, FTP, and HTTP use TCP, and VoIP, DHCP, and TFTP use UDP.

6. **C.** The acknowledgement number indicates that the data that has been received, the header length indicates the length of the TCP segment header, the window size specifies the number of bytes that can be received before an acknowledgement is required, and the checksum is used for error-checking the segment header and data.

7. port numbers

8. **B.** UDP does not track conversations and has the advantage of low overhead relative to TCP.

9. **C.** Well-known ports (numbers 0 to 1023) are commonly used to request a connection to that specific port, and its associated service. Registered ports (numbers 1024 to 49151) are assigned to user processes or applications. These processes are primarily individual applications that a user has chosen to install, rather than common applications that would receive a well-known port number. When not used for a server resource, these ports can also be dynamically selected by a client as its source port. Dynamic or private ports (numbers 49152 to 65535) are most often used to identify the client application during communication.

10. ephemeral or private

11. **B.** UDP reassembles the data in the order received and passes it to the application. It is up to the application to sort out the data. UDP has no mechanism for reordering of datagrams or requesting retransmission.

12. **F.** The FIN control bit indicates that there is no more data from the sender.

13. **A.** The three-way handshake starts when a client device sends an ISN to the server. The server responds with an acknowledgement of the client ISN+1 and its own ISN. The last step in the process is when the client acknowledges the server ISN by responding with a value of the server ISN+1.

14. **B.** FTP makes use of TCP, so when segments are lost in transit, the receiving device will send a decreased window size in returning segments.

15. selective acknowledgements (SACK)

Chapter 10

1. **B.** The functionality of the TCP/IP application layer protocols fit roughly into the framework of the top three layers of the OSI model: application, presentation, and session.

2. **B, C, E.** Email supports three separate protocols for operation: Simple Mail Transfer Protocol (SMTP), Post Office Protocol (POP), and Internet Message Access Protocol (IMAP).

3. **C.** DHCP allows a host to obtain an IP address dynamically when it connects to the network.

4. **A.** Application layer protocols are used to exchange data between programs running on the source and destination hosts.

5. The Domain Name System (DNS) provides domain name to address resolution for networks allowing end users to access resources with names rather than more difficult to remember IP addresses. This automated service matches resource names with the required numeric network addresses

Chapter 11

1. **B, C.** By carefully planning and documenting the address space, troubleshooting, access control, and security are greatly simplified.

2. **B, D.** Redundancy is eliminating any single point of failure. This could include equipment or links. Keeping a configured device as a spare will assist in the troubleshooting process but is not considered redundancy. Additionally having a switch that functions at both Layer 2 and Layer 3 is still a single point of failure and is not considered redundancy.

3. **A.** Voice traffic is very sensitive to delay and should be given the highest priority on the network.

4. **B, E.** The five focus areas when implementing a small network are cost, expandability, manageability, speed, and ports. Type of cable run would fall under cost, upgrades to network devices are part of expandability, prioritization of data traffic and IP addressing schemes are part of manageability, bandwidth requirement is part of speed, and number of interfaces required would be ports.

5. **B.** Application layer services prepare the data for transfer over the network; they are based on standards and do not provide any sort of human interface. Application programs interface with the user.

6. **D.** FTP and FTPS allow files to be moved on the network. HTTP and HTTPS allow communication between a host and a web server. Telnet and SSH both allow remote login to a device. FTPS, HTTPS, and SSH are the secure versions of FTP, HTTP, and Telnet, respectively, and should be used whenever possible.

7. VoIP

8. **B, C.** Traffic should be captured on different network segments during peak utilization times to ensure that all traffic types are collected.

9. **B.** The key cause of the failure was high humidity, which is an environmental threat.

10. **A.** Vulnerabilities are inherent weaknesses in the network that can be exploited by people and tools.

11. **B.** Configuring easily guessed passwords creates a vulnerability that can easily be exploited.

12. **B.** Making illegal online purchases by posing as another person is identity theft.

13. **B.** A virus is malicious software that is attached to another program to execute some unknown function. A Trojan horse is a program that is disguised as another program to trick the user into executing it. Worms are self-contained programs that attack a system to exploit a vulnerability.

14. **A.** The attacker is using the ping sweep to gather information on the network, making this a reconnaissance attack.

15. **C.** A smurf attack overloads a network link by causing multiple Echo Replies to be directed against a target, making it a denial of service attack.

16. **A.** With stateful packet inspection (SPI), only legitimate responses from internal requests are permitted through the firewall.

17. **C.** Strong passwords should mix uppercase and lowercase text, numbers, and symbols into a random pattern that cannot be easily guessed.

10. **D.** To enter extended ping mode, type **ping** and then press Enter.

19. **D.** The **show version** command will display the configuration register.

A

access method   A set of rules used by LAN hardware to direct traffic on the network. It determines which host or device uses the LAN next.

acknowledgement   Notification sent from one network device to another to acknowledge that some event (for example, receipt of a message) has occurred.

Address Resolution Protocol (ARP)   Internet protocol used to map an IP address to a MAC address. Defined in RFC 826.

adjacency table   A table in a router that contains a list of the relationship formed between selected neighboring routers and end nodes for the purpose of exchanging routing information. Adjacency is based upon the use of a common media segment.

American Standard Code for Information Interchange (ASCII)   An 8-bit code for character representation (7 bits plus parity).

AND (logical)   One of three basic binary logic operations. ANDing yields the following results: 1 AND 1 = 1, 1 AND 0 = 0, 0 AND 1 = 0, 1 AND 0 = 0.

ARP cache   Logical storage in a host's RAM to store ARP entries. *Also called ARP table.*

ARP table   Logical storage in a host's RAM to store ARP entries. *Also called ARP cache.*

assigned multicast   Reserved IPv6 multicast addresses for predefined groups of devices.

asymmetric switching   A switching technique used to allow for different data rates on different ports.

automatic medium-dependent interface cross-over (auto-MDIX)   A detection on a switch port or hub port to detect the type of cable used between switches or hubs. Once the cable type is detected, the port is connected and configured accordingly. With auto-MDIX, a crossover or a straight-through cable can be used for connections to a copper 10/100/1000 port on the switch, regardless of the type of device on the other end of the connection.

availability   The assurance of timely and reliable access to data services for authorized users. Network firewall devices, along with desktop and server antivirus software, can ensure system reliability and the robustness to detect, repel, and cope with breaches of network security. Building fully redundant network infrastructures, with few single points of failure, can reduce the impact of these threats.

B

bandwidth   The rated throughput capacity of a given network medium or protocol. Bandwidth is listed as available or consumed data communication resources expressed in bits/second.

best-effort delivery   Describes a network system that does not use a sophisticated acknowledgement system to guarantee reliable delivery of information.

Bootstrap Protocol (BOOTP)   Protocol used by a network node to determine the IP address of its Ethernet interfaces in order to facilitate network booting.

Bring Your Own Device (BYOD)   The concept of any device, to any content, in any way is a major global trend that requires significant changes to the way devices are used. This trend is about end users having the freedom to use personal tools to access information and communicate across a business or campus network.

broadcast   A form of transmission where one device transmits to all devices within the network or on another network.

broadcast address   Special address reserved for sending a message to all stations. Generally, a broadcast address is a MAC destination address of all ones. Compare with multicast address and unicast address.

burned-in address (BIA)   The MAC address that is permanently assigned to a LAN interface or NIC. It is called burned-in because the address is burned into a chip on the card, and the address cannot be changed. Also called universally administered address (UAA).

C

Carrier Sense Multiple Access (CSMA) Media-access mechanism wherein devices ready to transmit data first check the channel for a carrier. If no carrier is sensed for a specific period of time, a device can transmit. *See also* CSMA/CA and CSMA/CD.

channel   A communication path over a medium used to transport information from a sender to a receiver. Multiple channels can be multiplexed over a single cable.

circuit switched   Switching system in which a dedicated physical circuit path must exist between sender and receiver for the duration of the call. Used heavily in the telephone company network.

Cisco Express Forwarding (CEF)   A Layer 3 switching method. This technique speeds up packet forwarding by decoupling the usual strict interdependence between Layer 2 and Layer 3 decision making. The forwarding decision information is stored in several data structures for CEF switching. This forwarding information can be rapidly referenced to expedite packet forwarding decisions.

Cisco Internetwork Operating System (IOS)   Generic term for the collection of network operating systems used by Cisco networking devices.

classful addressing   A unicast IP address that is considered to have three parts: a network part, a subnet part, and a host part. The term classful refers to the fact that the classful network rules are first applied to the address, and then the rest of the address can be separated into a subnet and host part to perform subnetting. Originally, IPv4 addresses were divided into five classes, namely, Class A, Class B, Class C, Class D, and Class E. Classful addressing is not generally practiced in current network implementations.

classless addressing   An IPv4 addressing scheme that uses a subnet mask that does not follow classful addressing limitations. It provides increased flexibility when dividing ranges of IP addresses into separate networks. Classless addressing is considered the best in current network implementations. *See also* VLSM.

client   A network device that accesses a service on another computer remotely through a network.

client-server   A computer system setup in which tasks are distributed between a service provider (server) and a service user, such as a workstation (client). The server is used to store the applications and data and the majority of the computer processing is done on the server.

cloud computing   The use of computing resources (hardware and software) that are delivered as a service over a network. A company uses the hardware and software in the cloud and a service fee is charged.

coaxial cable/coax   Cable consisting of a hollow outer cylindrical conductor that surrounds a single inner wire conductor. Two types of coaxial cable are currently used in LANs: 50-ohm cable, which is used for digital signaling, and 75-ohm cable, which is used for analog signaling.

collaboration   The creation of a document or documents that can be edited by more than one person in real time across a network.

collision fragment   Any frame less than 64 bytes in length. These frames are automatically discarded by receiving stations. Also called runt frame.

command-line interface (CLI)   User interface to a computer operating system or application that depends on textual commands being entered by the user.

communication   Transmission and receipt of information.

communities   Consist of people who share common experiences and hobbies who exchange ideas and information. Communities allow for social interaction that is independent of location or time zone.

confidentiality   Insures that only the intended and authorized recipients—individuals, processes, or devices—can access and read data. Confidentiality is accomplished by having a strong system for user authentication, enforcing passwords that are difficult to guess, and requiring users to change them frequently. Encrypting data, so that only the intended recipient can read it, is also part of confidentiality.

congested   A condition where a network has more bits to transmit than what the bandwidth of the communication channel can deliver.

congestion   Traffic in excess of network capacity.

connectionless   Term used to describe data transfer without the existence of a virtual circuit.

connection-oriented   Term used to describe data transfer that requires the establishment of a virtual circuit.

console   Term used to describe data transfer that requires the establishment of a virtual circuit.

content addressable memory (CAM) table   Memory that is accessed based on its contents, not on its memory address. Also known as associative memory.

contention-based   A method of networking that is a non-deterministic method. That is, any device can try to transmit data across the shared medium whenever it has data to send.

converged network   A network that aggregates various forms of traffic such as voice, video, and data on the same network infrastructure.

crosstalk   Source of interference that occurs when cables are bundled together for long lengths. The signal from one cable can leak out and enter adjacent cables. *See also* electromagnetic interference (EMI).

CSMA/Collision Avoidance (CSMA/CA)
A mechanism that regulates the transmission of data onto a network medium. CSMA/CA is similar to CSMA/CD except the devices first request the right to send, which hopefully avoids collisions. CSMA/CA is used in 802.11 WLANs.

CSMA/Collision Detection (CSMA/CD)
Media-access mechanism that requires a node wishing to transmit to listen for a carrier signal before trying to send. If a carrier is sensed, the node waits for the transmission in progress to finish before initiating its own transmission. If a collision occurs and is detected, the sending node uses the backoff algorithm before retransmitting.

custom cloud   These are clouds built to meet the needs of a specific industry, such as healthcare or media. Custom clouds can be private or public.

cyclic redundancy check (CRC)   A type of hash function (one-way encryption) that is used to produce a small, fixed-size checksum of a block of data, such as a packet or a computer file. A CRC is computed and appended before transmission or storage and verified afterward by the recipient to confirm that no changes have happened in transit. Error-checking technique in which the frame recipient calculates a remainder by dividing frame contents by a prime binary divisor and compares the calculated remainder to a value stored in the frame by the sending node.

D

daemon   A computer program that runs in the background and is usually initiated as a process. Daemons often support server processes.

data center   A data center is a facility used to house computer systems and associated components, including redundant data communications connections, high-speed virtual servers, redundant storage systems, and security devices.

data networks   Infrastructure historically used by businesses to record and manage the business systems. Data networks have evolved to enable the transmission of many different types of information services, including email, video, messaging, and telephony.

datagram   Logical grouping of information sent as a network layer unit over a transmission medium without prior establishment of a virtual circuit. IP datagrams are the primary information units in the Internet. The terms frame, message, packet, and segment are also called datagrams. *See also* Protocol Data Unit PDU.

decapsulation (de-encapsulation)   A process by which an end device, after it receives data over some transmission medium, examines the headers and trailers at each successive higher layer, eventually handing the data to the correct application. Sometimes called de-encapsulation.

default gateway   A device on a network that serves as an access point to other networks.

A default gateway is used by a host to forward IP packets that have destination addresses outside the local subnet. A router interface typically is used as the default gateway. When the computer needs to send a packet to another subnet, it sends the packet to its default gateway. Also known as default router.

destination   The target host for a message. Ethernet/IP frames contain a destination MAC and IP address.

destination IP address   The Layer 3 address to which the data is going.

directed broadcast   A term that describes IPv4 packets sent to all hosts in a particular network. In a directed broadcast, a single copy of the packet is routed to the specified network, where it is broadcast to all hosts on that network.

Domain Name System (DNS)   An Internet-wide system by which a hierarchical set of DNS servers collectively holds all the name-IP address mappings, with DNS servers referring users to the correct DNS server to successfully resolve a DNS name.

dual stack   A device that is enabled for both IPv4 and IPv6 protocols.

duplex   Two types of settings used for communications on networks: half duplex and full duplex. Half-duplex communication relies on unidirectional data flow where sending and receiving data are not performed at the same time. In full-duplex communication, data flow is bidirectional, so data can be sent and received at the same time.

Dynamic Host Configuration Protocol (DHCP)   A protocol used to dynamically assign IP configurations to hosts. The services defined by the protocol are used to request and assign an IP address, default gateway, and DNS server address to a network host.

E

electromagnetic interference (EMI)   Interference by magnetic signals caused by the flow of electricity. EMI can cause reduced data integrity and increased error rates on transmission channels. The physics of this process are that electrical current creates magnetic fields, which in turn cause other electrical currents in nearby wires. The induced electrical currents can interfere with proper operation of the other wire.

enable password   Unencrypted password used to limit access to privileged EXEC mode from IOS user EXEC mode.

enable secret   Encrypted password used to limit access to privileged EXEC mode from IOS user EXEC mode.

encapsulation   The process by which a device adds networking headers and trailers to data from an application for the eventual transmission of the data onto a transmission medium.

encoding   Process by which bits are represented on a media.

end device   Either the source or destination of a message transmitted over the network.

EtherChannel   Logical interface on a Cisco device associated with a bundle of routed ports in order to aggregate bandwidth.

Ethernet   Baseband LAN specification invented by Xerox Corporation and developed jointly by

Xerox, Intel, and Digital Equipment Corporation. Ethernet networks use CSMA/CD and run over a variety of cable types at 10 Mbps. Ethernet is similar to the IEEE 802.3 series.

Expectational acknowledgement Acknowledgement used by TCP where the ACK number is sent back to the source to indicate the next byte that the receiver expects to receive.

Extended Unique Identifier (EUI-64) Process that uses a client's 48-bit Ethernet MAC address and inserts another 16 bits in the middle of the 48-bit MAC address to create a 64-bit Interface ID for an IPv6 global unicast address.

extranet Part of the network that provides secure and safe access to individuals who work for a different organization but require access to the organization's data.

F

fault tolerant Limits the impact of a failure so that the fewest number of devices are affected. It is also built in a way that allows quick recovery when such a failure occurs.

fiber-optic cable Physical medium that uses glass or plastic threads to transmit data. A fiber-optic cable consists of a bundle of these threads, each of which is capable of transmitting data into light waves.

File Transfer Protocol (FTP) Application protocol, part of the TCP/IP protocol stack, used for transferring files between network nodes. FTP is defined in RFC 959.

flash A removable component that has memory space for storage. Used on the router or switch for storing the compressed operating system image.

flow control The management of data flow between devices in a network. It is used to avoid too much data arriving before a device can handle it, causing data overflow.

Forwarding Information Base (FIB) A data structure that contains all routes known. Conceptually the FIB is similar to a routing table. A networking device uses the FIB lookup table to make destination-based switching decisions.

fragmentation The dividing of IP datagrams to meet the MTU requirements of a Layer 2 protocol.

full duplex Both devices can transmit and receive on the media at the same time.

G

gateway Normally, a relatively general term that refers to different kinds of networking devices. Historically, when routers were created, they were called gateways.

global configuration mode From the privileged mode, you can enter the device's global configuration mode. From global configuration mode, you can configure global parameters or enter other configuration submodes such as interface, router, and line configuration submodes.

global routing prefix IPv6 prefix, or network, portion of the address that is assigned by the provider, such as an ISP, to a customer or site.

global unicast address (GUA) An IPv6 address similar to a public IPv4 address. These are globally unique, Internet routable addresses. Global unicast addresses can be configured statically or assigned dynamically.

goodput   Application-level throughput. It is the number of useful bits per unit of time from a certain source address to a certain destination, excluding protocol overhead and excluding retransmitted data packets.

graphical user interface (GUI)   User-friendly interface that uses graphical images and widgets, along with text, to indicate the information and actions available to a user when interacting with a computer.

H

half duplex   Both devices can transmit and receive on the media but cannot do so simultaneously.

header   Control information added before data during the encapsulation for network transmission.

hexadecimal (Base 16)   A number system using the digits 0 through 9, with their usual meaning, plus the letters A through F to represent hexadecimal digits with values of 10 to 15. The rightmost digit counts ones, the next counts multiples of 16, then 162 = 256.

Hextet   The unofficial term used to refer to a segment of 16 bits or four hexadecimal values. For IPv6 addressing, each digit is a single hextet, 16 bits, or four hexadecimal digits.

host address   IPv4 address of a network host. When talking about host addresses, they are the network layer addresses.

Hybrid cloud   A hybrid cloud is made up of two or more clouds (example: part custom, part public), where each part remains a distinctive object but both are connected using a single architecture.

I

initial sequence number (ISN)   Randomly chosen number and is used to begin tracking the flow of data from the client to the server for this session. The ISN in the header of each segment is increased by one for each byte of data sent from the client to the server as the data conversation continues.

Institute of Electrical and Electronics Engineers (IEEE)   An international, nonprofit organization for the advancement of technology related to electricity. IEEE maintains the standards defining many LAN protocols.

integrity   The assurance that the information has not been altered in transmission, from origin to destination. Data integrity can be compromised when information has been corrupted—willfully or accidentally. Data integrity is made possible by requiring validation of the sender as well as using mechanisms to validate that the packet has not changed during transmission.

interface   Specialized ports on a networking device that connect to individual networks. Because routers are used to interconnect networks, the ports on a router are referred to as network interfaces.

Interface ID   Host portion of an IPv6 global unicast address.

intermediary device   Connects end devices to the network and can connect multiple individual networks to form an internetwork.

International Organization for Standardization (ISO)   An international standards body that defines many networking standards. Also, the standards body that created the OSI model.

International Telecommunications Union (ITU)   United Nations (UN) agency responsible for issues that concern information and communication technologies.

Internet   The network that combines enterprise networks, individual users, and ISPs into a single global IP network.

Internet Assigned Numbers Authority (IANA)   An organization that assigns the numbers important to the proper operation of the TCP/IP protocol and the Internet, including assigning globally unique IP addresses.

Internet Control Message Protocol (ICMP)   As part of the TCP/IP Internet layer, ICMP defines protocol messages used to inform network engineers of how well an internetwork is working. For example, the ping command sends ICMP messages to determine whether a host can send packets to another host.

Internet of Everything (IoE)   A reference to adding devices of all types onto the Internet. IOE brings together people, processes, data, and things to make networked connections more relevant and valuable.

Internet Message Access Protocol (IMAP)   Protocol that describes a method to retrieve email messages. Unlike POP, copies of the messages are downloaded to the client application but the original messages are kept on the server until manually deleted.

Internet Service Provider (ISP)   A company that helps create the Internet by providing connectivity to enterprises and individuals as well as interconnecting to other ISPs to create connectivity to all other ISPs.

intranet   A term often used to refer to a private connection of LANs and WANs that belongs to an organization and is designed to be accessible only by the organization's members, employees, or others with authorization.

IPv4 address   A 32-bit number, written in dotted decimal notation, used by the IPv4 protocol to uniquely identify an interface connected to an IP network. It is also used as a destination address in an IP header to allow routing. As a source address, it enables a computer to receive a packet and to know to which IP address a response should be sent.

J

jumbo frame   Ethernet frames with more than 1500 bytes of data.

K

kernel   The portion of the operating system that interacts directly with computer hardware.

L

latency   Refers to the amount of time, to include delays, for data to travel from one given point to another.

limited broadcast   A broadcast that is sent to a specific network or series of networks.

link-local IPv4 address   An IPv4 address in the range of 169.254.1.0 to 169.254.254.255. Communication using these addresses is used with a TTL of 1 and is limited to the local network.

link-local IPv6 address An IPv6 used to communicate with other devices on the same local link. With IPv6, the term link refers to a subnet. Link-local addresses are confined to a single link. Their uniqueness must only be confirmed on that link because they are not routable beyond the link.

local area network (LAN) A network infrastructure that provides access to users and end devices in a small geographical area, which is typically an enterprise, home, or small business network owned and managed by an individual or IT department.

Logical Link Control (LLC) The IEEE 802.2 standard that defines the upper sublayer of the Ethernet Layer 2 specifications (and other LAN standards).

logical topology diagram A map of the devices on a network representing how the devices communicate with each other. Identifies devices, ports, and addressing scheme.

Loopback A special reserved IPv4 address, 127.0.0.1 and IPv6 address of ::1, that can be used to test TCP/IP applications. Packets sent to 127.0.0.1 (::1) by a computer never leave the computer or even require a working NIC. Instead, the packet is processed by IP at the lowest layer and is then sent back up the TCP/IP stack to another application on that same computer.

M

MAC address table On a switch, a table that lists all known MAC addresses and the bridge/switch port out that the bridge/switch should use to forward frames sent to each MAC address.

Manchester encoding Line code in which each bit of data is signified by at least one voltage level transition.

maximum transmission unit (MTU) The largest IP packet size allowed to be sent out a particular interface. Ethernet interfaces default to an MTU of 1500 because the data field of a standard Ethernet frame should be limited to 1500 bytes, and the IP packet sits inside the Ethernet frame's data field. The Gigabit Ethernet standard supports "jumbo frames," which can be as large as 9216 including tagging.

Media Access Control (MAC) The lower of the two sublayers of the IEEE standard for Ethernet. It is also the name of that sublayer (as defined by the IEEE 802.3 subcommittee).

media independent The networking layers whose processes are not affected by the media being used. In Ethernet, these are all the layers from the LLC sublayer of data link upward.

medium Provides the channel over which the message travels from source to destination.

Medium to large network Networks used by corporations and schools, which can have many locations with hundreds or thousands of interconnected computers.

mobile learning An environment-supporting learning. This may be physical or virtual.

multicast Sending a message to selected hosts that are part of a group. A single packet is copied by the network and sent to a specific subset of network addresses. These addresses are specified in the destination address field. Compare with broadcast and unicast.

multicast group/client   A member of a multi-cast group. Every multicast client in each group has the same IP address. IPv4 multicast addresses begin with 224.*.*.* and end with 239.*.*.*. IPv6 multicast addresses have the prefix FF00::/8.

multiplexing   A process where multiple digital data streams are combined into one signal.

N

Neighbor Advertisement message   Similar to an ARP reply for IPv4, ICMPv6 messages are sent by devices in response to an ICMPv6 Neighbor Solicitation message containing the IPv6 address and the corresponding MAC address.

Neighbor Solicitation message   Similar to an ARP request for IPv4, ICMPv6 messages are sent by devices when they know the IPv6 address but need the corresponding MAC address.

network address   A dotted decimal number defined by the IPv4 protocol to represent a net-work or subnet. It represents the network that hosts reside in. Also called a network number or network ID.

Network Address Translation (NAT)   Trans-lation of IP addresses to different addresses. This is commonly used to translate RFC 1918 addresses that are not routed on the Internet to public domain addresses that can be routed on the Internet.

Network Address Translation 64 (NAT64) Allows IPv6-enabled devices to communicate with IPv4-enabled devices using a translation technique similar to NAT for IPv4. An IPv6 packet is translated to an IPv4 packet and vice versa

network architecture   Technologies that sup-port the infrastructure and the programmed services and rules, or protocols, that move data across the network.

network infrastructure   The architecture defin-ing the connection within a network; refers to the physical hardware and connections used to transmit data.

Network Interface Card (NIC)   Computer hard-ware, typically used for LANs, that allows the computer to connect to some networking cable. The NIC can then send and receive data over the cable at the direction of the computer.

network prefix   The initial part of a Layer 3 IP address. The network prefix is used by routers to forward the packet to the proper network.

next hop   The next gateway to which a Layer 3 packet is delivered, used to reach its destination.

nibble boundary   A nibble is 4 bits or one hexa-decimal digit. A nibble boundary is using nibble aligned for subnet masks. By borrowing bits from the interface ID, the best practice is to subnet on a nibble boundary.

nonreturn to zero (NRZ)   Line code in which 1s are represented by one significant condition and 0s are represented by another.

non-volatile RAM (NVRAM)   RAM that does not lose its contents when the device is powered off.

nslookup   A service or a program to look up information in the DNS (Domain Name System).

O

octet   A group of 8 binary bits. It is similar to, but not the same as, a byte. One application in computer networking is to use octets to divide IPv4 addresses into four components.

Octet boundary   The part of an IPv4 address that falls between an octet.

Organizationally Unique Identifier (OUI)   The first half of a MAC address. Manufacturers must ensure that the value of the OUI has been registered with the IEEE. This value identifies the manufacturer of any Ethernet NIC or interface.

overhead   Resources used to manage or operate the network. Overhead consumes bandwidth and reduces the amount of application data that can be transported across the network.

P

packet switched   Network architecture that routes packets along the path perceived as the most efficient and allows a communications channel to be shared by multiple connections.

peer-to-peer (P2P)   In peer-to-peer networking each device serves as both a client and a server portion of an application. P2P also describes a small local network where hosts can play the role of client and/or server.

peer-to-peer file sharing   allows people to share files with each other without having to store and download them from a central server. The user joins the P2P network by simply installing the P2P software. P2P file sharing has not been embraced by everyone. Many people are concerned about violating the laws of copyrighted materials.

physical media   The cabling and connectors used to interconnect the network devices.

physical port   A connector or outlet on a networking device where the media is connected to an end device or another networking device.

physical topology   The arrangement of the nodes in a network and the physical connections between them. This is the representation of how the media is used to connect the devices.

physical topology diagram   Identifies the physical location of intermediary devices and cable installation.

ping   A troubleshooting tool used to verify network connectivity by sending a packet to a specific IP address and waiting for the reply.

port   In networking, this term is used in several ways. With Ethernet hub and switch hardware, port is simply another name for interface, which is a physical connector in the switch into which a cable can be connected. With TCP and UDP, a port is a software function that uniquely identifies a software process on a computer that uses TCP or UDP. With PCs, a port can be a physical connector on the PC, like a parallel or USB port.

port number   A field in a TCP or UDP header that identifies the application that either send (source port) or should receive (destination port) the data inside the data segment.

Post Office Protocol (POP)   A protocol that allows a computer to retrieve email from a server.

power over Ethernet (PoE)   The powering of network devices over Ethernet cable. PoE is defined by two different standards: IEEE 802.3af and Cisco.

powerline technology   An emerging trend for home networking that uses existing electrical wiring to connect devices.

preferred format   Representing an IPv6 address is x:x:x:x:x:x:x:x, with each "x" consisting of four hexadecimal values.

prefix length   In IP subnetting, this refers to the portion of a set of IP addresses whose value must be identical for the addresses to be in the same subnet.

private address   Defined in RFC 1918, an IP address that does not have to be globally unique because the address exists inside packets only when the packets are inside a single private IP internetwork. Private IP addresses are popularly used in most companies today, with NAT translating the private IP addresses into globally unique IP addresses.

private cloud   Cloud-based applications and services offered in a private cloud are intended for a specific organization or entity, such as the government.

privileged executive (EXEC) mode   An IOS administrative level mode that supports access to configuration and management commands.

proprietary   One company or vendor controls the definition of the protocol and how it functions. Some proprietary protocols can be used by different organizations with permission from the owner. Others can only be implemented on equipment manufactured by the proprietary vendor.

protocol analyzer   Network monitoring device gathers information regarding the status of the network and devices attached to it. Also known as network analyzer, or packet sniffer.

protocol data unit (PDUs)   A generic term from OSI that refers to the data, headers, and trailers about which a particular networking layer is concerned.

protocol suite   A delineation of networking protocols and standards into different categories, called layers, along with definitions of which sets of standards and protocols need to be implemented to create products that can be used to create a working network.

protocols   Written specifications that define what tasks a service or device should perform. Each protocol defines messages, often in the form of headers, plus the rules and processes by which these messages are used to achieve some stated purpose.

public address   An IP address that has been registered with IANA or one of its member agencies, which guarantees that the address is globally unique. Globally unique public IP addresses can be used for packets sent through the Internet.

public cloud   Cloud-based applications and services offered in a public cloud are made available to the general population.

Q

Quality of Service (QoS)   A control mechanism that can provide different priorities to different users or data flows or guarantee a certain level of performance to a data flow in accordance with requests from the application program.

queuing   In routing and switching, a backlog of packets or frames waiting to be forwarded out an interface.

R

radio frequency interference (RFI) Radio frequencies that create noise that interferes with information being transmitted across unshielded copper cabling.

Random Access Memory (RAM) Also known as read-write memory, RAM can have new data written to it and can have stored data read from it. RAM is the main working area, or temporary storage, used by the CPU for most processing and operations. A drawback of RAM is that it requires electrical power to maintain data storage. If the computer is turned off or loses power, all data stored in RAM is lost unless the data was previously saved to disk. Memory boards with RAM chips plug into the motherboard.

real-time traffic Data traffic that carries signal output as it happens or as fast as possible. Real-time traffic is sensitive to latency and jitter.

redundancy In internetworking, a network architecture designed to eliminate network downtime caused by a single point of failure. Redundancy includes the replication of devices, services, or connections that support operations even in the occurrence of a failure. *See also* redundant system.

reference model A conceptual framework to help understand and implement the relationships between various protocols.

Regional Internet Registry (RIR) Five organizations responsible for allocating IP addresses within their geographic region.

reliable A characteristic of a protocol that uses mechanisms such as handshaking, timers, acknowledgement messages, and dynamic windowing to help ensure that the data received is the same as the data sent. Reliable protocols require additional overhead on the network in terms of much larger segment headers.

Requests for Comments (RFC) Series of documents and memoranda encompassing new research, innovations, and methodologies applicable to Internet technologies. RFCs are a reference for how technologies should work.

response timeout How long a service waits on a response before taking some action. How long service waits and what action is taken if a response timeout occurs are defined by the protocol.

Round-trip time (RTT) The time required for some networking PDUs to be sent and received, and a response PDU to be sent and received. In other words, the time between when a device sends data and when the same device receives a response.

Router Advertisement message ICMPv6 messages sent by routers to provide addressing information to hosts using SLAAC.

Router Solicitation message ICMPv6 messages sent by devices to request an ICMPv6 Router Advertisement message.

routing The process by which a router receives an incoming frame, discards the data-link header and trailer, makes a forwarding decision based on the destination IP address, adds a new data-link header and trailer based on the outgoing interface, and forwards the new frame out the outgoing interface.

runt frame Any frame less than 64 bytes in length. These frames are automatically discarded by receiving stations. Also called collision fragment.

S

scalable network   A network that expands quickly to support new users and applications without impacting the performance of the service being delivered to existing users.

Secure Shell (SSH)   A protocol that provides a secure remote connection to a host through a TCP application.

segment   (1) A collision domain that is a section of a LAN that is bound by bridges, routers, or switches. (2) In a LAN using a bus topology, a segment is a continuous electrical circuit that is often connected to other such segments with repeaters. (3) When used with TCP, the term segment (verb) refers to the work TCP does to accept a large piece of data from an application and break it into smaller pieces. Again with TCP, used as a noun, segment refers to one of those smaller pieces of data.

segmenting   In TCP, the process of taking a large chunk of data and breaking it into small-enough pieces to fit within a TCP segment without breaking any rules about the maximum amount of data allowed in a segment.

selective acknowledgement (SACK)   Optional TCP feature that makes it possible for the destination to acknowledge bytes in discontinuous segments. With SACK, the source host would only need to retransmit the specific unacknowledged data rather than retransmitting all data since the last acknowledged data.

sequence number   Information placed in a data header to ensure correct sequencing of the arriving data.

server   Can refer to computer hardware that is to be used by multiple concurrent users. Alternatively, this term can refer to computer software that provides services to many users. For example, a web server consists of web server software running on some computer.

Server Message Block (SMB)   An application level network protocol mainly applied to shared access to files, printers, serial ports, and miscellaneous communications between nodes on a network.

session   A related set of communications transactions between two or more network devices.

shell   The portion of the operating system that interfaces with applications and the user.

shielded twisted-pair (STP) cable   A type of network cabling that includes twisted-pair wires, with shielding around each pair of wires, as well as another shield around all wires in the cable.

Simple Mail Transfer Protocol (SMTP)   An application layer protocol providing electronic mail services to transfer mail from client to server and between servers.

slash notation   A method of expressing a network prefix. It uses a forward slash (/) followed by the network prefix, for example, 192.168.254.0 /24. This /24 represents the 24-bit network prefix in slash format.

Small Office/Home Office (SOHO) network   Enables computers within a home office or a remote office to connect to a corporate network or access centralized, shared resources

Smart home technology   Technology that is integrated into everyday appliances allowing them to interconnect with other devices, making them more 'smart' or automated.

socket   a logical communications end point within a network device. A socket is typically represented by a Layer 3 address and a Layer 4 port number.

solicited node multicast   IPv6 multicast address associated with an IPv6 unicast address and is mapped to a special Ethernet multicast address.

source   The device that is originating the PDU.

source IP address   The IP address of the originating host that is placed into the IP packet header.

spoofing   A person or program that masquerades as another to gain access to data and the network.

standard   An internationally recognized definition of technical specifications that ensure worldwide consistency.

stateful   Tracking of actual conversations and their state of the communication session for a protocol, such as TCP.

stateful DHCPv6   Similar to DHCP for IPv4, provides IPv6 address, prefix length, and other information such as DNS server and domain name. Does not provide a default gateway address.

Stateless Address Autoconfiguration (SLAAC)   Plug-and-play IPv6 feature that enables devices to connect themselves to the network without any configuration and without any servers (like DHCP servers).

stateless DHCPv6   Provides information other than the IPv6 address and prefix length, such as DNS server and domain name. Does not provide a default gateway address.

subnet   A group of IP addresses that have the same value in the first part of the IP addresses for the purpose of allowing routing to identify the group by that initial part of the addresses. IP addresses in the same subnet typically sit on the same network medium and are not separated from each other by any routers. IP addresses on different subnets are typically separated from one another by at least one router. Subnet is short for subnetwork.

subnet ID   Part of the IPv6 global unicast address used by an organization to identify subnets within its site. The larger the subnet ID, the more subnets available.

subnet mask   A dotted decimal number that helps identify the structure of IPv4 addresses. The mask represents the network and subnet parts of related IPv4 addresses with binary 1s and the host part of related IPv4 addresses with binary 0s.

subnetwork   See subnet.

switch fabric   The integrated circuits and the accompanying machine programming in a switch that allow the data paths through the switch to be controlled.

Switch Form-Factor Pluggable (SFP)   Removal modules used in routers and switches to support a number of different network media.

switch virtual interfaces (SVI)   Virtual interfaces for which there is no physical hardware on the device associated. An SVI is created in software. The virtual interfaces are used as a means to remotely manage a switch over a network. They are also used as a method of routing between VLANs.

T

Telecommunications Industry Association (TIA)   An organization that develops standards that relate to telecommunications technologies. Together, the TIA and the Electronic Industries Alliance (EIA) have formalized standards, such as EIA/TIA-232, for the electrical characteristics of data transmission.

TelePresence   Cisco multimedia products for business virtual meetings and collaboration.

Telnet   A non-secure network service that supports CLI access to a remote host. It also can be used to verify the application layer software between source and destination stations.

terminal emulation   Network application in which a computer runs software that makes it appear to a remote host as a directly attached terminal.

TEST-NET address   The IPv4 address block 192.0.2.0 to 192.0.2.255 (192.0.2.0 /24) that is set aside for teaching and learning purposes. These addresses can be used in documentation and network examples.

three-way handshake   The process used by TCP to establish a session.

throughput   The actual data transfer rate between two computers at some point in time. Throughput is impacted by the slowest-speed link used to send data between the two computers as well as myriad variables that might change during the course of a day.

Time to Live (TTL)   A field in the IP header that prevents a packet from indefinitely looping around an IP internetwork. Routers decrement the TTL field each time they forward a packet, and if they decrement the TTL to 0, the router discards the packet, which prevents it from looping forever.

topology   The arrangement of networking components or nodes. Examples include star, extended star, ring, and mesh.

traceroute (tracert)   A command on many computer operating systems that discovers the IP addresses, and possibly host names, of the routers used by the network when sending a packet from one computer to another.

traffic prioritization   A process in Quality of Service (QoS) where frames are forwarded in priority order based on their marking.

Transmission Control Protocol (TCP)   A Layer 4 protocol of the TCP/IP model, TCP lets applications guarantee delivery of data across a network.

Trivial File Transfer Protocol (TFTP)   A protocol similar to FTP that provides the transfer of files from one computer to another over a network. TFTP is supported by UDP where FTP is supported by TCP.

tunneling   Encapsulating an IP packet inside another IP packet.

U

unicast   Message sent to a single network destination. Compare with broadcast and multicast.

unique local address   IPv6 similar to RFC 1918 private addresses for IPv4. Unique local addresses are used for local addressing within a site or between a limited number of sites. These addresses should not be routable in the global IPv6 Internet. Unique local addresses are in the range of FC00::/7 to FDFF::/7.

Unknown unicast   An Ethernet frame that does not have an entry in the switch's MAC address table for the destination MAC address.

unshielded twisted-pair (UTP) cable   A general type of cable, with the cable holding twisted pairs of copper wires and the cable itself having little shielding.

unspecified address   An IPv6 all-0s address represented in the compressed format as ::/128 or just :: in the compressed format. It cannot be assigned to an interface and is only to be used as a source address in an IPv6 packet. An unspecified address is used as a source address when the device does not yet have a permanent IPv6 address or when the source of the packet is irrelevant to the destination.

User Datagram Protocol (UDP)   A connectionless transport layer protocol in the TCP/IP protocol stack. UDP is a simple protocol that exchanges datagrams without acknowledgements or guaranteed delivery, requiring that error processing and retransmission be handled.

user executive (EXEC) mode   The limited CLI mode where the commands available to the user are a subset of those available at the privileged level. In general, use the user EXEC commands to temporarily change terminal settings, perform basic tests, and list system information.

V

Variable Length Subnet Masking (VLSM)
Ability to specify a different subnet mask for the same network number on different subnets. VLSM can help optimize available address space.

virtual circuit   A logical connection created within a network between two network devices.

virtual classroom   A logical classroom environment created as a collaboration space without physical restraints.

Virtual Local Area Network (VLAN)   A network of end devices that behave as if they are connected to the same network segment, even though they might be physically located on different segments of a LAN. VLANs are configured through software on the switch and router (IOS on Cisco routers and switches).

virtual terminal line (vty)   The reference to text based logical interfaces on an IOS device. These are accessed using Telnet or SSH to perform administrative tasks. VTY lines are also called virtual type terminal.

virtualization   The creation of a virtual version of something, such as a hardware platform, operating system (OS), storage device, or network resources. As an example, a virtual machine consists of a set of files and programs running on an actual physical system.

Voice over IP (VoIP)   Voice data encapsulated in an IP packet that allows it to traverse already implemented IP networks without needing its own network infrastructure.

W

wide area network (WAN)   A network infrastructure that provides access to other networks over a wide geographical area, which is typically owned and managed by a telecommunications service provider.

window size   As filed in the TCP header that is set in a sent segment, signifies the maximum amount of unacknowledged data the host is willing to receive before the other sending host must wait for an acknowledgement. Used for flow control.

wireless access point (WAP)   A network device that provides connectivity of wireless clients to connect to a data network.

Wireless Internet Service Provider (WISP)   An ISP that connects subscribers to a designated access point or hot spot using similar wireless technologies found in home wireless local area networks (WLANs).

J

CISCO

Connect, Engage, Collaborate

The Award Winning Cisco Support Community

Attend and Participate in Events

Ask the Experts
Live Webcasts

Knowledge Sharing

Documents
Blogs
Videos

Top Contributor Programs

Cisco Designated VIP
Hall of Fame
Spotlight Awards

Multi-Language Support

https://supportforums.cisco.com